CW00707193

MORE JAVA GEMS

SIGS Reference Library

Additional Volumes in Preparation

MORE JAVA GEMS

edited by
Dwight Deugo, PhD

PUBLISHED BY THE PRESS SYNDICATE OF THE UNIVERSITY OF CAMBRIDGE
The Pitt Building, Trumpington Street, Cambridge, United Kingdom

CAMBRIDGE UNIVERSITY PRESS
The Edinburgh Building, Cambridge CB2 2RU, UK   http:\\www.cup.cam.ac.uk
40 West 20th Street, New York, NY 10011-4211, USA   http:\\www.cup.org
10 Stamford Road, Oakleigh, Melbourne 3166, Australia
Ruiz de Alarcón 13, 28014 Madrid, Spain

Published in association with SIGS Books

First published in 2000

Design and composition by Kevin Callahan /BNGO Books
Cover design by Andrea Cammarata

Printed in the United States of America

A catalog record for this book is available from the British Library.

Library of Congress Cataloging - in - Publication data is on record with the publisher.

ISBN 0 521 77477 2 Paperback

Contents

MODELING AND PATTERNS

JAVA IN A DISTRIBUTED WORLD

THREADS

USER INTERFACES

SECURITY

TESTING

PERFORMANCE

REALITY CHECK

INTRODUCTION
TO JAVA REPORT—
NOW AND BEYOND

T HE *JAVA REPORT* published its first issue in March 1996. This was a real accomplishment when you consider that it was only on May 23, 1995, that John Gage, director of the Science Office for Sun Microsystems, announced Java to the world at SunWorld. Later in 1995, Sun released the initial Java Development Kit (JDK) and a Java enabled Web Browser called HotJava. The rest is history, as Java is now firmly entrenched in the computing industry. Many of us who saw demonstrations of Java in 1995 knew that it was something new, something different, and something not to be ignored. Those behind the *Java Report* knew this too, and we have been reporting on Java ever since.

In his first editorial for *Java Report*, the original Editor-In-Chief, David Fisco, wrote:

> The Java community is becoming broader every day, encompassing CIOs, information technologists, market professionals, programmers, multimedia designers, educators, managers, and even hobbyists. ... However, many CIOs, developers, and even software experts are having a hard time getting a handle on Java. Some have said that it's just a neat way to run animations on the Web, others note that Java enables Web-based electronic transaction, and still others tout Java as the Holy Grail that will bring about the $500 PC and change the world of computing as we know it.

David's comments are as relevant today as they were back in 1996. To quote the lyrics of Pearl Jam, "it's evolution baby." This year's JavaOne conference

– Sun's original Java conference – had 20,000 attendees. I don't think anyone left JavaOne without being moved. The feeling started the moment you entered Halls A and B at the Moscone Center in San Francisco for the opening keynote. Imagine going to a technical conference and thinking that you were at a rock concert. With the huge conference attendance, the keynote was overflowing, the remaining people standing in lines that went for blocks waiting to get their conference materials or Palm V's selling for $199 – Java virtual machine included. As the lights went down and the main characters took the stage, one felt like holding up a lighter.

The message at the conference was clear: Java has arrived, it's real, it's not boring, it is not going away anytime soon, and it's a key ingredient for the enterprise, the desktop, and for small devices. These were more than just statements to take on faith; the proof was there for all to see. Endless companies demonstrated how they were using Java and how it was helping them to be successful in their specific lines of business.

So what's the evolution? Part of it is the fact that Java grants developers endless possibilities. Here is a language that works everywhere and on everything, opening a new world of applications limited only by the imaginations of developers and entrepreneurs. Not only does Java help with the development of applications for the Networked Economy. It is being used to develop applications that connect us at a personal level never seen before, as we beam information and applications back and forth. After all, it's great to do business with people and companies around the world, but it's even better to see a face behind the machine.

The *Java Report's* mission from the beginning has been to be your independent, objective source of information about Java. Its intent is to inform, enlighten, and entertain. Initially a bimonthly publication, *Java Report* has been a monthly publication since September 1997. Over the years, its page count has increased from 64 in the first issue to 80 in the latest one. This year, with the release of The Java 2 Platform (JDK 1.2), Java continues to grow in functionality and use. To keep pace, the *Java Report* is intending to do the same. Look for more news, reviews, interviews, columns, and feature articles as we reach the millennium. In one of my editorials, I asked, will anything derail the growth of Java? I believe now the answer is no. Sun is delivering on its Java promises and, provided people use it correctly, Java's future is very bright. The *Java Report* will continue to help technical managers and developers use Java correctly by providing up-to-date information on topics and issues that they face now and in the near future.

I officially took on the responsibility of Editor-In-Chief of *Java Report* in June 1996. If I knew then what I know now about the job, I think I still would have taken the position. For the most part, the job is fun, although in the magazine business deadlines are hard – something the software industry could learn from. Being Editor-In-Chief involves a number of tasks. I meet with companies or visit their homepages regularly to keep informed of what they are doing and what they plan to do next. There are product reviews and interviews to schedule, meetings with people who want to talk about the status of Java, and the magazine to edit. Then there is the task of getting developers to write for the magazine. Getting someone to say he will write an article is often easier than getting them to complete it. You would be surprised at how long it takes some people to write a 2000–3000 word article and the excuses for not doing so. I know everyone is busy. If you are not, you're not working hard enough. However, the problems and the issues that developers are dealing with now are ones of great interest to many in the Java community. More than a million people are new to Java and to object-oriented programming. If you have discovered, developed, used, or solved something interesting relating to Java, write about it. The pattern community has learned the benefits of this. What will it take to convince you to do the same? Along with the above tasks, many are surprised to hear that I am also an assistant professor at Carleton University in Ottawa, Canada. You don't think you can be the editor of a technical magazine without actually working with the technology, do you? For me this is a real benefit. Companies may be able to gloss over important technical details with some of the media. However, it does not take me long to get by the PR people and talk with the ones who are really doing the work: the developers.

At any one time, I am dealing with three different *Java Report* issues. There is the issue that just hit the streets where I am talking with people about its contents. There is the issue that is in production where I am checking its quality. Then, there is the next issue where I am looking for good articles that fit its theme. Thanks to your submissions, the number of quality articles available for publication is growing. I am always asking colleagues and leading members in the community to write for the *Java Report*. It may take a while to get them to agree, but I can be a very convincing person.

Java has grown up since I took over the helm of *Java Report* and so have the people that use it. To keep pace, the *Java Report* is written for and by colleagues in the Java community. Only you know the problems, solutions, details, and issues that are important. For example, you know why your Java projects succeed or fail. You know the types of projects being developed. Moreover, only you can help to keep *Java Report* continually focused on your needs. Aimed at knowledgeable Java users, feature articles explore different areas of the language, such as ways to use Java effectively, traps and pitfalls, novel uses, or arguments for and against particular language features. Articles containing descriptions of commercial products are normally excluded. In addition, in each issue an expert group of columnists explores in detail particular aspects of Java. Each issue provides book and product reviews, corporate profiles, one-on-one interviews with industry leaders and Java gurus, product announcements, and a survey of current trends in the industry.

This book is the second collection of articles from *Java Report* and covers the last twenty-four issues, from July 1997 to June 1999. Selecting articles proved difficult again because the *Java Report* had presented a wide range of interesting articles, including primer-style articles, enterprise articles, and those for Java power users. In addition, there were numerous great articles from columnists dealing with themes such as Java Means Business, Madison Avenue Java, ODMG, Effective Java, Durable APIs, Business Objects, Scott's Solutions, Modeling and Java, 2D Graphics and Distributed Computing. My task was to select 34 articles. I found it analogous to being in a candy store with only fifty cents and wondering where to start. Excellence alone was not a sufficient criterion to help prune the articles available to my target number. I used the following criteria to base my final decision:

- **Developer as intended reader.** I decided not to include any piece whose primary interest was business or managerial related, with the possible exception of Martin Schedlbauer and David Udin's article, "How to Successfully Migrate to Java." I wanted this collection to offer insights into Java for the developer.
- **Relevant issues for today's developer.** With the changes and additions made to Java over the last year, I decided not to include any piece that was dependent on releases of Java before 1.1. I wanted the topics addressed by the collection to match the concerns and issues of developers today.
- **Not readily available from other sources.** I also decided not to include introductory material easily found in other sources. The *Java Report* has had introductory pieces on APIs and techniques. However, many Java books deal with these topics at great length. If your bookshelf is not already filled with these types of books, I am sure it soon will be.

Using the above criteria, my first pass through the back issues left me with a list of 80 articles – more than twice as many as I required. I was proud of the quality of the articles I had selected and of the *Java Report* for its content, realizing it was going to be difficult to get that number to 34. On my second pass, I arranged the articles into sections relevant for today's developers and from that managed to get the number down to 50. Finally, I set a goal of no more than three articles per section and pruned the number of articles to 34. I could cut no more! I had not reached my goal, but I felt that to cut any more would take away from the overall flow of the collection.

The collection has eleven sections: "Getting Started with Java," "Migrating to Java," "Techniques 101, "Modeling and Patterns," "Java in a Distributed World," "Threads," "User Interfaces," "Security," "Testing," "Performance" and "Reality Check."

The collection begins with the section "Getting Started with Java," and it is only fitting that Richard Deadman's article on "A Guide to the Java Paradigm" leads the way. For many, Java was not their first object-oriented programming language. It was either C++ or Smalltalk. It is no secret that Java has a syntax similar to C++ and many classes similar to those in Smalltalk. However, that's where the similarities stop. As Richard puts it,

> Moving to a new language, even if it's one object-oriented language to another, involves some paradigm shifts in how you think about structuring and solving problems.

For example, you can't escape a discussion on pointers or cleaning up memory when working with C++. You can to a greater extent in Java, although even with it you can hold onto objects forever. Richard's article describes several good examples of what he calls "conceptual confusion" that you can avoid in order to write well-architected Java programs.

Known in the other languages, such as C and C++ as enumeration constants, the enum keyword permitted programmers to define new integer based types. However, there is no such keyword in Java. This does not imply that you can't build a similar mechanism into Java. The answer is always the same: build a class. Eric White's article on "Enumerating Types with Class" completes the section describing how to add Java type enumerations as object-oriented constructs to abstract the unsafe type enumerations of legacy procedural code.

Java has rapidly emerged for many as the language of choice for the enterprise, the desktop and small devices. To take advantage of Java's many capabilities, companies are faced with the task of migrating people that have never done any object-oriented programming or design. The collection's second section on "Migrating to Java" examines two different approaches to getting people to use Java.

The first article, by Martin Schedlbauer and David Udin, on "How to Successfully Migrate to Java" examines three different migration patterns addressing the unique training requirements of different groups of people, such as mainframe developers, system and application developers, and those with VisualBasic and C experience.

Rather than have developers go directly to using Java, another approach is to have them start with JavaScript. If you are already familiar with Web browsers and HTML, JavaScript is a natural step in your evolution to use Java. However, Java and JavaScript are not completely disjoint from one another, and as Steven Disbrow shows in his article, "Kissin' Cousins: Communicating Between Java and JavaScript," developers have a choice to use either one or both.

The next section in the collection, called "Techniques 101" contains three articles on techniques for building a developer's toolbox, designing by contract and internationalization. At the heart of any application a company has successfully built using object-oriented programming is a set of classes that developers trust and are willing to use over and over again. I am a firm believer of developing classes not only for today, but also for tomorrow. Since browsing source code is an essential task for an object-oriented developer, it should not be surprising to a developer that their classes will be scrutinized. Therefore, when you get the chance to build a class, do a good job. This is exactly what Steven Metsker did in his article on "Java Permutations and Combinations." He provides us with two excellent implementations of permutations and combinations and shows how to put them to good use by solving a logic puzzle using a generate-and-test technique.

When one thinks of Java interfaces, one thinks of a promise by a class to provide a body for the methods declared in the interface. However, this is only a syntactic construction. As Mike Mannion and Roy Phillips say in their article called "Prevention is Better than a Cure," "Design by contract is a specification that allows the designer or programmer to specify the semantics of a class's interface."

They describe how the addition of assertions to Java and designing by contract bring tremendous benefits, particularly for developers in the component market, by increasing the overall precision in handling pre-, post- and invariant conditions in your software.

The section's final article addresses the technique of developing software that can be deployed easily across a variety of world markets, with different languages and writing systems. The Network Economy is here, and if you do not think of your Java applications as being used internationally, you should. Mark Davis, Doug Felt, and John Raley discuss several problems posed by the different writing systems and describe how you can use the new TextLayout class in Java to handle these problems easily and efficiently.

The next section is called "Modeling and Patterns," and it is only appropriate that Craig Larman, *Java Report*'s resident modeling columnist, leads off the section. Any type of modeling activity, unless it can be of real value, is arguably not productive. As Craig says, "Modeling and diagramming should practically aid the development of better software."

In the section's first two articles, Craig describes how a conceptual model can help you succinctly visualize the vocabulary of a new or large problem space and can help you illustrate the important relationships between the key ideas and information it contains.

Two of the key goals of modeling are to help save time and to develop better designs. The use of software patterns is another excellent way to improve your designs. By applying them, you build into your software well-thought-out, proven designs that developers have used successfully in the past. The section concludes with two software patterns. The first by Andrew Smith, called "Distributed Observer Chains," extends the Model-View pattern to make distributed objects observable. The second pattern by Sachitra Gupta et al., called "Event Notifier," describes how to enable components to react to the occurrence of particular events in other components without knowledge of one another, while still allowing the dynamic participation of components and dynamic introduction of new events.

To develop software for a distributed environment forces one to consider several different architectures and components. You can make a great deal of money these days if you can present companies with end-to-end solutions for their applications. With so many options, the problem is to determine what items should be put together and when it is appropriate to do so.

In the section called "Java in a Distributed World," we give you advice on three such options. The section's first article by Steven Farley, called "Mobile Agent System Architectures," provides a new way of thinking about distributed computing: a mobile agent. Rather than sending messages between distributed objects, a mobile agent in a mobile agent system is an object that can autonomously move and execute where and when required.

The section's second article by Ron Repking, called "Deployment Strategies for Java Client Applications," compares and contrasts options available for client-side deployment of Java applications. The three strategies discussed include Web deployment, stand-alone application deployment, and using broadcast and push technology.

Not forgetting the server-side of distributed computing, the section's last article by John O'Shea from Iona, called "Locating CORBA Objects from Java," describes how your client applications and applets should bootstrap into the CORBA system and how CORBA servers should distribute CORBA object references so that clients can easily and efficiently find them.

The ability to do multithreaded programming in Java is a feature that most developers use to build robust applications. Conceptually, it is easy to understand Java threads and how to use them to build multithreaded applications. However, effectively using threads is often difficult. In the next section, called "Threads" we have four articles chosen from *Java Report* to help you use threads better.

The first article by Peter Bosch, called "Effective Multithreading," describes a framework to thread-separate servers from the clients that call them. Thread separation is useful for many reasons, including allowing the client to do other things while waiting on a response from the server and limiting the number of threads in use. As Steve Ball and John Crawford say in the section's second article, "A volatile brew is formed by mixing assignment and threads."

In their article, called "Multithreaded Assignment Surprises," the two examine the perils and surprises lurking within the most innocent-looking statements that use assignment. And the article called "Multithreaded Exception Handling in Java," Joe De Russo III and Peter Haggar describe how to use threads and exceptions together. As they say, "How effective is writing a multithreaded Java program if it is incapable of properly handling exceptions occurring on secondary threads?"

Bill Lewis completes the discussion on threads with his article called "Writing More Complex Synchronization in Java." In his article, he covers synchronization situations that are not obvious and shows you how to extend the synchronization primitives.

Good software is usually the result of good architecture. Therefore, it should not be difficult to understand that user interfaces should be easy to develop and maintain if they too are constructed with this principle in mind. However, for those early adopters of Java, building modular object-oriented user interfaces with the AWT was tough. With the addition of the delegation event model in JDK 1.1, the picture changed, providing the potential of separating the views for the control parts of the user interface. This separation, know and the model-view-controller (MVC) architecture was well known in the Smalltalk community. It just took Java a little longer to catch on.

In the next section, called "User Interfaces," we begin with two articles on MVC. The first by John Hunt, called "Constructing Modular User Interfaces in Java," discusses why MVC is so important to Java and how to apply it to build user interfaces that are robust, principled, and reusable. In David Geary's article, "JFC's Swing," he examines how MVC is used by Swing, Java's collection of lightweight components.

MVC is not the only architecture you can use for constructing user interfaces. The section's last article, by Roger Spall, "Panel States," describes an efficient architecture for presenting a group of user interface panels in a specific sequence to a user.

The next section examines the issue of security in Java. I still believe security is one of the most overlooked areas in application development. When I ask developers if they believe security is important for their software, they all answer "yes." When asked if they are adding it to their application, most say "no." With more education on security, I believe this situation will change.

The section's first two articles are by Steve Burnett, a crypto engineer at RSA Data Security, Inc.. In his first article, called "Using the JavaSoft Security Package," he describes how to sign or verify data using Digital Signal Algorithm (DSA) with Java's security package. His example will help you to get a better understanding of Java's Cryptography architecture.

In his second article, called "Using the Java Cryptographic Extensions," he demonstrates how to encrypt and decrypt data using DES and how to create an RSA digital envelop with the extensions package.

Signing, encryption, and decryption are security features that are provided by Sun. Developers can also add their own security mechanisms. In the section's final article by Greg Frascadore, called "Java Application Server Security Using Capabilities," he describes an approach to guarding sensitive server data. Often accomplished by access lists, his capability approach is less cluttered, more efficient,. and more failsafe.

There is no doubt that the first product to market in a given area captures a good slice of the market share. However, the only way it can keep or gain in its share of the market is if it has quality. There is no better way to achieve quality in a product than by making sure it is well tested BEFORE it hits the market. I don't know how many times I have told people that I would gladly use an application that has fewer features and works than one with hundreds of features that doesn't.

In the "Testing" section, we have three articles that examine different aspects of testing. The first article by Kamesh Pemmaraju takes a holistic approach. In his "Effective Test Strategies for Enterprise-Critical Applications" article, he presents a case-study of how testing was done on a Java-based financial application.

At the other side of the testing scale, we have David Houlding's article called "Putting Java Beans to the Test." He illustrates strategies for testing Java Beans, describing how to ensure that the beans you develop are verifiable through testing.

The final article in the section, by Kent Beck and Erich Gamma, describes how to structure your test cases and run them in a framework called JUnit. As they put it, "Code a little, test a little, code a little, ..." With their framework you can put these words to the test.

The one capability that Java must exceed in everyone's mind to become the premier language for development is performance. This is not to say that Java does not perform well. In fact, in most applications I have seen, Java performs fine. I am just tired of hearing that it is not as fast as C++. The point is that Java only has to be fast enough to run your applications and no faster. An analogy to this is that we don't drive cars that can go 200 m.p.h.; we don't need them to go that fast.

In the section titled "Performance," the articles look at different aspects of performance that Java developers have control over. It is up to Sun and the other virtual machine (VM) companies to make VMs execute Java code at the speed of light. However, there are many techniques you can use to make your code go faster. Allen Wirfs-Brock's article, called "Breaking the Speed Limits," describes ways to change your code to attack VM inefficiencies. Laura Werner's article, called "Efficient Text Searching in Java," shows you how to use Java's Collator class to help with searching. Finally, John Cerwin's article, called "Enterprise Applets and Archive Functionality," describes how to use Java's Zip classes to improve performance over the network. By using the right class for the right job and in the right way, developers can get the performance they need today.

There does not seem to be a feature or API that Java doesn't offer to developers. However, for all of the advantages and benefits of Java, it is still up to the developer to make sure that he uses Java correctly and when appropriate. In the last section, called "Reality Check," we look at two such areas: primitive types and math support.

Sherman Alpert describes the advantages and disadvantages of using types such as int, boolean, float, long, and short. Included with the language due to its similarity with C and C++, and for performance and verification reasons, primitive types break with Java's object-oriented nature. Sherman's discussion will help you decide whether they are worth using.

Related to primitive types is the issue of how accurate numerical computations are in Java. In the article, called "Getting the Numbers Right, A Cautionary Tale," Ken Dickey reflects on how math is done in Java, using a specific example of interval arithmetic. In sharing their experiences, both writers will help you to get the right answers, using the best classes for the job.

After reflecting on my task of selecting and introducing the articles in this collection, I have the same regret as I did with the previous collection. I wish that I were not limited as much by space. The *Java Report* has been fortunate in having an excellent group of writers and columnists from its conception. However, no one person represents its voice; it is their collective voices that make the magazine a success.

Our goal for the *Java Report* is to help you do it right. We want to keep you informed of the latest developments and products in the industry. We want to help you learn and use Java's new APIs. We want to provide you with tips, techniques, and patterns for Java. We want to help you understand Java and object-oriented programming issues, provide answers to difficult questions, and provide you with solutions to problems you will encounter. We want to help you and your projects succeed!

To help us achieve our goal, we need to hear from you. We need to know why your Java projects succeed or fail. We need to know the types of projects you are developing. We want your help keeping *Java Report* continually focused on your needs. *Java Report* is committed to you in being your premier source of information on Java. In return, I want to hear your views and any contributions you would like to make.

Dwight Deugo,
editor-in-chief
Java Report

GETTING STARTED
WITH JAVA

WHEN IN ROME:
A GUIDE TO THE JAVA PARADIGM

RICHARD DEADMAN

MOVING TO A NEW LANGUAGE involves some paradigm shifts in how you think about structuring programs and solving problems. Often we think in terms of solutions instead of problems and so ask questions like, "How do I pass a method pointer Java?" instead of "How do I encapsulate a behavior reference in Java?" This is particularly important for C++ programmers migrating to Java, because the similarity in syntax between the languages can lead to the assumption that the language paradigm is identical.

I'll discuss two classes of problems faced by developers. The first is what I call "Conceptual Confusion," where a user of one language carries their assumptions to another language and then gets confused when their assumptions are invalid. The second class is the desire for new features to be added to the language. This "Creeping Featurism" generally involves adding complexity to the language for the sake of mimicking another language's feature, often no more than syntactic sugar. That is, the proposed feature may reduce the typing without adding to the power of the language.

Let me warn you of my bias: I find that too many features in a language confuse me. I find that a simple language based on a single paradigm provides for less confusion, better maintainability, and quicker code development. You may understand that neat "constant reference" feature, but think of the person who may have to fix, reuse, or extend your code a year from now.

CONCEPTUAL CONFUSION

There are at least four good examples of conceptual confusion that I have run across. Mostly these affect people migrating from either C++ or Smalltalk.

VIRTUAL METHODS

A common mistake is to assume that casting an object in Java changes which methods are bound to that object. Java uses late binding; that is, the instance method invoked when a message is sent to an object is determined by the object's type, not the type of the handle to the object. If the object is a sub-type of a base-type, then the sub-type's instance method will always get called, whether or not the handle to the object is declared as of the base-type, an interface, or any sub-type between the base-type and the subtype. This obviously has to be true when the handle is declared to be of an interface type. So. . .

```
class Foo{
  public String toString(){
     return "An instance of class Foo";
}

class Bar extends Foo{
  public String toString(){
     return "An instance of class Bar";
}

public class FooBar{
  public static void main(String[] args) {
     Foo myPersonalFoo=new Bar();

     System.out.println(myPersonalFoo);
  }
}
```

will print "An instance of class Bar."

It should be up to the object to determine how messages sent to it will be handled. Note that this is the opposite of how static methods are bound in Java. More on this later.

Because the default in C++ is for non-virtual methods, some C++ programmers can inadvertently assume that early binding takes place and then not understand the behavior of their code.

All the compiler checks is that the message is supported by the handle's object type. To send a sub-type's message to an object handle that does not support that message, you must cast the handle to the proper sub-type:

```
import java.rmi.server.*;

…

Object vectorContent = aVector.firstElement();
if(vectorContent instanceof ServerRef) {
  System.out.println("Remote call from"+
    ((ServerRef)vectorContent.getHostName()));
}
```

PASS-BY-REFERENCE

Every variable in Java is a handle to either a basic type or an object instance. When you pass an object into a method, or out via a return value, you are actually passing a copy of the reference; the object pointed to stays the same. And there is no way to restrict access to that referenced object (see the discussion below on the "const" feature of C++). So, you can alter the state of the object pointed to (unless they are immutable—including basic types), but you cannot change someone else's reference to that object, because their reference was copied when it was given to you.

This is identical to Smalltalk's parameter passing but contrasts significantly with the C++ allowed modes:

- *Pass-by-reference.* This is the same as it is in Smalltalk and Java but involves passing the pointer to an object explicitly. The receiver must then explicitly de-reference the pointer. If you don't "get" pointers, you shouldn't be playing with C and C++.
- *Pass-by-value.* A copy is made of the parameter. In Java the equivalent can be accomplished by cloning the object before sending it.
- *Pass-by-reference-but-seem-like-a-value.* This is the most confusing C++ addition, the "Reference." Here you tell the method that you are passing a reference to the object, but you hide the syntax to make it seem like the object was passed as a value.

As long as you understand the paradigm, you can achieve your desired contract between objects within Java with the benefit of a simpler object model.

(Note: With RMI, the rules change for distributed objects. All parameters, which are not themselves remote handles, are serialized between the virtual machine, effectively implementing a pass-by-value paradigm for non-Remote objects.)

CLASS/STATIC METHODS

In Smalltalk, classes and instances are both first-class objects, and there is a name space separation between class methods and instance methods. If an instance wants to call a registration method on its class to add itself to some class-based cache of instances, it can perform:

```
addInstanceToCache
    self class addInstanceToCache: self.
```

Subclasses of the base class can override "addInstanceToCache" and they will be called by instances of the subclass that perform the "addInstance-ToCache" method. In other words, the class methods are dynamically bound in Smalltalk, as are all methods.

Smalltalkers moving to Java often mistake static methods and variables as being equivalent to "class" methods and variables in Smalltalk. This is not strictly true. While static methods and variables are bound to a class and not an instance, they are resolved "statically" to the type of the variable (or named class), by the compiler. If the variable type and instance class are different, the static method or variable is not overridden at runtime by the instance's class. Hence:

```
class Bar {
    static String getName() { return "Bar";}
}

class Baz extends Bar {
    static String getName() {return "Baz";}
}

public class Foo {
    public static void main(String[] args) {
        Bar myBar = new Baz();
        System.out.println(myBar.getName());
    }
}
```

will output "Bar" and not "Baz," even though "myBar" is of class Baz.

Here is one of Java's great inconsistencies: Instance methods involve late binding, but class methods involve early binding. Think of static as meaning "bound statically to the class at compile time." Now write it out fifty times.

A similar problem exists in the understanding of Interfaces…

No Static Interface Methods

Interfaces are often seen as contracts or signatures for classes. As such, interfaces can define instance methods that classes must implement. Obviously, instance variables cannot be defined in an interface, because the interface does not define behavior that could operate on such instance variables.

But people are often confused as to why interfaces can define static variables and cannot define static methods. After all, what is the purpose of a static variable if there is not static behavior? And why can't I use an interface to declare that all classes that implement this interface will implement these static methods?

Well, the answer gets back to understanding how static variables and methods work. They are bound at compile time against the class identified either by class name or variable type. For variables, this means that you can actually use interface state:

```
char doneCharacterForMyText = java.text.
    CharacterIterator.DONE;
```

Often interface variables are defined as final and given in uppercase to simulate the C "#define" feature, but they are not limited to this use. Note that if your class tries to implement multiple interfaces, which define the same static variable, the compiler will throw an exception—this is as close as you can get to the multiple-inheritance "Diamond of Death."

For methods, what does it mean to define a static method in the interface? Well, because static method calls are always bound to the type of the variable, it means that any calls to these static methods from variables, which are defined as instances of the interface, will try to invoke the interface's static method—and because, by definition, interfaces cannot have behavior, this would be a problem.

Some argue that this is an argument for static methods and variables being dynamically bound, but that moves us into the next section...

Creeping Featurism

Some features, like Inner Classes, are conceptually useful and can be added without altering the language paradigm. Providing Template support, while really syntactic sugar for automatic code generation, has proven so useful to data management that, given the anemic support in Java for different container types, is very likely on the list of future features being debated inside the bowels of JavaSoft. However, most of the additional language features being proposed on various newsgroups and mailing lists can already be solved within the language without adding the complexity of their syntactic sugar.

Here is a rundown of some of the features I have heard cries for within the last year:

FIRST-CLASS METHODS

JUSTIFICATION:

Sometimes we need to tell an entity which method to call in response to an asynchronous event. This is the so-called "callback" function pointer prevalent in so many C and C++ APIs. Methods should be first-class citizens in Java.

REBUTTAL:

Java is an OO language (unlike C++, which is an OO/Procedural mix). While Java's reflection mechanisms do allow you to find a method object, this method object is not bound to any particular instance. Because instance methods are useless out of the context of the object in which they reside, you really need to pass the context of the method, that is, the object. But method pointers would allow me to pass different methods into the same notifier, you say? Well here, the adapter pattern (Gamma, E., et al., *Design Patterns: Elements of Reusable Object-Oriented Software,* Addison-Wesley, 1995) comes in handy, mixed with the syntactic sugar of Inner classes.

Define a notification interface that the notifier understands and uses to notify clients. Now the object that needs to be notified can implement this interface and be passed to the notifier, or an Inner class can be used to create an adapter to the object that needs to be notifed. This is the basis of Java's Observer/Observable system, as well. In fact, now we can provide more than one notification method simply, which otherwise would require sending multiple callback function pointers.

An added benefit of registering objects through and observable pattern is that "user data" does not have to be registered with the event source. This context information can be saved with the observer object without having to break encapsulation and expose that data to the observable, which has no intrinsic interest in the data. In addition, a single instance can create and register multiple observer adapters for each context/event it is interested in.

AUTO-DELEGATION

JUSTIFICATION:

Because Java does not have multiple inheritance, the alternative approach to coalescing the behavior of two classes into one subclass is through delegation.

While Java provides interfaces that allow delegation contracting, the hooking up of the interface implementors to the delegate's methods is both trivial and laborious. Why not just add a flag to the Java source code that indicates that this interface's methods should be delegated to this internal instance variable?

REBUTTAL:
This is syntactic sugar in the highest form. No additional functionality is being added to the language, just automatic typing. In addition, you would then need to define how to resolve interface method intersections, and how to override automatic delegation. Because the design decisions are hidden from the designer, side effects of other changes to the object model may not be transparent. Say you implement both interface A and B, and delegate them to a and b, respectively. Now, a change in the object model moves a method from interface A to interface B. Even though your signature hasn't changed, you now need to recompile your source code, because the hidden delegation decisions are no longer valid.

This is not to say that the automatic generation of code does not have its place. IDEs use code generation to create GUIs; the BeanBox uses code generation to glue components together using adapter classes. The difference is that here the code generation is part of a tool and not part of the language. An automatic interface delegate tool would be a useful addition to an IDE toolset. The generated code would be Java source code and could be intelligently managed within the scope of the application builder.

SUPPORT FOR CONSTANT PARAMETERS

JUSTIFICATION:
When I send object to another object as a parameter or return value, I want to ensure that the other object does not change its state. By specifying that the variable is of type "const," I can ensure that the other object does not modify the object (unless, in C++, the method casts the object to a non-constant variable).

REBUTTAL:
If you want to protect the data from unauthorized changes, Java supplies at least three other options that do not add the conceptual complexity of const (which is not truly secure in C++ anyway):

1. *Cloning.* Here you clone the object before passing it to ensure that the receiver has a copy that is decoupled from the object you are pointing to. This is expensive, but much safer than the C++ "const" feature. Note, however, that by default, cloning in Java involves a shallow copy. Shallow

copy means that only the object is copied, not any objects contained within the object as instance variables. Because all variables are handles to other instances or to base types, if the referenced objects are not also cloned, the original instance and its shallow copy will both contain handles to the same entities. So the original object and the cloned object I passed you will share any contained objects, leaving the possibility of some shared state. Implementing your own deep-copy (which recursively clones all state to some specified level) is recommended if this is a serious problem. A simple form of deep-copy is performed by Java's Serialization facility.

2. *Protected interface.* Write an interface that does not modify your object's state and implement the interface within your object. If the object is passed as a type of this interface, the effect is equivalent to the C++ "const" feature—that is, you have protection but it can be cast aside.

3. *Protection Proxy.* (Gamma et al., p. 207). Wrap up the object within a protection proxy object, which checks and disallows certain access on the object. Here the whole interface is exported, but some methods will return a "Disallowed" exception. This also allows for capabilities-based dynamic authorization (i.e., user access can be more finely controlled). This protection strategy is probably the most secure, but may be the most work.

To add "const" to the language would not only add to the conceptual complexity, it would also require specifying which methods were safe to send to a "const" version of the class (essentially a parallel class, much like every class has a parallel array class)—at least as much work as defining a protection interface. This is particularly true because Java involves much more passing of objects instead of raw data types (int, long) than is often found in C++ programs.

IN/OUT PARAMETERS

JUSTIFICATION:
This is the flip side of the "const" issue. Because Java passes variables using a copied reference handle, I can send an object to another object, where it is modified. However, if the receiving object wants to replace the object, my reference still points to the old object. I want to be able to pass my reference indirectly, so that the receiver can modify my reference directly, pointing me to a new object.

REBUTTAL:
There are several ways to accomplish passing references without complicating the calling semantics of Java with "const," "by-reference," or "by-reference-but-look-like-value." The easiest way is to wrap up the passed object in a container object, such as one-element array of the object being passed.

Then, when the receiver changes the object in the array's first slot, the new object will be accessible to the sending object through the array.

As with many other issues on this list, this is an example of using OO patterns and techniques to solve problems instead of making the language more complex and incorporating the techniques into the language semantics. Kind of like RISC for programming languages.

INLINED GETTERS AND SETTERS

JUSTIFICATION:
For performance reasons, I would like to have access to my instance variables "inlined." That is, the byte code is copied from the receivers class to the senders to reduce runtime method lookup and invocation time.

REBUTTAL:
Inlining is difficult with polymorphic late-bound languages. You have to know that the object receiving the message has not overridden your inlined method, so the method had better be "final." If the method is final, many Java compilers will allow inlining as an optimization option. In essence, the inlining decision is removed from the language and moved to the compiler.

Note, however, that inlining may speed up your code at the cost of large class files. A classic computing time-space trade-off. Large class files may mean greater download times and even, if your memory is running low, slower performance due to memory swapping. Optimizing your code is rarely as simple as it first seems and often has side effects (such as extensibility and support problems). There are many rules to optimization, but I like:

1. Don't do it unless absolutely necessary
2. Don't do it yet
3. If you do optimize, make sure you're optimizing the system bottlenecks (run your system through a call tracer)

MULTI-VALUED RETURN PARAMETERS

JUSTIFICATION:
My method can take multiple parameters, why can't I specify return values?

REBUTTAL:
One of the key rules of object-oriented technology is that each method should do one and only one thing. This is a rule that should occasionally be broken,

particularly during distributed interface design. However, as a fundamental rule, it is a good one, and has led (along with the C and procedure history of many OO languages) to single-value return for Java methods. It is certainly semantically simple.

Enough with excuses. Multi-value return is sometimes useful. But if you are returning a collection of related objects, maybe you should take a more OO approach and encapsulate the data into an object. If the data is really unrelated and creating an encapsulation class doesn't make sense, you can always use arrays, Vectors, or some other generic collection class.

SATIRIC JAVA FEATURE REQUEST LIST

I first posted this list to a mailing list in December 1996 in response to a thread advocating the addition of Lisp-style multiple return values to Java methods. Additional contributions have been noted.

Golly gosh, now that we have spent time analyzing the syntactic sugar needed to add multiple-return values to the language, I have some other suggestions. I have programmed in Assembler, Machine (PDP-11), Fortran-77, COBOL, BASIC, and other powerful languages and would like to add some features to Java that will occasionally make it easier to think in my old ways.

Here are some features that Java needs now to become a serious programming language:

1. Goto statement. There's the code I want to do in that other class, so why can't I just:

        goto OtherClass.method()::line;

2. Push and Pop. Heck, in-line assembly code should be allowed. I know where those values I want are, let me get at 'em.

3. Turn off garbage collection and add free()/delete(). I can do a better job than any compiler/VM.

4. Pointers. Please, I finally understand these. Give 'em back.

5. Compile-time platform optimization, header files, #define, #pragma.

6. *More basic types modifiers.* Microsoft has the right idea.

        unsigned long FAR PASCAL *data.

DYNAMIC "STATIC"

JUSTIFICATION:

As I discussed in the previous section, static variables and methods are bound to the class or interface at compile time. This means that you cannot have calls to your static methods be overridden by subclass static methods based on the type of object your variable is pointing to. Dynamic class variables and methods are a nice clean feature, and they are implemented in languages such as Smalltalk.

7. Friend classes, methods, variables, Vector components. I would like to set up a Vector and say that only some of its members are available to other classes, i.e.,
     Vector data = newVector(3, 1::private, 2::friend, 3::public);

8. First-class methods. Who needs OO after all?

9. More passing mechanisms. Add Pass-by-reference, pass-by-value, pass-by-reference-but-look-like-a-value (C++ reference).

10. Multiple inheritance. Never used it, but someday I may...

11. Enforced Hungarian notation, which allows us to avoid declaring variables, something I liked in Fortran. Instead of:
     UserInfo user = new UserInfo();
   we could have:
     cUserInfo_data + new UserInfo();
   Mark Wutka (wutka@netcom.com) suggested **(http://MetaDigest.XCF.Berkeley.EDU/archive/ advanced-java/9611/0834.html)** an enhancement to this for either:

   a. Implicit typing. The first time a cUserInfo_data variable is used, the default constructor is automatically called.
   b. "Extended Hungarian notation" that could automatically define the class within the variable name.

12. More fluff words so that the code is more readable, *à la* COBOL:
     add iNative_first to iNative_second giving iNative_result;

Hmmm, maybe I should just forward 11 and 12 to the C++ committee; they're more responsive and understanding anyway.

REBUTTAL:

The problem is that you would have to either add a new keyword and a new type of class variable and method (try explaining to someone that we have both static and dynamic class methods and variables and the rules for using them with Interfaces) or break almost all code already in existence. The cows are out of the barn, so closing the barn door doesn't help at this point.

CONCLUSION

One of the strengths of great languages like C, Lisp, or Smalltalk is their conceptual simplicity. In C, you have pointers and the functions, and if you understand these, the rest is straightforward. In fact, a general programming language can solve any problem, the differences really lie in the conceptual paradigm they support and the syntactic sugar provided to make programming less error-prone. Often, there is a trade-off between power and maintainability that must be made by the language designers. For some domains, such as OS programming, low-level power is imperative; but for the vast majority of domains long-term maintainability, reuse, and extensibility are much more important. As faster processors and better compilers have become available, we have seen the progression of dominant paradigms migrate from Assembly to Functional to object-oriented simply because the dominant problem has changed from performance to manageability as the complexity of our systems increased.

In an effort to keep the language as simple and clean as possible, the Java language designers purposely chose to provide a simple programming paradigm. Some exceptions were made, notably the inclusion of basic data types that are not objects. But overall, the language is simple, elegant, and clean.

Programmers used to solving problems using the syntactic features of other languages often pine for the adoption of those features in Java. What they miss is that there is a conceptual cost to adding those features, both in complexity and in paradigm. This is particularly difficult for C++ programmers because the syntax of Java was purposely modeled on the syntax of C++, and this often leads new Java programmers to bring their C++ mindset with them to Java.

To write well-architected Java programs, a designer must have a good understanding of the language paradigm, remember to think of patterns and not techniques, and remember to ask him/herself "How do I solve this problem?" rather than "How do I apply this technique native to my old language?"

ENUMERATING TYPES WITH CLASS

ERIC WHITE

KNOWN IN THE C/C++ language world as "enumerations constants," the enum keyword permits C/C++ programmers to define new integer-based types. The following code fragment, (*The C Programming Language, 2nd ed.,* B. Kernigan and D. Ritchie, 1988) demonstrates the use of the C/C++ enum keyword:

```
enum months {JAN = 1, FEB, MAR, APR, MAY, JUN, JUL, AUG, SEP,
        OCT, NOV, DEC };
```

This code fragment establishes a new, integer-based type months that can be used to declare program variables or constants with type values of JAN . . . DEC. The C/C++ compiler will perform limited syntax checking with respect to months variables or constants and, so, provides the basic type enumeration construct for these languages.

The use of enumerations is much more prevalent in C-based applications than C++ programs, primarily because C++ has richer constructs for safely-typed variables and constants. Nonetheless, the need to understand and adhere to ANSI C enumerations in new Java code exists. In my particular case, I had to understand and decompose message-level enumerations built into network data packets that originated from a C-based application. Native method interfaces were unnecessary, since I could easily open a network socket in Java and just start listening for network traffic. Within my Java code, I wanted a robust and safe way of representing and manipulating enumeration types that started life as C enums.

Note that an enumeration type is a different concept from the Java Enumeration interface. The Java Enumeration interface describes a template for defining a new class, adhering to a minimum required set of public methods.

An enumeration type is a class that implements a well-known, closed set of type objects, where a runtime instantiation of the enumeration type class can only have a value that is a member of that closed set of object. For example, to instantiate a month object, that new object must have a value in the set [JAN...DEC]. Similarly, another type enumeration might describe the colors of the rainbow and an instantiated object of that type could not have the type value Monday.

The simple and "unsafe" Java approach is to declare static final ints that correspond to the integer-based C/C++ equivalents. However, to evolve from such basic type enumerations, exploit the power and safety of Java constructs, and basically write better code, an object-oriented approach to type enumerations is required.

MONTHS WITH CLASS

To establish a value-based month enumeration type, we encapsulate the values as private attributes within the class. To minimize code, we could easily eliminate the use of private constants to represent the numeric values of our enumerated type, but the private constants make for better code readablility:

```java
public class Month {

/*Declare constants for numeric month values */

    private final static int jan = 1;
    private final static int feb = 2;
    private final static int mar = 3;
... etc.
```

and, of course, a private attribute that holds the type value:

```java
private int numeric_value;
```

The internal value storage could really be of any type—from basic Java types to complex class types. This example implementation uses an integer for internal value storage. The new Month class needs a private constructor that accepts a numeric argument for initialization and sets the internal value attribute to the passed initialization argument.

```java
private Month(int value) { numeric_value = value; }
```

The private constructor prevents external object instantiations and ensures that only static objects created within the Month class can be instantiated.

Within an application program using the Month type enumeration, we can have a null object reference for which we must have application program logic, but we have a much more robust type enumeration than a set of static final ints. Now, we can declare the static class attributes that serve as the actual constant enumeration types, using the previously declared private constants as the initialization argument for the month class constructor. We also declare a private array of these enumerated types for use later:

```
public final static Month JAN = new Month(jan);
public final static Month FEB = new Month(feb);
public final static Month MAR = new Month(mar);
...etc.

protected final static Month [ ] element =
                {JAN,
                 FEB,
                 MAR,
    ... etc.
```

At this point, we have sufficient code to implement and use a value-based enumeration type, which is only a slight extension of Scott Oaks' original code. However, this fundamental class design has so much more potential that we really must extend it further.

We can encapsulate some useful informational and attribute access methods, providing discovery methods to users of these type enumeration objects. We'll use some of these methods later when we look at implementing a Java Enumerator:

```
private final static String [ ] StringRep =
                        {"January",
                         "February",
                         "March",
                         . . . etc.

public int numericValueOf () {
    return numeric_value;
}

    public String stringValueOf () {
    return StringRep [ numeric_value-1];

    }
```

```
public int size () {
return element. length;

}
```

We still don't have an "external" means of instantiating an enumeration type object, given an integer value. We need a public means of instantiating a Month object with a numeric value, but we cannot use a constructor, because the method signature will clash with the existing private constructor. So we'll provide a special function for instantiating value-based enumeration types:

```
public static final Month createMonth(int index)
            throws NoSuchElementException {
    if ((index>= lowerBoundOf()) && (index
        <= upperBoundOf ()))

        return element [index-1];

    throw new NoSuchElementException
            ("Month.createMonth(" +index
            +") index argument out of
            bounds");

}
```

Note that the createMonth method makes use of the Month array we declared previously. An alternate implementation (and one of my early prototypes) used a switch statement to return the individual static enumeration objects. Since this implementation could exploit the sequential nature of the enumerated type's numeric value, it seemed more efficient (with respect to memory consumption and access times) to use an array. Also not that the createMonth code depends upon another two methods for getting the upper and lower boundary values for the type value. These boundary access methods could be useful outside of the class, so we make them public methods, albeit final and static:

```
public final static int lowerBoundOf () {
return jan;
}

public final static int upperBoundOf () {
return dec;
}
```

At this point it's important to reinforce that, in this example, the legal values for the enumerated type are sequential, which makes it much easier to implement boundary checks. Type values, for other enumerated types, might not be so easily "bounded" and the logic for checking boundary conditions could be quite a bit more complex in the public createType method of your own enumerated type classes.

The last, useful functionality we could add is support for a Java Enumeration interface. To do so, we must enhance the month class a little more by adding a public method that returns an object that implements the Java Enumeration interface:

```
public final Enumeration getEnumeration () {
        return new MonthEnumerator (this);
}
```

The concrete methods required to implement a Java Enumeration interface are hasMoreElements() and nextElement(). Again, the sequential nature of the Month class numeric values is a key consideration in the implementation of the MonthEnumerator class. The Enumeration class is shown in its entirety in Listing 1.

With a complete class definition of Month and MonthEnumerator, we can instantiate enumeration type objects and test their values quite simply:

```
Month m = Month.createMonth (3);

If (m==Month.MAR)
```

Listing 1.

```
final class MonthEnumerator implements Enumeration {
    Month month;
    int index;

    MonthEnumerator (Month m) {
      month = m;
      index =  O; }

  public boolean hasMoreElements () {
    return index < month.element.length; }

  public Object nextElement () {
    if (index ++< month.size()) {
        month = month.nextMonth ();
        return month; }

    throw new NoSuchElementException ("Month
        Enumerator.nextElement
        ("+index+") out of bounds"); }

  public void reset (){
    index =  O; } }
```

```
System.out.printIn("Month is" + m.stringValueOf ());
```

A type-safe enumeration object can be a valuable means for Java programs to encapsulate and interact with "legacy" C/C++ code that employs the enum keyword to define enumeration constants. The Java enumeration class approach provides a software engineering improvement over the enum approach and abstracts the numeric value basis for such enumeration constants. I have found the enumeration class approach presented herein extremely valuable in creating network-centric Java applications that must interact with C/C++ programs via TCP/IP or UDP/IP protocols. As C/C++ network applications encode value-based enumerations via enum, the new Java applications can rely on an enumeration class to abstract the legacy implementation details and provide a clean and type-safe programming feature for newer, Java-based applications.

Java type enumerations are valuable object-oriented constructs to abstract the unsafe type enumeratins of legacy procedural code. Type enumeration classes can be useful in network application programming, native method interfaces, and wholesale code porting efforts.

MIGRATING TO JAVA

How to Successfully Migrate to Java

Martin Schedlbauer and David Udin

JAVA HAS RAPIDLY emerged as an important tool for the development of cross-platform, distributed applications. While Java has been primarily associated with the Web, it is a much broader technology with applications far beyond the Internet. To take advantage of the capabilities of Java and its wide range of application programming services, an organization must enhance the skill base of its workforce in several critical areas, among them object-oriented programming, interactive and event-driven application development, distributed (client/server) systems architecture, and coming up rapidly, design and use of components (beans) for Java's component architecture, *JavaBeans*.

To create an effective and successful migration strategy for its development and project management staff, a company must consider several factors. These factors are discussed in detail in this article.

AUDIENCE

Each group of potential Java users will likely need a different migration strategy. While one group, such as software developers, may need in-depth knowledge of the Java programming facilities, another group, such as project managers, need only a superficial understanding of the language features but a strong understanding of the impact that the use of Java has on a project. The audience for a migration effort can be broken into five distinct groups:

- Software Developers
- Web Masters
- Software Architects
- Project Managers
- Business Analysts

This report will closely examine how each group can successfully migrate to Java.

Experience

The technical background that a person migrating to Java brings to the table has a significant impact on the training approach to be taken. For example, developers that have experience in C++ or another object-oriented language tend to understand Java much faster than those migrating from traditional languages, such as COBOL. Similarly, the event-driven nature of the Java user interface packages AWT and Swing are easier to comprehend if one has exposure to event-driven GUI development, such as with Visual Basic or PowerBuilder. Finally, Java is an object-oriented language that requires a solid understanding of object technology to be used effectively.

Overall, the following dimensions impact any migration strategy to Java:

- Language background: 4GL (Visual Basic, PowerBuilder), C++, COBOL
- GUI development experience
- Distributed system development, including client/server development
- Object-oriented analysis & design

Objectives

Java has several roles in distributed application development: Web-based applets, remote business objects, stand-alone client/server applications, and components (beans), each of which greatly influences how a migration strategy to Java must be planned. Commonly, Java can be used to develop:

- Intranet or Internet client services in the form of applets
- Server objects to provide shared business services (Servlets)
- Component-based development (JavaBeans)
- Stand-alone applications

COMPANY CONTEXT

The environment in which Java will be deployed also influences the migration strategy, particularly if legacy systems must be integrated. For example, a mainframe application may need to be accessed through an object broker, such as CORBA.

We have identified the following company context variables that can sway the direction and scope of any migration strategy to Java:

- Legacy system integration
- Existing database management systems
- Security requirements
- Management and operations strategies

TRAINING APPROACHES

Migration to Java is possible with a variety of approaches, each with its benefits and drawbacks:

- Instructor-led training
- Web-based or computer-based courses
- Mentoring
- Self-study

The remainder of this article will address how to evaluate the current skills of a development team and how to design and implement an effective migration strategy for the development team that incorporates an appropriate mix of training, self-education, and mentoring.

WHAT ARE YOUR GOALS?

What do you want to train your staff to do? Build large-scale platform-independent distributed applications? Replace Visual Basic front ends in client-server applications? Replace CGI scripts with Java Servlets? Spice up a Web page with singing and dancing applets? Java has a role in all of these, but the training emphasis ranges from learning component assembly tools (bean assemblers) to the Java language and object-oriented development.

Your initial training goal should be to understand the new possibilities provided by Java and its family of packages. This requires an overview of the language and context, explaining the role it can play in network clients and servers, in embedded processing, on portability, in interfacing to legacy databases, and on component-based development. This training should be directed to system architects and IT managers. Because of the very broad subject area and the wide range of potential emphasis, such material is best delivered by instructor-led training. This allows maximum flexibility in adapting to your organization's background and needs.

Where Are You Starting from?

For the developer—programmer, architect, and even project manager—the most critical success factor for anything but the simplest application is understanding object-oriented and component-based programming. The programmer must understand programming with classes; the architect, object-oriented analysis and design; the business analyst, use case analysis; and the manager, evaluating and measuring progress in an object-oriented development project. One of the critical lessons learned from experience in adopting C++ is that learning the language is not the same as learning how to do object-oriented development. Java has many advantages over C++ in terms of its accessibility to the novice, but that will only reduce the time to learn the language—only part of the time required to learn the paradigm.

If a company's staff has experience with object-oriented programming, learning the Java *language* is relatively straightforward, but Java adds something to the mix: learning the ins and outs of its many packages. Java has powerful support for interactive and event-driven programming, multi-threaded applications, distributed applications, component architecture, database access, to name a few. Again, if one is coming from a background with experience in these areas, but using another language such as C++, learning a new set of interfaces is relatively straightforward. For developers with a related technological background in other programming languages, Web-based or computer-based training or self-training may suffice.

A background in Visual Basic is helpful if your goal is to adopt Java's event-driven component architecture—JavaBeans. C++ programmers may require extra training in this development paradigm. Furthermore, in our experience, there are many C++ programmers out there who have mainly learned to use C++ as a "better C" and lack a fundamental understanding of object-oriented development.

If one is trying to learn to write interactive, multi-threaded, Web-based applications at the same time one is learning Java and its packages, take great care not to multiply the risks in a major development project. As a rule, no project should try to adopt more than one new technology, and a "Java project" can be deceptive—two or three new technologies can sneak in under the cover of learning a new language.

Evaluation of your current situation is thus more complicated than just language experience. Evaluate the depth of experience in object-oriented programming, in interactive and event-driven applications, and in distributed applications. Pay special attention to project experience as opposed to simply having "taken a course" somewhere. With little project experience under your belt, a combination of preliminary instructor-led training and mentoring on pilot projects is the best combination. Developers who participate in the pilot projects can act as mentors in subsequent projects, with new developers requiring just preliminary classroom training.

WHO NEEDS TRAINING?

Where migrating to Java includes migrating to object-oriented development, or where the contemplated projects use significant new technology, managers as well as developers need to be trained. Managing an object-oriented project requires an understanding of at least the requirements definition aspect of object-oriented analysis, an understanding of iterative development, and a different set of progress measures and milestone evaluation metrics.

Staffing for object-oriented development requires software architects and class designers to acquire a thorough grounding in object-oriented analysis and design as well as the Java language and packages. Again, a simple language course covers only a fraction of the material.

Architects must understand a new application organization and a long list of issues: Web architecture and its architecture patterns, security of network transactions, and database integration.

WHAT IS THE BEST TRAINING MEDIUM?

For an experienced object-oriented developer with project experience in the kind of development you wish to undertake in Java, the simplest and most direct approach is often to use Web-based or computer-based training. Such a developer knows exactly what he needs to do; he is primarily interested in a quick overview of language and library features and pointers to where to find the details. Because of the very wide range of potential material, however, instructor-led training has the advantage that the instructor can adapt the material to the specific interests of the audience.

Learning to assemble applications out of beans with a bean editor and interface designer requires training in the principles—most easily acquired in a short period of instructor-led training—followed by extensively familiarizing oneself with the available components. This can be found in various repositories and vendor home pages around the Web.

TRAINING ALTERNATIVES

For one who is experienced in the technology area, whether it is object-oriented programming, interactive and event-driven application development, client-server architecture, or component-based development, the best medium is one that quickly imparts an overview of the newly available means to familiar ends. For this person, self-directed learning: Web-based, computer-based, book-based (remember those?), or a short, focused, instructor-led course is often the best approach.

For one who is learning both a new means and a new end, instructor-led training is important because the instructor can adjust the material to the student's experience and mind-set. Most students need to see a new concept expressed in a variety of ways before "the penny drops." Experienced instructors accumulate a large repertory of examples and analogies to get students over the many thresholds in learning a new topic.

When a whole new paradigm is being taught, instructor-led training goes only so far. Experience is the necessary teacher, and an experienced mentor guiding a pilot project will accelerate the process of absorbing a new discipline. In this approach, development staff usually participates in instructor-led training appropriate to their role before beginning the development project; thereafter a mentor will assist at each stage of development in adopting the lessons of the course.

MIGRATION PATTERNS

To clarify the training and migration approaches that can be taken, several *migration patterns* can be described. Each migration pattern addresses the unique training requirements for different groups. We'll present the different migration patterns by giving examples from our client base. For each pattern, we'll define the background of the group, their objectives, and a suggested migration *strategy*.

PATTERN 1: WEB-BASED APPLICATION DEVELOPMENT

Audience: Mainframe developers with COBOL experience.

Objectives: Develop applets and Java-based CGI programs or Servlets.

Company Context: Read data from a DB2 mainframe database.

Migration Strategy: Combination of CBT and Instructor-led training with mentoring.

- CBT: Internet Development and HTML.
- Instructor-led course: *Introduction to Java Programming* for developers and *Fundamentals of Java* for project managers.
- Instructor-led course: *Object-Oriented Development* for developers.
- Instructor-led course: *Advanced Java and Web Programming* for developers.
- Weekly meetings during which recently published material is presented in seminar form.

PATTERN 2: BROAD-BASED CLIENT/SERVER APPLICATIONS AND NETWORK MANAGEMENT

Audience: Systems and applications developers, most with C and some with C++ experience.

Objectives: Use Java applets in Web clients, Servlets in Web servers; write portable applications.

Company Context: Large range of hardware, software, and networking products requiring Web-based management; extensive use of Internet internally and externally.

Migration Strategy: Periodic internal course offerings; general availability of CBT and WBT.

- Instructor-led courses: *Introduction to Java Programming* for developers and *Fundamentals of Java* for project managers.
- WBT: *Intranet and Distributed Web Application Architecture Patterns*.
- Instructor-led course: *Object-Oriented Development in Java* for developers.

- Instructor-led courses: Half-day *Advanced Topics* (Threads, Coding and Design Patterns, JDBC, JavaBeans, RMI, Security, Management, Network Programming, etc.), as required for the specific project tasks at hand, for developers who have learned the Java basics.

PATTERN 3: CLIENT/SERVER CUSTOMER SERVICE APPLICATIONS

Audience: Analysts, architects, and developers primarily using Visual Basic and PowerBuilder for front ends, and using C and some C++ in servers.

Objectives: Use Java in clients and servers where appropriate. Adopt applets and Servlets for Intranet and Extranet applications.

Company Context: Developer of client/server database applications. Large internal investment in relational database skills and library support. Legacy relational databases that need to be accessed.

Migration Strategy: Broad adoption of object-oriented development; carefully targeted adoption of Java in specific client projects. Training usually applied in the context of specific projects using the new technology.

- Instructor-led course: *Object-Oriented Analysis and Design* for analysts, architects, and developers.
- Mentoring and workshops during requirements analysis.
- Instructor-led course: *Introduction to Java Programming* for developers and *Fundamentals of Java* for project managers.
- CBT or WBT: *HTML Programming and Web Page Design.*
- Instructor-led course: *Java Applet Programming* for Web GUI developers.
- Instructor-led course: *Distributed Application Development in Java* for developers with emphasis on JDBC, component technology, and JavaBeans.

CONCLUSION

The challenge in migrating to Java is the very wide range of technologies covered by the Java packages and the wide range of applications that can benefit from them. The keys to success are systematic exploration of the possibilities and a multi-faceted approach to training your staff that leverages their current skill set and background.

Kissin' Cousins: Communicating Between Java and JavaScript

Steven W. Disbrow

AFTER MY LAST ARTICLE for *Java Report* ("Tapping the Power of JavaScript," March 1997), I received a question from a reader asking if there was some way for a Java applet to call a JavaScript function. I knew that JavaScript could call Java funtions, but I wasn't sure if things would work the other way around. So, it was off to the Internet to investigate! I wound up at Netscape's official JavaScript documentation site and here's what I found....

The Basics

First, let's answer the question that started all this: Yes—Java methods *can* call JavaScript code, and JavaScript code *can* call Java methods. However, as you might expect, there are some exceptions and restrictions, and those depend on which browser you are using (we'll discuss these a bit later on).

The second question you might have is: "Why on earth would you *want* to do this?" Well, contrary to popular belief, JavaScript isn't just "Java lite," it's a powerful and useful language in its own right. However, because it's intended to execute inside a Web browser, it does have a few things missing from it. For example, in JavaScript, you have no way to play a sound or access a database. Java has both of these capabilities, and by making them available to JavaScript, we greatly enhance the types of tasks it can perform.

Java, while much more powerful, lacks JavaScript's close ties to the browser environment and its ability to interact with the individual elements of a Web page (text fields, buttons, etc.). Because of this, a lot of Java coding time is spent simply devising a user interface for each applet that you write, when, in most cases, a simple set of HTML controls would probably be sufficient. JavaScript, on the other hand, has direct access to all the different elements on a Web page, which can benefit a Java applet by eliminating the need to code a custom user interface.

CALLING JAVA FROM JAVASCRIPT

The nice thing about calling Java from JavaScript is that you can do it in both of the most popular browsers: Netscape Navigator v3.x and Microsoft Internet Explorer v3.x.

In Navigator, communication between Java and JavaScript is carried out by a mechanism called "LiveConnect." LiveConnect is a bridge between your

---

Table 1. Parameters of the JSObject applet.

SRC   Also used in the <BGSOUND> tag, this allows you to specify the path of the sound file you want to play. This path must be relative to the current HTML document and the file specified must be a Sun Audio (.au) format file. (Sorry, but Windows-style .wav files are not currently playable by Java.)

LOOP   Also used in the <BGSOUND> tag, this parameter allows you to specify the number of times to play the sound file. A value of "-1" specifies that the sound should be played indefinitely.

DELAY   This parameter specifies the number of milliseconds to wait between playings of the sound file. For example, if this value is "1000," the sound will be played, and then there will be a 1-second pause before the sound is played again. This parameter is required because Java does not give you any way to easily determine the playback time of a sound file. So, ideally, this value should represent the actual playback time of the sound file. Other values can be used, however, to produce various odd effects.

Java applets and your JavaScript code. LiveConnect takes care of things like name resolution and data conversion (i.e., turning JavaScript string objects into corresponding Java Strings). Navigator also provides a handy array called "applets" that lets you access all of the applets in a given document as if they were simply objects in an array. So, for example, if all of your applets contain a method called "getAppleInfo," you could use a simple for loop to return all of the information about the applets in a document, like so:

```
for (i=0; i<document.applets.length; i++)
    Document.write( document.applets[i].getAppletInfo());
```

Of course, referring to applets by number can be cumbersome, so Live-Connect also allows you to refer to an applet by name. Simply specify a "name=<appletName>" attribute inside the <applet> tag and you can then use <appletName> as an object name in your JavaScript code. For example, If you have an applet named "BGSound," and you want to write out the result of its getAppletInfo method, you would simply code:

```
document.write( document.BGSound.getAppletInfo());
```

In Microsoft's Internet Explorer v3.x you can still call your applets by name, but unfortunately, there is no applets array. This means that you *must* give your applets names if you want to talk to them via JavaScript from inside Internet Explorer.

Finally, in order to call a Java method, that method *must* be declared as "public." If a method isn't public, it can't be called from outside the applet, which means you can't call it from JavaScript. Other than this, calling Java methods from JavaScript is as simple as making a function call.

AN EXAMPLE—THE BGSOUND APPLET

As an example, let's look at a simple HTML page that uses JavaScript to help simplify the testing of an applet. Listing 1 shows the source for the HTML page, and Listing 2 shows the Java source for the applet. The applet in question is called "BGSound," which is short for "Background Sound." I wrote this applet because a client of mine wanted to be able to play sounds in both Navigator and Internet Explorer. Internet Explorer already supports a <BGSOUND> tag, but Navigator does not. So, the BGSound applet was written to add the capabilities for the <BGSOUND> tag to Navigator or any other Java-capable browser.

I've written this applet to be as close in operation to the <BGSOUND> tag as possible (Table 1 shows the parameters the applet takes), but I've also written it to be controllable from JavaScript. For example, consider the following lines from Listing 1:

```
<input type=text name=loop>

<input type=button value="Set Playback Count"
    onClick="document.BGSound.setLoopValue(
    this.form.loop.value)">
```

These lines define two HTML controls. The first is a text box that will hold the number of times to play our sound. The second is a button that, when clicked, executes a JavaScript command that calls the setLoopValue method in the BGSound applet. As the name implies, this sets the loop counter in the BGSound applet, which tells the applet how many times to play our sound.

In fact, there are seven different methods that you can use to interact with the BGSound applet (shown in Table 2). Three of these methods (the get methods) are used by the JavaScript doLoad function to fill our HTML fields with the appropriate values from the BGSound applet. Three others (the set methods) are used to set the corresponding variables in the BGSound applet using values that you type into the HTML fields. The last method, playSound, actually triggers the playing of the sound.

Table 2. The BGSound "Interface" Methods

playSound	Triggers the playing of the sound.
getSRC	Returns the path to our sound file.
setSRC	Sets the path to our sound file.
getLoopValue	Returns the number of times our sound will be played.
setLoopValue	Sets the number of times our sound will played.
getDelay	Returns the number of milliseconds between playings of our sound.
setDelay	Sets the number of milliseconds between playings of our sound.

All of the methods we've discussed so far are called by referencing the applet by its name. However, there is one other JavaScript function on this HTML page that you should look at: the allAppletInfo function. This function uses the applets array to loop through all of the applets in the current document and call each applet's getAppletInfo and getParameterInfo methods. (These are two methods that are generated automatically by Visual J++. However, you can easily add them to any applet.) The results of these methods are placed into a string (with line breaks provided by the JavaScript function lineBreak). The final string is then placed into the textarea control whose name is passed when you call the allAppletInfo function. (Notice that the first thing the allAppletInfo function does is to check and see if it's running inside of a Netscape browser. This is because, as of this writing, Netscape is the only browser that supports an applet's array. And, without the applet's array, this function can't, er. . .function.)

SECURITY CONCERNS

You may have noticed that in the setSRC method (near the end of Listing 2), I don't actually load the new sound file that is specified. Instead, I simply copy the path to the new sound into the appropriate variable and then set a flag variable (soundChanged) to mark that the sound source has been changed. This variable is later checked by the run method, and, if it's true, the new sound is loaded. I do this because, as a part of LiveConnect's security, JavaScript is not allowed to call any Java method that causes any sort of file activity. So, instead of loading the sound immediately, we defer that action until it's actually necessary to play the sound and then we handle the task inside a method that has not been "touched" by JavaScript.

OTHER POSSIBLE USES

In this example, I've used JavaScript-to-Java communication to simplify the testing of an applet. After all, it would have been silly to code a user interface for this applet in Java, and it would have been time-consuming to edit the HTML file over and over again to test different parameter values.

But this isn't the only use for this capability ... Imagine a Ticker Tape applet that you could feed display strings to via JavaScript. Or, you could create an applet that uses Java's database connectivity tools (JDBC) to return query results directly to a set of JavaScript functions that then display those results in standard HTML controls.

Calling JavaScript from Java

While calling Java from JavaScript is so easy it's almost a non-problem, calling JavaScript from Java is a bit more difficult. Actually, if you are using Internet Explorer, it's even worse than that: You simply can't call JavaScript from a Java applet executing in Internet Explorer v3.x. (Because of this, the remainder of this article will apply to Navigator only.)

Step 1

First, when creating your Java applet, you must include a special Netscape-created Java class called JSObject. JSObject is found in the Java class file that comes with Netscape Navigator v3.0 and 3.01. On the PC, this file can be found in the Netscape\Navigator\Program\Java\ Classes folder. (If you are using v3.0 of Navigator, the file will be named "java_30," and if you are using v3.01, the file will be named "java_301.") Once you've found this file, include the path to it in your **CLASSPATH**, and at the top of your Java code, include the statement:

```
import netscape.javascript.*;
```

Step 2

The second thing you have to do is to create a variable of type JSObject in your Java code. After you have a JSObject variable, you can fill it with a "handle" to the browser window that the applet is currently executing in. To get this window handle, you call the JSObject method getWindow and pass it the current applet. For example, the code:

```
JSObject myWin = JSObject.getWindow( this);
```

Returns a "handle" to the browser window object that this applet is currently executing in. With that handle safely stored in the myWin variable, you can then call any of the other JSObject methods. (All of the JSObject methods are shown in Table 3.)

Table 3. The Methods of JSObject.

Name	Description	Returns
getWindow	Gets a "handle" to browser window object.This handle should be stored in a JSObject variable for later use.	A JSObject representing the entire browser window.(Note that this is the only JSObject method that returns an actual JSObject. The results of the other methods must be cast to JSObject.)
call	Allows you to call a JavaScript function or method.	An object representing the result of the JavaScript function or method.
eval	Allows you to use the JavaScript eval method to execute a legal JavaScript statement inside your Java program.	An object representing the result of the JavaScript statement that was executed.
getMember	Retrieves the value of a single, named member in a JSObject. This value can be either another object or a scalar value.	An object representing the the named member.
getSlot	Same as getMember, except you access the member by an index number rather than by name.	An object representing the selected member.
removeMember	Removes a named member from the JSObject.	No return value.
setMember	Sets the value of named member to a specified value.	No return value.
setSlot	Same as setMember, but you access the member by an index number rather than by name.	No return value.
toString	Converts a JSObject into a Java String object. Useful for extracting scalar values from JSObjects.	A Java string representation of the JSObject variable.

STEP 3

In your HTML file, you must explicitly give your applet the ability to access your JavaScript code by including the "MAYSCRIPT" attribute in your <applet> tag. (an example of this is shown in Listing 4.) For example, if you had an applet called "BrowzaInfo" that you wanted to be able to call JavaScript, you would code something like:

```
<applet code="BrowzaInfo.class" name=
"BrowzaInfo"MAYSCRIPT></applet>
```

With these three steps taken care of, you are now ready to actually access JavaScript from your Java applet.

AN EXAMPLE—THE BROWZAINFO APPLET

Rather than simply list each JSObject method, let's look at a simple applet that uses some of these methods to obtain and display information about the browser it's running in.

Listing 3 shows the Java source for a very simple applet called "BrowzaInfo." At the top of the applet, you'll see the required include statement (Step 1), and at the top of the paint method, you'll see the call to the getWindow method that returns our browser window as a JSObject (Step 2).

Below that you'll see several lines that use various JSObject methods to interact with JavaScript in the current browser window. The first of these lines uses the "eval" method to find out how many forms are contained in the HTML document.

```
Integer formsLen = Integer.valueOf( myWin.eval(
"document.forms.length").toString());
```

If you are familiar with JavaScript, you'll be happy to know that this eval method is similar to the JavaScript eval method: You pass it a string representing a valid JavaScript statement and it executes that statement just as if you had hard-coded it in your JavaScript code. The main difference is that after eval executes the statement, you get a return value wrapped in a Java Object.

This is usually no problem, because a lot of the time your statements will resolve to actual JavaScript objects (arrays, forms, etc.), that you'll want to save off for later use. However, the problem with this scheme is that, as in this case, when the statement you are executing resolves to a simple scalar value, it's still returned to you inside a Java Object. So, to get it out, you have to do some type of conversion. In this case, the heart of our statement is:

```
...myWin.eval( "document.forms.length")...
```

which returns an Object that contains (in this example) the value "2." So, we then use the JSObject method toString to convert this object to a Java String. At this point, we can use the Integer.valueOf method to convert that String into an Integer that we can actually use in our Java applet.

Most of the time, you should be able to get the information you want with a single call to the eval method. However, those can get fairly complicated, so, in many cases, you'll want to "capture" a single JavaScript object to reuse in later statements. For example, the next statement:

```
JSObject Browza = (JSObject) myWin.eval(
"navigator");
```

retrieves the JavaScript "navigator" object and places it in a JSObject called "Browza." (Note the type cast that changes the generic "Object" into a "JSObject." You have to do this a lot to use JSObject and its methods.) Once we have this object in hand, we can use other JSObject methods to access the data in it. Specifically, in the next statement:

```
g.drawString("You are using" +
    Browza.getMember("appName")toString()+" "+
    Browza.getMember( "appVersion").toString(), 10, 20);
```

we use the getMember method to extract the value of the navigator object's "appName" and "appVersion" properties so that we can write them out (after converting them to Strings with toString). The getMember method is what you use to retrieve an object property by its name. Simply pass the name of the property (which might represent a scalar or another object), and you'll get it back as an Object.

Skipping down in the code a bit, you'll see a for loop that is used to report on the forms in the HTML document. The first line of code inside this loop is:

```
JSObject thisForm = (JSObject) myWin.eval(
    "document.forms["+i+"]");
```

The interesting thing to note here is that we are mixing Java variables (the loop index counter, "i") into the string that will be evaluated by the eval method. This may seem like a small point, but once you begin to use it, you'll find that this capability allows you to write some very flexible code.

Finally, let's look at how we can actually change the contents of HTML controls via JavaScript.

Near the bottom of the paint method, you'll see the statements:

```
String helloStr = "Greetings from Java!";
```

```
myWin.eval("document.forms[0].elements[0].
    value = '" + helloStr+ "';");
```

In the second statement, we've coded a simple JavaScript statement that directly sets the value of the first element (control) in the first form in our document. Very straightforward and very simple.

However, in the next two statements:

```
JSObject theTextArea = (JSObject) myWin.eval(
    "document.forms[0].elements[1]");
theTextArea.setMember( "value", getAppletInfo());
```

we take a more indirect route. First, we use the eval method to grab the Object that actually represents a control (in this case a textarea control) on the HTML page. Then, we use the setMember method to set the "value" property of that control to the string that is returned by the getAppletInfo method. As with the getMember method, setMember lets you access an object's property by name, but you are setting the property to a new value instead of retrieving the current value.

If you've looked at Table 3, you've probably noticed that there are several more JSObject methods. In my experience, the methods I've discussed here are the most useful, so I'll leave you to discover the use of these other methods as you need them. Which is a good excuse for me to mention again that, for the complete and final word on JSObject and its methods, you should check out Netscape's official documentation on LiveConnect.

OTHER POSSIBLE USES

Honestly, Java doesn't benefit from using JavaScript as much as JavaScript does from using Java. Besides the previously noted benefit of allowing direct access to the HTML page, one very useful thing I've found to do with Java-to-JavaScript communication is to use it to create a very simple debugging framework for my Java programs. If there's one thing I hate, it's constantly switching from my browser to my Java IDE to check the value of a variable. (I do a lot of development on my laptop, so my large monitor isn't available for placing the windows side by side.) I just place some text fields on my HTML page and then use some calls to the various JSObject methods to display the Java values I'm interested in right in my browser. It's a great time saver.

CONCLUSION

So that's just about all you need to know about Java-toJavaScript communication (and vice versa). Of course, I've glossed over some of the more technical details, like the exact rules for data conversion between Java and JavaScript, and how to use the JSException class to catch any errors thrown by the methods of JSObject. Again, for this detailed technical information, you should visit Netscape's Official JavaScript documentation site.

Listing 1. The BGSound.htm file.

```
<html>
<head>
<title>BGSound</title>
<script language=javascript>
/( This function creates and returns a line break character based on our plat-
   form...
function lineBreak(){
    return (navigator.appVersion.indexOf.("Win")! =-1)?"\r\n":; }

// This function returns the info for all of the applets on this page function
allAppletInfo( outPutField) {
    var infoStr = "";
    // Internet Explorer 3 doesn't support the applets array, so°
    if (navigator.appName =( "Netscape") {
    var numApplets = document.
    applets.length;
    for (var i=0; i<numApplets; i+() {
        infoStr += document.applets [i].getAppletInfo();
        infoStr += lineBreak ();
        infoStr += "Parameter List: <name> - <description>" + lineBreak ();
        appletInfo = document.applets [i].getParameterInfo ();
        for (var j=0; j<appletInfo.length; j+(){
         infoStr += appletInfo [j][0]+  "-"+ appletInfo[j][2];
         infoStr += lineBreak () ;
        }
        infoStr += "-((((";
        infoStr += lineBreak() + lineBreak() ;
        }}
    else
    alert("Sorry, but this feature does not work in "+navigator.appName +".");
    if (infoStr ! ="")
    eval( 'document.' + outPutField + .'value= infoStr;'); }

// This function displays various values from our applet
function doLoad( ) {
    document.form1.sndSrc.value=document.BGSound.getSRC() ;

    document.form1.loop.value = document.BGSound.getLoopValue();
```

(continued)

Listing 1. *(continued)*

```
        document.form1.loop.value = document.BGSound.getDelay(); }
</script>
</head>
<body bgcolor=red onLoad="doLoad()">
<H1 align=center>BGSound Applet Tester</H1><BR>

<applet code="BGSound.class" name="BGSound" width=2 height=0>
<param name=SRC value="bell.au" >
<param name=LOOP value="1">
<param name=DELAY value="1000">
</applet>

<form name=form1>
<input type=text name=sndSrc>

<input type=button value="Set Source .au File"
onClick="document.BGSound.setSRC( this.form.sndSrc.value)" ><P>

<input type=text name=loop>

<input type=button value="Set Playback Count"
onClick="document.BGSound.setLoopValue( this.form.loop.value)" ><P>
<input type=text name=delay>

<input type=button value="Set Delay"
onClick="document.BGSound.setDelay( this.form.delay.value)" ><P>

<input type=button value= "Info on Applets"onClick="allAppletInfo( 'form1.ap-
pletInfo')" >

<INPUT TYPE=button VALUE="PlaySound"
onClick="document.BGSound.playSound
( )" ><BR>

<textarea name="appletInfo"rows=10 cols=50></textarea>

</form>
</body>
</html>
```

Listing 2. BGSound.java.

```
//(*********************************************************************/
/* BGSound.java: Applet
By Steven W. Disbrow - Copyright 1997 by EGO Systems
The purpose of this applet is to emulate the <BGSound>Tag that is supported
by (Internet Explorer, but NOT by Netscape Navigator. */
//(*********************************************************************/
import java.applet.*;
import java.awt. *;

public class BGSound extends Applet implements Runnable{
```

(continued)

Listing 2. **BGSound.java.**

```
/( m_BGSound is the Thread object for the applet
Thread m_BGSound = null;

/* Loop Count - number of times to play the sound */
int m_LoopValue; /( Permanent storage for our loop value
int m_LoopCount; /( Temporary loop counter

/* m_DelayTime is the delay between each playing of the sound file, in
    milliseconds */
long m_DelayTime;

/*m_TheSound will hold the sound file object */
AudioClip m_TheSound = null;

/* Flag to tell if the source sound file had been changed */
boolean soundChanged = false;

/* Variables used to store the parameter values passed from the HTML file */
private String m_SRC = "";
private String m_LOOP = "1";
private String m_DELAYLEN = "500";

/* Parameter names that should be specified in the HTML file */
private final String PARAM_SRC = "SRC";
private final String PARAM_LOOP = "LOOP";
private final String PARAM_DELAYLEN = "DELAY";

/* BGSound Class Constructor */
public BGSound(){
    /* Nothing to do here } */

/* The getAppletInfo()method returns a string describing the applet's author,
   copyright date, and miscellaneous information. */
public String getAppletInfo(){
    return "Name: BGSound\r\n" +
    "Author: Steven W. Disbrow\r\n" +
    "Copyright 1997 by EGO Systems\r\n" +
    "Created with Microsoft Visual J+( Version 1.1"; }

/* The getParameterInfo()method returns an array of strings describing the
   parameters understood by this applet. BGSound Parameter Information: {
   "Name" , "Type" , "Description" }, */
public String[] [] getParameterInfo(){
    String [] [] info = {
        {PARAM_SRC, "String" , "Name of our source sound file (.au files only)" },
        {PARAM_LOOP, "String" , "Number of times to play the sound file (-1 is
        loop indefinitely)"},
        {PARAM_DELAYLEN, "String" , "The delay between each playing of the
            sound, in milliseconds" }, };
    return info; }

/* The init()method is used to load our parameters and get things set up to play
   our sound files. */
public void init(){
```
(continued)

Listing 2 *(continued)*

```
/* The following code retrieves the value of each parameter specified with
   the <PARAM> tag and stores it in a member variable. */

String param;

/* SRC: Name of our source sound file */
param = getParameter(PARAM_SRC);
if (param != null){
    this.setSRC( param); }

/* LOOP: Number of times to play the sound file */
param = getParameter(PARAM_LOOP);
if (param != null)
    setLoopValue( param);

/* DELAYLEN: The length between playings of the sound file, in milliseconds */
param = getParameter(PARAM_DELAYLEN);
if (param != null)
    this.setDelay( param); }
```

```
/* The start()method is called when the page containing the applet first
   appears on the screen. For this applet, we use this time to start up our
   thread and play our sound. */
public void start(){
    if (m_BGSound = ( null){
    m_BGSound = new Thread(this);
    m_BGSound.start();
    }
    playSound(); }
```

```
/* The stop()method is called when the page containing the applet is no longer
   on the screen. All we do here is stop the sound, and then stop the thread. */
public void stop(){
    /* Stop the sound
    if (m_TheSound != null){
    m_TheSound.stop();
    m_TheSound = null; }
    /* Stop the thread
    if(m_BGSound != null){
    m_BGSound.stop();
    m_BGSSound = null; } }
```

```
/* the run()method is called when the applet's thread is started. For our applet
   we first check to see if the path to the sound has changed. If it has, we load the
   new sound file. Then, we attempt to play the sound the appropriate number of
   times. */
public void run(){
    while(true){
        try{
        if(soundChanged){
            m_TheSound = getAudioClip(getDocumentBase(),
            m_SRC);
            soundChanged = false; }
```

(continued)

Listing 2. *(continued)*

```
        if (m_LoopCount>0) {
            m_LoopCount–;
            m_TheSound.play(); }
        if (m_LoopCount =( -1){
            m_TheSound.loop();
            m_LoopCount = 0; }
      Thread.sleep(m_DelayTime) ; }
    catch(InterruptException e) {
    stop(); } } }
/* This method sets the path to our source sound file */
public void setSRC( String the SRC) {
    m_SRC = theSRC;

    soundChanged = true; }

/* This method returns the path to our .au sound */
public String getSRC(){
    return m_SRC; }

/* This method sets our loop value */
public void setLoopValue( String loopVal){
    m_LOOP = loopVal;

    /* Should we loop the sound forever? */
    if (m_LOOP.toUpperCase().compareTo( "INFINITE")=( 0){
      m_LoopValue= -1;}
    else
      m_LoopValue = Integer.parseInt( m_Loop); }

/* This method returns our loop count */
public int getLoopValue(){
    return m_LoopValue; }

/* This method sets our delay value */
public void setDelay(String delayVal){
    m_DELAYLEN = delayVal;
    m_DelayTime = Long.parseLong(m_DELAYLEN); }

/* This method returns our delay time */
public long getDelay(){
    return m_DelayTime; }

/* This method caused the applet to play our sound by copying the number of
   times to pay the sound into the m_LoopCount variable. Because our thread is
   constantly checking this value, it will play the sound when it "notices" the
   change in the value. */
public void playSound(){
    m_LoopCount = m_LoopValue;}
}/* End of BGSound.java */
```

Listing 3.   The BrowzaInfo.java Source Code.

```
import java.applet.*;
import java.awt. *;
/* Step 1! Include the JSObject class! */
import netscape.javascript. *;

public class BrowzaInfo extends Applet{

    public BrowzaInfo(){ }

/* Return information about the applet */
public String getAppletInfo(){
    return "Name:BrowzaInfo\r"+
    "Author: Steven W. Disbrow\r\n" +
    "This applet gathers and displays information about" +
    "the current HTML page using JavaScript.\r\n" +
    "Created with Microsoft Visual J+( Version 1.1" ; }

/* Initialize the applet */
public void init(){
    resize(320, 240); }

/* Fill our display area with information about the browser window */
public void paint(Graphics g){
    /* Step 2! retrieve the browser window object This gives us the COMPLETE
        window object */
    JSObject myWin = JSObject.getWindow( this);

    /* Here's one way to resolve a single value form an object and place it into a
        Java variable. */
    Integer formsLen = Integer.valueOf( myWin.eval( "document.forms.length").
     toString()(;

    /* Normally however, you'll want to get a single object, and then, in the state-
        ments that follow, extract the values of the members in that object. For ex-
        ample, Here's how to get a SINGLE object from inside the window */
    JSObject Browza = (JSObject) myWin.eval ("navigator" );

    /* Now that we have the JavaScript navigator object, we use the
        getMember()method to get a couple of members out of it */
    g.drawString( " You are using " + Browza.getMember("appName" )
        .toString()+" "+
        Browza.getMember( "appVersion").toString(), 10, 20);

    g.drawString( "The title of this page is: " +
        myWin.eval( "document.title").toString(), 10,35);
    g.drawString( "Number of forms on this page: " + formsLen + ".",10, 50);

    /* Here's an example of how to 'dissect' an HTML document via JavaScript */
    int x = 15;
    int y = 65;
    for(int i=0; i<formsLen.intValue(); i+(){
        JSObject thisForm = (JSObject) myWin.eval("document.forms[" +i+ "]");
```

(continued)

Listing 3. *(continued)*

```
    g.drawString( "Form #" +(i+1)+
    "is named \""+ thisForm.getMember( "name").toString()+ "\"", x, y);
    /* Other details can be gathered here */
    y += 15; }

/* Now, we'll see a couple of ways to directly change an HTML element */
String helloStr = "Greetings from Java!";

/* First, the direct approach! */
myWin.eval( "document.forms[0].elements[0].value = "" + helloStr + ";");

/* Next, we extract an object representing the field we want to change
JSObject the TextArea = (JSObject)myWin.eval
("document.forms[0].elements[1]");
/* then we use the setMember()method to change it. */
the TextArea.setMember( "value", getAppletInfo ()(; }}
```

Listing 4.   The BrowzaInfo.htm file.

```
<html>
<head>
<title>BrowzaInfo</title>
</head>
<body bgcolor=white>
<hr>
<!- Step3! add the MAYSCRIPT attribute to your applet tag->
<applet code=BrowzaInfo.class name=BrowzaInfo width=320 height=240
MAYSCRIPT>
</applet>
<hr>
<form name=FirstForm >
<input type=text name=hello>
<BR>
<textarea name=appletInfo= rows=10 cols=50></textarea>
</form>
<form name=SecondForm >
</form>
</body>
</html>
```

TECHNIQUES 101

Java Permutations and Combinations

Steven J. Metsker

PERMUTATIONS AND combinations appear in problems that have more than one answer, where we want to know what all the possibilities are or just how many possibilities there are. For example, a basketball coach may need to select a team of 5 players from the 10 boys on his squad. How many possible teams is that? Is it more than we can reasonably put in a list? If the coach has statistics on the five starting players from a competing team, can he match up his players with them based on height, speed, and experience? You can address these questions with a handful of algorithms for permutations and combinations that are an important part of a Java developer's toolbox.

Counting Permutations

A permutation is an ordering of items. For example, we might have three errands to do, with a choice about what order to do them in. If we have to buy groceries, mail a package, and get an oil change, one possible ordering or *permutation* is {groceries, mail, oil}. Altogether, there are six possible orderings:

    groceries, mail, oil
    groceries, oil, mail
    mail, groceries, oil
    mail, oil, groceries
    oil, groceries, mail
    oil, mail, groceries

We can count these choices algorithmically, without necessarily listing them. Notice that once the errand runner completes one of the three errands, there are always two left. After the errand runner completes two errands, there is always one left. The total number of permutations is 3 times 2 times 1, which is also called 3 *factorial*, and written 3!. The formula for n! is:

$$n*(n-1)*(n-2)*\ldots*1$$

There are always n! ways to order n items, if we want to list all n items. We have to modify the algorithm if, say, we have 10 errands but only time to do 3. In this case, we could count the number of permutations by noting that there are 10 choices for the first errand, leaving 9 for the second, and 8 for the third. The total, then, is 10 times 9 times 8. Conventionally, the expression P(10, 3) represents the number of permutations of 3 items out of 10. In general,

$$P(n,m) = n*(n-1)*\ldots*(*n-m+1)$$

Or, compactly:

$$P(n,m) = n!/(n-m)!$$

Counts of permutations get big fast. For example, 20! is 2,432,902,008,176,640,000, which is much larger than 2,147,483,647, the value of Integer.MAX_VALUE. The code for this article uses Java's BigInteger class to avoid problems with overflow. All code for this article is available at *Java Report Online*. Listing 1 shows Combinatoric.java, which includes the following method for calculating P(n, m):

```
/**
 * @return BigInteger, the number of possible arrangements, or
   orderings, of m objects chosen
 * from a group of n objects.
 *
 * @param n int
 * @param m int
 * @exception combinatorics.CombinatoricException unless n >= m >=
   0
 */
public static BigInteger p(int n, int m)
      throws CombinatoricException {

      check(n, m);
```

Listing 1. **Combinatoric.**

```
package combinatorics;

import java.math.*;
/* The class Combinatoric contains methods for performing basic combinatoric
    operations such as counting numbers of permutations and combinations. */
public class Combinatoric {

/* @return BigInteger, the number of unordered subsets of m objects chosen from
    a group of n objects.

    @param n int
    @param m int
    @exception combinatorics.CombinatoricException unless n >= m >= 0 */
public static BigInteger c(int n, int m)
        throws CombinatoricException {

        check(n, m);
        int r = Math.min(m, n - m);
        return p(n, r).divide(factorial(r)); }
/* Check that 0 <= m <= n
    @param n int
    @param m int
    @exception combinatorics. CombinatoricException unless n >= m >= 0 */
static void check(int n, int m) throws CombinatoricException {
        if (n < 0) {
            throw new CombinatoricException(
                "n, the number of items, must be greater than 0"); }
        if (n < m) {
            throw new CombinatoricException(
                 "n, the number of items, must be >= m, the number selected"); }
        if (m < 0) {
            throw new CombinatoricException(
                 "m, the number of selected items, must be >= 0"); } }
/* @return BigInteger, the product of  * the numbers 1 ... n
    @param n int
    @exception combinatorics. CombinatoricException unless n >= 0 */
public static BigInteger factorial(int n)
        throws CombinatoricException {
        if (n < 0) {
            throw new CombinatoricException ("n must be >= 0");
        }
        BigInteger factorial = new BigInteger(new byte[]{1});
        for (int i = n; i > 1; i—) {
            factorial =
                factorial.multiply(new BigInteger(new byte[]{(byte)i})); }
        return factorial;
}
/* @return BigInteger, the number of  * possible ways of ordering n objects
    @param n int
    @exception combinatorics. CombinatoricException unless n >= 0 */
public static BigInteger p(int n) throws CombinatoricException {    (continued)
```

(continued)

Listing 1. *(continued)*

```
    return factorial(n); }
/* @return BigInteger, the number of possible arrangements, or orderings, of m
   objects chosen from a group of n objects.

 @param n int
 @param m int
 @exception combinatorics.CombinatoricException unless n >= m >= 0 */
public static BigInteger p(int n, int m)
    throws CombinatoricException {

    check(n, m);

    BigInteger product = new BigInteger(new byte[]{1});
    for (int i = n; i > n - m; i—) {
        product =
            product.multiply(new BigInteger(new byte[]{(byte)i})); }
    return product; } }
```

```
        BigInteger product = new BigInteger(new byte[]{1});
        for (int i = n; i > n - m; i—) {
            product =
                product.multiply(new BigInteger(new byte[]{(byte)i}));
        }
        return product;
    }
}
```

For example,

```
        System.out.println(combinatorics.Combinatoric.p(10,3));
```

will print out "720". The check() routine throws an exception if m > n or m < 0.

COUNTING COMBINATIONS

Combinations are essentially permutations where order doesn't matter. So, to count combinations, we count permutations of selecting m items from a list of n items, and then divide by the m! ways of ordering the selected items. For example, there are P(10,3) or 720 ways of doing 3 errands from a list of 10 errands. If we don't care about the order we do the errands in, we divide this number by 3! to get C(10,3) = 120, the number of combinations of 10 things taken 3 at a time. Algebraically:

$C(n,m)= P(n,m)/m\ !$

$C(n,m)= n!/((n-m!^{*}m\ !)$

The first equation captures the idea that combinations are permutations where

$$C(10,3) = \binom{10}{3}$$

order doesn't matter. The second equation shows the same formula, using just factorials. The final equation shows the conventional notation for combinations, dropping the C when the number n is written above the number m. The Combinatorics class includes the following method for calculating C(n, m):

```
/**
 * @return BigInteger, the number of unordered subsets of m objects
 * chosen from a group of n objects.
 *
 * @param n int
 * @param m int
 * @exception combinatorics.CombinatoricException unless n >= m
   >= 0
 */
public static BigInteger c(int n, int m)
      throws CombinatoricException {

      check(n, m);
      int r = Math.min(m, n - m);
      return p(n, r).divide(factorial(r));
}
```

For example, System.out.println(Combinatoric.c(10,2)) prints out 45.

The factorial method factorial(n) just returns n!. Notice that the calculation of C(n, m) makes use of the observation that C(n, m) will always equal C(n, n - m). One way of seeing this is to note that every choice of m items always leaves behind (n - m) items. For example, choosing 3 errands to run is the same as choosing 7 errands *not* to run. You may want to work through the mathematics, to prove to yourself that C(n, m) = C(n, n - m).

Working with the minimum of m and n - m makes a difference in the amount of computation we have to do. For example, we could calculate C(15,13) as P(15,13)/13!, which equals 653,837,184,000/6,227,020,800. But it is much easier to arrive at the same answer by calculating P(15,2)/2!, which is 210/2.

GENERATING PERMUTATIONS

Sometimes you need to actually generate lists of permutations and combinations, rather than just determining how long the lists may be. Examples of this come from the increasing popularity of advice software, that guides users through varieties of choices. Suppose you write a package for teachers that helps them design a curriculum. At runtime, you might have a History of Film teacher who assigns movies to 2 students each week for them to criticize orally for the class. This week's students are Hal and Alex, and the teacher wants to see the possible permutations of assigning two of four selected Stanley Kubrick movies to them. If the list of movies is {"2001: A Space Odyssey", "A Clockwork Orange", "Full Metal Jacket", "The Shining"}, the following code will show the teacher's choices:

```
Object[] students = {"Hal", "Alex"};
Object[] movies = {"2001", "Orange", "Jacket", "Shining"};
combinatorics.Permutations perms =
     new combinatorics.Permutations(movies, 2);

while (perms.hasMoreElements()) {
     Object[] perm = (Object[])perms.nextElement();
     for (int i = 0; i < perm.length; i++) {
          if (i > 0) System.out.print(", ");
          System.out.print(students[i] + ": " + perm[i]);
     }
     System.out.println();
}
```

This prints out:

```
Hal: 2001, Alex: Orange
Hal: 2001, Alex: Jacket
Hal: 2001, Alex: Shining
Hal: Orange, Alex: 2001
Hal: Orange, Alex: Jacket
Hal: Orange, Alex: Shining
Hal: Jacket, Alex: 2001
Hal: Jacket, Alex: Orange
Hal: Jacket, Alex: Shining
Hal: Shining, Alex: 2001
```

Hal: Shining, Alex: Orange
Hal: Shining, Alex: Jacket

Notice that the Permutations class, shown in Listing 2, implements the Enumeration interface, which includes the methods hasMoreElements() and nextElement(). The Enumeration interface is a perfect fit for the behavior of the Permutations class, which in fact enumerates all the permutations of the supplied array of Objects.

The Permutations class works by keeping an index array that it increments after each call to nextElement(). The constructor for Permutations accepts an array of Objects that it uses only for constructing the return Object array. The Permutations class does its real work on the index array. You can trace the steps of the array by running the following code scrap.

```
Object[] slots = new Object[4];
for (int i = 0; i < slots.length; i++) {
    slots[i] = new Integer(i);
}
combinatorics.Permutations perms =
    new combinatorics.Permutations(slots);
while (perms.hasMoreElements()) {
    Object[] perm = (Object[])perms.nextElement();
    for (int i = 0; i < perm.length; i++) {
        System.out.print(perm[i] + " ");
    }
    System.out.println();
}
```

This code outputs all the permutations of {0, 1, 2, 3}:

```
0 1 2 3
0 1 3 2
0 2 1 3
0 2 3 1
...
1 3 2 0
2 0 1 3
...
3 1 0 2
3 1 2 0
3 2 0 1
3 2 1 0
```

These are the 24 values that the index array will take on as it computes the permutations of any 4-element list. The constructor for Permutations initializes the index array so that index[i] contains i. That is, index initially contains {0, 1, 2, 3}. The algorithm moves index through the listed values as the code repeatedly sends the nextElement() message to the Permutations object.

The steps of the algorithm, from *Applied Combinatorics*,[1] are:

1. Find the rightmost position in the index array whose value is less than its neighbor to its right. This value is the "dip."
2. Find the position of smallest value to the right of the dip that is greater than the dip.
3. Swap this value with the dip.
4. Reverse all the values to the right of the position where the dip was found.

Consider the case when index contains:

{1, 3, 2, 0}

The "dip," or rightmost value less than its neighbor, is 1. Notice that there is no way to arrange the values to the right of 1 to get a permutation that should come after {1, 3, 2, 0}. To create a larger permutation, we have to change the number in the position occupied by 1.

The smallest element to the right of the dip is 2. Notice that we cannot just switch 1 with its neighbor. If we did, we would skip the permutations beginning with {2, ...}. Swapping 1 and 2 yields the temporary result:

{2, 3, 1, 0}

We know that the values to the right of the dip index are sorted biggest to smallest because of the way we found the dip. To find the smallest permutation beginning with {2, ...}, we reverse the list after the point where the dip was found:

{2, 0, 1, 3}

This is the next permutation after {1, 3, 2, 0}.

The algorithm in the code is somewhat more complex than this. The code handles the general case where the user requests only m elements from an n permutation. In this case, the algorithm takes the extra step of reversing again the elements from m to the end of the index. This ensures that the algorithm will find the next dip within the part of the permutation that we have been asked to generate.

GENERATING COMBINATIONS

The combinatorics package also includes a Combinations class, which, like Permutations, implements the Enumeration interface. Before listing all the combinations of an array of Objects, it may be a good idea to check the list's size. For example, how many ways are there to invite 50 of 100 Senators to a banquet? The answer is that there are:

Combinatoric.c(100,50) = 100,891,344,545,564,193,334,812,497,256

different choices, which is more than your user will want to scroll through. When a basketball coach asks to see all Combinatoric.c(10,5) ways of choosing his boys basketball team, he may shrink from browsing a list of all 252 possibilities. If he reduces his list of candidates to 7, then he can choose to consider the Combinatoric.c(7,5) choices that result. A code scrap that generates this 21-element list is:

```
Object[] boys =
     {"Alfred", "Ben", "Carl", "Drew", "Edwin", "Franklin",
      "Gregor"};
combinatorics.Combinations c =
new combinatorics.Combinations(boys, 5);
while (c.hasMoreElements()) {
     Object[] combo = (Object[])c.
                      nextElement();
     for (int i = 0; i < combo.length; i++) {
          System.out.print(combo[i] + " ");
     }
System.out.println();
}
```

Which results in:

```
Alfred Ben Carl Drew Edwin
Alfred Ben Carl Drew Franklin
Alfred Ben Carl Drew Gregor
...
Ben Carl Edwin Franklin Gregor
Ben Drew Edwin Franklin Gregor
Carl Drew Edwin Franklin Gregor
```

Observe how this list is sorted. Within each combination, the names appear in sorted order. This is because the algorithm retains the order of the starting list. Regarding the overall ordering of the list, combination c1 appears before combination c2 if the leftmost index where they differ is less in c1 than c2. Notice that, in the example, the first name in the list never advances beyond Carl. This is because 4 other names greater than "Carl" have to come to Carl's right. In general, the largest element possible at index 0 is whatever occupies the (n - m) position of the starting array. In this case, (n - m) = (7 - 5), and boys[2] contains "Carl". For any index i, the maximum value of index[i] is n - m + i. The algorithm for finding the next combination proceeds as follows:

1. Find the rightmost element of the index that can be incremented.
2. Increment that element.
3. Set each element to the right of that element to be 1 plus the element on their left.

For example, an index of 5 things taken 3 at a time will, at some point, contain {0 3 4}. In this case, only the 0 can be incremented without running out of room. Steps 1 and 2 of the algorithm find and increment the 0. Step three fills in the index simply by counting up. The next index is {1, 1+1, 1+2} or {1, 2, 3}. This index will be followed by {1, 2, 4}, {1, 3, 4}, and {2, 3, 4}.

Listing 3 contains the code for Combinations.java, which provides the ability to successively list all combinations of n things taken m at a time. This is a useful service, but our coach would probably appreciate some support for attaching skill metrics to each boy and comparing these to the skills of the opponents' team. The idea of generating all the combinations or permutations of a group of objects often widens in an application to including measuring or testing each solution. You can use the Permutations and Combinations classes as the foundation of a wide variety of generate-and-test algorithms.

GENERATE AND TEST

For a final example, we will see that we can solve the type of puzzles known as "Logic" puzzles using a generate-and-test technique. To solve a logic puzzle, generate all possible solutions, and test each solution to see if it passes a set of criteria or "clues." Consider the karate student problem:

Each of four martial arts students has a different specialty. From the following clues, can you determine each student's full name and her special skill?

1. Ms. Ellis (whose instructor is Mr. Caldwell), Amy, and Ms. Fowler are all martial arts students.

2. Sparring isn't the specialty of either Carla or Dianne.
3. Neither the shoot fighting expert nor the pressure point fighter is named Fowler.
4. Children's techniques aren't the specialty of Dianne (whose instructor is Ms. Sherman).
5. Amy, who disdains pressure point fighting, isn't Ms. Goodrich.
6. Betti and Ms. Fowler are roommates.
7. Ms. Hightower avoids sparring because of its point scoring nature.

Listing 4 shows the code for solving this problem. The KaratePuzzle class takes the approach that the four Student objects {amy betti carla dianne} will be given different last names and different karate specialties until together they match all the given clues. The Student class, shown in Listing 5, is just a data structure used by KaratePuzzle.

In KaratePuzzle.solve() method, two nested while loops walk through all permutations of last names and specialties, assigning them to the students. Then the code runs this mixture of first names, last names, and specialties through the gauntlet of clues. The program prints out:

```
Solution:
    Amy Hightower: Shoot Fighting
    Betti Ellis: Sparring
    Carla Fowler: Childrens
    Dianne Goodrich: Pressure Points
```

This example employs the important technique of assigning an arbitrary order to part of the problem and then generating permutations for the rest of the program. We set the girls' first names in a fixed order and then combine them with all permutations of last names and specialties. A basketball coach could use the same technique to consider all the ways to match up his 5 starters against another team: Line up the opponents in any order and then line up the home team starters next to them in each of 5! possible orderings.

Becoming comfortable with generating and analyzing permutations and combinations usually takes some practice, but your efforts will be repaid. With skill in this branch of mathematics, you can size, generate, and analyze solutions to a wide variety of ordering and selection problems.

REFERENCE

1. Tucker, A., *Applied Combinatorics*, John Wiley & Sons, 1984.

Listing 2. Permutations.

package combinatorics;

/* Copyright (c) 1998 Steven J. Metsker. All Rights Reserved. */

/* The Permutations class provides an enumeration of all permutations of an array of objects. Each "permutation" is simply an ordered list of the group.
<p>
  For example, to see all of the ways we can select a school representative and an alternate from a list of 4 children, begin with an array of names::
<blockquote><pre>
    Object[] children = {"Leonardo", "Monica", "Nathan", "Olivia"};
</pre></blockquote>
To see all 2-permutations of these 4 names, create and use a Permutations enumeration:
<blockquote><pre>
  Permutations c = new Permutations(children, 2); while (c.hasMoreElements()) {
      Object[] perm = (Object[])c.
      nextElement();
      for (int i = 0; i < perm.length; i++) {
            System.out.print(perm[i] + " "); }
  System.out.println(); }
*</pre></blockquote>
This will print out:
<blockquote><pre>
  Leonardo Monica
  Leonardo Nathan
  Leonardo Olivia
  Monica Leonardo
  Monica Nathan
  Monica Olivia
  Nathan Leonardo
  Nathan Monica
  Nathan Olivia
  Olivia Leonardo
  Olivia Monica
  Olivia Nathan
 </pre></blockquote> */

public class Permutations implements java.util.Enumeration {
      private Object[] inArray;
      private int n, m;
      private int[] index;
      private boolean hasMore = true;

/* Create a Permutation to enumerate through all possible lineups of the supplied array of Objects. @param Object[] inArray the group to line up @exception combinatorics.CombinatoricException Should never happen with this interface */
public Permutations(Object[] inArray) throws CombinatoricException {
      this(inArray, inArray.length); }
/* Create a Permutation to enumerate through all possible lineups of the supplied array of Objects. @param Object[] inArray the group to line up

Listing 2. *(continued)*

@param inArray java.lang.Object[], the group to line up @param m int, the number of objects to use @exception combinatorics.CombinatoricException if m is greater than the length of inArray, or less than 0. */
```
public Permutations(Object[] inArray, int m) throws CombinatoricException {
    this.inArray = inArray;
    this.n = inArray.length;
    this.m = m;
```

// throw exception unless n >= m >= 0
```
    Combinatoric.check(n, m);
```

/* "index" is an array of ints that keep track of the next permutation to return. For example, an index on a permutation of 3 things might contain {1 2 0}. This index will be followed by {2 0 1} and {2 1 0}.Initially, the index is {0 ... n - 1}. */

```
    index = new int[n];
    for (int i = 0; i < n; i++) {
        index[i] = i; }
```

/* The elements from m to n are always kept ascending right to left. This keeps the "dip" in the interesting region. */
```
    reverseAfter(m - 1); }
```
/* @return true, unless we have already returned the last permutation. */
```
public boolean hasMoreElements() {
    return hasMore; }
```
/* Move the index forward a notch. The algorithm first finds the rightmost index that is less than its neighbor to the right. This is the "dip" point. The algorithm next finds the least element to the right of the dip that is greater than the dip. That element is switched with the dip. Finally, the list of elements to the right of the dip is reversed.
<p>
For example, in a permutation of 5 items, the index may be {1, 2, 4, 3, 0}. The "dip" is 2 — the rightmost element less than its neighbor on its right. The least element to the right of 2 that is greater than 2 is 3. These elements are swapped, yielding {1, 3, 4, 2, 0}, and the list right of the dip point is reversed, yielding {1, 3, 0, 2, 4}.
<p>
The algorithm is from Applied Combinatorics, by Alan Tucker. */
```
private void moveIndex() {

    // find the index of the first element that dips
    int i = rightmostDip();
    if (i < 0) {
        hasMore = false;
        return; }

    // find the least greater element to the right of the dip
    int leastToRightIndex = i + 1;
    for (int j = i + 2; j < n; j++) {
        if (index[j] < index[leastToRightIndex] &&
        index[j] > index[i]) {
            leastToRightIndex = j; } }
```

(continued)

Listing 2. *(continued)*

```
// switch dip element with least greater element to its right
int t = index[i];
index[i] = index[leastToRightIndex];
index[leastToRightIndex] = t;

if (m - 1 > i) {
// reverse the elements to the right of the dip
    reverseAfter(i);
// reverse the elements to the right of m - 1
    reverseAfter(m - 1); } }
/* @return java.lang.Object, the next permutation of the original Object array.
  <p>
    Actually, an array of Objects is returned. The declaration must say just
    "Object," because the Permutations class implements Enumeration, which
    declares that the "nextElement()" returns a plain Object. Users must cast the
    returned object to (Object[]). */
public Object nextElement() {
    if (!hasMore) {
        return null; }

        Object[] out = new Object[m];
        for (int i = 0; i < m; i++) {
            out[i] = inArray[index[i]]; }

    moveIndex();
    return out; }
/* Reverse the index elements to the right of the specified index. */
private void reverseAfter(int i) {

    int start = i + 1;
    int end = n - 1;
    while (start < end) {
        int t = index[start];
        index[start] = index[end];
        index[end] = t;
        start++;
        end—; } }
/* @return int the index of the first element from the right that is less than its
    neighbor on the right. */
private int rightmostDip() {
    for (int i = n - 2; i >= 0; i—) {
        if (index[i] < index[i+1]) {
            return i; } }
    return -1; } }
```

Listing 3. **Combinations.**

```
package combinatorics;

/* Copyright (c) 1998 Steven J. Metsker. All Rights Reserved. */
/* The Combinations class provides an enumeration of all subsets of a group of n
   objects taken r at a time. The constructor for Combinations accepts the group
   as an array of Objects, along with the number to select.
<p>
   For example, to choose 3 boys from a list of 5, begin with an array of names:
<p>
<blockquote><pre>
   Object[] boys = {"Alfred", "Ben", "Carl", "Drew", "Edwin"};
</pre></blockquote>
To see all combinations of these 5 names taken 3 at a time, create and use a
Combinations enumeration:
<blockquote><pre>
     Combinations c = new Combinations(boys, 3);
   while (c.hasMoreElements()) {
     Object[] combo = (Object[])c.nextElement();
     for (int i = 0; i < combo.length; i++) {
        System.out.print((String)combo[i] + " "); }
   System.out.println(); }
</pre></blockquote>
<p>
This will print out a 10 line list:
<blockquote><pre>
   Alfred Ben Carl
   Alfred Ben Drew
   Alfred Ben Edwin
   Alfred Carl Drew
   Alfred Carl Edwin
   Alfred Drew Edwin
   Ben Carl Drew
   Ben Carl Edwin
   Ben Drew Edwin
   Carl Drew Edwin
 *</pre></blockquote> */

public class Combinations implements java.util.Enumeration {
     private Object[] inArray;
     private int n, m;
     private int[] index;
     private boolean hasMore = true;

/* Create a Combination to enumerate through all subsets of the supplied Object
   array, selecting "m" at a time.

   @param Object[] inArray the group to choose from @param m int the number to
   select in each choice @exception combinatorics. * CombinatoricException if m
   is greater than the length of inArray, or less than 0. */
public Combinations(Object[] inArray, int m) throws CombinatoricException {
     this.inArray = inArray;
     this.n = inArray.length;
     this.m = m;
```

(continued)

Listing 3. *(continued)*

```
// throw exception unless n >= m >= 0
   Combinatoric.check(n, m);

   /* "index" is an array of ints that keep track of the next combination to return.

   For example, an index on 5 things taken 3 at a time might contain {0 3 4}. index
   will be followed by {1 2 3}. Initially, the index is {0 ... m - 1}. */

   index = new int[m];
   for (int i = 0; i < m; i++) {
      index[i] = i; } }
/* @return true, unless we have already returned the last combination. */
public boolean hasMoreElements() {
   return hasMore;
}
/* Move the index forward a notch. The algorithm finds the rightmost index ele-
   ment that can be incremented, increments it, and then changes the elements
   to the right to each be 1 plus the element on their left.
   <p>
   For example, if an index of 5 things taken 3 at a time is at {0 3 4}, only the 0 can
   be incremented without running out of room. The next index is {1, 1+1, 1+2} or
   {1, 2, 3}. This will be followed by {1, 2, 4}, {1, 3, 4}, and {2, 3, 4}.
   <p>
   The algorithm is from Applied Combinatorics, by Alan Tucker. */
private void moveIndex() {
   int i = rightmostIndexBelowMax();
   if (i >= 0) {
         index[i] = index[i] + 1;
         for (int j = i + 1; j < m; j++) {
            index[j] = index[j-1] + 1; } }
   else {
         hasMore = false; } }
/* @return java.lang.Object, the next combination from the supplied Object array.
   <p>
   Actually, an array of Objects is returned. The declaration must say just
   "Object," because the Combinations class implements Enumeration, which
   declares that the "nextElement()" returns a plain Object. Users must cast the
   returned object to (Object[]). */
public Object nextElement() {
   if (!hasMore) {
      return null; }

   Object[] out = new Object[m];
   for (int i = 0; i < m; i++) {
      out[i] = inArray[index[i]]; }

   moveIndex();
   return out; }
/* @return int, the index which can be bumped up. */
private int rightmostIndexBelowMax() {

   for (int i = m - 1; i >= 0; i—) {
      if (index[i] < n - m + i) {
            return i; } }
   return -1; } }
```

Listing 4. **KaratePuzzle.**

```
package karatePuzzle;

import combinatorics.*;
/* Each of four martial arts students has a different specialty. From the following
   clues, can you determine each student's full name and her special skill?
<ol>
<li>Ms. Ellis (whose instructor is Mr. Caldwell), Amy, and Ms.
   Fowler are all martial arts students.
<li>Sparring isn't the specialty of either Carla or Dianne.
<li>Neither the shoot-fighting expert nor the pressure point fighter is named
   Fowler.
<li>Children's techniques aren't the specialty of Dianne (whose instructor is Ms.
   Sherman).
<li>Amy, who disdains pressure point fighting, isn't Ms. Goodrich.
<li>Betti and Ms. Fowler are roommates.
<li>Ms. Hightower avoids sparring because of its point scoring nature.
</ol> */
public class KaratePuzzle {
   private Student amy = new Student("Amy");
   private Student betti = new Student("Betti");
   private Student carla = new Student("Carla");
   private Student dianne = new Student("Dianne");
   private Student[] students = {amy, betti, carla, dianne};
   private String[] lastNames =
      {"Ellis", "Fowler", "Goodrich", "Hightower"};
   private String[] specialties =
      {"Sparring", "Shoot Fighting", "Pressure Points", "Childrens"};

/* Solve the karate puzzle. @exception combinatorics.CombinatoricException
   Shouldn't happen */
public static void main(String[] args) throws CombinatoricException {
   new KaratePuzzle().solve(); }
/* Generate all permutations of last names and specialties, and check each
   arrangement to see if it passes all the clues that the puzzle specifies.
   @exception combinatorics.CombinatoricException Shouldn't happen */
public void solve() throws CombinatoricException {
   Permutations lastNamePerm = new Permutations(lastNames);
   while (lastNamePerm.hasMoreElements()) {
      Object[] lasts = (Object[])lastNamePerm.nextElement();

      Permutations specPerm = new Permutations(specialties);
      while (specPerm.hasMoreElements()) {
         Object[] specs = (Object[])specPerm.nextElement();

         for (int i = 0; i < students.length; i++) {
            students[i].lastName = (String)lasts[i];
            students[i].specialty = (String)specs[i];
         }

            if (
            // Clue 1
            amy.lastName != "Ellis" &&
```

(continued)

Listing 4. *(continued)*

```
        amy.lastName != "Fowler" &&
        // Clue 2
        carla.specialty != "Sparring" &&
        dianne.specialty != "Sparring" &&
        // Clue 3
        studentNamed("Fowler").specialty != "Shoot Fighting" &&
        studentNamed("Fowler").specialty != "Pressure Points" &&
        // Clue 4
        dianne.specialty != "Childrens" &&
        // Clue 5
        amy.lastName != "Goodrich" &&
        amy.specialty != "Pressure Points" &&
        // Clue 6
        betti.lastName != "Fowler" &&
        // Clue 7
        studentNamed("Hightower").specialty != "Sparring" &&
        // Clue 4, 1
        dianne.lastName != "Ellis")
        {
        System.out.println("Solution:");
        for (int i = 0; i < students.length; i++)
            System.out.println("\t" + students[i] + " "); } } } }
/* Return the Student who has the given last name @return Student, the Student
   with the given last name @param lastName java.lang.String */
public Student studentNamed(String lastName) {
    for (int i = 0; i < students.length; i++) {
        if (students[i].lastName.equals(lastName)) {
            return students[i]; } }
    throw new InternalError("Bad last name"); } }
```

Prevention Is Better Than a Cure

Mike Mannion and Roy Phillips

W E HAVE TWO goals for this article: first, to briefly explain Design by Contract™ (Note: "Design by Contract" is a trademark of Interactive Software Engineering, Goleta, CA)—its benefits and application to software development. The second goal of the article is to examine its impact on Java, describe how Design by Contract (DBC) can be used to complement Java's exception mechanism, and to provide an overview of various techniques for implementing DBC in Java.

What Is Design by Contract?

Design by Contract (DBC) is a specification and programming technique that allows the designer or programmer to specify the *semantics* of a class's interface: an *Abstract Behavioral Specification*. As well as specifying the signature of say, a method (the name, the return type, and any arguments) DBC allows us to specify the abstract behavior that the method will or should implement.

In DBC, we take the view that an interface is a service provider: a piece of software that does something for us, such as displaying a widget, setting a port, or adding a new member to a club. As with any contract between a *client* and the *supplier* of a service, it is wise to specify the conditions of that contract for the benefit of both parties. This contract can be viewed as *requirements* on both the supplier and the client, and a statement of work—what is to be done.

In the following code fragment, a service newMember, provided by a class Club, is used to add a new member to a club.

```
Club brfc = new Club ( " Basel RFC" );
Person cw = new Person ( " C. Williams" ," 12-Dec-1972" );
brfc.newMember ( cw);
```

This service is specified by the Javadoc entry from class Club:

> **newMember**
> **public void newMember   (Person candidate)**
>   Add "candidate" to list of club members
> **Parameters:**
>   candidate—person to add to club's membership
> **See Also:**
>   members

But this isn't the full story: the Javadoc entry tells us what we need to know *syntactically* to use this service, but does not tell us anything about the conditions under which the service can be provided (a bit like buying a ski-pass in the summer). So, what are these conditions? Generally, we need to know the state of all objects involved before the service is invoked: what state should "candidate" and "club" be in? These are the *preconditions* for the service. In addition, we need a specification of what the service will do, which can be viewed as the state of involved objects after the call to this service: these are the *postconditions* for the service. A complete contract for the newMember service can be expressed in terms of these conditions as follows:

PRECONDITIONS

- The "candidate" object should not be null and the details in it must be complete.
- There should be room in the club for a new member.
- The candidate should not already be a member of the club.

POSTCONDITIONS

- Good candidate should have been made a member.

Extending the documentation for newMember to include these conditions—written as *assertions* on the state of the object and any arguments, we have a full specification for the interface:

newMember

public void newMember   (Person candidate)

    Add "candidate" to list of club members

Parameters:

    candidate—person to add to club's membership

Require:

    Candidate OK candidate **!= null &&** candidate.complete();

    Room in Club members.size() < membershipLimit;

    Not a member !isMember(candidate);

Ensure:

    Added if good !goodCandidate(candidate) || isMember(candidate);

See Also:

    members, membershipLimit

Note: As the client is expected to make certain that the precondition is true before calling a service, then all methods or attributes used to define the precondition should be visible to the client—no "hidden clauses" as it were. The same concern does not apply to postconditions, because if the supplier decides to conform to hidden postconditions, this is no one else's concern.

OBLIGATIONS AND BENEFITS

OK, we have specified the conditions under which the call to newMember is valid (candidate is valid, room in club) and stated what that service will do (if acceptable, candidate made a member of the club). These conditions can be expressed as a table showing the contract as the obligations of and benefits to, the client and supplier: The contract can be formulated as in Table 1 (using the style in *Building Bug-Free O-O Software: An Introduction to Design by Contract*).

Specifying the contract in this manner tells us:

- *What the service does.* The abstract behavior of a method can be thought of as a statement of conditions that hold before the call (preconditions), and those that should hold after the call (postconditions). Well formu-

Table 1. Obligations and benefits.

	Obligations	Benefits
Client	*(Must ensure pre-condition.)* Provide a valid candidate to club, if room for a new member	*(May benefit from post-condition.)* Candidate becomes club member
Supplier	*(Must ensure post-condition.)* If the candidate was acceptable and there is room in the club, then candidate must be made a member	*(May assume pre-condition.)* No need to attempt to add a member if no room in club, or if candidate is already a member

lated pre- and postconditions are an invaluable help when looking for a class to do a job. Although what a method does can often be inferred from its name, return type, arguments, and any comments (if present *and* correct), explicit and executable assertions that raise exceptions if false, are a far better guarantee.

- *How to use the service.* As well as specifying the behavior of a method (what the method does), DBC states the assumptions that the service will make about the state of the involved objects (its environment) when the service is called. Ensuring that these assumptions are correct is the job of the caller, the client.

Implementing an interface specified in this way becomes a case of transitioning the state of the involved objects (essentially the supplier object plus any arguments) before the call, to the state specified in the postcondition (the state of the supplier object and any returned values after the call). If the interface is well specified—that is, all important states are accurately defined in the pre- and postconditions—then the programming logic needed to implement that interface becomes clearer to write, to validate, and to maintain.

Until now, we have considered only conditions relating to single methods. In practice, it quickly becomes apparent when working out the postconditions that some conditions should *always* hold true. Such conditions defining the "correct" states of an object are known as the *class invariant*. As well as ensuring that the postconditions hold true, each and every method should also ensure that the class invariant is not violated. The "ensure" clauses in the interface specification above can be read to mean: (postconditions) && invariant(), assuming that the class implements a Boolean function "invariant" that checks and reports on the "correctness" of the object's current state. In fact, it is not required that an object must maintain the invariant at all times, only that it must always leave the object in a valid state after an operation is completed.

Working out the Contract

We have reviewed how specifying the contract enhances the depth of specification of an interface, but where do these conditions come from? How can we work out what the contract should be? One of the most useful sources of rules and axioms from which the contract can be derived is the problem domain being addressed: In our Club example, we have assumed the existence of a set of club membership rules. In other domains, this information might be taken from user requirements, an API manual, or observations made by the developer.

Having defined the boundaries of what a method must do in this way, we leave the developer complete freedom of *how* that contract is maintained: the most ingenious, efficient, and portable implementations can be created, within the well marked-out borders of the pre- and postconditions.

Inheritance

A lot of the benefit of OO is that a general class of object can be specialized or extended in a sub-class to deal with the specifics of a particular case. In our Club example, we may wish to create a specialization of a general club, in which the membership conditions are more specific: A sports club may allow two categories of membership, social and player, and members may join as both. In this case, the precondition !isMember(candidate) no longer applies, so when we re-implement newMember in class SportsClub, we will have to relax the precondition. In addition, we may wish to specify in the postcondition that a member may appear a maximum of two times in the memberships list.

Pre- and postconditions should always be inherited—it would not make sense to allow a sub-class to ignore the promises of the more general superclass. But if the new preconditions were stricter than the original conditions, code that so far worked well with the general Club class would break when it encounters an object of the SportsClub class: this is clearly unacceptable, and violates the Open-Closed principle (see the Open-Closed Principle sidebar).

For this reason then, it makes sense that the only changes to the preconditions are to make them less onerous. The opposite is true for postconditions—

Listing 1.   A simple Assertion class (does not satisfy all DBC Requirements).

```
public class Assertion
{
static private boolean preconditionsOn = true;
static private boolean postconditionsOn = true;
static private boolean invariantsOn = true;

static public void setPreconditionsEnabled(boolean pre)
{ preconditionsOn = pre; }

static public void setPostconditionsEnabled(boolean post)
{ postconditionsOn = post; }

static public void setInvariantsEnabled(boolean invar)
{ invariantsOn = invar; }

static public void pre(String label, boolean expr)
{ if (preconditionsOn)
   { System.out.println(" Assertion/pre:" +label);
   if (!expr) throw new PreconditionException(); }
}

static public void post(String label, boolean expr)
{ if (postconditionsOn)
   { System.out.println(" Assertion/post:" + label);
   if (!expr) throw new PostConditionException(); }
}

static public void invar(String label, boolean expr)
{ if (invariantssOn)
   { System.out.println(" Assertion/invar:" + label);
   if (!expr)
     throw new InvariantConditionException(); } } }
```

---

as that is what the supplier has promised, it would not be fair to deliver less. So postconditions may be left as they were or strengthened, in a sub-class.

CONSTRAINT LANGUAGE

We have given the expressions used to define the assertions in a contract as normal Java language statements evaluating to a Boolean value. It has been suggested (see "Further Reading") that a formal constraint language should be used for this purpose, providing predicates such as "forall" (iterate over a collection, asserting something about each element), taken from formal method practice, as found in the Z language. But as we have stated that it is the responsibility of the client to make sure that preconditions are met, expressing them in a language that is not available to the client is not reasonable: a contract should be expressed in a mutually-understood language. In practice, assertions about members of a collection can easily be

---

The Open-Closed Principle

An important property of a reusable software module is that it is *closed*: it is available for use by other modules by virtue of the fact that its interface is defined—the user knows how to invoke it (syntax) and what it will accomplish (semantics). At the same time, a module should be *open* for extension: future changes in requirements and usage should not be ruled out, thus fostering reusability.

This topic is covered in more detail by Bertrand Meyer in *Object-Oriented Software Construction* (Prentice Hall, 1997).

---

provided for by writing a Boolean function that performs that check. Such a function is often of general use as well.

In our "club" example, imagine we wanted to write an assertion that a given member is in the collection "members," which could be expressed in a constraint language as:

    member ∈ members

which reads as: "member *is in set* members." This can be expressed by providing a Java Boolean method check for containment in a list of members, for example:

    members.contains (member);

It now can be checked by the caller, and provides a method that may possibly be of use by other clients of the "members" class. Of course, as a basic design principle, query functions should not usually cause side-effects, i.e., they should not change the concrete state of the object.

Benefits for Developers

Pre- and postconditions are a specific form of *assertion*, using Boolean statements (Predicates), which enable us to define the abstract behavior of some software element. The immediate advantages of this are:

- To component writers (suppliers): It is not necessary to consider cases where our software is abused, provided we define the correct usage by providing adequate assertions.
- To component users (clients): A precise definition of what we need to do in order to use the service. Specification of what the service will do for us.

Listing 2. Using the Assertion class.

```
public void newMember(Person candidate)
{
Assertion.pre(" Candidate OK" ,
   candidate != null && candidate.complete() );
   Assertion.pre(" Room in Club" , members.size() < membershipLimit);
   Assertion.pre(" Not a member" , !isMember() );

   members.addElement(candidate);

   Assertion.post(" Added if good" ,
      !goodCandidate(candidate) || isMember(candidate));
   Assertion.invar(" Capacity OK" , invariant() );  }
protected boolean invariant()
{ return members.size() <=membershipLimit; }}
```

In addition, a rigorous use of DBC benefits the software life-cycle in other ways:

- *Traceability*: Business or problem-domain rules and axioms can be represented directly in the code, "proving" that the software system obeys those rules. The contracts should be updated to reflect changes in requirements, ensuring that the software system conforms.
- *Reusability*: Combats the "not invented here" syndrome, by helping us understand what a class does, and by building confidence in the performance of such classes (that it actually does what it claims).
- *Robustness*: Uncovers incorrect code (client or supplier) earlier, and provides a basis for unit testing; supports "cleanroom" software development. The ability to select the assertions to check is useful (often, "trusted" code can be left with assertion checking off, while new, untried code will usually be run with full checking). Leads to exceptions being raised at the point of error, better highlighting the misbehaving code.
- *Extendibility*: Supports Open–Closed principle. Specifying the interface fully (including the semantics) allows a module to be considered closed (available for use by other modules), while still open for extension, providing the contract is maintained (see the Open–Closed Principle sidebar).

In the DBC paradigm, the basic "Law of (software) Acquisition" (with apologies to Quark) is:

my colleague Al Goerner phrases it, "Squeeze diagrams out of text."

The third technique draws on published catalogs of conceptual models or partial models in well-understood domains, such as accounting, inventory, and insurance. Fascinating books such as *Analysis Patterns: Reusable Object Models* by Martin Fowler (Addison-Wesley, 1996) and *Data Model Patterns: Conventions of Thought* by David C. Hay (Dorset House, 1995) are highly recommended, not only as catalogs, but as learning resources to improve skills in modeling.

STRATEGIES TO IDENTIFY ASSOCIATIONS

An *association* is a relationship between concepts that indicate some meaningful and interesting connection. It is illustrated in the UML with a labeled line between the type boxes.

There are many *possible* associations between concepts in a model, but which ones are worth showing? A danger exists in overwhelming the diagram reader with an abundance of lines between boxes—we always need to be mindful that,

Table 1. Common concept categories.

Concept category	Examples
physical or tangible objects	Video
specifications, designs, or descriptions of things	VideoDescription
places	VideoStore
transactions	Sale, Payment, RentalTransaction
transaction line items	VideoRental (or VideoRentalLineItem)
roles of people	Customer
containers of other things	VideoStore
things in a container	Video
organizations	VideoStore
rules and policies	LoanPolicy
catalogs	VideoCatalog

when drawing diagrams, they can become so busy that they are hard to read and thus unusable. Given a desire to limit associations to those of high value, a practical criterion for including them is:

Only include associations for which memory of the relationship needs to be preserved for some duration according to the requirements and business rules.

For example, in Figure 3 there is a *Rents* association between Customer and Video because there is a need to remember what videos are being rented by a customer—not doing so would cause a problem. This association communicates an important relationship that software developers in this domain need to pay attention to. In contrast, there is an *Influenced-by* association between Customer and LoanPolicy. This is a legal and possible relationship, but what value does it add? There is probably no need to remember an instance of this relationship between a particular customer and policy. By following this heuristic when adding associations, you will tend to create models that emphasize only the really high-interest relationships, without swamping the diagrams with excessive low-interest information.

Another technique to help identify associations is to use the "common association categories" list presented in Table 2. However, the possible choices suggested by this list should still be tempered with the "need to remember" criterion just discussed.

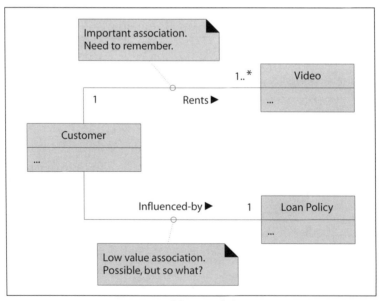

Figure 3. More and less useful associations.

MULTIPLICITY

At each end of an association a multiplicity value is shown. Multiplicity defines how many instances of type A can be associated with one instance of type B, usually considered at a particular moment in time. Including multiplicity values in a conceptual model increases our comprehension of the nature and constraints of an association. Figure 4 illustrates the basic UML notation.

ADDING ATTRIBUTES

An *attribute* is a logical data value of an object. It is illustrated in the UML in the second compartment of the type box (Figure 5).

Add attributes to a conceptual model to illustrate the information that is important to understanding the problem domain, such as information that needs to be remembered and reasoned with, based on the current use cases under development.

PUTTING IT ALL TOGETHER

Figure 6 illustrates a conceptual model that attempts to communicate the noteworthy concepts, associations, and attributes related to the domain of the video store and a use case related to borrowing videos. Considered as a "visual dictio-

Table 2. Common association categories.

Category	*Examples*
A is contained in B	VideoDescription—Catalog
A is a description for B	VideoDescription-Video
A is a line item of a transaction or report B	VideoRental—RentalTransaction
A is known/logged/recorded/reported/ captured in B	Video—VideoRental
A is a member of B	Customer—VideoStore

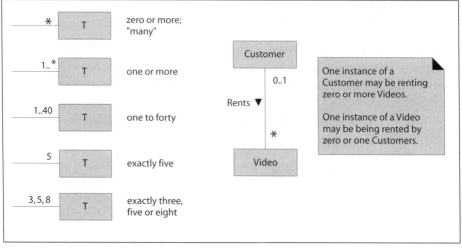

Figure 4. Multiplicity examples.

Figure 5.
Sample attribute
notation.

nary", this model concisely and expressively depicts many of the interesting things in this domain. In addition, it will serve as an excellent source of inspiration for the names of some of the software objects in the domain layer of the solution.

This model can be improved on to yield even more information and visual clues pertaining to the problem domain. In the future, we will dig a little deeper, both in terms of some common idioms in conceptual model, and some other notation available in the UML to portray these models.

RELATING TO OTHER ARTIFACTS AND JAVA

A conceptual model has a central role in influencing later models and the Java code itself. In particular, the concept and attribute names often are duplicated in the Java class definitions, and the connections between Java objects often mirror the important "need to remember" associations.

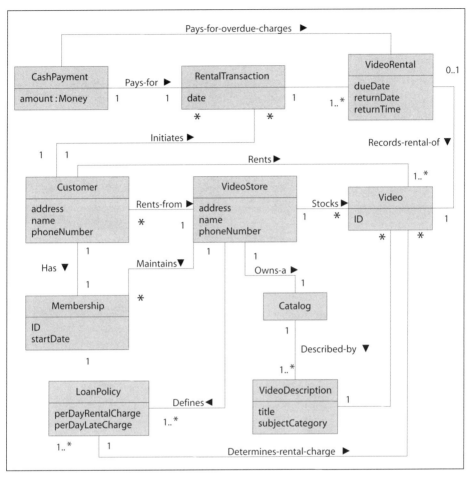

Figure 6.   A sample conceptual model.

NEXT TIME

In the next installment, we explore further topics in conceptual modeling. After that, we will investigate the creation of a system behavior model using sequence diagrams and contracts.

REFINING SKILLS FOR EXPRESSIVE CONCEPTUAL MODELS

CRAIG LARMAN

FOR THOSE WHO are just joining us, welcome! We are exploring common and useful object-oriented analysis and design modeling activities that ultimately lead to the creation of a system implemented in Java.

By definition, because analysis focuses on investigation of the problem space, the analysis models do not directly relate to Java. However, as we move on to design, we will explore more Java-related issues that impact the design of the architecture and software classes. When diagrams are used, we illustrate them in the Unified Modeling Language (UML) notation. However, this is *not* a column about the UML (which is "simply" a useful, standard diagramming notation—no small feat), rather it is a column about skills and heuristics in analysis and design, which is a more critical concern than notation. My usual disclaimer applies: modeling and diagramming should practically aid the development of "better" software—better in meeting the desires of the client or in being easier to change and extend. If it doesn't, question its value.

In our last column on conceptual (or domain object) models (see "The Conceptual Model—What's the Object?," *Java Report*, Vol. 3, No. 10) we focused on the fundamentals of this classic object-oriented analysis model: identifying concepts, attributes, and associations. It is *not* a picture of software components or classes; it is an analysis-oriented set of diagrams that depict abstractions of things of interest in the problem domain. You can think of it as a "visual dictionary" of the terminology of a domain.

A conceptual model may be helpful in a new or large domain that is unfamiliar to the developers. It succinctly visualizes the vocabulary of the problem space and expressively illustrates the important relationships between key ideas and information of interest to the stakeholders. The content of a conceptual model is primarily driven by the use cases currently under consideration—they suggest the meaningful concepts of interest to model. Also, it is the main source of inspiration for the names and properties of the software classes representing the "domain layer."

The objective is to help deepen our skills in making expressive conceptual models that capture the noteworthy terms/objects/concepts in the problem domain related to those we need to build a software system. Our ongoing example is a video store software system that will support the use cases discussed earlier.

KEEP ATTRIBUTES SIMPLE

Informally, we define simple attributes to include common "primitive" types, such as:

- Numbers, String (Text), Boolean, Character, and Enumeration types

and other basic types such as:

- Address, PhoneNumber, Name, Quantity (and its specializations, such as Money), Date/Time, and Color.

These simple categories are suitable to include in the attribute compartment of a type box. Other potential attributes, which represent *complex* types, are better not shown as attributes but rather indicated via associations. Figure 1 illustrates that the *destination* attribute of **Flight** is better modeled via an association, and that in the video store, it is better to model the **manager** as a **Person** concept than as an attribute.

IF IT'S NOT TEXT IN THE REAL WORLD . . .

A common weakness in conceptual modeling is to model complex concepts as simple Text/String attributes. If a potential attribute is not thought of as text or text-like in the real world, better to model it as a concept with associations rather than as an attribute. For example, in Figure 1, the *destination* of a Flight is really a complex thing in the real world—an airport occupying physical space. It is not a piece of text.

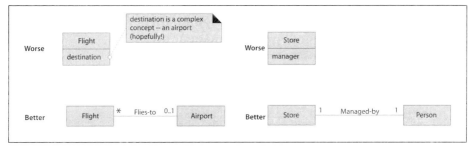

Figure 1.   Modeling attributes as separate concepts.

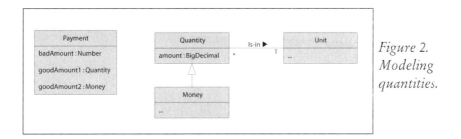

*Figure 2.
Modeling
quantities.*

MODEL QUANTITIES AS QUANTITIES

In his excellent book *Analysis Patterns* (Addison-Wesley, 1996), Martin Fowler re-emphasizes a heuristic that has been recognized for many years but all too often ignored in software development: most "numbers" are not just numbers. Ward Cunningham also described this in his Whole-Value pattern (*Pattern Languages of Program Design*, Volume 1, Addison-Wesley, 1995). What does it mean to have a weight of 50? A price of 27? Not much. What is needed is a unit. This is the Quantity pattern—to model (and ultimately to implement in Java) numeric values with units as Quantity types, rather than Integer, Float, and so on. Money is a kind of quantity. For example, in Java, monetary values should not be represented by just a float or a BigDecimal, rather, there should be something like a Money class, with a unit indicating the currency. This is both more accurate and allows for reasoning in varying units. One may express all kinds of quantities as just of type Quantity, or one may be more specific, such as Money, Weight, and so on. Quantities are "simple" types that may be shown in the attribute compartment (see Figure 2).

By the way, in Java, the *amount* of Money should be BigDecimal, to provide the least possible loss of precision in calculations.

ADDING GENERALIZATION/SPECIALIZATION

As a rule of thumb, generalization and specialization are useful to show in a conceptual model when:

- A potential subtype has additional attributes of interest.
- The subtype has additional associations of interest.
- The subtype concept is operated on, handled, reacted to, or manipulated differently than the supertype or other subtypes, in ways that are of interest.

For example, a video rental can be paid for by a variety of means (cash, credit, and so on), and we handle the payment types differently. In addition, the payment types have varying associations. This is motivation to specify the payments as different subtypes, as shown in Figure 3.

As expected, subtypes conform to the definitions of their supertypes, which is to say that they have the attributes and associations of their supertypes.

Notice also in Figure 3 that the set of concepts is broken down into a relatively fine-grained level of detail, such as CreditCard, Check, DriversLicense, and GeoPoliticalRegion. This fine level of detail is desirable both in an analysis conceptual model and later in the design and implementation of the software classes.

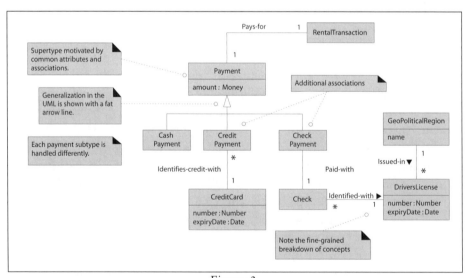

Figure 3.
Generalization and specialization, and fine-grained concept analysis.

WHEN TO SHOW AGGREGATION

Aggregation is a kind of association used to model whole–part relationships between things. The whole is usually called the *composite* or the *aggregate*, but the parts have no standard name—part or component is common. For instance, physical assemblies are organized in aggregation relationships, such as a Hand aggregates Fingers. As another example, a video RentalTransaction contains as its parts one or more VideoRentals. There is a very strong whole–part kind of relationship between these two concepts.

Showing aggregation is not critical. It could be left off a conceptual model without any significant loss of information. It does visually clarify the domain constraint (or "business rule") that (usually) the existence of the part is not possible or legal without the existence of the composite. And during the later design phase, it may be used to inspire an obvious "creator" software object of the parts, and to suggest referential integrity in a database schema.

Aggregation is shown in the UML with a hollow or filled diamond symbol at the composite end of a whole-part association (Figure 4).

Consider showing aggregation when:

- The lifetime of the part is bound within the lifetime of the composite—there is a create–delete dependency of the part on the whole.
- There is an obvious whole–part physical or logical assembly.
- Some properties of the composite propagate to the parts, such as its location.
- Operations applied to the composite propagate to the parts, such as destruction, movement, or recording.

PARTITIONING A CONCEPTUAL MODEL

For any significant application domain, and especially in "enterprise" modeling, a conceptual model is going to be quite large—easily in the hundreds of concepts. To

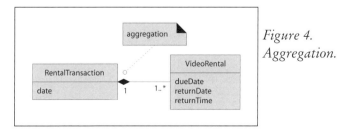

Figure 4.
Aggregation.

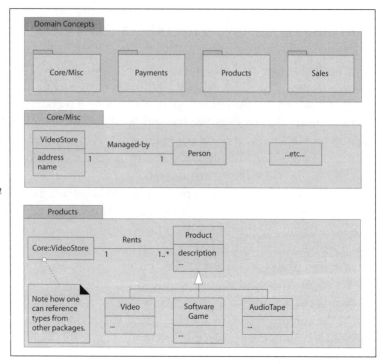

Figure 5. Organizing the model in packages.

visually and mentally group this detail into manageable chunks, we can use the UML package notation to group concepts with strong associations and common sub-domain membership. An UML package may contain any UML element: other packages (subpackages), types, use cases, and so on.

I recommend grouping your conceptual model into packages as soon as possible and drawing each package in a separate diagram. Figure 5 illustrates the salient notation in an example from the video store domain.

NEXT TIME

In a future installment, we will review the definition of a system behavior model in which we identify the external system operations and write operation contracts that specify the pre- and post-conditions for those operations.

DISTRIBUTED Observer CHAINS

ANDREW SMITH

OBJECTS ARE GOOD. Patterns are good. Networks are good.

These statements have almost become IT axioms in the last few years. I'm not going to buck the trend here. Objects are indeed good. Networks and patterns help to make them even better. I'm going to show a relatively easy way to link these three things together.

Well designed object-oriented applications share a common topology (see Riel, A. *Object-Oriented Design Heuristics*. Addison-Wesley, 1996.) By topology I mean the natural features of an entity and their structural relationships. A well-planned object model will spread out the application logic within a system. Related data and behavior will be kept in logical, isolated units. Structuring applications in this way promotes reuse, facilitates comprehension, and minimizes the effects of change.

One side effect of partitioning a system in this way is the need for these "logical isolated units" to communicate with each other. Using controller classes to organize the communication is not a viable solution because it concentrates the system's intelligence in a single place. How can we share information without cluttering our design?

The Observer pattern (see Gamma, E., R. Helm, R. Johnson, and J. Vlissides, *Design Patterns: Elements of Reusable Object-Oriented Software*. Addison-Wesley, 1995.) provides a possible answer to our question. In the applicability section of the pattern description we find that Observer is a good way to "notify other objects without making assumptions about who these objects are. In other words, you don't want these objects tightly coupled." This pattern is widely used and an implementation is even included as part of the standard JDK in the java.util package.

That takes care of objects and patterns. Now, how do networks fit into the picture? With a decentralized design we can start pulling out classes and plunking them down on different machines, servicing requests on the objects we instantiate via an Object Request Broker (ORB).

When we move to the ORB we want to be able to take our pattern with us. This is a fairly straightforward operation, but there are a few issues that come up. The code in this article was written and tested using the JDK1.1.4 and the OrbixWeb3.0 Beta (see IONA Technologies Web site).

The balance of this article will provide a roadmap to implementing the Observer pattern in a distributed environment. In addition, the notion of Observer Chaining will be discussed (see Smith, A., D. Pfister, and P. Arnold, *EDL, Rhymes with Wheedle: An Event Description Language for Distributed Systems*, Internal memorandum, May 1997). Observer Chaining is a useful extension to the Observer pattern that makes it easier to watch over many objects without knowing when or how they were created.

Listing 1 shows the IDL for the Observer pattern. The two interfaces that make up the Observer pattern have been included in a module called ModelView in deference to this pattern's Smalltalk origins. One change from the java. util.Observable interface was necessary. The notifyObservers method is only provided with the Object argument included. This is due to the fact that IDL does not support overloaded methods. We opt for the notifyObservers method with an argument because it will come in handy later. Clients who do not wish to send an argument can simply pass null and get the same functionality that the excluded method provided.

After compiling the IDL we have to provide an implementation class for the interfaces we defined. Listing 2 (Warth, C. "Observer.java," Sun Microsystems, JDK Source Code Web page) shows what should be very familiar code. This is basically the source code provided with the JDK for java.util.Observable. The implementation for the Observer interface will be done later on the client side. The most significant change to the Observable implementation is the addition of an abstract method called ref. This method must be implemented in distributed classes that want to make themselves observable. The reason for this method is that everything in CORBA must be done through object references.

WHAT IS A REFERENCE?

Wait just a minute. Aren't all objects in Java accessed through object references? Well yes, that is what the language spec says (see Arnold, K. and J. Gosling, *The Java Programming Language*, Addison-Wesley, 1996.) But when you start doing distributed computing you have to expand your concept of the word "reference."

When dealing with CORBA you can talk about references and mean any of the following things (see Siegel, J., *CORBA Fundamentals and Programming*, John Wiley & Sons, 1996.)

1. *Interoperable Object Reference or IOR*: This type of reference is never really seen by clients. It is used to allow method invocations to pass between ORBs from different vendors. IORs contain information about the object being referenced to make this possible. Some of the information in an IOR includes the type of the object, what protocols can be used by the ORB sending the request, what ORB services can be used, and whether this object reference is null.

2. Stringified Object Reference: Object references obtained from the ORB can be converted to strings by using a method provided by the ORB called object_to_string(). The result can be stored somewhere and used later to get the object back from the ORB at some arbitrary point in the future.

3. Object Reference: Every object created by an ORB is assigned an object reference. The reference is valid for the lifetime of the object. When the object gets deleted so does the reference. This is the reference that you hand to the ORB when you want to use a distributed obect. The ORB takes care of finding the target object and invoking methods for you.

Due to these different notions of what a reference actually is, we had to make our **Observable** class abstract. When we sit down to write an observable object that resides on the ORB, we have to provide an object reference as just defined. Listing 2.1 shows a typical implementation of **ref**.

Listing 1. ModelView.idl.

```
#ifndef MODELVIEW_IDL
#define MODELVIEW_IDL

module ModelView {
    interface Observable;

    interface Observer {
        void update ( in Observable observable, in Object argument ); };

    interface Observable {
        void addObserver     ( in Observer observer );
        void deleteObserver  ( in Observer observer );
        void notifyObservers ( in Object argument );
        void deleteObservers ( );
        long countObservers ( );
        boolean hasChanged ( ); }; };

#endif
```

Listing 2. **Observable.java.**

```java
package ModelView;
import java.util.Vector;

public abstract class __Observable implements _ObservableOperations {

    private boolean changed = false;
    protected Vector objects;
    protected Observer[] observerArray = new Observer[2];

    //Implement this method in your CORBA objects to make them observable
    //cf. Listing 2.1, Listing 4, Listing 5
    protected abstract Observable ref();

    public __Observable() {
        objects = new Vector(); }

    public synchronized void addObserver(Observer observer) {
        if (!objects.contains(observer)) {
            objects.addElement(observer); } }

    public synchronized void deleteObserver(Observer observer) {
        objects.removeElement(observer); }

    protected synchronized void clearChanged() {
        changed = false; }

    public synchronized int countObservers() {
        return objects.size(); }

    public synchronized void deleteObservers() {
        objects.removeAllElements(); }

    public synchronized boolean hasChanged() {
        return changed; }

    public void notifyObservers(org.omg.CORBA.Object argument) {
        int size=0;

        synchronized (this) {
            /* We don't want the Observer doing callbacks into arbitrary code while
               holding its own Monitor. The code where we extract each Observable
               from the Vector and store the state of the Observer needs synchro-
               nization, but notifying observersdoes not (should not). The worst re-
               sult of any potential race-condition here is that: 1) a newly-added
               Observer will miss a notification in progress 2) a recently unregistered
               Observer will be wrongly notified when it doesn't care */
            if (!hasChanged())
                return;
            size = objects.size();
            if (size > observerArray.length) {
                observerArray = new Observer[size]; }
            objects.copyInto(observerArray);
            clearChanged(); }

        for (int i = size -1; i>=0; i—) {
            if (observerArray[i] != null) {
                observerArray[i].update(ref(), argument); } } }

    protected synchronized void setChanged() {
        changed = true; } }
```

Observer Chaining

We now have a framework for making distributed objects observable. Before presenting an example application, consider the following. If you wanted to find out what was going on in New York City you could spend the day running around watching all the things that you were interested in. After a day or two you would probably discover that there had to be a better way to get the job done. You could, for example, buy a newspaper. You still get the job done, but your task has been greatly simplified. The newspaper watches all the things you are interested in, and all you have to do is watch the newspaper. This is an example of **Observer Chaining**. Table 1 shows the relevant classes and interfaces implemented in the previous scenario.

Let's call the objects that implement the **Observer** interface, Clients. Then call objects implementing the **Observable** interface Sources. If **Source** objects are implemented in an ORB and **Client** objects are implemented somewhere else across the network, it becomes difficult to bridge the gap between **Source** and **Client**. In addition, if **Source** objects are logical collections of objects it can be inconvenient to monitor them all separately. What is needed is a way to attach an **Observer** to a **Source** object at construction and then publish that **Observer** as a way for **Client** objects to get at the **Source**. Let's call that **Observer** a **RelayAgent**. Table 2 shows the new classes we have defined and the interfaces that they implement.

When multiple clients share interest in source events a **RelayAgent** *can be used to mediate the relationship.*

This simplifies creation routines for the source object.

Example

An example of **Observer Chaining** can be found at the trading desk in a securities brokerage firm.

- **Orders** are requests to buy or sell securities at a given price.
- **Accounts** are where **Orders** originate from.
- **Blotters** are views of the **Orders** in an **Account**.

A **Blotter** might contain several different **Accounts**. For example, a head trader might want to have a **Blotter** available that showed him the **Orders** in all of his traders' **Accounts**. **Orders** change state over time. Over the course of its lifetime

---

Listing 2.1.   Typical implementation of ref.

```
//Provide this object's CORBA object reference

protected Observable ref()
{
    // tell the ORB to create an object reference to "this" object// later when the
        ORB needs to invoke methods on// "this" it will use the reference created
        here to // get at our implementation return new _tie_MyObject(this);
}
```

Listing 3.   ObserverChain.idl.

```
#ifndef OBSERVERCHAIN_IDL
#define OBSERVERCHAIN_IDL

#include <ModelView.idl>

module ObserverChain {
    interface Order;
    typedef sequence<Order> OrderList;

    interface Blotter : ModelView::Observer {
        //client side implementation };

    interface Account : ModelView::Observer, ModelView::Observable {
        readonly attribute OrderList orders;
        void newOrder(); };

    interface Order : ModelView::Observable {
        //OrbixWeb3.0 beta 2 requires defining set method here instead of using
            attributes
        readonly attribute string status;
        void   setStatus(in string status); }; };

#endif
```

---

an Order may be canceled, filled, partially filled, rejected, etc. A Blotter should show this activity to give the trader an up-to-date view of where his Orders stand.

Before going into detail about Listing 3, I want to say something about inheritance in IDL. In IDL you can derive a new interface from an existing one. The new interface has all the same operations that its base interface had, plus any others that you define. Multiple inheritance of interfaces is also allowed in IDL. If you inherit from an interface you are required to provide an implementation for all the base interface operations as well as your newly defined operations when you write your implementation class.

Listing 3 shows the IDL for our Blotter-Account-Order Observer Chain. You can see that Blotter will be a client side implementation of an Observer. By inheriting the ModelView::Observer interface we can avoid duplicating it here.

Table 1. Newspaper example of Observer chaining.

	Observer	*Observable*
You	X	
Newspaper	X	X
Goings on About Town		X

Table 2. Implementations of the Observer and Observable interfaces.

	Observer	*Observable*
Client	X	
RelayAgent	X	X
Source		X

Because this is IDL, inheritance here means inheriting the operation signatures that were defined in Listing 1. Account acts as the RelayAgent. Because the account must be both an Observer and Observable we multiply inherit from the two ModelView interfaces. Order is the Source object and therefore inherits the Observable interface. Table 3 shows the classes in this example and the interfaces that they implement. Listings 4–6 provide the implementation for our Observer Chain.

To implement the Account and Order objects we can inherit the Observable implementation we provided earlier in Listing 2. Because multiple inheritance is not allowed in Java we use a feature in OrbixWeb called the TIE approach. This method allows us to implement a Java interface for our distributed objects instead of inheriting from an ORB generated ImplBase object.

The interesting thing about our implementation of the Observer Chain is the way the upcalls work from Order to Account to Blotter. Keep in mind that the implementation of notifyObservers passes the Observable object that called it as the first argument to the update method of the Observer that has registered interest. Figure 1 shows how Observer Chaining allows Clients to access Source objects via RelayAgents.

Our Source object, Order, calls notifyObservers with a null argument. It sim-

Table 3. Implementations of the Blotter-Account-Order chain.

	Observer	Observable
Blotter	X	
Account	X	X
Order		X

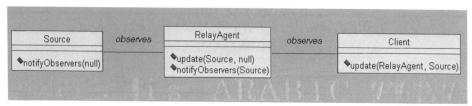

Figure 1.
Observer Chaining allows Clients to access Source objects via RelayAgents.

```
                        Listing 4.  Order.java.
package ObserverChain;

import ModelView.*;

public class __Order extends    __Observable
            implements _OrderOperations
{
    private String status_;

    public __Order() {
        status_ = new String("NEW"); }

    public String status() {
        return status_; }

    public void setStatus(String status) {
        status_ = status;
        setChanged();
        notifyObservers(null); }

    protected Observable ref() {
        return new _tie_Order(this); } }
```

ply lets the RelayAgent, Account, know that something happened. Now for the good stuff. The update method in Account calls notifyObservers with the Order object as an argument. This means that when the update method gets called at the Blotter, we can ignore the Account object that was passed in as the first parameter, and narrow the Object reference passed in as an argument to get at the Order. The nice thing about this is that we can have access to the Order object's functionality without duplicating its interface in the Account.

CONCLUSION

Objects, networks, and patterns are useful tools in constructing systems. When moving to a distributed architecture there are several hurdles to overcome. By

---

Listing 5. Account.java.

```
package ObserverChain;

import COM.objectspace.jgl.Array;
import ModelView.*;

public class __Account extends__Observable
             implements_ObserverOperations,
                _AccountOperations
{
    private Array orders_ = null;
    private Order[] sequence_;

    public __Account() {
        orders_ = new Array(); }

    public void newOrder() {
        Order order = new _tie_Order(new __Order());
        order.addObserver(new _tie_Account(this));

        orders_.pushBack(order); }
    public Order[] orders() {
        sequence_ = new Order[orders_.size()];
        orders_.copyTo(sequence_);
        return sequence_; }

    protected Observable ref() {
        return new _tie_Account(this); }

    public void update(ModelView.Observable observable,
          org.omg.CORBA.Object argument) {
        setChanged();
        //send the observable as an argument
        //this allows access to the source interface from the client
        notifyObservers(observable); } }
```

bringing some of the time-tested patterns of traditional object-oriented design to the process we can make the transition a little easier. Distributed Observer Chaining is a dressed up version of the old Model/View pattern. This pattern should be familiar to most developers and give some frame of reference to work from while exploring the other details of working within a distributed environment.

Listing 6.   Blotter.java.

```java
package ObserverChain;

import org.omg.CORBA.ORB;
import org.omg.CORBA.SystemException;
import COM.objectspace.jgl.Array;
import ModelView.*;

public class __Blotter implements _ObserverOperations
{
    public void update(ModelView.Observable observable, org.omg.CORBA.
      Object argument) {
        Order order = null;
        try {
            order = OrderHelper.narrow(argument);
            System.out.println("Status: " + order.status()); }
        catch (SystemException se) {
            System.out.println("illegal cast");
            System.exit(1); } }

    public Observer ref() {
        return new _tie_Observer(this); }

    public static void main(String args[]) {
        Account account_;
        Array orders_;

        __Blotter blotter_ = new __Blotter();

        ORB orb = ORB.init();

        account_ = AccountHelper.bind(":OCAccount", "orbhost");
        account_.addObserver(blotter_.ref());
        account_.newOrder();
        orders_ = new Array(account_.orders());
        Order order = (Order)orders_.at(0);
        order.setStatus("Partial");
        order.setStatus("Cancel Leaves");
        order.setStatus("Canceled");
        System.exit(1); } }
```

EVENT NOTIFIER:
A PATTERN FOR EVENT
NOTIFICATION

SUCHITRA GUPTA, JEFFREY M. HARTKOPF, AND SURESH RAMASWAMY

I N OUR COMPLEX world, events are constantly occurring. Any one person is only interested in a very small subset of all these events, so humans have worked out ways of getting just the information of interest, which works to a degree. We may periodically check to see if the event has occurred, or we ask someone to notify us when the event occurs. Often there is more than one source of a particular type of event such as disaster-related events, but we do not typically care about *who* notifies us, just that the event has occurred. Ideally, we would subscribe to just those types of events in which we are interested and be notified of them when they occur.

Event notification is a useful communication paradigm in computing systems as in real life. This article documents general event notification in the form of a design pattern, which provides a useful way of exposing readers to the important concepts and issues involved in event notification, and provides a language-neutral pattern for implementing event notification in a variety of scenarios. Concurrently, we discuss design issues using examples as appropriate to demonstrate effective use of event notification. Diagrams use the Unified Modeling Notation (UML) (see *Unified Modeling Language User Guide*, Booch, G. et al., Addison-Wesley, 1997).

INTENT

Event Notifier enables components to react to the occurrence of particular events in other components without knowledge of one another, while allowing dynamic participation of components and dynamic introduction of new kinds of events.

ALSO KNOWN AS

It is also known as Dispatcher, Decoupler, and Publish-Subscribe.

MOTIVATION

To understand the need for **Event Notifier**, we will take a simple example of a network management system, and implement it in a simplistic way. Then we will look at the problems with this approach, and incrementally show how we might solve them using **Event Notifier**.

Consider a large network of distributed components, such as computers, hubs, routers, software programs, and so forth. We wish to monitor and manage these components from a central location. We will refer to the components being managed as *managed objects*. Problems are typically infrequent and unpredictable, but when they do occur we wish to be notified without having to constantly poll the managed objects. The notification may appear on a *management system* such as a central console, pager, or electronic mail reader. For our example, suppose we have both a console and a paging system. In the simplistic implementation, shown in Figure 1a, a managed object must send notification of problems to both the console and the paging system. If we later wish to change the interface to the console or paging system, or add an electronic mail system, every managed object must be modified. Apart from being unscalable, this approach is very error prone, because each managed object must essentially duplicate the same sequence for notification, making consistency difficult to achieve. Encapsulating the notification behavior in a common superclass only partially mitigates the problem.

In a system of any size, we would like to minimize the number of dependencies and interconnections between objects to keep the system from becoming brittle and hard to change. The more dependencies there are, the more a change in any particular point in the system propagates to other points in the

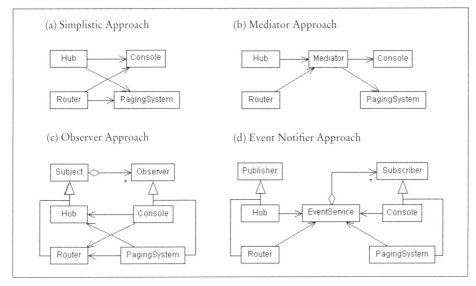

Figure 1. Approaches to a network management system.

system. The simplistic approach requires each managed object to maintain a reference to each management system. The number of these references increases geometrically with the number of managed objects and management systems. A better approach that keeps this to a linear increase is to have a mediator that encapsulates and coordinates the communication, as shown in Figure 1b. To report a problem, each managed object notifies the mediator, which in turn notifies the console and paging system as appropriate. Now, to modify an existing management system or add a new one, such as an electronic mail system, we need only to modify the mediator. This is a use of the Mediator design pattern (see *Design Patterns: Elements of Reusable Object-Oriented Software*, Gamma, E. et al., Addison-Wesley, 1997).

An alternative approach to solving the dependency problem is to introduce the notion of notification to the system in a generic way, using the Observer design pattern (see Gamma et al.). As shown in Figure 1c, each managed object implements a common "subject" interface, which allows interested observers such as the paging system and console to register interest in its events. When a managed object has a problem to report, it traverses its internal list of interested observers, calling each in turn. Unlike in the simplistic approach, the managed object does not need to know *a priori* which systems to notify; the management systems themselves are responsible for dynamically registering with the managed objects for notification. However, we have introduced a new problem: now the management systems need to know about each managed object, to register interest in them. If anything, this is worse, because there may be an arbitrarily large number of managed objects on a large network, and they may come and go frequently. We need a mechanism that requires neither the managed objects nor the management system to have *a priori* knowledge of each other, but to still be able to communicate problems.

The Observer approach has the benefit of allowing more dynamic behavior than the Mediator approach: new management systems may be added without impacting the rest of the system, although we cannot do the same with managed objects. It also does not require the presence of an omniscient mediator that understands and controls the flow of interactions: behavior that naturally fits in the managed objects or management systems may stay there. However, each subject has the burden of maintaining a list of observers and calling them as necessary, which the mediator approach nicely centralizes. It is possible to implement the system in a way that combines the benefits of both the Mediator and Observer approaches, as shown in Figure 1d. Like in the Mediator approach, we have a central event service that mediates notification, so that managed objects and management systems do not need to know about each other. Like in the Observer approach, a registration system allows us to add and remove observers (called *subscribers*) dynamically. Unlike the Observer approach, however, this functionality is centralized in the event service, relieving subjects (called *publishers*) of this burden. We give the name Event Notifier to this best-of-both-worlds approach.

Event Notifier derives many of its benefits from the fact that subscribers only know about *events*, not about publishers. For example, routers and hubs might both generate events of the same type, say FaultEvent, when problems occur. In an Observer implementation, each management system needs to know which managed objects generate fault events and register with each. The same is essentially true of Mediator, except that the mediator encapsulates this knowledge. However, using Event Notifier, a management system needs only to register interest in the FaultEvent type to get all fault events, regardless of who publishes them.

Applicability

Use the Event Notifier pattern in any of the following situations:

- When an object should be able to notify other objects of an event without needing to know who these objects are or what they do in response.

- When an object needs to be notified of an event, but does not need to know where the event originated.
- When more than one object can generate the same kind of event.
- When some objects are interested in a broader classification of events, while others are interested in a narrower classification.
- When an object may be interested in more than one kind of event.
- When you need to dynamically introduce new kinds of events.
- When objects participating in notification may be dynamically introduced or removed, as in distributed systems.
- When you need to filter out events based on arbitrary criteria.

STRUCTURE

The class diagram in Figure 2 shows the structure of the **Event Notifier** pattern. Details on the purpose of each class and the interactions between them, are discussed later in this article.

The **EventService** class contains the aggregations **filters**, **subscribers**, and

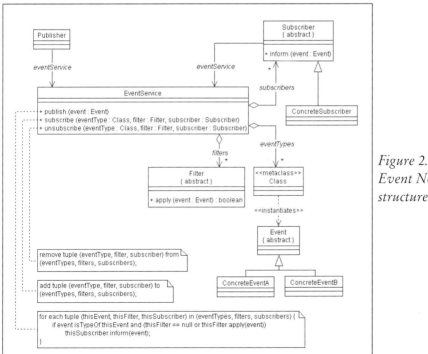

*Figure 2.
Event Notifier
structure.*

eventTypes. Although not readily apparent from the structure, corresponding elements from these aggregations comprise a tuple. Each tuple corresponds to the parameters passed to a single call to subscribe.

PARTICIPANTS

This section describes the responsibilities of the classes shown in the Event Notifier structure.

- **Event** A common ancestor type for all events.
- **ConcreteEvent** (FaultEvent) Represents a specific occurrence, possibly containing data about that occurrence.
- **Publisher** (Hub, Router) Emits or produces events.
- **Subscriber** Defines an interface for all objects that need to handle events.
- **ConcreteSubscriber** (Console, PagingSystem) Registers for events, and handles events by implementing the Subscriber interface.
- **EventService** Brokers events between subscriber and publisher.
- **Filter** Responsible for discarding events not of interest to a subscriber.
- **Class** A metaclass (a class whose instances are classes). **Event Notifier** uses an instance of this class to identify the type of event of interest.

COLLABORATIONS

The collaboration diagram in Figure 3 shows the typical sequence of interactions between participating objects.

The subscriber invokes the subscribe method on the event service (1) specifying the event type it is interested in and passes a reference to itself (or possibly another object) and a filter. The eventType argument represents the type of the event. When an event occurs, the publisher invokes the publish method on the event service (2) passing an event object. The event service determines which subscribers are interested in this event, and for each of them applies the filter (3) provided by the subscriber. If no filter is provided, or if application of the filter results in true, then the event service invokes the inform method of the subscriber (4), passing the event as an argument.

Notice that all publication and subscription is done through the event service. The event service maintains all information about which subscribers are interested in which events, so that publishers and subscribers need not be

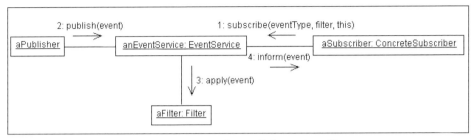

Figure 3. Event Notifier collaboration diagram.

aware of each other. Moreover, anyone may publish or subscribe to events using the well-defined interface provided by the event service without having to implement any special logic to handle interaction with other entities for which it has no other reason to communicate.

CONSEQUENCES

This section discusses the results and tradeoffs associated with the use of **Event Notifier**.

Subscription is based on event type rather than publisher. In some event notification models, a subscriber registers interest in receiving events from a particular publisher or type of publisher. This is useful when subscribers have knowledge of the publisher. When processing events from a graphical user interface (GUI), for example, the event handler knows about the individual controls that can publish events. In **Event Notifier**, a subscriber registers interest based solely on event type, without regard to publisher. This is more suitable for services in a distributed environment that are not coupled and may cooperate using an enterprise-wide event hierarchy without any knowledge of each other at compile time or run time. For those cases where subscribers are interested in events from a particular publisher, include an event attribute that identifies the source, and define a filter that uses this attribute to discard uninteresting events.

Subscribing to an event type automatically subscribes to all its subtypes. Because event types are structured in an inheritance hierarchy, when a subscriber subscribes to a particular event type, the event service notifies it of all events of that type or any subtype in the hierarchy. This enables subscribers to specify interest in events as broadly or narrowly as necessary. This feature is easier to implement in languages like Java and Smalltalk that provide rich run-time type information.

Events can be filtered. Filtering allows a subscriber to programmatically select the events of interest. By specifying an event type at subscription time, the subscriber narrows its interest to a certain class of events. An explicit filter allows further selection of events prior to notification, based on custom criteria such as the values of certain event attributes. For example, a filter might use an event source attribute to restrict events to those from a certain source. In the network management example described earlier, regional monitoring centers could use filters to limit events to those received from the regions of interest.

Subscribers and publishers can vary independently. Event subscribers and publishers do not have knowledge of each other and can vary independently. The understanding between the two is via agreement on a set of legal event types, the semantics of what an event means, and event data associated with an event type.

There can be multiple publishers and subscribers for a given kind of event. Some patterns for event notification require a subscriber to "know" each publisher of an event type. This can be difficult or impossible if the publishers of an event cannot be determined at compile time.

Subscribers can be interested in events for a limited duration. They can subscribe and unsubscribe at will. Support for dynamic registration and unregistration allows for this freedom.

Subscribers and publishers may be transient. A new subscriber or publisher can appear or disappear without impacting other components of the system. This is particularly important because it allows relocation of services in a distributed environment.

Event types can be introduced with minimal impact. In languages like Java that support dynamic loading of classes, one can add new event types to an existing application dynamically. Existing subscribers will receive events of the new event type if they are already subscribing to a supertype. One can dynamically add publishers for the new event type without having to rebuild the entire application. In environments without support for dynamic class loading, one may need to rebuild the application to add new event types, but no changes to subscriber or event service code are required.

Event Notifier makes a tradeoff between genericity and static type safety. In large distributed systems, change can entail recompilation and redistribution of many components to multiple locations in a network. It is imperative to design such systems to be resilient to change, minimizing the impact of change to the smallest number of components possible. Using **Event Notifier** helps accomplish this goal by keeping components decoupled from the beginning and allowing for change by keeping interfaces generic in terms of the types they deal with. However, this genericity and extensibility comes at the cost of some type safety provided by compile-time type checking. If the same event can emanate from one of many sources then this flexibility pays off. The Reclaiming Type Safety subsection under Implementation describes one way to mitigate the lack of static type checking for events.

The event service could be a single point of failure or bottleneck. This could be the case if a single event service brokers all events. However, we can mitigate these and other problems associated with centralization by distributing the work without changing the semantics, as discussed in the Enhancing Fault Tolerance and Performance section of Implementation.

IMPLEMENTATION

This section discusses specific issues that one must address when implementing Event Notifier in a real situation. We divide the issues into more or less autonomous sections, discussing implementation techniques where appropriate.

ACCESSING THE EVENT SERVICE

An event service always has a well-known point of access so that subscribers and publishers in a given environment can share the same event service. One can provide this well-known point of access using the Singleton or Abstract Factory pattern (see Gamma et al.), or by registering the event service with a well-known naming service.

MODELING EVENTS

When modeling events, one must think about how to decompose communication in a system into generic messages that convey certain standard information in the form of an event object. Such an object could be of any type, but there are certain advantages to requiring event types to be subclasses of an Event base class as shown in Figure 4. One advantage is that the Event class can enforce a common interface or set of attributes on all events, such as a time stamp, which captures the time of occurrence of an event. Such an event hierarchy also enables type-based subscription: subscribers can specify a non-leaf node in the event tree to be informed of all events of that type or below.

The natural way to implement an event hierarchy in an object-oriented language is by using inheritance. However, it could also be implemented using a string

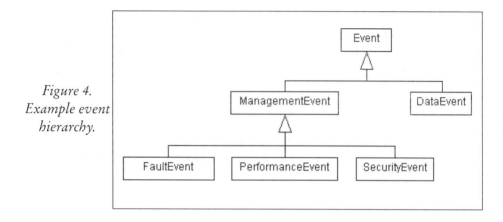

Figure 4.
Example event
hierarchy.

representation, with the levels of the hierarchy separated by colons. For example, the event types in Figure 4 might be represented as Event, Event:ManagementEvent, Event:ManagementEvent:FaultEvent, and so forth. The inheritance mechanism, not surprisingly, has several advantages. Principally, it allows an event subscriber to more easily subscribe to all events in a subtree of the type hierarchy. One subscriber may want all management events, while another may only be interested in data events. This is expressed simply by subscribing to the event at the root of the hierarchy of interest. Furthermore, because events are objects, attributes may be packaged naturally with them, so the subscriber need not invoke methods on (say) the publisher to retrieve those attributes. The inheritance mechanism also takes advantage of compile-time type checking. The compiler will not catch errors in string representations, such as a misspelled event type, but it will catch errors in class names. The advantages to the string technique are that it works in languages that are not object-oriented, and strings may be generated dynamically, while in many languages, objects in an event hierarchy must have classes that are defined at compile time.

Events can have various characteristics, which may lead to alternative ways of arranging them into a single hierarchy. Figure 5 shows two ways to model management events. To take advantage of type-based event notification, it is useful to choose a model based on the kind of events in which one anticipates subscribers having interest. If subscribers need to be informed of all fault events, regardless of whether they are hardware or software faults, then modeling the events as in Figure 5a would be appropriate. On the other hand, if subscribers are interested in all hardware events regardless of whether they are fault or performance events, devising an event hierarchy as shown in Figure 5b makes sense.

Event characteristics may appear as attributes of events instead of being modeled as types in the event hierarchy. However, this approach prevents

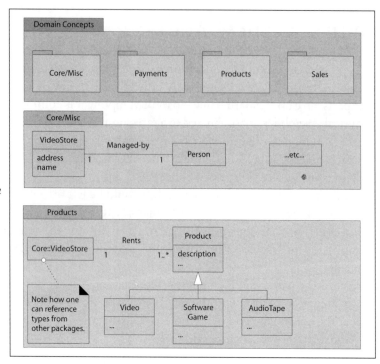

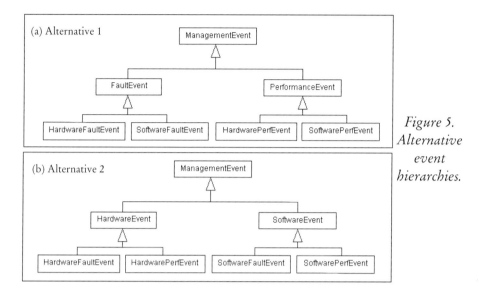

Figure 5. Alternative event hierarchies.

subscription based on that characteristic. Filters can be used to achieve a similar effect, although they are less efficient and not as type safe.

Identification of event source (publisher) is useful in certain situations. As alluded to earlier, when processing events from a GUI, the action taken by a subscriber in response to an event may depend on the source of the event. On a button click event, the subscriber would want to known which button was clicked. Event source could also be used to advantage in situations where one would otherwise need to specify a number of attributes that have information related to the source. In this case, storing an event source handle as an event attribute will allow a subscriber to get the information it needs about the event source from the event source directly. The tradeoff is that including the event source as an attribute leads to coupling between subscriber and publisher.

DETERMINING EVENT TYPE AT RUN TIME

To subscribe to events of a particular type, a subscriber passes an instance of a metaclass. When an event is published, the event service checks whether any subscribers are interested in it. Different implementation languages support the notion of a metaclass and the ability to check if an object is of a certain type to varying degrees.

In Java, the Class class is like a metaclass. One can check whether an object is of a certain type by invoking the isAssignableFrom method on the type's Class object, passing the Class object for the object in question. If an instance of the class specified as an argument to isAssignableFrom could be assigned to an instance of the class on which this method is invoked, then the class specified in the argument must be the same class as, or a subclass of, the class on which the method is invoked. This is the essential mechanism for supporting type-based notification in Event Notifier.

Smalltalk supports a similar mechanism as part of its Class class for determining if an object is of a certain type.

C++ also provides run-time type information. To check if an event object is of a certain event type, one might think of using the dynamic_cast operator. However, this is not sufficient, because the event service only knows the event type to which to cast at run time. We would prefer to implement the event service generically, without the need to modify it each time we use it in a different environment with a different set of event types. Even in a single environment, we would prefer not to have to alter the implementation of the event service whenever we introduce a new event type, so as to promote reuse.

A second alternative for C++ uses the type_info class as an approximation of a metaclass. Using the typeid operator, the event service can check whether an event is of the same type as that specified by the type_info object. This technique, however, does not fully address the requirement because the published event could be a subtype of the type in the type_info object. Dealing with this issue requires type information beyond that supported in C++. However, there are well-known ways to accomplish getting the additional type information. One technique is for each class in the event hierarchy to implement an isKindOf method. The NIH class library (see *Data Abstraction and Object-Oriented Programming in C++*, Wiley, J., Wiley and Sons, 1990) provides a good example of how this can be done. Every NIH class has a private static member variable named classDesc that is an instance of a class named Class. This class descriptor object contains items of information about an object's class such as its name and superclass(es). Objects instantiated from NIH classes support an isKindOf method that in turn relies on information in the corresponding Class object to ascertain whether an object is of a certain type.

RECLAIMING TYPE SAFETY

As mentioned in Consequences, the genericity of Event Notifier comes at the expense of some type safety. This problem manifests itself in the implementation of the subscriber's inform method and the filter's apply method. Below, we describe the problem and potential solutions in terms of the subscriber, but the same applies to the filter.

The subscriber receives an event of type Event, which it must downcast to the type of event it is expecting. If a subscriber subscribes to more than one type of

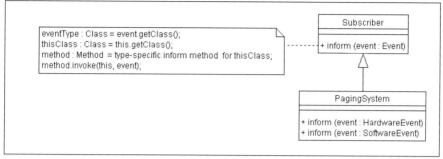

Figure 6. Type safety.

event, it first needs to check the event type. Even if it subscribes to only a single event type, it should first validate the event type to prevent run-time errors due to improper coding. For example, the subscriber may inadvertently have given the wrong event type at the time of subscription.

In a language like Java, it is possible to eliminate the need for each subscriber to downcast by relying on the extensive run-time type information and the reflection API provided by the language. For each event type to which a concrete subscriber subscribes, it implements a type-specific inform method that takes as an argument an event of that type. The abstract Subscriber class implements an inform method that takes a parameter of type Event. When an event occurs, the event service calls this inform method. The inform method uses the reflection API to invoke the appropriate type-specific inform method provided by the concrete subscriber, passing the event as an argument. If there is no appropriate type-specific inform method, the abstract subscriber throws an exception. Alternatively, this error could be caught even earlier by the event service at subscription time. Figure 6 illustrates a paging system that subscribes to two event types and provides type-specific inform methods to handle them. Note that the concrete subscriber must not override the inform method that takes an Event type as a parameter, because this will neutralize the dispatching mechanism described.

ADVERTISEMENT AND DISCOVERY

In some situations, it may be useful for the subscriber to be able to query the event service as to which event types are currently available. For example, a management console might present a list of all possible event types to the user, allow the user to pick those of interest, and then subscribe to those events on the user's behalf.

Support for this capability requires a simple modification to Event Notifier. Publishers could explicitly advertise the types of events they can publish with the event service by calling an **advertise** method, and the event service could provide an interface that allows subscribers to discover the list of advertised events.

DISTRIBUTED EVENT NOTIFICATION

The **Event Notifier** pattern is well suited to a distributed implementation, where publishers, subscribers, and the event service itself reside on distinct machines. A distributed system can realize additional benefits by using **Event Notifier** in conjunction with the **Proxy** pattern (see Gamma et al.), as shown in Figure 7.

The **RemoteEventService** is an event service in a distributed environment. An **EventProxy** resides locally and serves as a proxy for the remote event service, and is implemented as a singleton. It maintains a list of local subscriptions, and subscribes to events from the remote event service on behalf of the local subscribers.

For simplicity, we show the common **EventService** superclass maintaining the aggregations. It may be necessary to actually implement **EventService** as an abstract class, with the aggregations implemented in the subclasses **RemoteEventService** and **EventProxy**. For example, the event proxy may choose not to maintain a list of subscribers, but to delegate all operations directly to the remote event service. Alternatively, the type of objects stored in the aggregations may be different for the event proxy and the remote event service: the former may store local subscribers, and the latter may store remote subscribers (proxies).

Figure 8 shows a typical interaction between the various objects.

Use of an event proxy insulates publishers from the issues that arise in a distributed environment. In particular, an event proxy can yield the following benefits:

- Encapsulates failures that result in the inaccessibility of the remote event service. For example, if the network or event service is down, the event proxy can queue events and publish them later.
- Ensures that events are delivered to the remote event service in the order in which they are published. This could be used to ensure that events from a specific proxy are delivered from the event service to the subscriber in the order they were published.
- Eliminates the need for publishers and subscribers to know about the location of the remote event service.
- Simplifies the implementation of subscribers by eliminating the need to be remotely accessible by the remote event service.
- Provides a place to add additional behavior such as logging or security, in a manner transparent to subscribers and publishers.

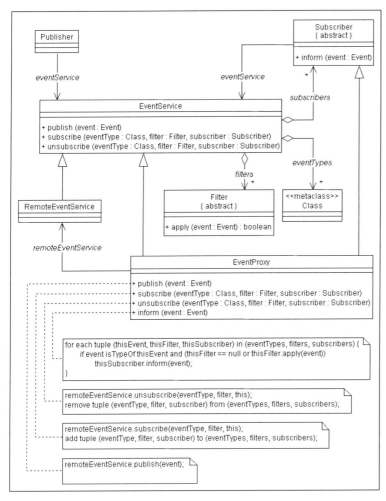

*Figure 7.
Event
Proxy
structure.*

*Figure 8 (below).
Event Proxy
collaboration
diagram.*

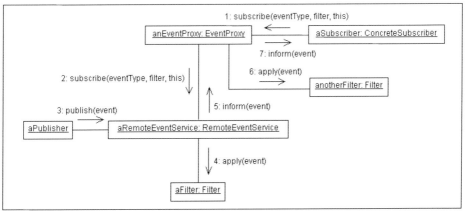

- Reduces network traffic by subscribing for an event on behalf of multiple local subscribers.
- Improves performance from the point of view of the publisher in a multithreaded environment, because the event proxy can return control to the publisher before publishing the event remotely.

Sometimes certain events are only of interest in a local environment, and others are of interest to the entire remote community. For example, GUI events are typically of interest locally, while fault events are of interest remotely. An event proxy can double as a stand-alone local event service if there is some way to specify whether to publish an event remotely or locally. One can specify this as an event attribute or as part of the event type hierarchy. The former allows the programmer to determine how to use the event, while the latter allows the designer of the event hierarchy to enforce this as part of the design. If only local events are published and subscribed to, the proxy can function in the absence of the remote event service.

ENHANCING FAULT TOLERANCE AND PERFORMANCE

Large scale use of **Event Notifier** can potentially result in the event service being a single point of failure and a performance bottleneck. One solution to this problem is to have multiple event services, where each brokers a group of related events; for example, one event service for network management, and another for financial services. The failure of the event service for one area will not impact the systems dependent only on events from the other area.

Another way to deal with the problem is to use a variation of **Event Notifier** in which the subscription list is not stored in the event service, but is instead distributed across publishers. One can achieve this without breaking the semantics of a centralized event service by having publishers advertise the event types they intend to publish. The event service would maintain this association of publishers and event types. On subscription to an event type, the event service would pass the subscriber to the publishers of that event type. Now publishers can inform subscribers directly.

Because the subscription list is distributed among the set of publishers instead of being stored centrally in the event service, failure of any single component is likely to have less impact on the system as a whole. Because the frequency of publication is typically much higher than the frequency of subscription, and at publication time events are not being channeled through a single point, there is no single point that could become a bottleneck.

Because the publication list changes less frequently than the subscription list, it is feasible to maintain a "hot spare" for the event service. Whenever an advertisement occurs, the event service updates the hot spare, thus keeping the information current in both places. If the event service goes down, the hot spare can take over.

Asynchronous Notification

If one implements the event service as a synchronous service, when a publisher publishes an event, the event service returns control to the publisher only after it informs each of the interested subscribers. If there are a large number of subscribers, or if subscribers do not return control to the event service in a timely manner, the publisher is blocked, and the event service cannot process other requests. One can fix this problem by providing asynchronous notification. For example, the event service could use a separate thread to handle the publication, and return control to the publisher immediately. The event service could start a separate thread to inform each subscriber, or rely on a thread pool.

Push and Pull Semantics

Event Notifier supports the canonical *push model* semantics (see "The OMG Events Service," *C++ Report*, Vol. 9, No. 2, 1997), in which the publisher pushes events to the event service, and the event service pushes events to the subscriber. It is possible to have an active subscriber that pulls information from the event service, or a passive publisher from which information is pulled by the event service. If a pull model is desired at either leg, event notification semantics can be reestablished from the user's point of view by hiding it behind a proxy.

Subscriber Anchoring

Generally in distributed environments, the subscriber executes the response to an event within its own address space. We refer to this type of subscriber as *anchored*, and it passes its own remote handle to the event service at subscription time. At other times, it is not important where the inform method is executed. An example of such an *unanchored* subscriber is one that pages an appropriate person, which can execute on its own. An unanchored subscriber passes a copy of itself to the event service, and the event service executes the inform method in its own address space. The process that called subscribe no longer needs to exist to process the events. An unanchored subscriber acts as an agent, which takes action in response to events independently of the process that called subscribe.

SAMPLE CODE

This section provides a skeletal implementation of Event Notifier in Java, and shows how it can be used.

EVENT SERVICE

The EventService class is implemented as a singleton, providing a well-known point of access and implementations for publish, subscribe, and unsubscribe.

```java
public class EventService {
/* Prevents direct instantiation */
  private EventService() {
    eventClass = Event.class;
    subscriptions = new Vector();
  }

  static private EventService singleton = null;

  /* Provides well-known access point to singleton EventService */
  static public EventService instance() {
    if (singleton == null)
      singleton = new EventService();
    return singleton;
  }

  public void publish(Event event) {
    for (Enumeration elems =
        subscriptions.elements();
        elems.hasMoreElements(); ) {
      Subscription subscription =
        (Subscription) elems.nextElement();
      if (subscription.eventType.
        isAssignableFrom(event.getClass())
        && (subscription.filter == null
        || subscription.filter.apply(event)))
        subscription.subscriber.inform(event);
    }
  }
  public void subscribe(Class eventType,
      Filter filter, Subscriber subscriber)
```

```
   throws InvalidEventTypeException {
  if (!eventClass.isAssignableFrom(eventType))
   throw new InvalidEventTypeException();

  // Prevent duplicate subscriptions
  Subscription subscription =
   new Subscription(eventType, filter,
   subscriber);
  if (!subscriptions.contains(subscription))
   subscriptions.addElement(subscription);
 }

 public void unsubscribe(Class eventType,
   Filter filter, Subscriber subscriber)
   throws InvalidEventTypeException {
  if (!eventClass.isAssignableFrom(eventType))
   throw new InvalidEventTypeException();
  subscriptions.removeElement(
   new Subscription(eventType, filter,
   subscriber));
 }

 private Class eventClass;
 protected Vector subscriptions;
}
/* Stores information about a single subscription */
class Subscription {
 public Subscription(Class anEventType,
   Filter aFilter, Subscriber aSubscriber) {
  eventType = anEventType;
  filter = aFilter;
  subscriber = aSubscriber;
 }

 public Class eventType;
 public Filter filter;
 public Subscriber subscriber;
}
public class InvalidEventTypeException
   extends RuntimeException {}
```

EVENT

The interface construct in Java is used to implement the abstract Event class shown in the Event Notifier structure.

```
public interface Event {}
public interface ManagementEvent
    extends Event {}

public class FaultEvent
    implements ManagementEvent {
public static final int CRITICAL = 1;
public static final int MODERATE = 2;
public static final int LOW = 3;

public int severity;

FaultEvent() {
  severity = LOW;
}

FaultEvent(int aSeverity) {
  severity = aSeverity;
}
}
```

FILTER

When the apply method on the CriticalFaultFilter class is called with an event, it returns true if the event is a critical fault event. A subscriber that provides this filter thus manages to filter out all but the critical fault events.

```
public interface Filter {
  public boolean apply(Event event);
}

public class CriticalFaultFilter implements Filter {
  public boolean apply(Event event) {
    /* Assumes that this filter is used only with subscriptions to
        FaultEvent */
    FaultEvent faultEvent = (FaultEvent) event;
    return (faultEvent.severity == FaultEvent.CRITICAL);
```

```
    }
  }
```

SUBSCRIBER

An abstract subscriber class and an example concrete subscriber are shown below. The PagingSystem subscriber subscribes to and handles FaultEvent.

```
public abstract class Subscriber {
  abstract void inform(Event event);
}

public class PagingSystem extends Subscriber {
  public PagingSystem() {
    FaultEvent event = new FaultEvent();
    CriticalFaultFilter filter = new CriticalFaultFilter();
    EventService.instance().subscribe( filter.getClass(), filter, this);
  }

  public void inform(Event event) {
    /* Assumes that this subscriber has only subscribed
       to FaultEvent */
    FaultEvent faultEvent = (FaultEvent) event;

    /* Respond to the event */
    System.out.println("Critical Fault Event " + faultEvent);
  }
}
```

PUBLISHER

The Router class is an example publisher, which publishes a critical fault event.

```
public class Router {
  public static void triggerPublication() {
    Event event = new FaultEvent(FaultEvent.CRITICAL);
    EventService.instance().publish(event);
  }
}
```

USING DYNAMIC TYPING TO RESTORE TYPE SAFETY

As described in the Reclaiming Type Safety subsection of Implementation, it is possible for the abstract subscriber's inform method to determine at run time which inform method of a concrete subscriber to invoke using the Java reflection API. Notice that the PagingSystem provides a type-specific inform method for handling fault events, which does not need to downcast the event.

```java
public abstract class Subscriber {
  public void inform(Event event) {
    Class paramTypes[] = new Class[1];
    paramTypes[0] = event.getClass();
    try {
      /* Look for an inform method in the current object that takes the
         event subtype as a parameter */
      Method method = getClass().getDeclaredMethod(
        "inform", paramTypes);
      Object paramList[] = new Object[1];
      paramList[0] = event;
      method.invoke(this, paramList);
    }
    /* Catch appropriate exceptions */
  }
}

public class PagingSystem extends Subscriber {
  public void inform(FaultEvent event) {
    /* Handle fault event without downcasting */
  }
}
```

KNOWN USES

In this section, we compare two other event notification models with the Event Notifier model.

JavaBeans

The JavaBeans API defined as part of the Java platform introduces reusable software components called *JavaBeans.* The user can connect and manipulate beans programmatically or visually using a bean builder. Beans communicate with each other via event notification. JavaBeans event notification is type safe, instance based, synchronous, and multicasting. It is restricted to a single process. For every event, there is a corresponding EventListener interface. The event source (publisher) advertises one or more EventListener interfaces that EventListener beans (subscribers) implement to receive events directly from the source beans. Source and listener beans know about each other, and the source handle is always passed as part of an event. Each source bean is responsible for maintaining a list of interested listeners. In Event Notifier, a well-known event service takes on this responsibility. Using Java's introspection API, beans can discover listener interfaces advertised by a source and implemented by a listener. Unless one uses an event adapter, the subscriber and publisher are coupled.

CORBA

The CORBA Event Service (see *C++ Report,* Vol. 9, No. 2) provides a way of delivering event data from supplier (publisher) to consumer (subscriber) without them knowing about each other. It supports typed and untyped event systems, neither of which allows events as objects.

The CORBA Event Service supports both pull and push models, which allow suppliers and consumers to play active or passive roles. This results in unnecessary complexity. Furthermore, the CORBA Event Service provides no filtering.

Related Patterns

As mentioned in the Motivation section, Event Notifier is closely related to the Observer and Mediator patterns (see Gamma et al.), and in fact, can be viewed as a cross between them. The Multicast pattern (see "Pattern Hatching: Multicast," *C++ Report*, Vol. 9, No. 8) is also related, but emphasizes static type checking at the expense of genericity and extensibility.

Analysis Patterns

MARTIN FOWLER

R ECENTLY, THE SUBJECT of patterns has become one of the hottest topics in object-oriented development. The most well-known patterns are the design patterns of the *Gang of Four* (Gamma, E., R. Helm, R. Johnson, and J. Vlissides, *Design Patterns: Elements of Reusable Object-Oriented Software*, Addison-Wesley, 1994), fundamental implementation patterns that are widely useful in object-oriented implementations. An important part of most OO systems is the domain model—those classes which model the underlying business that the software is supporting. We can see patterns in domain models too, patterns that often recur in surprising places. I will provide a short introduction to some *analysis patterns* that I have come across.

I'm not going to do this by surveying the field, or discussing theory—patterns don't really lend themselves to that. Rather, I'll show you some examples of patterns and illustrate them with UML diagrams (Fowler, M., *UML Distilled: Applying the Standard Object Modeling Language*, Addison-Wesley, 1997) and Java interface declarations.

REPRESENTING QUANTITIES

Imagine you are writing a computerized medical record system for a hospital. You have to record several measurements about your patients, such as their height, weight, and blood-glucose level. You might choose to model this using numeric attributes (see Figure 1 and Listing 1).*

This approach is quite common, but may present several problems. One major problem is with using numbers. I vividly remember a physics teacher at my

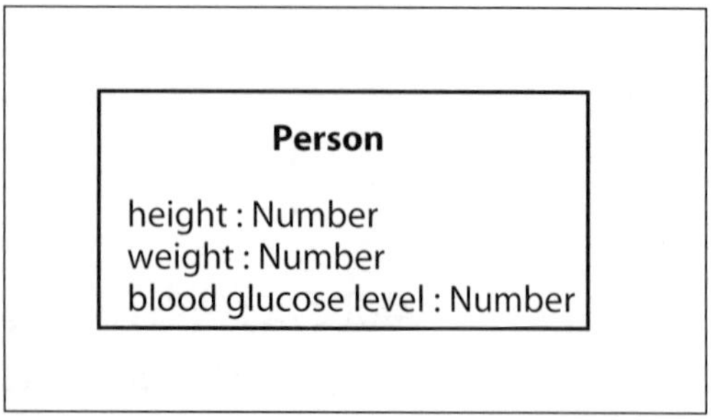

Figure 1. Measurements of a person using numeric attributes.

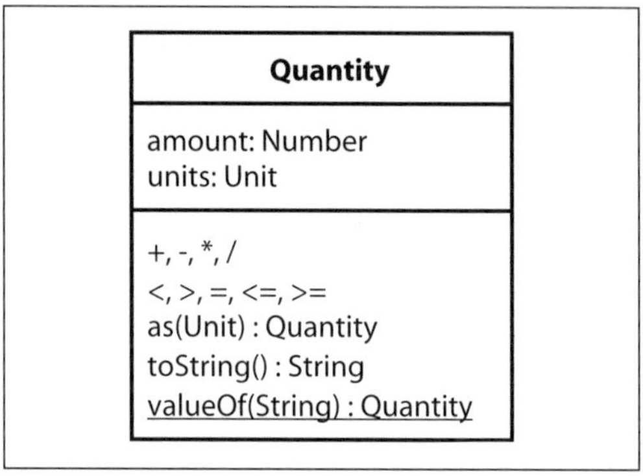

Person
height : Number
weight : Number
blood glucose level : Number

Figure 2. UML class diagram of the Quantity pattern.

Quantity
amount: Number units: Unit
+, -, *, / <, >, =, <=, >= as(Unit) : Quantity toString() : String valueOf(String) : Quantity

grammar school—we called him "Barney Rubble" (not to his face, of course)—who would often ask a question in class and someone would volunteer, or be volunteered, to answer it. If you answered his question about the speed of some falling body, for instance, as "4.7 sir," he would stop in his tracks, walk over to your desk, glare at you, and shout at the top of his voice "UNITS, U NIT!"

Now in pre-object systems, you have a good excuse to represent quantities as numbers because it is very awkward to do anything else. But in an object-oriented system you can easily do better by creating a Quantity class to deal with the problem (see Figure 2 and Listing 2). A proper Quantity class makes it much easier to represent things. If you're using a U.S.-based system, it can record height in inches; while European-based systems can record it in cm—it's not too difficult to extend Quantity to handle feet and inches. Furthermore, when you use the quantities in calculations the system can check that you do appropriate things. At the simplest level it can stop you from adding together two quantities with different units. If you need more sophistication you can get it to do conversions to add inches to cm. Or you can set it up so it knows that if you divide miles by hours your answer is in MPH. Most of the time you don't need all that complication, but at times it can be useful.

> **Listing 1. Java interface for Figure 1.**
>
> ```java
> class Person {
>   public double height();
>   public double weight();
>   public double bloodGlucoseLevel();
> ```

> **Listing 2. Java interface for Figure 2.**
>
> ```java
> class Quantity
>   public Quantity (double amount, Unit units);
>   public Quantity plus (Quantity arg);
>   public Quantity minus (Quantity arg);
>   public Quantity times (double arg);
>   public Quantity divide (double arg);
>   public boolean greaterThan (Quantity arg);
>   public boolean lessThan (Quantity arg);
>   public boolean greaterThanOrEquals (Quantity arg);
>   public boolean lessThanOrEquals (Quantity arg);
>   public boolean equals (Quantity arg);
>   public Quantity as (Unit newUnits);
>   public String toString ();
>   public static Quantity valueOf(String arg);
> ```

THE Quantity PATTERN

A common application of the Quantity pattern is in modeling money. Here you can use a Money class with a currency as a unit. As well as handling the arithmetic in a safe way, it is also a good place to ensure proper rounding behavior.

I'm calling Quantity a pattern rather than a class because I'm discussing the general idea of using a quantity, rather than prescribing a particular interface, or even class name. When someone uses a class called CurrencyAmount with a currency and a value, and puts arithmetic operations on it, then they are using the Quantity pattern. You don't have to follow a particular interface to use a pattern, although it helps to use the names suggested by the pattern—if they are appropriate. People find code interfaces, such as Listing 2, useful in understanding the pattern—which is why I include them—but the interfaces are neither mandatory nor complete.

One key benefit of objects is that they allow you to create new fundamental types such as this, and use them as if they were built into the language. Currently, Java does let us down a bit because it doesn't allow us to overload operators. Those plus and minus methods are awkward in many expressions.

MEASUREMENTS

Using quantities is an improvement over numbers, but still leads to some problems. In particular, there is a problem with the amount of different things we need to measure for a person. A single hospital department could have hundreds of different measurements we'd have to make for a person. An entire hospital would require thousands of measurements. A **Person** class with hundreds of methods for the various measurements would be too fat an interface to be practical. Furthermore, such a class would be very brittle. Frequently, we add new things that we want to measure and each such change would need recompilation of the **Person** class—this could get painful.

You've all heard that an additional level of indirection can solve any problem in computer science. So you won't be surprised by the next pattern. In Figure 3 I have replaced the separate attributes of **Person** with a collection of measurement objects, where each measurement represents some single value of some **Phenomenon Type**. The **Phenomenon Type** represents something we want to measure about the person. For each thing we want to measure, we add a new instance of **Phenomenon Type**. We can now add measurements and get values using that instance as a parameter (see Listing 3 and Listing 4).

The **Measurement** pattern is useful because it means that we can support hundreds or thousands of **Phenomenon Types** without increasing the interface of **Person**. We can also add new **Phenomenon Types** without changing the interface of **Person**. This is good, but it comes at a price. The price is that the **Person** interface is no longer as explicit as it was. To see what I can ask for **Person** I need to know about the instances of **Phenomenon Type**. I also have to support the mechanisms of dealing with measurements. With this pat-

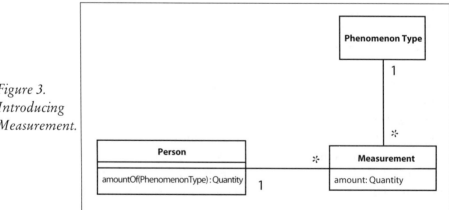

Figure 3.
Introducing
Measurement.

tern it is important to understand the trade-offs. Having fixed properties is much better if you only have a few things to measure. Don't use the **Measurement** pattern unless you really need it.

This issue of trade-offs is central to patterns. A pattern is much more than just showing a model. A pattern also includes guidance about when and where to use it, and what the benefits and liabilities are. Understanding these guidelines is essential to help you use the pattern effectively.

(Another value of the **Measurement** pattern is that it helps provide a good base to describe measurements that change over time, but for the moment I'll leave that as an exercise for the reader.)

The **Measurement** pattern deals well with quantitative statements about a **person**. But in healthcare we also have to deal with qualitative values, such as that **Martin** has blood group O. To cope with this we need to extend the **Measurement** pattern.

Figure 4 shows the essential conceptual picture of the **Observation** pattern. I have factored out that part of **Measurement** that deals with the relationship with **Person**, and put that in a new superclass called **Observation**. With that factoring, **Measurement** works just the same. To handle the qualitative statements, I have added two new classes: **CategoryObservation** and **Phenomenon**. The **Phenomenon** class is used to represent the qualitative values of some phenomenon type. Listing 5 and Listing 6 show how these might be used.

You may have noticed that **Phenomenon Type** is doing two things. First, it is

---

Listing 3   Java interface for Figure 3.

```
class Person {
    public Quantity amountOf (PhenomenonType arg);
    ...
class Measurement {
    public Measurement (PhenomenonType phenomenonType, Person person,
        Quantity amount);
    public Quantity amount();
```

Listing 4.   Using the Measurement pattern.

```
Unit feet = new Unit("ft");
Unit pounds = new Unit("lb");
PhenomenonType height = new PhenomenonType("height");
PhenomenonType weight = new PhenomenonType("weight");
Person martin = new Person("martin");
new Measurement (height, martin, new Quantity (6, feet);
new Measurement (weight, martin, new Quantity (180, pounds);
Quantity martinHeight = martin.amountOf(height)    // martinHeight is now 6 feet
```

Listing 5.   Additional interfaces for the Observation pattern.

```
class PhenomenonType {
   public PhenomenonType (String name);
   public Enumeration phenomena();
   public String[] phenomenaNames();  //useful for UI choice menus
   public void addPhenomenonNamed (String name);
   public Phenomenon phenomenonNamed (String name);
   ...
class CategoryObservation extends Observation {
   public CategoryObservation (Phenomenon phenomenon, Person person);

Class Person
   public Phenomenon valueOf(PhenomenonType type);
```

Listing 6.   Using CategoryObservations.

```
PhenomenonType gender = new PhenomenonType("Gender");
gender.addPhenomenonNamed("Male");
gender.addPhenomenonNamed
("Female");
Person martin = new Person ("martin");
new CategoryObservation (gender.phenomenonNamed("Male"), martin);
Phenomenon martinGender = martin.valueOf(gender);
// martinGender is male
```

---

the thing that a Measurement is measuring and second, it acts as a grouping mechanism for phenomena. Why are these two roles combined into a single class? The answer lies in the fact that you can describe a Phenomenon Type both quantitatively and qualitatively. A clinician can measure heart rate with a Measurement, but she might also want to state that heart rates can be described as "fast," "slow," or "normal." In this case, the heart rate Phenomenon would have both measurements and phenomena.

We would ideally like an observation of heart rate to be both a measurement (e.g., 98 beats per minute) and a CategoryObservation (e.g., fast). Indeed, that is what Figure 4 indicates when it marks the generalization as *overlapping*. However, this conceptual statement cannot be directly modeled in Java. A Java object is of only one class (and that class may have superclasses)— a style of classification which is called *single classification*. Our conceptual picture describes *multiple classification*: allowing an object to have multiple classes that are not related by inheritance. So how do we get around this?

There are several ways to deal with multiple classification in a single classification language. In this case, I will implement the CategoryObservation concept directly in the Observation class using Figure 5, Listing 7 and Listing 8.

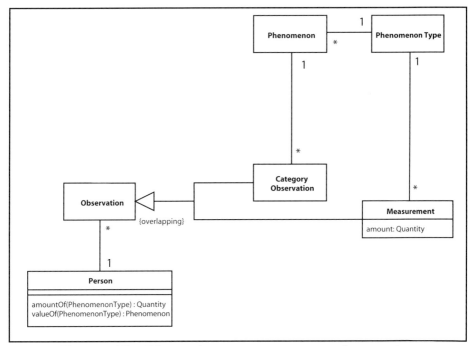

Figure 4. The Observation pattern—a conceptual perspective.

This kind of adaptation often occurs when you are implementing a conceptual model or pattern. I find it useful to model the conceptual situation first, because that makes it clear in my own mind what is going on. Once I have that clear, I then implement as I need to. This is a good example of the difference between the conceptual model (how we think) and the specification model (the class interfaces). In my projects I usually only document the latter; I describe the former, in my book, because the trade-offs will vary with implementation environment and the actual use cases in a specific situation.

I also prefer writing analysis patterns in the conceptual form—so that the user of the pattern can make the trade-offs that they need. But I do like to give some examples about how to do the trade-offs, so that the user has an overview of the options. I haven't given an exhaustive list here—to find more information about dealing with multiple and dynamic classification you can find some thoughts in *Analysis Patterns: Reusable Object Models* (Fowler, M., Addison-Wesley, 1997).

Use the Observation pattern when you want to handle both qualitative and quantitative statements about something. If you only want quantitative statements you can just use the Measurement pattern. If you only need qualita-

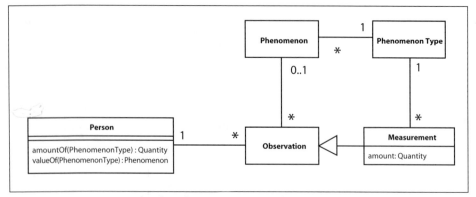

Figure 5. A single classification version of the Observation pattern.

tive statements you can just use a `CategoryObservation` without the Measurement.

ASSIGNING Ranges AUTOMATICALLY

Often you find situations where you can assign a **Phenomenon**—based on its measurement—to an **Observation** automatically. For instance, you might say that for **heart rates**: 60-80 beats per minute is normal, less than 60 is slow, and more than 80 is high. It shouldn't be too difficult to teach a computer to do this.

This step requires two patterns. The first, **Range**, is a fundamental pattern much in the same way that **Quantity** is. When I see people dealing with ranges, they usually take some domain object, and give that domain object an upper and a lower value, or a start and end pair of dates. That's a shame, because they are missing out on the idea of making the range itself an object—and thus giving all sorts of useful behavior (see Figure 6).

The basic idea of **Range** is to combine the upper and lower into a single object. We can then easily add methods to determine if some value is included within a range, and whether two ranges overlap or abut.

You can use any object in a **Range** that understands how to compare itself to another object, i.e., that supports an interface as defined in Figure 6 as a **Magnitude**. This can be done several ways in different languages. In Smalltalk you just have to ensure that the operations are defined in the appropriate class (or subclass class **Magnitude**), in C++ you can use templates, but using Java is more problematic. Currently, I prefer creating specific **Range** classes for those classes

---

Listing 7. Operations on the Single Classification version of Observation.

```
class Observation {
    public Phenomenon (Phenomenon phenomenon, Person person);
    public void setPhenomenon(Phenomenon arg);
```

Listing 8. Adding a Phenomenon to a Measurement.

```
PhenomenonType heartRate = new Phenomenon ("Heart Rate");
Unit bps = new Unit ("Beats / min");
heartRate.addPhenomenonNamed("fast");
heartRate.addPhenomenonNamed("normal");
heartRate.addPhenomenonNamed("slow");
Person martin = new Person("Martin");
newMeasurement = new Measurement(heartRate, martin,
        new Quantity (98, bps));
newMeasurement.setPhenomenon(heartRate.phenomenonNamed("fast");
Quantity martinRate = martin.amountOf(heartRate); //martinRate is 98 beats/min
Phenomenon martinRateValue = martin.valueOf(heartRate); //martinRateValue is fast
```

---

that I want to work with (e.g., QuantityRange—see Listing 9). You could define Magnitude as an interface and work with that. The problem is that the existing Java types and classes (e.g., int, double, and Date) don't implement such an interface. Also, any queries about the Range will involve downcasting.

For discrete values (e.g., integers or dates), the only attributes you need are the upper and lower. Continuous values (e.g., doubles), need the two booleans. This is so that you can express a range like "greater than 80 BPM" (see Listing 10). I also find it a useful convention to use nulls to indicate open-ended ranges (e.g., "greater than 80 BPM"). An empty Range is one whose lower is greater than its upper.

I find Ranges a great help in development. I can't remember how many times I've coded tests between beginning and ending values. Now I do it once in a Range class and don't bother again—I do like avoiding work!

Once we've defined Range we can use it to provide standard Ranges by attaching a Range to a Phenomenon (see Figure 7). Now, whenever we create a Measurement, we check the phenomena of that Phenomenon Type to see if any include the amount, if any do, we can attach that Phenomenon to the Measurement (see Figure 8).

I call this pattern Phenomenon with Range and it represents the simplest and most direct case of assigning a Phenomenon to an Observation based on a Range. However, it does not work for all cases. This is because many Ranges are dependent on other factors. Normal Ranges often depend on age, or on the

Figure 6.
Range.

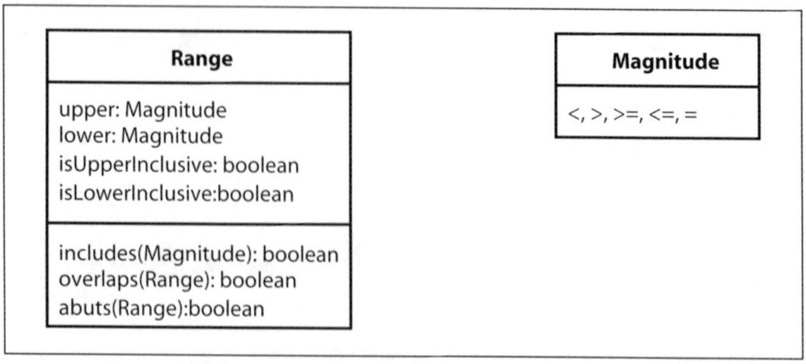

Range
upper: Magnitude
lower: Magnitude
isUpperInclusive: boolean
isLowerInclusive:boolean
includes(Magnitude): boolean
overlaps(Range): boolean
abuts(Range):boolean

Magnitude
<, >, >=, <=, =

Listing 9. Implementing the Range pattern for ranges of quantities.

```
class QuantityRange
    public Range (Quantity upper, Quantity lower);
    public Range (Quantity upper, Quantity lower,
        boolean isUpperInclusive, boolean isLowerInclusive);
    public boolean includes (Quantity arg);
    public boolean overlaps (Range arg);
    public boolean abuts (Range arg);
    public Quantity upper();
    public Quantity lower();
    public boolean isUpperInclusive();
    public boolean isLowerInclusive();
```

Listing 10. Using QuantityRange.

```
Unit bps = new Unit ("beats / minute");
normalHeartRate = new Range (new Quantity (80, bpm), new Quantity (60, bpm));
fastHeartRate = new Range (null, new Quantity (80, bpm), false, false);
slowHeartRate = new Range (new Quantity (60, bpm), null, false, false);
```

---

presence of other conditions. For more complex cases you need another pattern: Range Function. But I'll just tease you with the name because I don't have the space to discuss it.

These patterns are the first few of several that explore patterns of Observation in healthcare. I don't have much space left, so rather than go into more of them, I'll tell you how I ended up finding them useful in an unexpected place.

Sometime after I finished the healthcare project, I was doing a class with a large manufacturing company. Part of the class was an example modeling session, where the instructor would do some analysis of a domain familiar to some of the students. The idea being that the students get to see how an experienced modeler goes through building a model of some domain. The

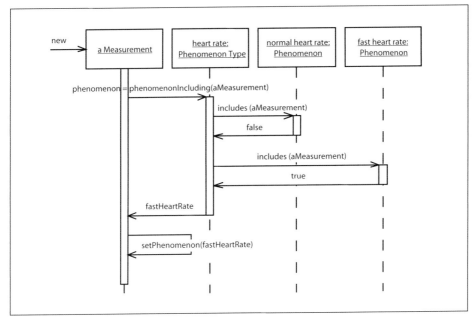

Figure 8. Setting a Phenomenon for a Measurement.

problem they gave me had to do with corporate finance. They were building a system where they got various high-level financial data about the company's performance and needed to look at this data and then indicate areas of good and poor performance.

The students were quite impressed with how quickly I got to the heart of their problem; how I seemed to understand it so well despite only just being introduced to it. I explained that I did it by applying the patterns I had come across in the healthcare project. The elements of financial data were **Mea-surements**, the classification of the measurements into various grades of good and poor used the **Phenomenon** with **Range** pattern, and in fact, the similarities went much deeper than that. Many other healthcare patterns, going beyond those I've talked about here, were present. There were also differences too (e.g., breaking a company down along different dimensions, calculating some measurements based on other measurements, comparing actuals versus planned or historic data). The healthcare patterns did not solve the whole problem by any means, but they did give us a good start, and we found them very useful as we explored the ground further.

I hope all of this has given you a sense of what analysis patterns are all about, and maybe piqued your curiosity to discover more. At the moment I know of only two books about analysis patterns: my own—*Analysis Patterns: Reusable Object Models*, Addison-Wesley, 1997—and David Hay's—*Data Model Patterns: Conventions of Thought*, Dorset House, 1996. Hay's book is about relational data modeling patterns, but his patterns are very conceptual and thus useful even if you are into objects rather than databases. As more materials are made available I will post the information on my Web site.

For information on the book, *Analysis Patterns*, by Martin Fowler visit http://www.amazon.com/exec/obidos/ASIN/0202895420

JAVA IN A
DISTRIBUTED WORLD

MOBILE AGENT SYSTEM
ARCHITECTURE

STEVEN R. FARLEY

YOU HAVE PROBABLY HEARD or read something about software agents; they have been a hot topic for some time now and agent-based commercial products are available. There are several schools of thought on what the term "agent" really means. For example, in the context of artificial intelligence, an agent is often described as an autonomous, intelligent entity: They can make decisions and perform actions based on perceived inputs in order to achieve some goal (Russell, S., and P. Norvig, *Artificial Intelligence: A Modern Approach,* 1995).

Mobility is a common characteristic of many agent definitions. A *mobile agent* is an active object that can move both data and functionality (code) to multiple places within a distributed system. It doesn't matter what the ultimate purpose of the agent is or whether or not it can be classified as "intelligent."

A mobile agent should be able to execute on any machine within a network, regardless of the processor type or operating system. In addition, the agent code should not have to be installed on every machine that the agent could potentially visit; it should move with the agent's data automatically. Therefore, it is desirable to implement agents on top of a mobile code system, such as Java virtual machine (VM). The dynamic nature of Java classes and objects, combined with advanced networking capabilities, makes Java highly qualified for use as a mobile agent platform. Just as an applet's classes are loaded dynamically from the Web server into the browser, an agent's classes are loaded at runtime over the network as it travels from one location to another.

This article discusses mobile agents in the context of system architecture.

For some applications, an agent architecture should be employed as the core around which the rest of the system is built. An *agent system* provides a framework in which mobile agents can operate. Just as distributed objects within a CORBA-based system rely on Object Request Brokers (ORBs), agents require *agent hosts*, which provide an environment in which the agent may execute. In the case of a Java implementation, the agent environment is a Java VM containing server objects on which the agent operates. Other agents may be present as well, and they can communicate with each other if the implementation allows. We will show the design and implementation of a simple agent system that takes advantage of some new JDK 1.1 features.

WHY USE AN AGENT ARCHITECTURE?

If client-server systems are the currently established norm and distributed object systems such as CORBA are defining the future standards, why bother with agents? Agent architectures have certain advantages over these types. Three of the most important advantages are:

1. An agent performs much processing at the server where local bandwidth is high, thus reducing the amount of network bandwidth consumed and increasing overall performance. In contrast, a CORBA client object with the equivalent functionality of a given agent must make repeated remote method calls to the server object because CORBA objects cannot move across the network at runtime.

2. An agent operates independently of the application from which the agent was invoked. The agent operates asynchronously, meaning that the client application does not need to wait for the results. This is especially important for mobile users who are not always connected to the network.

3. The use of agents allows for the injection of new functionality into a system at runtime. An agent system essentially contains its own automatic software distribution mechanism. Since CORBA has no built-in support for mobile code, new functionality generally has to be installed manually.

Of course a non-agent system can exhibit these same features with some work. But the mobile code paradigm supports the transfer of executable code to a remote location for asynchronous execution from the start. An agent architecture should be considered for systems where the above features are primary requirements.

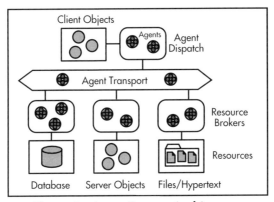

Figure 1. Agent System Architecture.

AN EXAMPLE AGENT SYSTEM

Figure 1 shows an example system based on an agent architecture that contains a dispatch host and multiple resource brokers. The agent dispatch provides an API that the client application uses to invoke agent transactions. This host creates and configures the agent, sets its agenda, and sends it on its way. A resource broker is a fancy name for an agent host that provides access to any type of local resource, such as databases and "live" stationary objects. The bus-like shape labeled "agent transport" represents the protocol used to move agents around the system.

Here's the typical agent life cycle: A client application operation causes an agent object to be created within a dispatch host. Based on the particular needs of the client application, the agent is given an agenda containing the list of resource brokers (or other types of hosts) to visit and the tasks to perform at each site. The dispatch sends the agent to its first destination. Once inside the resource broker, the agent gets it own thread of execution in which to perform its duties, and is limited by the broker's security manager (just like an applet inside a browser). In many cases, the agent is not allowed to do anything but talk to its current broker, which may have operations that provide access to the underlying resources. One of the advantages of an agent system, especially for applications that require intensive data processing, is that network bandwidth is preserved. This is because the agent may repeatedly query the broker locally instead of executing a series of remote operations as in a distributed object system. The agent eventually returns to the dispatch host, which extracts the results from the agent.

Figure 2 contains the object model diagram in Coad notation (Coad, P., and M. Mayfield, *Java Design: Building Better Apps and Applets,* 1997). This

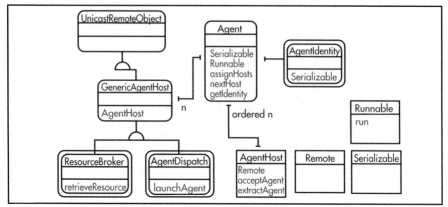

Figure 2. Agent System Object Model.

notation is used because of its clean representation of the Java interface, drawn as a box with square edges. Objects that implement the interface simply include its name in their method list.

This agent system takes advantage of two new JDK 1.1 features: Remote Method Invocation (RMI) and Object Serialization. The **Agent** and **AgentIdentity** objects implement the **Serializable** interface so that they may be transferred across the network from the address space of one agent host to another. RMI is used to accomplish the agent transfer. This actually results in two copies of the same **Agent**, so the transmitting host must insure that it is dormant and let the garbage collector clean it up.

Serialization takes care of streaming the contents of the agent and its objects from host to host. If the receiving host does not have these class files stored locally, RMI takes care of retrieving the classes automatically as they are needed. When the classes are loaded, they are cached locally, so if the host has previously loaded an agent type, then reloading the classes is not necessary.

Listings 1, 2, and 3 contain the Java source code for the **AgentHost** interface, the **GenericAgentHost** and the **Agent** class. If you wish to use this code in your own application, remember to run the RMI stub and skeleton compiler, rmic, on subclasses of **UnicastRemoteObject**. See the JDK1.1 documentation for details.

An agent begins its life in an **AgentDispatch**. This host must have previously acquired the RMI client stubs that represent the remote **AgentHost** objects. The stubs are returned by the RMI **Naming** object, which returns a stub for a named server object at a given IP address. The dispatch instantiates the specific **Agent** subclass, calls **assignHosts()** to set its travel path (a

Listing 1 AgentHost.java

```
import java.rmi.Remote;
import java.rmi.RemoteException;

/* All agent hosts must implement this remote interface.*/
public interface AgentHost extends Remote
{
    /* Called by a remote agent host that wants to send an agent to this host.
       This host follows with an extractAgent() call to the remote host, which
       "pulls" the agent into this address space. */
    public void acceptAgent(AgentIdentity agent_id, AgentHost sender)
        throws RemoteException;
    /* Called by a remote agent host that wants to retrieve an agent from this
       host. Usually called in response to acceptAgent(). */
    public Agent extractAgent(AgentIdentity agent_id)
        throws RemoteException;
```

Vector of AgentHost stubs), and additionally assigns tasks to be performed at each location. The agent is then sent to its first destination by calling the AgentHost.acceptAgent() method of the first AgentHost object in the list. This triggers a chain of agent transfers and execution, until the Agent is eventually sent back to the dispatch host.

When an agent is ready to be transferred, its receiving host is notified by calling AgentHost.acceptAgent(), which passes the agent identity to be sent along with the sending AgentHost object (which is actually a stub). The receiver then "pulls" the agent from the sender by calling AgentHost.extractAgent(), which returns the Agent object. A separate thread is created for the agent and started. The agent, thread, and a thread monitor that waits for the thread to finish are all stored in hash tables using the agent identity as a key. When the agent's thread is finished (the Agent.run() method has completed), the monitor calls Agent.nextHost() and the transfer process repeats.

A developer can write a custom agent by creating a subclass of Agent and implementing the run() method. But the Agent class described here is just a basic example. In order to be more useful, it needs methods that subclasses could use for getting information about the agent's current location, etc. Also, important events need to be handled by the agent so that it may react gracefully to exceptional conditions. For example, if the creator of the agent cancels the task before it is complete, the agent should finish what it is doing and return with whatever results it might have.

Listing 2.   GenericAgentHost.java

```java
import java.util.Hashtable;
import java.rmi.RemoteException;
import java.rmi.server.UnicastRemoteObject;

/* This class implements the basic mechanism for agent transfers over a network. */
public abstract class GenericAgentHost extends UnicastRemoteObject
        implements AgentHost
{
    public GenericAgentHost() throws RemoteExeption {
            super();
            /* Agents, their execution threads, and thread monitors are stored in
                hast tables using the unique agent identity as a key. */
            agent_ = new Hashtable();
            threads_ = new Hashtable();
            monitors_ = new Hashtable(); }
    /* Called by a remote agent host that wants to send an agent to this host.
       This host follows with an ExtractAgent() call to the remote host, which
       "pulls" the agent into this address space. */
    public void acceptAgent(Agent Identity agent_id, AgentHost sender)
        throws RemoteException
    {
        /* Extract the agent from the sending host and store it. RMI handles seri-
            alization of the agent and its contents. */
        Agent agent = sender.extractAgent(agent_id);
        agents_.put(agent_id, agent);

        /* Create a thread in which this agent will run and store thread. */
        Thread thread = new Thread(agent);
        threads_.put(agent_id, thread);

        /* Create a thread monitor that detects when the agent is finished and is
            ready to move to its host, and store the monitor. */
        AgentThreadMonitor monitor = new AgentThreadMonitor (agent, this,
                                            thread);
        monitors_.put(agent_id, monitor);

        /* Start the threads. */
        thread.start();
        monitor.start(); }
    /* Called by a remote agent host that wants to retrieve an agent from this
       host. Usually called in response to acceptAgent().*/

    public Agent extractAgent(AgentIdentity agent_id)
        throws RemoteException
    {
        /* Stop the agent's thread and remove it. The only time the agent's
            thread would still be running is when extractAgent() was not called in
            response to acceptAgent(). */
```

(continued)

Listing 2. *(continued)*

```
        Thread thread = (Thread) threads_.remove(agent_id);
        thread.stop();

        /* Remove the thread monitor. It stops automatically. */
        monitors_.remove(agent_id);

        /* Remove the agent and return it. It will be returned over the network
            to the requesting host. RMI handles serialization of the agent and its
            contents. */
        Agent agent = (Agent) agents_.remove(agent_id);
        return agent; }
    private Hashtable agents_;
    private Hashtable threads_;
    private Hashtable monitors_; }
class AgentThreadMonitor extends Thread{
    AgentThreadMonitor(Agent agent, AgentHost host, Thread thread){
        super();
        agent_ = agent;
        host_ = host;
        thread_ = thread; }

    public void run()
    {
        try
        {
            /* Wait for the Agent's thread to finish. */
            thread_.join();

            /* Get the agent's next destination host. */
            AgentHost next = agent_.nextHost();

            /* Ask the remote host to accept this agent. it should respond with an
                extractAgent() call to this host. */
            next.acceptAgent(agent_.getIdentity(), host_); }
        catch (Exception e)
        {
            // Handle errors. } }
    private Agent agent_;
    private AgentHost host_;
    private Thread thread_; }
```

SECURITY ISSUES

Security in an agent system is not something that can be initially ignored and
dealt with later. After all, an agent host is letting an active object (the agent) run
within its address space. (A computer virus is essentially a malicious mobile
agent.) No agent system should be deployed without a robust security mech-

anism in place. Trust must be established between the agent and the host. A host must be able to recognize an agent's identity and then enforce appropriate constraints on what the agent is allowed to do based on its access privileges. Likewise, an agent must insure that a host that is to be visited is not a spoofed version of the host waiting to capture the agent and compromise the information contained within.

AGENT STANDARDS

Just as CORBA defines a standard for distributed object interoperability, standard are needed for a universal agent platform that would allow any server to accept and execute an agent from any vendor. As it turns out, the Object Management Group (OMG) is working on an agent standard in the form of a CORBA Common Facility. The resulting standard will specify language-independent interfaces for dealing with agents, but will probably not go as far as specifying any particular mobile code implementation.

For software developers, this means that there will be competing agent systems to choose from. It is good to have a choice, but when it comes to interoperability on the Internet, it would be nice to have a single standard that is as universally accepted as HTTP. The Java platform is a prime candidate for an agent system standard.

One of the most promising candidates for a Java-based agent standard is IBM's Aglets. The Aglets Workbench provides class libraries for creating custom agents, along with an agent host environment. See the links section at the end of this article for the Web address. IBM has submitted their Mobile Agent Facility (MAF) Specification in response to the OMG Common Facilities RFP3. The IBM MAF is largely based on the Aglet API and is one of the top contenders for standardization within CORBA.

CONCLUSION

An agent architecture provides a flexible alternative to client/server and distributed object architectures. Java is a natural choice for implementing such a system because it is a mobile code platform with built-in support for networking. With the emergence of agent standards, we may soon see more agent systems deployed. But before an agent system is used for real-world applications, robust se-

Listing 3. **Agent.java**

```java
import java.util.Vector;
import java.util.Enumeration;
import java.io.Serializable;
/*A base class for Agents. New agents can be created by overriding the run()
   method. This method will be called by each agent host when it arrives. All
   references to AgentHost objects are actually RMI stubs. */
public abstract class Agent implements Runnable, Serializable
{
    /* Create the agent with a unique identity and give it a handle to its origin. */
    public Agent(AgentIdentity identity, AgentHost home)
    {
        identity_ = identity;
        home_ = home; }
    /*
     * Tell the agent where to go.
     */
    public void assignHosts(Vector hosts)
    {
        hosts_ = hosts;
        host_enum_ = hosts_.elements(); }
    /* Return the next agent host. Called by the current host when the agent
       finished there. The agent sends itself home when all hosts have been
       visited. */
    public AgentHost nextHost()
    {
        if (host_enum_.hasMoreElements())
        {
        return (AgentHost) host_enum_.nextElement();
        } else
        {
            return home_; } }
    /* Return this agent's unique identity. */
    public AgentIdentity getIdentity()
    {
        return identity_; }
    /* From Runnable interface. Execute appropriate tasks based on current
       host. */
    public abstract void run();

    private Vector hosts_;
    private AgentHost home_;
    private Enumeration host_enum_;
    private AgentIdentity identity_; }
```

curity mechanisms must be embedded directly into the framework. A secure agent architecture becomes a powerful solution for enterprises looking to implement scalable distributed software systems, especially over the Internet.

DEPLOYMENT STRATEGIES FOR JAVA CLIENT APPLICATIONS

RON REPKING

BUSINESS APPLICATION development and deployment using Java has become much more popular in the past year. This is partly because of the redesigned java.awt library in the JDK 1.1, as well as other third-party JDK 1.1-compliant GUI class libraries and IDEs. Developers can now build sophisticated and complex GUI interface front-ends for their applications. As these front-ends become heavier, special consideration needs to be given to the deployment strategy used to deploy the client side of a client/server application.

There are several different options available for deploying Java client applications. Some of the options are fairly familiar, while others are not. Even if you understand what options are available, it is not always as obvious which should be used in a given situation. This article reviews options available for client-side deployment of Java applications along with the advantages and disadvantages of each strategy.

TRADITIONAL DEPLOYMENT

In most client/server applications, the deployment options for the client piece of the application is fairly limited. Usually, a client platform and programming language are chosen before development begins and the application is built with the target platform in mind. For example, a telephone invoicing client GUI application could be built using C++ on a Windows NT machine. On completion of the coding for the application, it would have to be manually or remotely installed on every Windows NT client machine that needed to use the application. When the application is updated to a new version, another manual or remote reinstall on every client machine is required.

The 3 major problems with this approach are:

1. There can be a substantial overhead cost associated with the install and maintenance of the client machines, especially if there are thousands of them.

2. There is a lag time from the time the application is completed and when the end user can use it.

3. The application has to be ported to the new platform, if the client application needs to run on a different platform than the one targeted.

This not only creates extra work, but also a new version of the software to manage and update. Because of Java's inherent cross-platform capability, Problem 3 is taken care of automatically by the language. Depending on how a Java application is deployed, Problems 1 and 2 may also be resolved.

JAVA CLIENT DEPLOYMENT OPTIONS

Currently, there are 3 major options available for deploying Java-based client applications:

1. Through a Web browser such as Netscape Navigator or Microsoft Internet Explorer.

2. As a stand-alone application.

3. Using broadcast or "push" technology such as in Marimba's Castanet.

Each of these approaches has its distinct advantages and disadvantages (see Table 1). Armed with this information, you should be able to make an educated decision on how to deploy your Java client application.

DEPLOYING VIA A WEB BROWSER

Deploying an application through a Web browser is probably the most common form of deployment today. The simple browser access of an HTML page embedded with a Java applet starts the Java client application. Java windows (Frames and Dialogs) may be displayed and destroyed while the application is running. This gives the application the general look and feel of a normal stand-alone GUI application. However, the big difference is that the browser is the starting point and the application cannot run unless the browser is also running.

As the Java application is running, Java objects are created (instantiated) as needed. When Java objects of a specific class type are created for the first time, the Web browser looks for the corresponding Java class files. These class files provide the definition for the particular class. All class files in the core JDK API are already resident in the browser and therefore are not loaded over the network. These classes are recognizable because they start with a package name of "java" (e.g., java.awt.Frame).

Class files that are not resident in the browser must be downloaded from the Web server. Class files that need to be downloaded include any third-party libraries (such as GUI widget libraries, collection classes, etc.) and any custom developed code. Once the class files are downloaded, they are cached on the client machine and therefore do not need to be downloaded again during that particular browser session. However, once the browser's cache is deleted or fills up, the class files are deleted and will need to be downloaded the next time the application is restarted.

When deploying in a browser, it is also important to consider the "sandbox" security model imposed by the browsers. In particular, browsers currently only allow connections to be opened to the Web server from which the application was served. This means that connections cannot be made to the local client machine to perform functions such as printing or reading/writing data on the local file system. For some applications, this can be a huge limitation.

Advantages of Browser Deployment

One advantage of this approach over the traditional approach is that there is no need to install or upgrade the application on the client machine. The application is automatically installed and updated when accessed in the browser by the Web server. This alone could save a corporation a tremendous amount of maintenance costs. Because the update happens immediately, there is no lag time between versions of the application. Once the application is installed on the Web server, the new version will automatically be run the next time that the application is accessed.

Because many people are already familiar with browsers and how to use them, there are generally very little up front training costs. The only training needed is for the application itself, which is the case for all deployment strategies.

Finally, because the application is running in the browser, it can be directly integrated with the World Wide Web. This can provide users with seamless access to related information such as other complimentary applications or products or even general information about the company who created the application.

DISADVANTAGES OF BROWSER DEPLOYMENT

The biggest disadvantage of browser deployment is runtime performance. Depending on the remote access capabilities of the client (e.g., 28.8K modem), there can be serious performance issues when downloading numerous class files or class files that are fairly large in size. Robust, large applications that use third-party libraries and a lot of custom code can take a long time to download and run in this environment. For example, on a 28.8K modem, you can expect a transfer rate of about 2K bytes per second. This means that if your application is 500K in size (which is not unreasonable for a rich GUI interface with much functionality), a user must wait more than 4 minutes to download the application!

To help minimize this download time there are several different techniques that may be used to help, however, for large applications these techniques may still not be enough.

Another disadvantage of browser deployment is the dependence on the browser for support of language features and extensions. When new releases of the JDK are introduced, it usually takes the browser vendors several months to implement and support the new features. In the case of JDK 1.1, there was about a 6-month lag time between the time that the JDK 1.1 was released and the time that IE and Navigator supported it in their virtual machine (VM). In addition, as the new versions of the browsers are released, there is extra maintenance in upgrading existing desktops with the new browser.

Closely related to the previous issue is the lack of support of major pieces of the Java language by certain browsers. For example, as of this writing, Microsoft's IE browser does not support Java Remote Method Invocation (RMI) for making remote calls on Java objects, the Java Native Interface (JNI) for calling non-Java methods, and has no plans to support the Java Foundation Classes (JFC).

Sun Microsystems, Inc. has recently made available an early access release of Java Activator, a product that alleviates the above JDK-related browser problems. The Java Activator allows users to specify the use of Sun's implementation of the Java Runtime Environment (JRE) in a browser instead of the default JVM built into the browser. Thus, a browser that has been activated will fully support all features of the version of the JDK for which the JRE is installed. Keep in mind, however, that the Activator also comes with its own problems. Its several MB size takes a long time to download and install, and the activator itself isn't yet supported for all browsers or platforms.

Summary of Browser Deployment

Browser deployment is ideally suited for Intranet or Extranet applications with high-speed connections or for small applications deployed over the Internet. These scenarios eliminate the concern over the slow performance of the download of the application. On internal systems, there is also usually more control over the types and versions of the browsers in these environments so that it is known up front which browsers will be supported, and easier to keep application and browser versions in sync. Finally, the use of these applications in this environment can be used seamlessly with corporate Intranets and WWW access.

Deploying as a Stand-alone Application

Deploying Java applications as stand-alone applications is very similar to the traditional forms of deployment. When the code for the application is completed, the Java source code is compiled into class files (which could be then packaged into jar files) and is installed on the client's local machine. For example, for Windows clients, this installation can take the form of a windows "install shield" program. Once installed, the application runs as any other normal GUI application; there is no browser or other third-party software required to run the application (other than the JVM, which may be installed with the application itself). This also means that there are no "sandbox" restrictions either.

Besides just installing class files/jar files on the client machines, there are other options for stand-alone deployment. The first alternative is to use a "native" compiler to compile and link the class files into an executable program. In this case, only the executable program needs to be deployed. The advantage of this

approach is that because the code is not interpreted at runtime, the runtime performance of the application will be faster. The downside of this approach is that
the compiled code can only run on the platform for which it was compiled. This
may be acceptable in cases where the target machines are known—such as for
Intranet applications. Another factor to consider is that native compilers are
not free and are not yet available on all platforms. There are several JDK 1.1-
compliant native compilers available for the Windows platform including
Asymmetrics' Supercede and Symantec's Visual Café. In addition, Tower
Technology's TowerJ 2.0 native compiler supports both the Windows NT
platform and most UNIX platforms.

Another alternative is to use the Java Runtime Environment (JRE) to deploy the application. Using the JRE also creates an executable that is also platform dependent. The difference between JRE and native deployment is that
the JRE is not tuned for the particular platform so there is no performance
gain. But, on the plus side, the JRE is freely available and is released at the
same time as each new release of the JDK, so you do not have to wait for a
native compiler to be built to run with a new version of the JDK.

ADVANTAGES OF JAVA STAND-ALONE DEPLOYMENT

Stand-alone deployment is ideal for the user who is already familiar with, and
likes, the look and feel of Windows applications. There are no third-party software products needed to run the application (aside from the JVM), so there are
no extra installation or training issues as with the other approaches. In addition, the application will be able to support new versions and functionality of
the JDK immediately.

Because the class files are local, there are no initial download performance
implications as with the browser deployment. All necessary class files are already resident on the client machine.

DISADVANTAGES OF JAVA STAND-ALONE DEPLOYMENT

The downside of this approach is that the class files must be manually updated when new versions of the application are released. This leads to the main-

tenance costs and lag time problems mentioned at the beginning of this article. There is also no automatic notification to the user to let them know that a new release is even available. Lastly, there is no built-in integration with the World Wide Web. All integration must be custom-built.

Summary of Stand-alone Deployment

Stand-alone deployment is ideal for an internal application with a relatively small user base. The small user base will keep maintenance costs of updating the application with new versions at a minimum. Stand-alone deployment should be seriously considered when the application is not updated very often or the application requires access to the local client machine such as for printing. In general, avoid using stand-alone deployment for Internet-based applications with an unknown user base.

Deploying as a Channel

Another deployment strategy for Java client applications is using a "broadcast" or "push" technology product. For easier understanding, this section will cover deployment using a product that supports this technology—Marimba's Castanet. Additional information about Marimba and their products may be found at their Web site.

In this approach, the application to be deployed is converted to, and deployed as, a Castanet *channel*. A channel is similar to the concept of a television channel. The application is broadcast via a transmitter to interested parties who use a tuner to receive and run the application. A tuner in this analogy is similar to a television. The tuner is the user device (actually a GUI application), which can listen to anything that is broadcast via a transmitter, assuming appropriate permissions.

When a user tunes to a particular application channel, the entire application, all class files, HTML files, etc., is downloaded to the client's machine. Once the application is downloaded, there is no need to ever download any class files from the transmitter. All subsequent runs of the application occur without the download performance problem that can plague browser deployment.

The tuner takes the place of the Web browser for running the application. It basically has the same security restrictions (sandbox) as the browser. Much like browsers, Castanet applications can only open connections back to the server, however, they do allow an application to read and write to a special directory on the local file system. (Browsers will provide this same functionality through the use of signed applets.)

Advantages of Channel Deployment

The big advantage of using this technology, (similar to the browser), is there is no need to manually install the client application on any client machine. However, (unlike the browser), there is only one performance penalty taken up front for downloading the application. This download can be lessened even further if running on an internal corporate network. The application can be downloaded from a remote server to a main server machine that can then feed the local client machines.

Another huge advantage of this approach is the update technology built into Castanet. When the application is changed at the transmitter, it is automatically updated on the client machine by the tuner when the application is run. Castanet performs a checksum to determine if the application is out of date. This is equivalent in performance to a regular "ping" operation to the server machine. If the checksums show that the application is out of date, Castanet determines which files have changed and uses binary differences to only download and update the portions of the files that have changed. This saves the extra overhead of downloading completely new files making this approach incredibly efficient.

The tuner also doesn't have the same upgrade problems as browsers. When the tuner needs to be updated, it can update itself automatically in much the same way as its applications. This saves the maintenance of the tuner application, effectively creating a maintenance-free client. In addition, the tuner isn't tied to any particular version of the JDK because applications may be deployed using the JRE as mentioned above. This means that applications built with a new version of the JDK may be deployed immediately without having to wait for third-party software to support the new JDK version.

Disadvantages of Channel Deployment

The problems with channel deployment mainly center on the tuner. The tuner itself must be installed on the client machine, which may be a concern for large IT shops that have standard desktop configurations.

Although the tuner is freely available, the transmitter is not. Depending on how the application is deployed (Internet, Intranet, and Extranet) and how many users will be connecting to the transmitter, the price of the software can become an issue. For smaller scale applications, this added cost may be significant enough to rule Castanet out as an option. For applications with large user bases, Castanet can pay for itself quickly in maintenance costs.

As was mentioned earlier, the tuner is the replacement for the browser for this form of deployment. It has its own sandbox model, which is very similar to the browser's sandbox. It also does not allow connections to be opened on the client machine thus preventing access to services such as printing.

Because Castanet is a relatively new product, there are extra training considerations for both end users and developers. However, the tuner is fairly easy to use and for developers, Marimba offers training courses on how to build and deploy Java applications that can ease some of this concern.

Lastly, because the tuner is in itself not a true browser, it cannot display HTML pages. So, if you wanted your application to integrate with the Web, you would have to do so through the launching of a Web browser from Castanet.

SUMMARY OF CHANNEL DEPLOYMENT

Channel deployment is the most ideal type of deployments for all environments—Internet, Intranet, and Extranet. However, think twice before using only channel deployment for unsophisticated users who may be afraid of this "new" technology. It also might not be the right option if your budget is tight. If these are not concerns for your project, channel deployment is the best option for deployment.

COMBINING BROWSER AND CHANNEL DEPLOYMENT

There is one more type of client deployment that is just becoming available and is important enough to be mentioned. The basic premise of this approach is combining the best of both the browser and the channel technologies. The channel technology is integrated directly in the browser and is transparent to the user. This gives the user the benefits of both the channel technology—permanent caching, and fast, transparent update of the application—and the browser

Table 1. Summary of advantages and disadvantages of Java deployment options.

	Advantages	Disadvantages
Web browser	• No client application installation necessary	• Potential runtime performance issues
	• Immediate update of client application	• Dependence on browser for support of JDK features
	• Familiar client environment	• Sandbox restrictions on printing, et al.
	• Integration with WWW	• Must upgrade browser to new version
Stand-alone application	• Standard GUI application look and feel	• Client installation required
	• No download runtime performance overhead	• No automatic update of application
	• No client software required	• No direct integation with WWW
	• Immediate support for new versions of JDK	
Channel	• No client application installation necessary	• Requires installation of tuner
	• Configurable update of client application	• Unfamiliar client environment
	• Download runtime performance minimized	• Cost
	• Automatic update of tuner	• Training considerations
	• Immediate support for new versions	• Only indirect integration with WWW of JDK through JRE

technology—familiar environment, readily available, and inexpensive.

Be careful before choosing this approach, however. This technology is brand new, having just been embedded into the latest releases of both the Microsoft and Netscape browsers. Because of this, there have yet to be any documented cases of business applications that use this strategy. Also, the push technology that is supported in the browser is currently proprietary. Both Netscape's Netcaster (based on Marimba's Castanet Channel) and Microsoft (CDF format) have their own approaches. This is currently being worked out though. Recently an announcement was made between Marimba, Microsoft, and Netscape to standardize on the format of how objects will be distributed on a network connection. Hopefully, this will clear up some of the confusion.

Summary

There are several strategies for deployment of Java client applications. For robust, large-scale Internet applications over slow connections, deploying as a stand-alone application or as a channel are the best choices. For smaller applications deployed on Intranets or Extranets with high-speed connections, browser deployment should be seriously considered in addition to the other approaches. It is important to keep a close eye on the channel technology in browsers. Depending on the timing of your application deployment, this technology might be a viable option. The ultimate selection that you make will rely heavily on the needs of your particular application and environment in which the application will run.

Finally, when should this deployment decision be made? To help alleviate the impact on the overall project, this decision should ideally be made as early in the development cycle as possible. This is because there are several design and coding techniques and alternatives that can be used to help alleviate some of the different disadvantages of each approach. However, most techniques require minimal, if any, coding changes so the actual impact to the development process itself may be minimal, making it possible to put off this decision until close to deployment time.

Locating CORBA Objects from Java

John O'Shea

J AVA AND CORBA fit together. With Java, you have portability of code and platform independence. With CORBA you add location transparency and an enterprise level object model that allows us to interoperate with a multitude of existing languages and integrated or legacy systems.

One of the most important steps when designing your client applications and applets is how they should bootstrap into the CORBA system. With a good system design, you can make this bootstrapping phase straightforward and avoid any bottlenecks along the way. You need to consider how CORBA servers should distribute CORBA object references so that clients can easily and efficiently find them. Some of your decisions may be made at the relatively early IDL design phase, while others can be implemented as late as when you deploy your clients and servers.

Bootstrapping a CORBA Application

A CORBA application only needs to obtain one CORBA Object reference (otherwise known as an Interoperable Object Reference (IOR)) for it to be able to connect to and participate in a CORBA system. From then on, a CORBA client or server should be able to obtain new IORs through normal IDL invocations. Therefore, it is the mechanism by which a client or server obtains this initial object reference that can be vital for a CORBA system's overall accessibility and scalability. The most interoperable and scalable solution to locating CORBA objects is to use the CORBA Naming Service.

THE CORBA NAMING SERVICE

The Object Naming Service is the principal mechanism for objects on an ORB to locate remote objects. A Naming Service typically runs on a network node that is available to all clients and servers throughout the system.

Conceptually, the Naming service can be viewed as a graph of objects (nodes), each of which is called a Naming Context. Naming Contexts are containers for two types of objects:

- Application IORs—CORBA servers can publish the IORs of the objects they wish to expose to the rest of the CORBA system under any Naming Context.
- Other Naming Contexts—Sub Naming Contexts can in turn contain both IORs and other Naming Contexts.

The graph itself can be extended and reorganized dynamically by either CORBA clients or servers or perhaps an administrator.

CONNECTING TO THE NAMING SERVICE

The core CORBA specification defines an operation resolve_initial_references() that all ORBs implement and that allows application code to bootstrap to well known services, such as the Naming Service, in a consistent and compliant way. The operation takes one parameter, a string, which identifies what CORBAService is required. How an ORB implementation of resolve_initial_references() works is not specified by CORBA but usually ORB configuration information specifies which host and port to connect to for the required service.

Typically, when a client application starts up, it will initialize its ORB by calling ORB.init(). After calling resolve_initial_references() on the ORB, a generic org.omg.CORBA.Object is handed back. Because this is the base class of all CORBA objects, you need to cast it to an object reference of type Naming-Context. The IDL to Java mapping provides us with a typesafe method, narrow(), for doing exactly this. Here's how to connect to the Naming Service:

```
import org.omg.CORBA.ORB;
import org.omg.CosNaming.NamingContext;
import org.omg.CosNaming.NamingContextHelper;
...
```

```
ORB myORB = ORB.init(args, null);
        // static—initializes the ORB
org.omg.CORBA.Object objRef;
NamingContext rootContextRef;
try {
      objRef  = myORB.resolve_initial_references("NameService");
      rootContextRef = NamingContextHelper.narrow(objRef);
}
catch (org.omg.CORBA.SystemException se) {
      //Something went wrong—comms failure
      //or config issue
}
```

All code that can make a remote invocation is encapsulated within a try…catch block in case anything should go wrong within the ORB level. The exception class SystemException inherits from java.lang.RuntimeException and so doesn't have to be caught. Subclasses of this class can be used to catch particular types of exceptions. For example, if you were only interested in detecting communications failures, then you would specify the exception class org.omg. CORBA.COMM_FAILURE. When writing CORBA applications, it is good practice to always be prepared to catch network or server side exceptions and deal with them appropriately.

CosNaming.idl

You now have a reference to the "root" Naming Context. You'll probably have noticed by now that each Naming Context is a CORBA object of type NamingContext. The OMG defined CosNaming IDL module contains the definition of the NamingContext interface. Here's what it looks like:

```
//IDL code, not java!
interface NamingContext {

//definitions of exceptions
// NotFound, CannotProceed, InvalidName,
//AlreadyBound and NotEmpty
//omitted
```

```
void bind(in Name n, in Object obj)
        raises(NotFound, CannotProceed,
            InvalidName, AlreadyBound);

void rebind(in Name n, in Object obj)
        raises(NotFound, CannotProceed, InvalidName);

void bind_context(in Name n, in NamingContext nc)
        raises(NotFound, CannotProceed,
            InvalidName, AlreadyBound);

void rebind_context(in Name n, in NamingContext nc)
        raises(NotFound, CannotProceed, InvalidName);

Object resolve (in Name n)
        raises(NotFound, CannotProceed, InvalidName);

void unbind(in Name n)
        raises(NotFound, CannotProceed, InvalidName);

NamingContext new_context();

NamingContext bind_new_context(in Name n)
        raises(NotFound, AlreadyBound, Cannot
            Proceed, InvalidName);

void destroy( )
        raises(NotEmpty);

void list (in unsigned long how_many,
        out BindingList bl, out BindingIterator bi);
};
```

The two operations that you use to insert and extract IORs into the Naming Service are bind() and resolve(), respectively. Servers *bind* IORs to a name within the Naming Service while clients ask the Naming Service to *resolve* an IOR from a supplied name.

What's In An Interoperable Object Reference?

A CORBA object reference identifies a CORBA Object that is unique throughout the system. Because you are using Java to talk to your CORBA system, your ORB will be using the Internet Inter-ORB Protocol, which is a specialization of the General Inter-ORB Protocol designed for TCP/IP networks (hence the word "Internet" in the name.) To identify a unique endpoint in a TCP/IP network, IORs use a network address and a port number. However, IORs must also point to a specific instance of an object at that location, so an IOR also contains an object key, the format of which is ORB vendor specific but doesn't concern the users of the IOR because it should never be examined by them.

NAMES

So what's in a **Name?** The **CosNaming** IDL module, where **Name** is defined, may make this clear:

```
// a placeholder for a future IDL
// internationalized string data type.
typedef string Istring;

struct NameComponent {
        Istring id;
        Istring kind;
};
typedef sequence <NameComponent> Name;
```

Names are in fact compound names, consisting of one or more Name Components, each of which represents a node in the Naming Context Graph. To work out what a **Name** looks like to a Java programmer, you need to use three of the rules of the IDL to Java language mapping specification:

1. A typedef of a basic type in IDL is mapped to the original type in Java. Istring will therefore map to a Java.lang.String.
2. A struct in IDL maps to a class containing equivalent data types in Java. The class is automatically generated by the IDL compiler and has a default constructor and also a constructor that initializes all the member variables of the class.
3. A sequence in IDL maps to an array of the equivalent type in Java.

So, to create a Name in Java, you will be creating an array of NameComponent instances, with each instance containing two strings, an identifier ("id") and the type ("kind"). Application developers are free to assign any naming conventions they like when creating both identifier and kind attributes—the Naming Service itself doesn't interpret either attribute. Typically, developers use the kind field to pass some application level type information to the client (for example "object," "context," "transient," "persistent" and so on.)

BINDING AN IOR TO A Name

Servers need to populate the Naming Service with application IORs so that client processes can retrieve them at some later stage. *When* the server should bind IORs to Names in the Naming Service depends on the type of IORs that the server is producing:

- **Transient IORs** point to CORBA Objects that are defined to be valid for the lifetime of the server process in which they were created and, specifically, should remain valid for the lifetime of that process only. If a client attempts to access a transient CORBA object after its server has exited, the client ORB should throw an exception. A server that wishes to make transient IORs available to clients should re-bind those IORs to Names in the Naming Service every time the server process is started.
- **Persistent IORs** also point to CORBA Objects but are designed to re-main valid even after the original server process that created the object and exported the IOR has exited. CORBA ORBs have a number of features that help facilitate the support of persistent IORs. In particular, the Implementation Repository (for example, the orbixd in OrbixWeb) is responsible for the transparent re-activation of server process on demand. This would occur if a client attempts to use a persistent IOR and the server process in which the CORBA Object resides isn't running. The client ORB itself has the capabilities to transparently wait and redirect the CORBA request once the server has been relaunched.

A server that publishes persistent IORs only needs to do so once—when it is installed on the host on which it will run.

Note that the term "persistent IOR" doesn't imply that the CORBA Object to which they point also has persistent state!

Here's example code for binding the Name "Dublin:Office/Chris:Manager" to a "Person" object, which is in your server (the delimeters ':' and '/' used above are only used for text representation of a Name!):

```
import org.omg.CosNaming.NameComponent;

        // Assume rootContextRef was found (as
        //in previous code snippet)
        // Also assume that a CORBA Object
        //"managerRef" exists in this server
        // "managerRef" is an IDL "Person" object

        // a CosNaming.Name is a sequence of IDL
        //NameComponents
        NameComponent[] name =
          new NameComponent[1];
        name[0] = new NameComponent("Dublin", "Office");

        // create new context and bind it relative
        //to the "root" context
        try {
        companyContextRef =
        rootContextRef.bind_new_context(name);
        }
        // catch clauses not shown

        // just re-set and reuse the Name object
        //"name"
        name[0].id = "Chris";
        name[0].kind = "Manager";

        try {
             // bind "name" to object
             //"managerRef"
             // relative to the "company"
             //context
             companyContextRef.bind(name, managerRef);
        }
        // catch clauses not shown
```

Here the server does two things—first you create a new Naming Context and then attach it to the graph below the "root" node. These steps are both done by the IDL operation bind_new_context(). Then using the reference returned to your new "company" Naming Context, you insert the IOR of your application object "Chris" (the manager of the Dublin office) into the Naming Service.

RESOLVING AN IOR FROM A Name

For a client to access "Chris", the manager of the Dublin office's IOR, the code is as follows:

```
import org.omg.CosNaming.NameComponent;

        //Assume rootContextRef was found
        Person managerRef = null;

        NameComponent[] name = new NameComponent[2];
        name[0] = new NameComponent("Dublin","Office");
        name[1] = new NameComponent("Chris","Manager");

        try {
        //Ask the Naming Service for the IOR
        objRef = rootContextRef.resolve(name);

        // you need to cast to be able to
        //call operations
        // on the Person IDL interface
        managerRef = PersonHelper.narrow(objRef);
    }
        //catch clauses not shown
```

The code is fairly simple. First you need to construct the **Name** of the IOR that you are looking for in the Naming Service and then you ask the Naming Service to find it. Note that the Naming Service only stores IORs as an org.omg. CORBA.Object. As an off-the-shelf component, the Naming Service couldn't possibly know about (and therefore have the necessary Java code for storing) all the IDL interfaces that exist within your system. When you get back your IOR, you need to narrow or cast it down to a particular Java interface (**Person**) that matches the CORBA object's IDL interface. You can then use this reference to invoke the remote object.

NAVIGATION

The fact that each Naming Service Naming Context is itself a full-fledged COR-
BA object leads to a few interesting observations:

- Clients can connect to their "root" Naming Context, construct the full
  Name of the IOR that it wants and then call resolve() on their root context object. The "root" context node is then responsible for navigation
  through other naming context objects until the Name is fully resolved
  and the IOR is found. The IOR is then returned to the client via the
  "root" naming context Object.
- Clients can use list() to explicitly navigate through the Naming Context graph to any location. They can then attempt to resolve() a Name
  starting from that location. The IOR they are looking for could be at
  that location, or it could be still several hops away, through other Naming Contexts.

Each individual Naming Service server can expose a "root" Naming Context for CORBA applications to connect directly to and start resolving or binding names. However, there is no global "root" of the Naming Service.

Because each Naming Context is a full CORBA Object, then it is possible
that the Naming Service can be provided by a collection of CORBA server
processes running on multiple hosts. Each server would implement the Cos-
Naming module with each server maintaining certain NamingContexts within
the overall Naming Context graph. It is possible that an attempt to resolve a
Name could be distributed across multiple servers, each responsible for nav-

---

How Else Can Clients And Servers Get Object References?

1. ORB proprietary extensions such as OrbixWeb's bind() method. Although these extensions are useful for small scale, relatively static systems, these connection mechanisms are
   not ORB-interoperable so they are not described here.

2. A stringified IOR can be converted into an object reference using the standard method
   string_to_object(), which is available on the ORB object. The returned object must be nar-
   rowed to a particular CORBA interface before use.

3. CORBA object references can be passed as "out" parameters or return values from invocations on other CORBA objects. This is the most dynamic approach to discovering COR-
   BA objects. See the "Factory" pattern described in this article.

igation through nodes of the graph, which it maintains until, ultimately, the IOR is found.

FEDERATION

The last point is interesting and introduces the notion of a "federated" Naming Service. With a little thought and organization when constructing the Naming Service graph, it is possible to easily introduce some simple load balancing and fault tolerance policies. The way the Naming Service graph can be partitioned is totally application dependent.

Let's take an example whereby a large corporation has three subsidiaries. In each subsidiary, there exists a Naming Service that contains a graph of IORs representing each employee of that subsidiary. The graph would look something like Table 1.

Now, for the head office to gain access to all of its world-wide employees, it simply needs to set up a local Naming Service server and create links to the relevant contexts of each remote Naming Context (by using bind_context()). The head office's view of the Naming Context graph is presented as a seamless connection of the combination of the three subsidiaries' graphs.

If each office occasionally needed access to a remote office's personnel data, they could also create Naming Contexts that map to the remote Naming Service contexts. Alternatively, each Naming Service server could regularly mirror its graph to the other remote servers to reduce response time and increase availability.

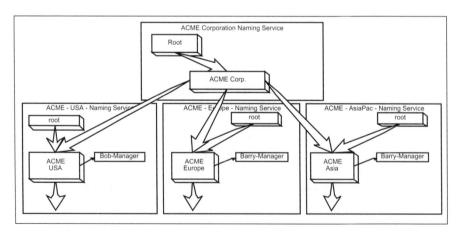

Table 1. Example of partitioning of the Naming Server.

You'll notice that there are a lot of options to choose from, and the best choice usually depends on the type of application that is being distributed.

FACTORIES

The Naming Service gives us a CORBA-compliant way to bootstrap into your CORBA system, but if all of your CORBA severs and clients are using the Naming Service, then it could become a potential bottleneck in your distributed system. One solution would be to upgrade to a different Naming Service (anyone can write them!), perhaps one that integrates with a directory or storage system that has proven to be scalable.

Alternatively, you could choose to utilize the **Factory Object** design pattern when designing your system. The pattern is simple to understand: A factory object is an object whose purpose is to create a different type of object on request. How the object is created isn't visible to the client process—the factory may find the required object in memory, it may recreate the object from persistent store or it may be a new object instance. Here's an example factory for **Person Objects**:

```
interface PersonFinder {
    Person find(in string lastName, in string firstName)
};
```

By binding only the factory object's IOR to a **Name** in the Naming Service, you will significantly reduce the load on the Naming Service—once a client resolves a factory object's IOR from the Naming Service it can then call on the factory directly to create as many application objects as it needs.

IMPLEMENTING THE CosNaming MODULE

An alternative to creating a non-standard IDL interface for your factory object is to use the **CosNaming** module to expose your factory. Instead of implementing the interface **PersonFinder** above, your server will implement CosNaming::NamingContext. You could then choose to use a very simple "flat" implementation with only resolve() for simple names—other operations in **NamingContext** could throw an org.omg.CORBA.NO_IMPLEMENT system exception, indicating that operation isn't implemented.

This is almost exactly the same amount of work as your **PersonFinder** but now you have the following additional benefits:

- No non-standard interfaces: clients use a single naming service method **resolve()** to find objects.
- If desired, a richer Naming Context could be implemented. For example, the method **list()** could be provided to access the Naming hierarchy. However, you have no obligation to do this.
- Finally, as CORBA becomes more integrated into existing directory and database solutions, Naming Service implementations with the right performance will come along (e.g., a Naming Service interface to a LDAP server) and you will be able to replace your custom version with something out of the box, because you used standard interfaces.

CONCLUSION

The CORBA Naming Service, at first glance, provides a directory service that allows us to distribute and find CORBA Object References in a language-, location-, and vendor-neutral manner. With some planning, the Naming Service can be extended to unobtrusively add load balancing and fault tolerance features to an existing distributed system, while scaling to provide a true enterprise-wide object location mechanism.

REFERENCES

CORBA 2.3 Specifications

FTP: //fpt.ongle/PUB/DOCS/FORMAL/98-07-0/.pdf

Orbix Web Programmer's Reference

www.iona.com

Orbix Web Programmer's Guide

www.iona.com

THREADS

EFFECTIVE MULTITHREADING

PETER BOSCH

T HIS IS THE second of a two-part series on thread separation. The first, published in *Java Report's* August 1998 issue, dealt with general issues and techniques for addressing them. This installment describes a simple framework to thread-separate servers from the clients that call them. This thread separation is useful if the request being served is a lengthy one, such as to retrieve an image from a large image database. The client may go on doing other things and be called back by the server when the requested task is complete. Thread separation of servers is also useful when (e.g., in a Web server), you have chosen a thread-pooling solution to limit the number of concurrent threads running in your server. All client requests are transferred to one or more controlled server threads for execution. Finally, thread separation is useful when you take advantage of the "liveness" rationale for threading, in effect, making tasks in a system "live," because it allows them better to embody the behaviors of their real-world counterparts. Thread separation allows different components to each live and run within their own thread or threads, with control and notification between components being as brief and shallow as the designer desires.

PROBLEM DOMAIN

I recently worked on a heavyweight component model that simplified the creation of system servers. Most of the top-level components in our system were built on this model and most of these components had presentation objects that commanded them based on user actions. The design team discussed the fact that, because all

Dispatch Thread: The thread from which other threads are launched to perform tasks.

Handler Thread: A thread launched to perform a specific task for a dispatch thread.

Calling Object: The object that uses the dispatch thread to determine a need to launch handler threads.

Task Object: The object that performs a task for the calling object.

system activity was ultimately traceable back to a user action, we would, for all practical purposes, be running the system off the AWT thread. There was ample concern that this would starve the system for performance. I offered to investigate thread separation, and proposed a mechanism from which to build a solution.

We needed a way to select some or all of a component's API and specify that, while anyone might *invoke* one of these methods, the actual execution of the method's body would take place on a separate thread. This separate thread could be owned and controlled by the component itself. We wanted to be able to vary the number of threads controlled by the component so that a (properly designed) simple, single-threaded component could easily become multithreaded at minimum code-rework cost.

GENERAL DESIGN APPROACH

The approach to solving this problem is to replace the methods being invoked in your server with proxy methods having the same signature. When a method is called by a client, the arguments and a method selector are packaged up into a thread-separated call (ThreadSeparatedCall) object and placed in a queue (ThreadSeparatedQueue). The calling thread then returns. If there are any idle handler threads, one of them then wakes up, pulls a ThreadSeparatedCall object off the ThreadSeparatedQueue and handles it. If all handler threads are processing client requests, the next one to complete its task checks the ThreadSeparatedQueue before idling itself. The handler thread's dispatch method pulls the ThreadSeparatedCall object off the ThreadSeparatedQueue, unpacks the arguments and method selector, applies necessary typecasts to the arguments, and invokes the method indicated by the method selector.

This mechanism combines thread-pooling, token-based task selection, and callbacks into one flexible, easily implemented framework. The framework includes code for a thread pool, and by creating a child class of the ThreadSepa-rator as an inner class to the server itself, simplifies the integration between the ThreadSeparator and your server.

SOLUTION DOMAINS

There are several areas of technical design in this architecture. They are the proxy methods, the ThreadSeparatedCall, the ThreadSeparatedFifo, the Han-dlerThread, and the ThreadPool. All but the proxy methods are bundled into the Thread-Separator. To use the thread separator, you derive from it in an inner class to your server object. We discuss each separate design area and provide examples of how the ThreadSeparator can be applied to both new and existing servers.

PROXY METHODS

A proxy method has the same signature as the method it replaces except that it does not usually return any value. Values are returned in the thread that executes the body of the method rather than being returned in the dispatch thread. Therefore, if a return value is desired, it will generally be fed back to the calling object by way of an interface or object reference supplied in the method's arguments. See the first part of my series (Aug. 1998, Vol. 3, No. 8) for more detail. Here, we discuss a gen-eral mechanism for allowing the thread-separated server to still return a value in the caller's thread. This completes the transparency of the thread separation.

Listing 1 shows a method in a non-thread-separated object, and then shows its proxy-method construct.

ThreadSeparatedCall

A ThreadSeparatedCall's purpose is to store an integer that is later used to select which method to invoke, and an array of objects that represent the arguments to be used in the deferred call to the actual method. Listing 1 shows the MyThread-Separator::enqueueCall(ThreadSeparatedCall theCall) method. This method will cause the creation of a ThreadSeparatedCall object which is then placed into a ThreadSeparatedFifo. The ThreadSeparatedCall is a very simple object, main-taining a method ID number and an object array of arguments. Both properties are set in the ThreadSeparatedCall's constructor and each property has an accessor.

Listing 1.

```
// A plain-old method
public class MyServer {
    public void doSomething( Thing aThing, Double aDouble ) {
        /* Actually do something with aThing and aDouble. */ }; }
// A proxy-method construct in a thread-separated server:
protected MyThreadSeparator myThreadSeparator; // Initted in the server's ctor.
protected final static void int DO_SOMETHING = 0; // A Method ID number
public class MyThreadSeparatedServer {
    public void doSomething( Thing aThing, Double aDouble ) {
        myThreadSeparator.enqueueCall(DO_SOMETHING,
                              new Object[]{aThing,aDouble}); } }
```

ThreadSeparatedFifo

The class ThreadSeparatedFifo is a first-in-first-out queue for ThreadSeparatedCall objects. ThreadSeparatedFifo wraps a vector, and has a void add(ThreadSeparatedCall threadSeparatedCall) and a ThreadSeparatedCall remove() method. However, the ThreadSeparatedFifo also maintains a reference to a ThreadGroup—the ThreadGroup shared by the HandlerThread objects. The reason for this is so that on adding a ThreadSeparatedCall to the ThreadSeparatedFifo, the ThreadSeparatedFifo can inform the handler threads' ThreadGroup (via the ThreadGroup::resume() API) of the newly arrived ThreadSeparatedCall object. This method call causes the ThreadGroup to call the resume method on all of its member threads, which happen to be the HandlerThreads. As a result of this call, any HandlerThread that was suspended (due to completing a prior task) is awakened, so that it may attempt to pull the new task off the FIFO. A HandlerThread that awoke and did not find a ThreadSeparatedCall on the FIFO, will simply suspend itself again.

The vector wrapped by the ThreadSeparatedFifo provides synchronization in the add() method, so that two clients making a request "at the same time" will be prevented from clobbering each others' ThreadSeparatedCall objects, and each will be taken completely, as an atomic submission to the ThreadSeparatedFifo.

HandlerThread

Handler threads are created as inner classes to the ThreadSeparator object and therefore have inherent access to all protected methods in the ThreadSeparator. Their run method consists of one simple sequence—they try to take a ThreadSeparatedCall off the ThreadSeparatedFifo. If there are any on the queue, they are

<table>
<tr><td colspan="1" align="center">**Listing 2.**</td></tr>
</table>

```
// protected TSepFIFO calls;
public void run(){
  while (true) {
    while ( (threadSeparatedCall =
(ThreadSeparatedCall)calls.remove()) != null ) {

        handleNextCall(threadSeparatedCall.getWhichCall(),
        threadSeparatedCall.getArguments());

    }
    suspend(); } }
```

successful in doing so, and they will handle it by calling the handleNextCall method in the ThreadSeparator. If they are unsuccessful, or after executing handleNextCall, they suspend themselves. The handleNextCall() API takes a method selector and an array of objects as arguments and is responsible for selecting the worker method and calling it. The proxy method is the method that put the ThreadSeparatedCall object on the ThreadSeparatedFifo. Listing 2 describes the lifecycle of the HandlerThread.

Thread Pool

The Thread Pool is just a set of HandlerThreads started by the ThreadSeparator all belonging to the same ThreadGroup. These threads are declared as inner classes to the ThreadSeparator, and therefore have implicit access to the same ThreadSeparatedFifo, the one declared by the ThreadSeparator. The fact that they are all members of the same ThreadGroup means that they can all be resumed at the same time. The fact that the ThreadSeparatedFifo is synchronized means that only one HandlerThread will be able to pull a given ThreadSeparatedCall off the ThreadSeparatedFifo. This means that when the ThreadGroup is resumed, all HandlerThreads will resume, and each one will pick off and handle a ThreadSeparatedCall object until there are no more to be had. Those that got ThreadSeparatedCalls will handle them, and then, whether they handled a ThreadSeparatedCall or not, they will all eventually suspend themselves again.

ThreadSeparator

The ThreadSeparator, although actually an abstract class, really ties the whole mechanism together. It declares a single ThreadSeparatedFifo instance for holding thread separated calls (ThreadSeparatedCall objects) until a handler thread can execute them. It also creates a number of instances of HandlerThread. The HandlerThread is defined as an inner class to the ThreadSeparator, so that all of the instances of HandlerThread can have implicit access to the ThreadSeparatedFifo and, most importantly, the abstract HandleNextCall() method.

While the ThreadSeparatedFifo and the HandlerThread don't need to be inner classes, we made them inner classes to the ThreadSeparator more for packaging reasons than functional ones. If you integrate ThreadSeparator into a broader utility or thread management package, as I have, you may want to do a little work to make them package protected separate classes instead.

PUTTING IT ALL TOGETHER—
CREATING A THREAD-SEPARATED SERVER

To create a thread-separated server, you must create a class that contains proxy methods and the worker methods they represent. This class can be the actual server or you can use the delegation pattern to wrap an existent or third-party server. Your class must declare and instantiate an inner class, which extends ThreadSeparator. In extending ThreadSeparator, you will provide a definition for the abstract method handleNextCall(), consisting of a switch statement that dispatches the thread-separated calls, based on their method ID values, to the worker methods.

As an illustration, Listing 3 displays how you would create a simple server, with the desired public API.

A client will call a public method, doSomething(), and the only thing that happens on the client's thread is that the call's arguments and a method ID are packed up in a ThreadSeparatedCall and added to the ThreadSeparator's ThreadSeparatedFifo. The client's thread then returns. As a result of the ThreadSeparatedCall object being added to the ThreadSeparatedFifo, the HandlerThread objects wake up and check the ThreadSeparatedFifo. The first one there takes the newly arrived ThreadSeparatedCall object, and all the others, finding nothing, go back to sleep. The HandlerThread that got the ThreadSeparatedCall unpacks it and then calls the ThreadSeparator object's handleNextCall() API. This causes the worker method to be executed, on the HandlerThread's thread. Voilà, thread separation. Let's look at the code. Listing 4 shows a simple server designed as a user of ThreadSeparator.

```
                          Listing 3.
// The desired publicly exposed API
public class MyServer {
    public MyServer( ... ) { ... };
    public void doSomething( String str, Hashtable htbl ){ ... }
    public void doSomethingElse( Observer obsv, Event evt ){ ... } }
```

RETURNING VALUES TO CLIENTS

While there are many variations, there are really just two mechanisms for returning values from server methods to clients.

The first mechanism is to pass in an object or interface reference as an argument to the server proxy method and then have the server's worker method call a well-known method in that object or interface. This technique is supported directly by the framework we have described so far. This mechanism has the advantage of being simple to implement in the server, and allowing the client to go off and do other things, but has the disadvantage of being a bit more complicated in the client. The client may need to have a means for matching the return value being supplied via callback to the past invocation that produced it.

The second mechanism is to block the calling thread until the call (which is executed in the HandlerThread) completes, and then return the value in the caller's thread. This, of course, does not allow your server's client to go off and do other things while your server processes. The benefits of this mechanism lie in the controllability of the client threads. The handler threads are all in the same Thread-Group and can be stopped and started and have their priorities manipulated simply and in unison. Your thread pool is performing the work so you have control over how many clients are afforded access at any given time.

ThreadSepRetValAdapter

The code distributed with this article includes a utility class, ThreadSepRetVal-Adapter. This class is used to receive a callback from a handler thread, and block a calling thread until that callback is received. This simplifies implementation of the second of the two return value mechanisms described. It is used in the proxy method and in the handleNextCall() method as described in Listings 5 and 6. Although the RetValAdapter comes only with a waitForObject() and returnObject() method, it is a simple matter to add a waitFor_int() and return_int(), as well as handlers for other primitives.

A WORD OF WARNING

Doug Lea's book, *Concurrent Programming in Java: Design Principles and Patterns* (Addison-Wesley, 1996), is excellent, and if you're thinking of doing multithreaded programming, it is quite worthy of a cover-to-cover read. Paraphrasing Mr. Lea, one of the great strengths of Java is how easy it makes it to do multithreaded programming, but one of its greatest weaknesses is how easy it makes it to do multithreaded programming. The point he is making is that multithreaded programming is hard. With Java, it is not tactically hard, inasmuch as the coding constructs are simple, but it is still strategically hard, in that very complex design issues must usually be sought out, analyzed, and unwanted interactions prevented. Java may have simplified the use of the forceps, scalpel, and skull saw, but it's still brain surgery. If you want results you can be proud of, you'd better know what you're doing—practice on a grapefruit first. Work your way through cantaloupes, squirrels, lawyers, and finally, maybe, real humans. Don't take a first jump into heavy multithreading on a large, important project for your best client.

CONCLUSION

We presented a framework that uses tokens and a thread pool to simplify the creation of a thread-separated server and we discussed a mechanism for returning values from thread separated methods to callers in their own threads.

The framework is provided as a Symantec Visual Café project, but of course, the Java files can be imported into almost any tool. There is a sample server and a test driver that creates clients and starts them calling into the server. The Thread-Separator class has a static final debug constant that causes printout of progress so you can see what is going on in it. The class, MyThreadSepTester has a main method that provides comprehensive testing and illustration of the mechanism. The class MyServer contains the code provided in the listings here, including a rudimentary exercise of the ThreadSepRetValAdapter.

I hope the discussion has been interesting, and that the framework, in some form, will be useful. Thanks for reading, and please, multithread carefully.

Listing 4.

```
import java.util.Hashtable;
import java.util.Observer;
import java.awt.Event;

public class MyServer {
    protected MyThreadSeparator myThreadSep;
    protected static final int NUM_HANDLER_THREADS = 5;

    // Server Method ID Values
    protected static final int DO_SOMETHING      = 0;
    protected static final int DO_SOMETHING_ELSE = 1;

    public MyServer() {
        myThreadSep = new MyThreadSeparator(NUM_HANDLER_THREADS);
        // Maybe do some other things, too. }

    /* These are the proxy methods, and are a part of the public API. */
    public void doSomething( String str, Hashtable htbl ){
        myThreadSep.enqueueCall(DO_SOMETHING, new Object[]
        {str, htbl}); }

    public void doSomethingElse( Observer obs, Event ev ){
        myThreadSep.enqueueCall(DO_SOMETHING_ELSE,
            new Object[]{obs, ev}); }

    /* Now, the actual worker methods. These are protected, or maybe private. */
    public void doSomething_( String str, Hashtable htbl ){ /* actual work */ }
    public void doSomethingElse_( Observer obs, Event ev ){ /* actual work */ }

    /* And finally, we create the inner class derived from ThreadSeparator,
       defining the handleNextCall() specifically to our server. */
    class MyThreadSeparator extends ThreadSeparator {

        public MyThreadSeparator(int numThreads){super(numThreads);}

        /* handleNextCall() is called by HandlerThreads upon getting a new
           ThreadSeparatedCall object */
        protected void handleNextCall(int whichCall, Object args[]){
            switch(whichCall){
                case DO_SOMETHING:{
                    doSomething_((String)args[0],(Hashtable)args[1]);
                    break; }
                case DO_SOMETHING_ELSE:{
                    doSomethingElse_((Observer)args[0],(Event)args[1]);
                    break; }
                default:{
                    // Hey, this part is bombproofing—your pain, your choice! } } } } }
```

Listing 5.

```
public String doSomethingSynchronous( String str ){
      ThreadSepRetValAdapter retValAdapter = new ThreadSepRetValAdapter();
      int methodID = DO_SOMETHING_SYNCHRONOUS;
      Object[] args = new Object[]{str, retValAdapter};
      myThreadSep.enqueueCall(methodID,args);
      String s = null;
      try {
         s = (String)retValAdapter.waitForObject();
      } catch (InterruptedException ie){}
      return s; }
```

Listing 6.

```
protected void handleNextCall(int whichCall, Object args[]){
      switch(whichCall){
            case DO_SOMETHING_SYNCHRONOUS:{
                ThreadSepRetValAdapter retValAdapter =
                    (ThreadSepRetValAdapter)args[1];
                Object o = doSomethingSynchronous_((String)args[0]);
                retValAdapter.returnObject(o);
                break; }
            // Eliminated other cases and a default for brevity. } }
```

Multi-Threaded Assignment Surprises

John Miller Crawford
Steve Ball

A VOLATILE BREW is formed by mixing assignment (topic of our previous column— "Assignment surprises," Vol. 3, No. 7) and threads. Perils and surprises lurk within the most innocent-looking statement. This time, we expose those perils and surprises and point out where you need to proceed with due caution if you are to ensure the effective use of locked objects.

Maxim 2: Never Assign to a Locked Object

We'll examine these pitfalls and their unhappy consequences within the setting of an aircraft ground service system. In this system, "checking out" an **Airplane** object and performing a large number of checks and modifications corresponds to the real-world allocation of an actual airplane to one of a number of service crews for refueling, repair, and refurbishment. For safety reasons, only one service crew is permitted to work on the airplane at the same time.

Because of that limitation, the methods for each service operation acquire exclusive access to the **Airplane** object for the duration of the task, locking the object with the synchronized statement. This forces all the other crews to have to wait until the airplane has been released for its next service operation.*

```
public class ParkingBay {
    Airplane airplane = null;
```

```
public void parkPlane(Airplane airplane) {
   this.airplane = airplane;
}

public void mechanicalService() {
   synchronized (airplane) {
      if (airplane.isAirWorthy())
         airplane.carryOutMaintenance();
      else
         airplane = new Airplane();

      airplane.refuel();
   }
}
```

Let's say that the mechanical service crew is the first to get to work today and is currently checking the airplane's airworthiness. Meanwhile the hospitality crew is waiting for access to the airplane so that they can give it a cleaning and load the next flight's meals.

```
public void hospitalityService() {
   synchronized (airplane) {
      airplane.loadMeals();
      airplane.vacuum();
      airplane.replaceAirSicknessBags();
   }
}
```

Because the mechanicalService() method started first, the hospitalityService() method is blocked and will not resume until the mechanicalService() method releases its lock on the Airplane object when it completes.

The advantage of this resource contention scheme is its simplicity. (Its disadvantage is that it does not permit the service crews to work in parallel on the same airplane). Because the Airplane class has so many methods that would require synchronization, the designer of the class chose not to add any synchro-

---

* Requiring the service crews to wait idly for the airplane to become available (in our code, to block in the synchronized statement) is far from ideal. A more sophisticated scheme would allow a service crew to inquire as to the airplane's availability and move on to a different airplane if appropriate.

nization at all within the class. This requires its users to provide these checks themselves at a higher level, as we've done in the ParkingBay class.

This is a perfectly reasonable compromise to make. On the one hand, placing multi-threaded checks in a class may complicate its implementation enormously. On the other hand, controlling access to objects of the class at a higher level places the responsibility for ensuring serialized access onto the users of the class and also reduces the amount of possible sharing of the class because it increases the granularity of the locking scope.

However, despite the simplicity of this scheme, it demonstrates the trickiness of working with multiple threads, as the peril we spoke of is lurking within the mechanicalService() method. The problem arises when the maintenance crew determines that the airplane is not airworthy and decides to replace it with a new plane that the airline keeps for just this sort of contingency:

```
airplane = new Airplane();
```

This new instance is not locked—that's okay though, because only the mechanical crew is privy to this exchange of airplanes (the other crews will go about their tasks unaware that the planes have been switched).

But what happens when the blocked hospitalityService() method proceeds, having acquired exclusive access to the Airplane object? Figure 1 shows the sequence of events.

The *T0* point on the timeline represents the state of the parking bay just after the airplane has been parked there and before any service crews have started. The instance variable airplane refers to the parked plane (Instance 1).

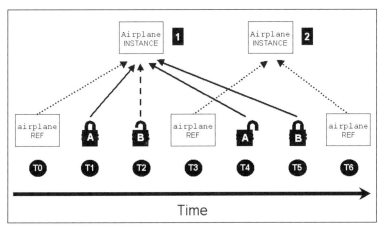

Figure 1. Assignment to locked object.

At *T1*, the mechanicalService() method is invoked and it acquires an exclusive lock on the Airplane instance using the synchronized statement.

The hospitality crew arrives later at point *T2* but discovers that the mechanical crew is not yet finished. The hospitalityService() method attempts to lock the Airplane instance and blocks.

At point *T3*, the mechanical crew concludes that the airplane is not fit to fly and decides to swap in a replacement. A new Airplane instance (Instance 2) is assigned to the airplane instance variable. The refueling of the new plane is completed and so at point *T4*, by exiting the synchronized block, the mechanicalService() method releases its lock on the first Airplane instance, the one that was previously referred to by airplane. Now remember, at the point that the mechanicalService() method released its lock the airplane instance variable had already been modified to refer to Instance 2 so the airplane switch should have been transparent to the other crews.

However, the hospitalityService() method has been waiting since the airworthiness checks started to get a lock on the original Airplane instance. At point *T5* (which occurs very shortly after the release of the lock at point *T4*) the hospitalityService() method acquires access to the original Airplane instance on which it synchronized at point *T2*. Unfortunately, the airplane instance variable now refers to a different Airplane object.

The resulting situation at point *T6* is obviously not a desirable one. The Airplane object now referenced by the airplane instance variable (and the one on which the hospitality crew will be working) has not been not locked by the hospitalityService() method, and the one on which that method does hold an exclusive lock is now being melted down in a local foundry.†

Things get worse. Suppose a further ParkingBay method, performTestFlight(), has been invoked in order to check the new airplane's ability to get off the ground after having been mothballed for so long. This method will also attempt to get exclusive access to the airplane by locking the instance now referred to by the airplane instance variable. This will immediately succeed because no thread currently has that instance locked. One hopes that the pilot would think to disconnect the vacuum cleaner power leads trailing out the back door before taxiing off down the runway!

---

† If the hospitalityService() method were to invoke the wait() or notify() methods on the airplane instance variable these methods would throw an IllegalMonitorStateException exception even though the methods would be invoked on the same reference as the one used with the synchronized statement that contains them!

We can trace the origin of this misfortune back to a failure to realize the implications of Java's distinction between object instances and object references. The lock held by a thread is a lock on the *instance*, not the reference. On the other hand, assignment acts on the *reference*, not the instance, as we emphasized in our last column ("Assignment surprises," Vol. 3, No. 7). Applied to a locked object in a threaded environment, assignment switches the reference to another instance, while any currently blocked lock requests will eventually be granted on the *original instance*; hence, our maxim warning you against assigning to a locked object.

There is a solution that will allow a method to gain a lock on the current instance associated with an object reference even when other threads may perform assignment on it. Applied to the hospitalityService() method, it looks like this:

```
public void hospitalityService() {
    for (;;) {
        Airplane local = airplane;

        synchronized (local) {
            if (local != airplane)
                continue;

            airplane.loadMeals();
            airplane.vacuum();
            airplane.replaceAirSicknessBags();

            break;
        }
    }
}
```

We loop around locking the instances referred to by airplane until the locked instance matches the current value of the reference. If assignments to airplane always occur while the instance it refers to is locked, then this method will operate on the latest instance referred to by airplane and *that instance will have been locked by the method.*

A better solution would be one that avoids needing to make assignments to locked objects in the first place. Accepting that the assignment performs a vital action that cannot be avoided, to solve the problem we will have to eliminate locking on the same object, which brings us to the next maxim.

MAXIM 3: LOCK WITH ONE CLASS AND ASSIGN WITH ANOTHER

Despite its problems, the simplicity of the original scheme has some appeal, as we still want to avoid placing the locking code into the Airplane class. The solution entails taking a lock not just on the right object but on the right object of the *right class*.

Let's review what went wrong with the airplane servicing. The hospitality crew requested a lock on a particular airplane scheduled for service. By the time that airplane had become available (and the lock granted), it had already been consigned to the scrap heap. The hospitality crew unwittingly carried out their duties on an airplane different from the one they'd locked. The designers of this system could have prevented this mishap if they'd arranged for the lock to be obtained on the parking bay instead of the airplane. This is safer because, even though airplanes may be swapped into and out of service unpredictably, the number of parking bays an airport has is generally fixed. Presumably, the Airport class is defined something like this:

```
public class Airport {
    private ParkingBay[] parkingBays;

    Airport(int nbParkingBays) {
        parkingBays = new ParkingBay[nbParkingBays];
    }
}
```

Applied to the ParkingBay class, the solution simply requires, in each method, the replacement of

```
synchronized (airplane) {
```

with a lock on the ParkingBay object itself

```
synchronized (this) {
```

or simply to make the relevant methods synchronized, which is a functionally equivalent form:

```
public synchronized void hospitalityService() {
    airplane.loadMeals();
    airplane.vacuum();
    airplane.replaceAirSicknessBags();
}
```

The problems of assigning to locked objects cannot arise when the this reference is locked or **synchronized** methods are invoked because assignment to the this reference is not permitted.

The mechanical crew, having carried out their tasks in drastic fashion by substituting the airplane in the parking bay, in due course would have released their lock on that bay. This would have allowed the hospitality crew to enter and lock the parking bay (and the replacement airplane now in it) and obstruct the actions of the test flight crew, who would then be compelled to wait their turn.

This solution works by ensuring that the layer of abstraction that is subjected to synchronization constraints is a different one than the layer at which new instances are assigned to existing references. We achieved this by moving the locking up to a higher level of abstraction—from **Airplane** class to **ParkingBay** class.

MAXIM 4: ENCAPSULATE YOUR LOCKING MECHANISMS IN SEPARATE CLASSES

An alternative application of *Maxim 3* could separate the locking from the assignment by creating a peer class for the **Airplane** class that would handle the synchronization issues for it.

To do this we'll need the assistance of a separate locking class. Listing 1 defines a **Mutex** (mutual exclusion) class that can be used for this purpose.

Using separate locking classes introduces its own problems—most notably that stand-alone locking objects are not automatically unlocked—but is generally a good idea in any non-trivial application. It also provides the opportunity we've been waiting for (no pun intended) to signal that the airplane is not yet ready for the next crew and would allow them to perform some other task other than merely wait for the airplane to become available.

```
public class ParkingBay {
    static Mutex available = new Mutex();

    public boolean hospitalityService(boolean wait) {
        if (!available.lock(false)) { // return if unavailable
            if (!wait)
                return false;
            available.lock(true); // block if unavailable
        }
```

```
                    Listing 1.  A Mutex class.
public class Mutex
{
    public boolean lock(boolean block) {
        synchronized (signal) {
            if (block)
                while (locked)
                    try {
                        signal.wait();
                    } catch (InterruptedException e) { }

            return locked ? false : locked = true; } }
    public boolean unlock() {
        synchronized (signal) {
            if (!locked)
                return false;

            locked = false;
            signal.notify();
            return true; } }

    private Object signal = new Object();
    private boolean locked; }
```

```
        airplane.loadMeals();
        airplane.vacuum();
        airplane.replaceAirSicknessBags();

        available.unlock();
        return true;
    }
}
```

Writing thread-safe code requires special vigilance, especially when contention is over objects that may be assigned new instances. An awareness of the difference between object instances and object references is, as always, key. When you face that type of resource contention look for other related objects that can be locked instead so that you will never need to assign to a locked object.

MULTITHREADED EXCEPTION HANDLING IN JAVA

JOE DE RUSSO III AND PETER HAGGAR

MULTITHREADED PROGRAMMING has been with us for many years and is considered to be a feature that many robust applications utilize. Exception handling is another feature of many languages considered to be necessary for proper and complete error handling. Each of these technologies stands very well on their own. In fact, you cannot pick up a book about Java programming without finding a chapter devoted to each of these topics. Many of these books do a good job defining and describing how to use them properly in your programs. What is missing is the information on how to use these two technologies together effectively. After all, how effective is writing a multithreaded Java program if it is incapable of properly handling exceptions occurring on secondary threads? We will present a solution for effectively dealing with this problem.

To solve this problem, we introduce two new classes and two new interfaces to be used when writing multithreaded Java programs. These classes are small, easy to use and understand, and effectively enable you to handle exceptions occurring on secondary threads.

Writing robust code implies many things. One of them is the proper and effective way in which your program deals with error situations. The approach you take can vary from doing nothing to handling any and all problems. The approach you choose is more than likely dictated by the type of application you are writing. For example, if you are writing an application that must run uninterrupted for many hours, days, or months at a time, you will need to effectively employ an error handling strategy that will ensure your software can run un-

223

interrupted when errors occur. Even if you are not writing such a program, effectively dealing with errors is just good programming practice.

One of the main areas of importance for dealing with exceptions is what we call *state management*. This involves ensuring that when an exception occurs, the state of the object the exception occurs in remains valid such that if the code recovers from the exception, the object can be reliably used again. Doing so in single-threaded applications is challenging enough without introducing multiple threads of execution.

The core problem that must be dealt with is how to manage concurrent threads of execution when one, or many, of those threads may terminate abnormally. We need a way to be notified of any errors occurring on secondary threads, and a solution that enables us to terminate gracefully while optionally preserving object state. Java is currently being considered as a platform for deploying mission-critical applications. Multithreaded exception handling is a reality in this environment. While much documentation exists on the virtues of using threads of execution and exceptions in Java, there is little documentation on how to integrate the two. One such solution to these problems is presented here. We designed our solution to be as generic as possible. Our design goals were to provide a solution that:

- Does not tightly couple the objects and code running on secondary threads with the objects and code that need to know if an exception occurs. For example, we do not implement a simple callback interface.
- Requires a minimum amount of maintenance when the code is changed to throw additional exceptions from the secondary threads.
- Minimizes the number of try/catch blocks.
- Works even if the code to be executed on secondary threads is not owned by the developer calling it. This could occur if you are implementing a run() method that calls code you obtained from a third party, and you want to catch any exception thrown from it.
- Works for all exceptions, both checked and unchecked, that may be thrown from within a secondary thread.

Note: Throughout this article we will be using the notion of checked and unchecked exceptions.

Checked exceptions are generally related to conditions that are specific to an operation being performed, such as trying to construct an invalid URL. The compiler requires that you take action on all checked exceptions that may occur in your method in one of two ways: either by handling them yourself with a try/catch block or by advertising to your callers that your method throws this exception by listing them in that method's *throws* clause. In contrast, unchecked exceptions could occur anywhere in your program, such as an out-of-memory condition. Although it may be useful to be aware of these problems in certain situations, the compiler does not require you to address unchecked exceptions.

The solution identified in this article satisfies all of the afforementioned design goals and is straightforward and generic enough to be used in production systems. All of the code presented here was compiled and run using the Sun JDK 1.1.4 on the Windows NT 4.0 Operating System.

MULTITHREADED EXCEPTION HANDLING

We present our solution to this problem in the following manner: Appendix A (posted at *Java Report* Online) contains a complete multithreaded program that attempts to open separate files on two threads. Listings 1-4 examine this code, point out the problems contained in it, and offer some initial attempts at solving them. Listings 5-8 introduce two new classes and two new interfaces to provide a solution to these problems. Appendix B (see *Java Report* Online) contains the program in Appendix A modified with the classes and interfaces introduced in Listings 5-8 such that it correctly deals with exceptions occurring on secondary threads. Listings 9-11 examine, more closely, Appendix B and offer commentary on how it was developed to solve these problems.

THE INITIAL CODE

The code in Appendix A contains a user interface that has two buttons and two listboxes. The listboxes are used to display the files and the buttons are used to fill the first listbox on the main thread and start the secondary thread to attempt to fill the second listbox. The code uses a **FileOpener** class to attempt to open the file on the secondary thread. The main thread will open the file and fill the first listbox without any errors. The second listbox will not fill up due to the exceptions occurring on the secondary thread.

Listing 1 contains some relevant code fragments from this program. Pressing the first button will result in an invalid filename at //4, being sent to the **FileOpener** class causing the secondary thread to generate a checked exception, **FileNotFoundException** at //1. Pressing the other button will result in a null pointer at

> **Listing 1.   Traditional multithreaded coding techniques.**
>
> ```
> class FileOpener implements Runnable {
> //...
>    public FileOpener(PrimaryFrame primaryFrame, String file) {
>    frame = primaryFrame;
>    fileName = file; }
>    public void run() {
>    try {
>       FileReader filReader = new FileReader(fileName); //1
>       BufferedReader bufReader = new BufferedReader(filReader);
>       String str = bufReader.readLine();
>       while (str != null) {
>       frame.list2.add(str); // will throw NullPointerException if frame is null //2
>       str = bufReader.readLine(); } }
>    catch (FileNotFoundException FileNotFoundExc) {} //3
>    catch (IOException IOExc) {} } }
> //...
> class PrimaryFrame extends Frame implements ActionListener {
> //...
>    public void actionPerformed(ActionEvent event) {
>    //...
>    if (event.getSource() == startButton1) {
>       primaryFrame = this;
>       fileName = new String("dummy.fil"); //4
>       threadName = new String("Regular Java Thread #1");
>    } else if (event.getSource() == startButton2) {
>       primaryFrame = null; //5
>       fileName = new String("layoutmanager2.java");
>       threadName = new String("Regular Java Thread #2"); }
>    FileOpener runnable = new FileOpener(pf, fileName);
>    Thread thread = new Thread(runnable, threadName);
>
>    /* An exception will occur in our runnable sometime after the call to start().
>    Because we have [passsed a file that does not exist, a FileNotFoundEx-
>    ception will be thrown, However, it must be caught inside of run() because
>    run() can't throw any checked exceptions. We currently have no way to
>    know that our secondary thread failed with this exception. */
>    thread.start();
>    //...}} }
> ```

//5, being sent to the **FileOpener** class at making the secondary thread throw an unchecked, NullPointerException at //2.

A key point to note is the primary thread must be able to determine the status of the secondary thread. This can be difficult particularly when the secondary thread may terminate due to an exception. What if you were writing a mission-critical application? How would you report failures in secondary threads to the calling code? After all, the calling code may be able to recover from the problem and try again. At a minimum, the calling code can inform the user that there is an unrecoverable problem and advise them to take some appropriate action. The worst thing that can happen is the calling code will continue as if the secondary thread completed successfully. This will result in errors occurring later, that will be much more difficult to track down.

So, what do we do? You may notice at //3 we are catching the **FileNot-FoundException** generated at //1. Why not catch it and let it pass through our run() method? The answer to this requires some explanation.

Why Not Use the Traditional Try/Catch Technique?

Our first attempt at solving the multithreaded exception handling problem was to devise a solution using traditional exception handling techniques. We simply placed a try/catch block around the start() method. After all, start() instantiates the secondary thread and calls its run() method and the use of try/catch is the natural way of dealing with exceptions. If the code in run() throws any exceptions we should be able to catch them. Let's see what happens if we try to solve our problem this way. Listing 2 shows some of the code from Listing 1 modified with this dubious idea.

Looking at this code we notice at //1 and //2 we are trying to catch exceptions thrown from the secondary thread by attempting to catch exceptions thrown from the call to start(). Because this code compiles cleanly, your next step may be to get the exception to propagate from the run() method so it can be caught at //2. Listing 3 shows our **Runnable** class modified with the changes you may make to accomplish this.

Instead of catching the **FileNotFoundException** in run() as we did in Listing 1, we have removed the try/catch block to let the caller of the run() method handle it. Because the **FileNotFoundException** is a checked exception, we are required to advertise the fact that our run() method throws this exception by specifying it in the method's *throws* clause at //3.

On closer examination, Listings 2 and 3 are ill-fated for two reasons. First, the code in Listing 3 will not even compile because you are not allowed to throw checked exceptions from the run() method. The reason for this is because an override method can only throw exceptions of the same type of the method being overridden or specializations of those types. In other words, because the run() method of the **Runnable** class does not specify that it throws any checked exceptions, you cannot throw any checked exceptions from your overridden version of run().

The second problem is at //1 and //2 in Listing 2. Even though this code compiles cleanly, it is doomed to fail. Remember that start() instantiates a secondary thread and calls the run() method of the **Runnable** object asynchronously. Exceptions signal back only to some point on the stack of the affected thread. Because start() creates a new stack, the primary thread will never be notified of any exceptions that occur. What the code in Listing 2 is actually doing is catching exceptions that occur when calling start(), not exceptions that occur in the run() method, which is what you are trying to accomplish.

MAKING Try/Catch AROUND START() "WORK"

One way to attempt to solve these problems is by creating a special class that acts like a thread, but also enables us to employ the try/catch model around the start() method for handling exceptions occurring on secondary threads. To accomplish this, we introduce a new class, shown in Listing 4, which will extend java.lang.Thread-Group. ThreadGroup contains a key method, uncaughtException(), which is called on a thread when an exception occurs that is not handled, that is, caught. When the uncaughtException() method ends, the thread is terminated.

To make our try/catch around start() scheme work, one may attempt to extend the **ThreadGroup** class at //1, provide a custom version of the start() method at //2, and override the uncaughtException() method at //4. We called this new class a **ThreadWrapper**. The steps outlined seem necessary so we can intercept the exception occurring on the secondary thread and then have

---

Listing 2. try/catch around start().

```
//...
FileOpener runnable = new FileOpener(this, "dummy.fil");
Thread thread = new Thread(runnable, "Regular Java Thread #1");
try {              //1
   thread.start(); }
catch(FileNotFoundException FileNotFoundExc) { //... } //2
```

Listing 3 Throws clause on public void run().

```
class FileOpener implements Runnable {
//...
public void run() throws FileNotFoundException { //3
     FileReader filReader = new FileReader(fileName);
   //... } }
```

our custom start() method throw it. This will enable the try/catch code from Listing 2 to actually catch the exception that occurred in the secondary thread.

There is one major drawback to the code in Listing 4. This is the use of the join() method at //3. The call to join() is needed in order to support the try/catch technique around the call to start(). The big problem with this is the use of join() effectively makes your code single-threaded again. The join() method will block the main thread until the secondary thread has finished. This completely defeats the purpose of multithreaded programming but was necessary to make the try/catch around start() technique work.

There does not exist a way in Java to use try/catch around your start() method to catch the exceptions thrown from a secondary thread and remain multithreaded. There does, however, exist an elegant way to handle exceptions thrown from secondary threads, that is derived from some of what we have seen so far. A new paradigm for dealing with exceptions is used which builds on the ideas of the JDK 1.1 event model.

LISTENING FOR EXCEPTIONS

As we have seen, the try/catch model does not extend well into a multithreaded scenario. We need a generic mechanism that allows a main thread to have an arbitrary number of concurrently running secondary threads, each with the ability to communicate exceptions to objects that can deal with these exceptions. This mechanism must allow us to catch and propagate both checked and unchecked exceptions. Unchecked exceptions are relatively straightforward, as the compiler does not force us to either catch these or explicitly declare that we are passing them on to our clients. Checked exceptions are more challenging. Although we are required to handle these programmatically, it still may be desirable to pass this information on for possible recovery (or at least soft shutdown).

The Java 1.1 Event Model introduces the notion of listener classes that can register with GUI components to be notified when events occur on those components. If we abstractly consider exceptions to be events, we can extend this paradigm to address our multithreaded exception handling issues. When an exception occurs in a secondary thread, notification could be sent to one or more other objects that are registered as listeners on that thread. Next, we discuss our approach and introduce the classes used to achieve our goal. For a complete solution, we have three fundamental requirements:

- We need a type of thread that is capable of intercepting ALL of its ex-

---

Listing 4. Thread wrapper that uses join().

```
class ThreadWrapper extends ThreadGroup { //1
    private Thread _thread;
    private Thread _sourceThread;        // Thread in which exception occurred
    private Throwable _threadException; // Exception caught by uncaughtException()
    private boolean exceptionThrown = false;

    public ThreadWrapper(Runnable target, String name) {
        super("ThreadWrapper thread group");
        _thread = new Thread(this,target,name); }// Create this thread as a member
                                                 // in our thread group
    public void start() throws CatchableThreadException { //2
        _thread.start();
        try { _thread.join(); } catch (InterruptedException InteruptedExc) {} //3

        if (exceptionThrown)
            throw new CatchableThreadException(_sourceThread,_threadException); }
    public void uncaughtException(Thread sourceThread,
            Throwable threadException) { //4
    /* On return from the join() in start(), we want to rethrow an exception back
    to the calling code for appropriate handling. Save pertinent information,
    and set a boolean to inform start(). */
    _sourceThread = sourceThread;
    _threadException = threadException;
    exceptionThrown = true; } }
```

---

ceptions, both checked and unchecked. This will allow us to consistently and comprehensively alert listeners of exceptions.
- We need a conduit between the secondary thread and one or more listener objects through which we can pass exception information.
- We need a mechanism that allows one or more listener objects to communicate back to the **Runnable** object on the thread where the exception occurred. This could be used to attempt recovery, preserve object state, or to perform some cleanup for soft termination.

THE SmartThread CLASS... A BETTER Thread THAN Thread

To address the first fundamental requirement, we introduce the **SmartThread** class in Listing 5. Like the **ThreadWrapper** class previously discussed, our **SmartThread** class extends **ThreadGroup** at //1. By overriding the **Thread-Group's** uncaughtException() method at //6, the **SmartThread** is able to intercept all unhandled, unchecked, and checked exceptions. The **SmartThread** can then notify all registered listener objects of the exception.

In order for **SmartThread** to notify listener objects of exceptions, it needs to provide an interface for listener objects to register interest. This is done via addThreadExceptionListener() at //4. This method will support multiple listener objects because it is implemented with a Java **Vector**. When the uncaughtException() method is called, it will iterate over the **Vector** of listeners at //7 calling their exceptionOccurred() methods. (The astute reader may observe that addThreadExceptionListener() could also be implemented with a **Multicaster**. We have chosen to use a **Vector** here for simplicity of illustration. However, the final working program implements a **Multicaster**.)

Each registered listener's exceptionOccured() method will be called from //8 with the **Runnable** object the exception occurred in, the thread the exception occurred on, and the exception thrown that was not handled. It is important to pass the thread because one listener could be listening to multiple threads.

Note that **SmartThread** is not truly a thread because it extends **ThreadGroup** by necessity.

It does, however, compose a thread at //2 and //3. In order to avoid the pain of reimplementing the entire thread interface, but still give programmatic access to the composed thread, **SmartThread** provides a thread getter, getThread(), at //5. For example, the following would allow you to change the priority of the thread composed by the **SmartThread** to 1.

```
//...
SmartThread smartThread = new SmartThread(someRunnable,
  "My Smart Java Thread");
smartThread.getThread().setPriority(1);
//...
```

THE ThreadExceptionListener INTERFACE

Exceptions in secondary threads are communicated to listeners through the exceptionOccurred() method, which is defined in the ThreadExceptionListener interface in Listing 6. This addresses our second fundamental requirement.

Classes that wish to be informed of exceptions occurring in other threads should implement this interface. In addition, they should utilize a **SmartThread**, rather than a regular Java **Thread**, because the **SmartThread** class knows how to notify the **ThreadExceptionListener** of exceptions.

Listing 5.   The SmartThread class.

```
/** Class: SmartThread
 This class wrappers the thread class to allow exceptions that are thrown from its
run() method to be caught and passed to a listener object. The wrapper actually is a
subclass of (is-a) ThreadGroup, because we have to override its uncaught Exception()
method. To achieve thread functionality, the wrapper aggregates (has-a) Thread. This
wrapper version is designed to handle multiple asynchronous secondary threads.
The main thread must implement the ThreadExceptionListener interface. Any
exception intercepted in any thread is routed back to the calling code through the
exceptionOccurred() method (defined in the ThreadExceptionListener interface). */
import java.lang.ThreadGroup;
import java.lang.Throwable;
import java.util.Vector;

class SmartThread extends ThreadGroup { //1
    private Runnable _runnable;
    private Thread _thread; //2
    private Vector _exceptionListenerList;

    public SmartThread(Runnable runnable, String name) {
        super("SmartThread thread group");
        _exceptionListenerList = new Vector(2,2);
        _runnable = runnable;
        _thread = new Thread(this, runnable, name);  } //Create this thread as a
            //member in our thread group //3
    public void addThreadExceptionListener(ThreadExceptionListener
                                    exceptionListener) { //4
        _exceptionListenerList.addElement(exceptionListener); }
    public Thread getThread() { //5
        return _thread; }
    public void start() {
        _thread.start(); }
    public void uncaughtException(Thread sourceThread,
      Throwable threadException) { //6
        int numElem = _exceptionListenerList.size();
        for (int i = 0; i<numElem; i++) { //7
            ThreadExceptionListener listener =
                ((ThreadExceptionListener)_exceptionListenerList.elementAt(i));
            listener.exceptionOccurred(_runnable, sourceThread,
                threadException); } } } //8
```

THE ThreadExceptionCleanup INTERFACE

A **ThreadExceptionListener** that wishes to communicate back to the **Runnable** in which the exception occurred, can call its cleanupOnException() method, which is defined in the **ThreadExceptionCleanup** interface in Listing 7. This addresses our third fundamental requirement. **Runnables** should implement this interface to participate in cleanup requests originating from a **ThreadExceptionListener**.

This enables reentry into the **Runnable** object. When an exception is thrown and not handled, and the uncaughtException() method called, you have left your **Runnable** object. This class gives you a way to get back into your **Runnable** object to perform any cleanup or state preservation.

THE CheckedThreadException CLASS

This class allows checked exceptions occurring in a secondary thread to be propagated to listeners in the same manner as unchecked exceptions. Recall that the occurrence of an unhandled unchecked exception results in a direct call to the **SmartThread's** implementation of uncaughtException(). From here it is propagated to listeners via our exceptionOccurred() conduit. Because checked exceptions must be explicitly caught (we can't rethrow them in the run() implementation for reasons discussed earlier), by definition they will never find their way directly to uncaughtException(). We need an indirect way to accomplish this.

CheckedThreadException, shown in Listing 8, extends the unchecked **RuntimeException** class. **CheckedThreadException** is a special exception that allows us to throw checked exceptions from a method without requiring a throws clause. When we want to alert our listeners of the occurrence of a checked exception in a secondary thread, we wrapper this exception in a **CheckedThreadException** and rethrow it. This will result in a call to uncaughtException(), allowing us to propagate both checked and unchecked exceptions through the same interface. The **CheckedThreadException** class also provides access to the original checked exception at //2 and the thread the exception occurred on at //1. This addresses our final fundamental requirement.

PUTTING IT ALL TOGETHER

Using the classes we have introduced, we have modified our initial multithreaded program from Appendix A to effectively deal with the exceptions generated on its secondary threads. The entire modified program is provided in Appendix B with the changes indicated in bold font. Let's now examine the specific areas we modified utilizing our new classes.

Listing 9 shows the modified **FileOpener** class. At //1 you will notice that our **FileOpener** class is implementing our **ThreadExceptionCleanup** interface. This also requires us to implement the cleanupOnException() method at //5. The cleanupOnException() method will be called if an exception is thrown from our **Runnable** object and not handled by that object. We are also utilizing the **CheckedThreadException** class at //4. As discussed, this enables us to throw checked exceptions out of our run() method. We must first catch the checked exception at //3, then wrapper it as an unchecked exception via the **CheckedThreadException** class. The "decoding" of this exception will occur later in the exceptionOccurred() method.

The cleanupOnExeption() method proves to be very useful at //2. Depending on where the exception was thrown from in the run() method, a **BufferedReader** object may have been left open and need to be closed. If the exception was due to a file not found, then the **BufferedReader** would not yet have been opened, as this happens after it is determined that the file was found. However, what if the exception was thrown after //2? If an exception is thrown after //2, the **BufferedReader** is left open and we have created a resource leak. The

---

Listing 6.   The ThreadExceptionListener interface.

```
/* interface: ThreadExceptionListener
This interface defines the method that a class should implement to handle
exceptions that are thrown in its secondary threads. This method will be called
after an exception has occurred in the run() method of a Runnable object, but
before the thread has been terminated. Implementing this method will allow
you to execute code inside of the class that created the secondary thread. You
can then optionally call the cleanupOnException() method of the Runnable. See
the ThreadExceptionCleanup interface for details. */
interface ThreadExceptionListener {
 public void exceptionOccurred(Runnable sourceRunnable, Thread
sourceThread,    Throwable   threadException); }
```

Listing 7.   The ThreadExceptionCleanup interface.

```
/* interface: ThreadExceptionCleanup
This interface defines the method that a class should implement to cleanup for an
object running on a thread after it has thrown an exception and before it is shut
down by the system. This method will be called after an exception has occurred
on a secondary thread, but before the thread has been terminated. Implementing
this method will allow you to execute code inside of your runnable object after an
exception was thrown from its run() method. This method is called from
exceptionOccurred() method of the ThreadExceptionListener class. See the
ThreadExceptionListener interface for details. */
interface ThreadExceptionCleanup {
   public void cleanupOnException(Throwable threadException);
}
```

cleanupOnException() method at //5 is called by exceptionOccurred() in this case to close the **BufferedReader** at //6, prior to this thread shutting down.

This particular example could have been accomplished through the proper use of a *finally* clause, however, in other implementations you may not have a try/catch block to work with because you may not be dealing with checked exceptions, only unchecked exceptions. Therefore, you would not have a try block in which to attach a *finally* clause.

Listing 10 shows the initial changes made to the **PrimaryFrame** class. **PrimaryFrame** now implements the **ThreadExceptionListener** interface at //1. This enables the **PrimaryFrame** class to register itself as a listener of uncaught exceptions occurring on its secondary threads via the addThreadExceptionListener() method shown at //3. However, for all of this to work, you must use the **SmartThread** class instead of the standard Java **Thread** class. This is accomplished at //2.

The last area to examine is the exceptionOccurred() method. Listing 11 shows the implementation of this method and what we do when we are notified of an exception. This method is called after:

- Creating a **SmartThread** class.
- Adding a **ThreadExceptionListener** object.
- Overriding the exceptionOccurred() method in your **ThreadExceptionListener** object.
- An exception is thrown from your **Runnable** object.

We see at //1 the exceptionOccurred() method is provided the necessary information to properly deal with the problem being reported. This method knows the **Runnable** object and the thread the exception occurred on, along with the actual exception thrown. First, we want to know if the exception was really a checked or unchecked exception. At //2 we are checking if the exception is wrappered in a **CheckedThreadException**, indicating the exception we caught is a checked exception. We then "decode" our CheckedThreadException to see what type of checked exception it is at //3. If we determine the exception was a **FileNotFoundException**, we attempt to open another file at //4.

Notice here that we don't register another exception listener. You can register another one, and may want to do so depending on what you would like to happen if this second file is not found. However, be warned that if you register this same class as the listener, you can get the code into an infinite loop fairly easily. It is suggested that in cases like this you register another object as the listener, not the same object. Registering the same object would

Listing 8. The CheckedThreadException class.

```
/* Class: CheckedThreadException
This class is used by a code inside the public void run() method of a Runnable to
enable it to throw a checked exception. Because public void run() does not
advertise that it throws any exceptions, you cannot throw any checked exceptions from
run(). All checked exceptions must be handled in the run() method with a catch()
clause. This class enables you to wrapper your checked exception  inside an
unchecked exception and propagate this exception out of run(). It will then be
caught by uncaughtException() and passed back to the object instantiating
the thread. Two getters are provided to make the additional information
available. */
class CheckedThreadException extends RuntimeException {
    private Thread _sourceThread;     // Thread in which exception occurred
    private Throwable _threadException; // Actual checked exception that was caught

    public CheckedThreadException(Thread sourceThread, Throwable
        threadException) {
        super("Exception caught in thread ["+sourceThread.getName()+"]");

    _sourceThread = sourceThread;
    _threadException = threadException; }
    public Thread getSourceThread() {
        return _sourceThread; } //1
    public Throwable getThreadException() {
        return _threadException; } } //2
```

require some special case code to avoid the infinite loop scenario.

If the exception caught here was not a checked exception, we know it was an unchecked exception. Therefore, we fall to the *else* clause and call back to our **Runnable** object via cleanupOnException() at //5. This is done to free the **BufferedReader** resource allocated in our **Runnable** object. This was discussed earlier in reference to Listing 9.

Figure 1 represents the flow of control through the final version of our program. Note that when execution returns from the uncaughtException method, the thread will terminate immediately.

ALTERNATE SOLUTION

In the course of our research for this article, we uncovered an alternate solution for multithreaded exception handling in Java published in *CurrentProgramming with Java* (Lea, D., Addison–Wesley, 1997) This method is called *Completion Callbacks*. Completion Callbacks involve a predefined interface which an object implements. Secondary threads then must call this interface to indicate success

---

Listing 9. Modified FileOpener class.

```
class FileOpener implements Runnable, ThreadExceptionCleanup { //1
//...
    public void run() {
    try {
        FileReader filReader = new FileReader(fileName);
        bufReader = new BufferedReader(); //2
        String str = bufReader.readLine();
        while (str != null) {
            frame.list2.add(str); //will throw NullPointerException if frame is null
            str = bufReader.readLine(); } }
        catch (FileNotFoundException FileNotFoundExc) { //3
            /* Because we can't throw checked exceptions out of run(), wrapper it
               in an unchecked exception. */
            throw new CheckedThreadException(Thread.currentThread(),
                                             FileNotFoundExc); } //4
        catch (IOException IOExc) {} }
    public void cleanupOnException(Throwable threadException) //5
    {
        frame.status.add("Thread: "+ Thread.currentThread().getName() +
        ". IncleanupOnException "+
            "calling close() on the bufferedReader.");
        try {
            bufReader.close(); //6 }
        catch (IOException IOExc){} } }
```

---

or failure. This allows the object implementing the interface to know whether the secondary thread completed successfully or with an exception.

Completion Callbacks are an excellent approach to the problem addressed in this article but they do require a more tightly coupled relationship between the primary object(s) and the secondary thread(s). In cases where you don't own the code to be executed in the secondary thread, this could be a problem. The Completion Callback solution also requires the developer to take explicit actions to address both checked and unchecked exceptions. By extending **ThreadGroup** and overriding the uncaughtException() method the developer is relieved of some of this work, and is also provided with a uniform and generic way of routing exception information to an object able to process it.

SUMMARY

We have shown a solution to enable Java programs to effectively deal with exceptions occurring in a multithreaded environment. We have done so, in part, by using the listener paradigm devised by the JDK 1.1 event model. We have

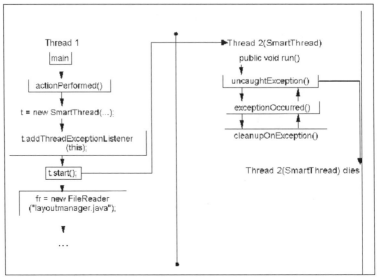

Figure 1. Control flow through final design.

Listing 10. Modified PrimaryFrame class.

```java
class PrimaryFrame extends Frame implements ActionListener,
  ThreadExceptionListener { //1
//...
  public void actionPerformed(ActionEvent event) {
  //...
    if (event.getSource() == startButton1)
    //...
    else if (event.getSource() == startButton2)
    //...

    FileOpener runnable = new FileOpener(primaryFrame, fileName);
    SmartThread smartThread = new SmartThread(runnable, threadName); //2
    status.add("Thread: "+ Thread.currentThread().getName() +
     ". Creating Secondary Thread");

    /* We register this object as an exception listener. This will ensure that
       exceptionOccurred() will be called if ANY exceptions occur on our
       secondary thread. */
    smartThread.addThreadExceptionListener(this); //3

    /* An exception will occur in our runnable sometime after the call to start().
       Because we have passed a file that does not exist a FileNotFoundException
       will be thrown. However, it must be caught inside of run() because run()
       can't throw any checked exceptions. To propagate it out of run() we wrapper it
       in an unchecked Exception so our exceptionOccurred() method will be
       called. */
    smartThread.start();
    //...
```

Listing 11 exceptionOccurred method.

```
class PrimaryFrame extends Frame implements ActionListener,
        ThreadExceptionListener
{
//...
    /* This method is called whenever an exception occurs on a secondary
       thread that this object has been registered a listener for. */
    public void exceptionOccurred(Runnable sourceRunnable,
            Thread sourceThread,
                Throwable threadException) { //1
    /* If we get a CheckedThreadException, we need to figure out exactly what
       type of exception it is. */
    if (threadException instanceof CheckedThreadException) //2
    {
        if (((CheckedThreadException)threadException).getThreadException()
                instanceof FileNotFoundException) { //3
            /* Don't add ourselves as a listener if this file is not found because
               that would cause an infinite loop without some special code. You
               can of course add another object as a listener. Create another
               thread and give it another try with another file. */
            FileOpener runnable2 = new FileOpener(this, "layoutmanager2.java");
                //4
            SmartThread smartThread2 = new SmartThread(runnable2,
                "Smart Java Thread #3");
            smartThread2.start(); } }
        else {
        //Call back into our runnable object to execute some cleanup code before
        this secondary thread is terminated by the system.
        ((FileOpener)sourceRunnable).cleanupOnException(threadException); //5
        } }
```

---

met all of our design goals with our solution and solved all of the problems we
have identified relating to completion callbacks. Our solution solves many of
the problems of dealing with exceptions in a multithreaded environment. This
solution allows you to throw checked and unchecked exceptions from run()
methods at will, while ensuring these exceptions will be caught and communicated to predefined listener objects.

This solution is more involved than a callback solution. The callback solution will work fine for certain cases but does not solve all of the problems
associated with multithread exception handling. The solution we have provided is complete, robust, and follows the common listener paradigm familiar to Java developers. We have also provided a complete running code example
of our final implementation utilizing our classes.

ACKNOWLEDGMENTS

The authors wish to thank Gary Craig, Art Jolin, and Bob Love for their efforts reviewing the first draft of this article and for their many useful comments and suggestions. (Appendices A and B are available at Java Report Online—www.javareport.com)

WRITING MORE COMPLEX SYNCHRONIZATION IN JAVA

BILL LEWIS

THE BASIC SYNCHRONIZATION primitives provided in Java are very easy to use, and well-suited to the majority of situations a programmer sees. In many respects they are simpler, easier to use, and less prone to errors than their counterparts in POSIX threads (Pthreads). They do not, however, cover all situations and extending them is not always obvious.

PROVIDING PROTECTION

The first thing that synchronization techniques must provide is a method to ensure that updates to shared data are done in a correct fashion. In particular, many updates comprise several distinct operations and those operations must be done together, atomically. The canonical example is a program that updates your bank account. In Listing 1, it should be obvious that thread number 1 could overwrite the data that thread number 2 had just saved.

The solution to this is to ensure that each of those operations happen atomically. In Java, this is done with a synchronized method (objects with such synchronization are known as *monitors*). Now the second method will have to wait for the one called first to complete before it can start. The code in Listing 2 will operate correctly.

Pthreads accomplishes the same behavior by using explicit mutex locks. While functionally equivalent, using explicit mutexes suffers from the added complexity of the programmer having to remember which locks to use and to unlock them after

241

use. This is not a big problem, but when writing complex code that has numerous branches and return statements, mistakes do happen (I speak from experience!) and it can be irritating to track down.

Listing 3 shows an example of synchronized updates in Pthreads.

So that's the good part about Java. The bad part is that monitors are not adequate to all situations. There are times when you need different behavior. For example, there are times when you want to do "chained locking." An example of this is where you want to manipulate a linked list and each element on that list is to be locked independently (see Figure 1 and Listing 4).

Listing 1. Non-synchronized updates.

```
        thread 1                              thread 2

void calculateInterest()            void addDeposit(int deposit)
{temp = account.getBalance();       {temp = account.getBalance();
 temp = temp * interestRate;         temp = temp + deposit;
                                     account.putBalance(temp);
 account.putBalance(temp);          } }
```

Listing 2. Synchronized updates.

```
thread 1                                      thread 2

void synchronized calculateInterest()   void synchronized addDeposit(int deposit)
{temp = account.getBalance();           // T2 must wait for T1 to finish
 temp = temp * interestRate;
 account.putBalance(temp);
}
                                        {temp = account.getBalance();
                                         temp = temp + deposit;
                                         account.putBalance(temp);
                                        }
```

Listing 3. Synchronized updates in Pthreads.

```
        thread 1                              thread 2

void calculateInterest()            void addDeposit(int deposit)
{pthread_mutex_lock(&mutex);        // T2 must wait for T1 to finish
 temp = account.getBalance();
 temp = temp * interestRate;
 account.putBalance(temp);
 pthread_mutex_unlock(&mutex);
}
                                    {pthread_mutex_lock(&mutex);
                                     temp = account.getBalance();
                                     temp = temp + deposit;
                                     account.putBalance(temp);
                                     pthread_mutex_unlock(&mutex);
                                    }
```

To do this, you must lock the first element of the list and check to see if the second one is the one you're interested in. If not, you must then lock the next element of the list BEFORE you release the current lock. (If you didn't do this, another thread could change that next element before you got to it.) Clearly, monitors cannot be used in this case. The only way to do chained locking is to have explicit mutexes. Happily, this is not particularly difficult to implement. A simple mutex class is shown in Listing 5. (Note that this is a variant of the "BusyFlag" class found in *Java Threads* by Scott Oaks and Henry Wong, (O'Reilly & Associates, 1997).

This class is functionally identical to Pthread mutexes: The first thread that calls lock() on a Mutex gets ownership, any subsequent threads will have to wait until it calls unlock(). There is no guarantee that a waiting thread will be the next one to get ownership and if the owner calls lock() a second time, it will deadlock. A sufficiently intelligent compiler could optimize this down to be identical to Pthread mutexes with identical performance. (I do not know of any

POSIX Threads and Java Threads

POSIX threads (Pthreads) is part of the IEEE/ISO standard for portable operating systems (1003.1). It was agreed on by about a hundred highly experienced programmers representing all major software companies. It defines a basic interface for threads in C, supplying little more than the absolute minimally sufficient functionality. As such, its semantics are simple and clear, but more sophisticated programs require more programmer effort. Pthreads were ratified in June '95 and are implemented (or being implemented) on almost all UNIX systems, Linux, VMS, AS/400, and some effort has been made to implement most of it on top of Win32.

Java is a sophisticated, high-level language designed to ease the programmer's burden at the cost of performance and memory. C (and thus Pthreads) is just the opposite—low-level, simple, it allows optimal performance and minimal memory requirements at the expense of programming effort and complexity.

A successful call to pthread_mutex_lock() requires a single instruction. For Java to do the same requires many. Pthreads handles signals, allows realtime scheduling, requires active memory management, and offers few fancy features. Java is the opposite.

The actual functionality of Pthreads and Java threads is almost identical, and any program you can write in one, you can write in the other (some issues exist concerning efficiency and bounded-time termination). Pthreads are generally the native programming interface on the operating system and Java threads are often implemented using Pthreads.

In terms of designing programs, all of the same issues exist for both. Understanding concurrency in Java is the same as understanding concurrency in Pthreads, only the APIs are different.

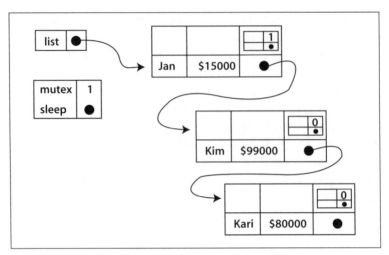

Figure 1. Chained locking.

compilers sufficiently intelligent, however, and the best code currently imagin-able would be many times slower than Pthreads. A native mutex class would be a very good thing.)

Such a mutex object could now be embedded into our list object and used for chained locking.

WHEN TO RUN

The other thing that synchronization must provide for is the ability to tell a thread when to sleep and when to wake up. For example, if you want to pull items off of a list for processing, you need to know when that list has items on it. When empty, you want to sleep. When an item appears, you want to wake up to process it. The Java primitives **wait()** and **notify()** provide exactly this functionality. In the produc-er/consumer example shown in Figure 2 and Listing 6, any number of threads may be running the consumer code and producer code. That's the good news.

The bad news is that there's a little problem with this code. Should the consumers be slower at consuming than the producers are at producing, then the list of pend-ing work requests will grow longer and longer and longer. You get the picture.

For a well-running program, this kind of behavior should be avoided. The obvious technique for doing this is to limit the list to some finite size. It's easy enough for the producers to check the length and wait when the list is full. The problem comes when it's time to wake them up (see Listing 7).

You see, in this design, both consumers and producers will be sleeping on the same synchronized object. It would be unfortunate should a consumer take an item off of the list and wake up another consumer instead of a producer as intended.

Listing 4. **Chained locking in Pthreads.**

```
int find_salary(List l, char *name)
{pthread_mutex_lock(l->lock);
 /* 1st element is a placeholder */
while (!empty(l->next))
{pthread_mutex_lock(l->next->lock);
   pthread_mutex_unlock(l->lock);
   l = l->next;
   if (equal(l->name, name))
   {s = l->salary;
   pthread_mutex_unlock(l->lock);
   return (s); } }
   pthread_mutex_unlock(l->lock);
   return(-1);
}
```

Listing 5. **The Mutex class.**

```
public class Mutex
{Thread owner = null;

public synchronized void lock()
{while (owner != null)
   {try
   {wait();}
   catch (InterruptedException ie) {} // Ignore
     interrupts!
   }
   owner = Thread.currentThread();
   }

public synchronized void unlock()
{owner = null;
notify();
}
}
```

With the right combination of list lengths, number of producers and consumers, this code is likely to be inefficient, and it is even possible that it will deadlock. (This is NOT an obvious situation and requires some careful analysis to figure out. Moreover, it is possible that this program will work well on one platform, while hanging on another. Part of the logic here relies on the order of wake up for sleeping threads, something that is not guaranteed by the JVM. This, by the way, is a good thing, as the programmer should NEVER rely on wake up order.) The solution is simple: consumers should only wake up producers, and producers should only wake up consumers. Unfortunately, the Java method notify() is directly linked to the synchronized object, so there's no way to direct wake ups as we'd like. We could wake up everybody by calling notifyAll(), but that would be abysmally inefficent. We must abandon the Java model once again and implement our own.

CONDITION VARIABLES

A condition variable in Pthreads is basically a queue for sleeping, threads which are independent of the locking mechanism. It operates exactly like Java wait() does, save that it is not dependent on the locked object. Just like Java, it is used by a thread, which locks a region, tests a condition, then releases that lock and goes to sleep (should the condition be false). On wake up, the lock is reacquired and the thread then repeats the test.

Because POSIX CVs are independent of the specific mutex, it is possible to have multiple CVs use the same mutex and wake up only the desired threads (either consumers or producers). Implementing a CV in Java is not particularly difficult, but there are a few subtle nuances. Listing 8 shows how we'll write our producer/consumer using CVs. This code is perfectly correct and will work correctly on all platforms for any number of producers, consumers, and size limits. Note that we now are forced to use explicit mutexes instead of synchronized methods. The reason is that the data must be protected by the same lock in every instance. If we tried to use synchronized methods, we'd be unable to have our two CVs both release that synchronization.

The CV class (see Listing 9) itself requires just two methods, condWait() (equivalent to Java's wait()) and condSignal() (Java's notify()). (Adding notifyAll() and a timed wait() is a simple exercise left to the reader.) The subtleties are in the cond-Wait() method. The mutex must be released and the thread sent to sleep ATOM-

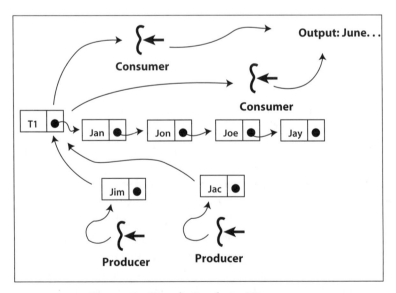

Figure 2. Simple Producer/Consumer.

ICALLY with respect to the condSignal(), hence, the synchronized section. (Exactly the same issue comes up for Java's wait() / notify(). There it's handled internally (see *Java Threads*, p. 75.)

Consider what would happen if these were not done atomically. With a bit of (bad) luck, thread 1 could call condWait(), release the mutex, and at just that instant thread 2 could be running on a different CPU. Thread 2 could then lock the mutex, change the condition to true, and call condSignal(). Thread 1 would not yet be asleep, so it wouldn't be awakened. It would subsequently go to sleep even though the condition is now true, and the wake up from thread 2 would be lost. Having done its work, thread 2 might never send another wake up (it might be waiting for thread 1 to finish!) and the entire program would hang. This would be a bad thing. It's known as the "Lost Wake up Problem."

The synchronized section in condWait() does not include the relocking of the mutex. This is also essential. Consider what could happen if it did (see Listing 10).

Listing 6. "Simplistic" Producer/Consumer.

```
public class Consumer implements Runnable
{Workpile workpile;
   Server server;

   public void run()
   {Item item;

   try
      {while (true)
         {synchronized (workpile)
            {while (workpile.empty())
                workpile.wait();      // Sleep while empty
                    item = workpile.remove(); }
                    server.process(item);} }
   catch (InterruptedException ie)
   {System.exit(1);} }

   public class Producer implements Runnable
   {Workpile workpile;
   Server server;

   public void run()
   {Item item;

   try
      {while (true)
         {item = server.getFromNet();
         synchronized (workpile)
            {workpile.add(item);
         workpile.notify();      // Wakeup one sleeper (if any) } } }
         catch (InterruptedException ie) {System.exit(1);} } } }
```

Running the producer/consumer code above, thread 1 might call condWait(), release the mutex and go to sleep. Thread 2 could then lock the mutex, call condSignal(), waking up thread 1. Thread 1 could then reacquire the synchronized section for the CV and call mutex.lock(). At this time, thread 2 has released the mutex, hurried back to the top, and relocked that mutex. Thread 1 would have to go to sleep to wait for thread 2 to release it. Thread 2, however, needs to call condSignal() before it releases the mutex. To run condSignal(), it needs to obtain the synchronization for the CV, which is still held by thread 1. Deadlock. (By moving the condSignal() call in the P/C code outside of the call to mutex.unlock(), this particular version of the problem could be resolved, but slightly more subtle versions of it would still be there for other situations. Consider having two consumers and one producer.)

Now that we have the POSIX-style primitives in our **Mutex** and **Condition-Var** classes, we can build anything at all quite simply. We'll finish by building a

Listing 7. "Realistic" Producer/Consumer (bad!).

```java
public class Consumer implements Runnable
{Workpile workpile;
 Server server;

public void run()
   {Item item;

   try
      {while (true)
      {synchronized (workpile)
      {while (workpile.empty())
         workpile.wait();   // Sleep while empty
      item = workpile.remove();
      workpile.notify();     // Wakeup a producer?! }
      server.process(item); } }
   catch (InterruptedException ie){System.exit(1);} } }

public class Producer implements Runnable
{Workpile workpile;
   Server server;

   public void run()
   {Item item;

   try
   {while (true)
   item = server.get();
      synchronized (workpile)
      {while (workpile.full())
         workpile.wait(); // Sleep while full
      workpile.add(item);
      workpile.notify();         // Wakeup a consumer?! } } }
   catch (InterruptedException ie) {System.exit(1);} } }
```

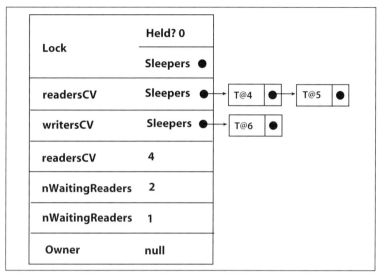

Figure 3. Readers/Writer lock structure.

Wake up order

It is often a concern of beginning programmers to know which thread will run when. When there are two threads blocked on the same mutex, which one will get that mutex when it's released? When many threads are waiting on a condition variable, what order will they run it, should they all be woken up at once?

The answer to all of these questions is the same: "You don't know, and you don't care!" (Folks doing realtime programming is a whole different kettle of fish, and I am not a realtime Trout.) The point is that a correctly written program will operate correctly no matter what order the threads run in. If there are two threads both processing requests, it doesn't make any difference which thread does the processing. It only matters that the answer is correct.

In the extreme case, it is not even possible to assure scheduling order on MP machines without additional hardware. The JavaVM does not specify wake up order for threads sleeping on wait() calls. In the "Realistic Producer/Consumer (bad!)" example, it does not define which thread will wake up when. As a matter of fact, on my single CPU SS4, using Java 1.02, that example runs flawlessly. On another platform it may not.

So, write your program so that no matter which threads are sleeping, the ones you wake up will always be the correct ones. If this means you have to use the ConditionVar class above, so be it. If you find yourself asking "What order will these threads wake up in?" you're making a mistake!

Listing 8. "Realistic" Producer/Consumer (good).

```
public class Consumer implements Runnable
{Workpile workpile;
   Server server;

   public void run()
   {Item item;

   while (true)
   {workpile.mutex.lock();
   {while (workpile.empty())
      {workpile.consumerCV.condWait(workpile.mutex);}
      item = workpile.remove();
      workpile.producerCV.condSignal();     // Normally unlock first
      workpile.mutex.unlock();}
      server.process(item);}}}

public class Producer implements Runnable
{Workpile workpile;
   Server server;

   public void run()
   {Item item;

   while (true)
   {item = server.get();
   workpile.mutex.lock();
   {while (workpile.full())
    {workpile.producerCV.condWait(workpile.mutex);}
      workpile.add(item);
      workpile.consumerCV.condSignal();  // Normally unlock first
      workpile.mutex.unlock(); } } } }
```

Listing 9. try/catch around start().

ConditionVar class.

```
public class ConditionVar
{Thread owner = null;

 public void condWait(Mutex mutex)
 {try
    {synchronized (this)
   {mutex.unlock();
    wait(); } }
 catch (InterruptedException ie) {}
  // Allow Spurious interrupts
 finally {mutex.lock();}
  // *Always* lock before returning!
 }

 public synchronized void condSignal()
 {
 notify(); }}
```

Listing 10. ConditionVar method (bad!).

```
public void condWait(Mutex mutex) throws
  InterruptedException
  {
    synchronized (this)
    {mutex.unlock();
       wait();
       mutex.lock(); } }
```

---

readers/writer lock. This is a synchronization variable, which will allow any number of threads to obtain a lock to read data at the same time but restricts changing that data to a single thread at a time. This is useful for things like the New York telephone directory assistance department.

Every day, thousands of people want to find phone numbers. It takes a little while to look up each one, and it would be absurd to force everyone to wait in a queue to look them up one by one. At the same time, it wouldn't work for lookups to occur while the monthly update was going on. So, with a readers/writer lock, 10,000 operators can obtain a read lock, and do a lookup. When it's time to update the book, the IR department will request a write lock. At that point, all new requests for read locks will have to wait. When the last current reader is finished, the write lock will be granted to IR, who will do the update. When complete, the write lock will be released and all the waiting readers will then be able to obtain their read locks and continue.

Here's the code (see Listing 11; also Figure 3). Using CVs, it's short, simple, and straight-forward. It's particularly interesting to contrast this code to the implementation of readers/writer locks which Oaks and Wong show in their book, done without using CVs.

Two comments about this Listing 11. First, readers may suffer starvation should there be a continuous stream of writers. Second, writers cannot request the lock recursively (i.e., if one thread calls writeLock() twice in a row, it will deadlock). The first bears some serious consideration. You could redefine the semantics of RWLocks to ensure some sense of "fairness." However, the use of RWLocks is predicated on the assumption that there will be extended periods with many readers and no writers at all. If your program does not behave like this, it doesn't make sense to be using RWLocks! In that (unusual) case, you should be considering your choice of algorithm carefully, and you may well need to write your own, specialized form of synchronization. Sometimes the correct answer is "Don't do that!"

The second issue is more trivial. Making the write lock recursive is a fairly simple task (left to the reader as an exercise). The motivation for making it recursive demands scrutiny. My personal feeling (widely held, though not universal) is that you should be writing your code so this situation never occurs. (Recursive locks

of any kind are never "required," and are generally the result of poor programming design earlier in the process. There's a better way to do it.)

Listing 11.   Readers/Writer Lock Class.

```
public class RWLock
{ Thread owner = null;     // Only writers set this.
   int nCurrentReaders = 0;
   int nWaitingWriters = 0;
   int nWaitingReaders = 0;
   Mutex m = new Mutex();
   ConditionVar readersCV = new ConditionVar();
   ConditionVar writersCV = new ConditionVar();

   public void readLock()
   {Thread t = Thread.currentThread();

   m.lock();
   nWaitingReaders++;
   while ((owner != null) || (nWaitingWriters > 0))
   {readersCV.condWait(m);}
   nWaitingReaders—;
   nCurrentReaders++;
   m.unlock(); }

   public void writeLock()
   {
   m.lock();
   nWaitingWriters++;
   while ((owner != null) || (nCurrentReaders > 0))
      {writersCV.condWait(m);}
   nWaitingWriters—;
   owner = Thread.currentThread();
   m.unlock(); }

   public void unlock()
   {
   m.lock();
   if (owner != null)
      {owner = null;}
   else
      nCurrentReaders—;

   if ((nWaitingWriters > 0) && (nCurrentReaders == 0))
      {writersCV.condSignal();}
   else
      if ((nWaitingWriters == 0) &&
        (nWaitingReaders > 0))
        {readersCV.condBroadcast();}
   m.unlock(); } }
```

USER INTERFACES

CONSTRUCTING MODULAR USER INTERFACES IN JAVA

JOHN HUNT

A NYONE WHO has ever tried to construct modular, object-oriented user interfaces using the AWT knows how hard it can be. The result can easily end up being difficult to debug, complex to understand and maintain, and certainly not reusable (except by cutting and pasting!). However, huge benefits can be obtained by separating out the user interface from the application code. This has been acknowledged for a long time and the Java Development Kit included the Observer class and the Observable interface to support this. However, with the addition of the delegation event model in the JDK 1.1, the potential for separating the view and control parts of the interface was provided. This allows the separation of the interface from the control elements (i.e., what to do when a user presses a button) and from the application code. Such a separation is often referred to as a model-view-controller architecture (or just as the MVC for short). The MVC originated in Smalltalk, but the concept has been used in many places. This article considers what the MVC is, why it is a good approach to GUI construction, and what features in Java support it. It then describes a GUI application which has been built using the MVC architecture. The source code for this application is provided as an appendix.

WHAT IS THE MODEL-VIEW-CONTROLLER ARCHITECTURE?

With the advent of JDK 1.1, a new event model was introduced into Java. This event model is much cleaner than the previous approach and can result in simpler, clearer, and more maintainable code. The introduction of this event model, along with existing Java facilities, allows the construction of modular user interfaces. In particular, it allows the separation of the display of information from the control or the user input to that display, as well as from the application. This separation is not a new idea, and it allows the construction of GUI applications that mirror the Model-View-Controller architecture. The intention of the MVC architecture is the separation of the user display from the control of user input as well as from the underlying information model as illustrated in Figure 1 (see "A Cookbook for Using the Model-View Controller User Interface Paradigm in Smalltalk-80," by G.E. Krashner and S.T. Pope in *JOOP*, 1(3), 1988). There are several reasons why this is useful:

- Reusability of application and/or user interface components
- Ability to develop the application and user interface separately
- Ability to inherit from different parts of the class hierarchy
- Ability to define control style classes that provide common features separately from how these features may be displayed.

This means that different interfaces can be used with the same application—without the application knowing about it. It also means that any part of the system can be changed without affecting the operation of the others. For example, the way that the graphical interface (the look) displays the information could be changed without modifying the actual application or how input is handled (the feel). Indeed, the application need not know what type of interface in currently connected to it at all.

WHAT JAVA FACILITIES SUPPORT THE MVC?

Java provides two facilities that together allow the separation of the application, interface, and control elements. These are:

- *The observer/observable model.* This allows application programs and user interfaces to be loosely coupled.

- *The delegation event model.* This provides listeners that act as controllers handling various events which may occur.

In JDK 1.0 and 1.0.2, Java could only really support the Model-View relationship, which used the dependency mechanism implemented by the Observable class and the Observer interface. However, in JDK 1.1, a delegation event mechanism was introduced that allows the controller to be separated from the user inter-

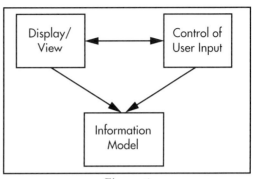

Figure 1.
The Model-View-Controller
architecture.

face. Thus, it is now possible to have a separate model, view, and controller objects. Next, we review these two mechanisms before considering how they are used to implement Java's MVC framework.

OBSERVERS AND OBSERVABLES

In Java, dependency is a relationship that can be used to relate two objects such that as the state of one changes, the state of the other automatically changes in an appropriate manner. In such a relationship we say that one object is dependent on another. The dependency mechanism is implemented in the class Observable within the util package (see *The Java Programming Language,* K. Arnold and J. Gosling, 1996). This class is a direct subclass of Object. This means that any class can inherit from Observable and thus take part in a dependency relationship. In Java terminology the object that is the head of the dependent relationship (i.e., the object on which other objects depend) is referred to as the *observable object*, while the dependent object is referred to as the *observer object.* This is because the observable object allows other objects to observe its current state. An observable object can have zero or more observers, all of which are notified of changes to its state via the notify Observers() method.

The basic implementation inherited from Observable, associates a Vector of other objects with the observable object. This Vector holds the objects that are dependent on the object (collectively, these objects are known as the object's observers "dependents"). For example, in Figure 2 the ObjectA has two observers, ObjectB and ObjectC. The links to the dependent objects are held

by ObjectA in a Vector of observers called obs. The add Observer() "ad-
dDependent/:" message is used to add an object to another object's dependency Vector.

We can use this mechanism to tell one object that another object has changed
in some way. To do this we use two sets of methods. One set is used to state
that something has changed. These are called *changed* methods. The other
set is used to state what type of update is required. These are called *update*
methods. They work as illustrated in Figure 3.

Figure 3 displays the sequence of messages that are sent in response to
the changed messages being sent to an object. That is, when ObjectA is sent,
the setChanged() and notifyObservers() messages (usually by itself) all of
its observers are sent an update() message. Again, from the viewpoint of
ObjectA much of this behavior is hidden.

The other end of this relationship is the Observer object (see Arnold &
Gosling). The Observer interface defines the abstract update method that
must be implemented by objects that wish to take part in a dependency relationship. The actual Observer interface definition is essentially:

```
public interface Observer{
    void update(Observable observable, Object arg);

}
```

As with all interfaces, any concrete class implementing this interface must
provide the body of the update method. Thus, any class implementing this
interface can be guaranteed to work with the notification methods used in an
observer object.

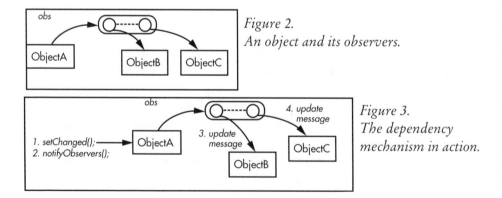

Figure 2.
An object and its observers.

Figure 3.
The dependency
mechanism in action.

The Delegation Event Model

The Java delegation event model introduced the concept of listeners (see "The JDK 1.1's New Delegation Event Model," by J. Sevareid, *Java* Report, April 1997). Listeners are effectively objects that "listen" for a particular event to occur. When it does, they react to it. For example, the event associated with the button might be that it has been "pressed." The listener would then be notified that the button had been pressed and would decide what action to take. This approach involves delegation, because the responsibility for handling an event generated by one object may belong to another object.

The delegation model changes the way in which users create GUIs. Using this model they define the graphic objects to be displayed, add them to the display, and associate them with a listener object. The listener object then handles the events that are generated for that object.

For example, if we wish to creat a button that will be displayed on an interface and allow the user to exit without using the border frame buttons, then we would need to create a button and a listener for the action on the button. For example,

```
exitButtonController = new ExitButtonController();
exitButton = new Button("Exit");
exitButton.addActionListener(exitButtonController);
```

This code creates a new user-defined listener object, ExitButtonController, then creates a new button (with a label exit). It then adds the exitButtonController as the action listener for the button, i.e., it is the object that will listen for action events (e.g., the button being pressed). The ExitButtonController class (presented next) provides a single instance method actionPerformed() that will initiate the System.exit(0) method.

Figure 4 illustrates the resulting class and instance structures and you can see from this diagram, the separation of interface and control is conceptually very clean.

The ExitButtonController class definition is now presented. There is, of course, no reason why you should call such a class controller, you could equally have called it an ExitButtonEventListener. However, the Listeners are the interface definitions. By choosing a different type of name, we make it clear we are talking about the classes intended to provide the execution control:

```
class ExitButtonController implements ActionListener {
```

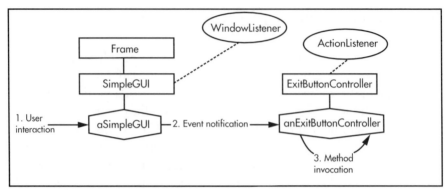

Figure 4.
The class and object diagram using the delegation event model.

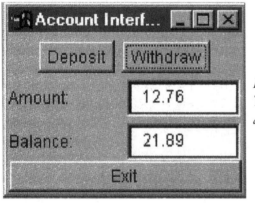

Figure 5.
The GUI for the account application.

```
public void actionPerformed(ActionEvent event) {
    System.exit(0);}
}
```

THE MVC IN JAVA

The application we will construct is illustrated in Figure 5. This application allows a user to keep track of his or her current bank balance. This is done using two buttons which indicate whether the amount input should be treated as a deposit or a withdrawal. The amount to be used in the current transaction is input by the user in the first of the text fields, while the current

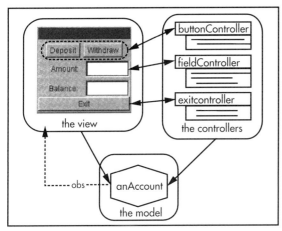

Figure 6.
The MVC architecture
as it is implemented by the
account application.

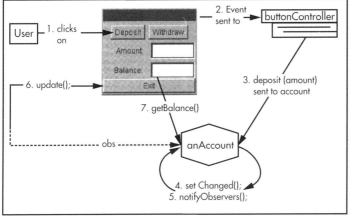

Figure 7.
Interaction in
the MVC.

balance is displayed in the second text field. The user can exit from the application in a controlled manner using the Exit button.

The overall structure of the application is shown in Figure 6. Note that the interface object and the controller objects have direct links between them. However, although the interface and the controller objects have links to the application (anAccount), the application knows nothing directly about the interface or the controllers. This means that the application is independent of the interface and its controllers and may actually have various different interfaces associated with it. One of the advantages of this approach is that any one of the three elements can be modified without the need to change the others.

The system interaction is illustrated in Figure 7. This figure illustrates the various messages sent once a user clicks on the deposit button. There are several points you should note about this example:

- Neither the display nor the controller hold on to the balance. It is obtained from the account whenever it is needed.
- The controller relies on the delegation event model to determine that it should do something.
- When the controller asks the model to change, it doesn't tell the display—the diplay learns about the change through the observer/observable mechanism.
- The account is unaware that the message deposit(amount); came from the controller. Thus, any object could send a deposit message and the account would still inform its dependents about the change.

EVENT LISTENERS

In this system, the controllers are registered as event listeners for the various input elements on the interface. This means that the buttonController deals with inputs associated with the deposit and withdraw buttons, and in turn, the fieldController deals with inputs to the amount field (when return is pressed). Finally, the exitController deals with inputs associated with the exit button.

OBSERVERS AND OBSERVABLES

Figure 6 shows that there is no direct link from the account object to the interface. However, the dependency mechanism defined by Java can be used to inform any object interested in the state of the account object that a change has occurred. Thus, the interface object can register itself as an observer of the account object. Then when a deposit or withdrawal is made, the account object can inform its observers that its balance has changed and they should update themselves. In this way, the interface object can be told when to update its balance display, without the account object knowing that it even exists.

FRAMES, PANELS, AND LAYOUT MANAGERS

The interface object consists of a number of objects (such as a frame) and panels, as well as graphic components such as buttons and text fields. In turn, layout managers are used to control the way in which these objects are arranged within the window frame. An interesting point to note is that the exit button controller is used without any modification from previous examples. In addition, the abstract `buttonController` class (from which the `buttonPanelController` class inherits) is a reusable class for any object acting as a controller within an MVC style architecture.

THE APPLICATION CODE

The application source code is provided as an annotated appendix, which can be found online (www.sigs.com/jro). The instance diagram which reflects the instantiation of the application is presented in Figure 8. The dashed boxes indicate the relationship between the source code and concepts such as model, view, and controller. Note that this application (like many applications) has a view made up of other views, each with its own controller. Of course, if this was a real application we might well have very many classes representing the application, rather than just the single class presented here.

DISCUSSION

I have tried to describe a way of constructing graphical user interface applications (and, of course, applets) that are robust, principled, and reusable. It al-

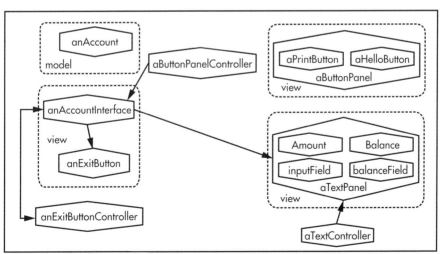

Figure 8.
The instance structure of the application.

lows the various classes to inherit from different parts of the class hierarchy, to implement different interfaces, and to provide clearly defined functionality; all of which lead to clearer, more comprehensible code. Such an approach allows GUI to be structured in an object-oriented manner. It would, of course, be possible to place all of the application within a single class. This class would hold the application code, the window definition, and the event handling code. However, we would have lost the following advantages:

- Reusability of parts of the system
- The ability to inherit from different parts of the class hierarchy
- Modularity of system code
- Resilience to change
- Encapsulation of the application

Although these issues might not be a problem for an application as simple as the one presented here, for real-world systems they would certainly be significant. I hope that you are now aware of the benefits of adopting the MVC architecture, and will try to adopt this approach in your own systems.

Appendix A: The Source Code

The classes defined are: AccountInterface, Button Controller, TextController, ExitButtonController, ButtonPanel Controller, ButtonPanel, TextPanel, and Account. Each of these is considered. The complete documentation can be found on jro online (www.sigs.com/jro).

JFC's Swing, Part 1
Model/View/Controller

David Geary

T HIS THE FIRST first in a series of articles focusing on the Swing components that will be released as part of the Java Foundation Classes in JDK 1.2. I'll review the underlying infrastructure for the Swing components, in addition to some of the components Swing has to offer, in my next few installments. This month, after a brief history of the Java Foundation Classes, I'll discuss Swing's implementation of the Model/View/Controller (MVC) architecture.

The Java Foundation Classes

In addition to being a vast improvement over its predecessor, the 1.1 AWT lays the foundation for one of the most visible core Java APIs: Foundation Classes (JFC). The JFC consists of the 1.1 (and later) AWT, the Swing components, the 2D API, and the Accessibility API.

History of the JFC

Back in 1995, no one overestimated the impact that Java was about to have on the modern computing world. As a language originally designed for consumer electronic devices, Java was suddenly catapulted into the stratosphere as the language for developing Web software. Over the next couple of years,

Java would mature quickly; not only the language but also core packages, such as the AWT.

The original AWT was not designed to be a high powered UI toolkit—instead it was envisioned as providing support for developing simple user interfaces for simple applets. The original AWT was fitted with an inheritance-based event model that did not scale well. The AWT also lacked a great many features that one would expect in an object-oriented UI toolkit, for instance: printing support, keyboard navigation, clipboard support, a scroll pane, etc.

The worst blemish for the original AWT, though, was a high incidence of bugs, most of which were related to the AWT's Achilles' heel—its peer-based approach. The peer-based approach employs native components (peers) to adopt native look-and-feel. Additionally, the peer approach afforded the AWT a quick time to market, because peer functionality did not have to be rewritten in Java. The downside of peers is that it is incredibly difficult to maintain them across different platforms. Instead of implementing badly needed new components, AWT engineers were mired in bug fixing native peers in C++. It was apparent that the peer-based approach did not scale well, and in order to support sophisticated applications, an alternative would have to be found.

The AWT was hurting, and it was beginning to show; Third parties were coming up with their own toolkits that provided more solid functionality than the AWT offered. One of those toolkits was Netscape's Internet Foundation Classes, a nice set of lightweight classes loosely based on concepts from NEXTSTEP's user interface classes. The IFC was peerless and outshined the AWT in many respects.

Realizing that the Java community was likely to split over a standard user interface toolkit, JavaSoft struck a deal with Netscape to implement the Java Foundation Classes (Sun and Netscape are also working with Apple and IBM on the JFC). Netscape developers have worked with AWT engineers to implement much of the IFC's functionality into lightweight Swing components. Additionally, JavaSoft provides a migration guide from the IFC to the JFC (see Sun's JFC Web site).

What is the JFC?

The Java Foundation Classes consists of the following APIs:

- 1.1 (and beyond) AWT
- Swing components

- Java 2D API
- Accessibility API

The core of the JFC is the 1.1 AWT. The AWT already provides some JFC features, such as:

- Delegation event model
- Lightweight components
- Clipboard and data transfer support
- Printing and mouseless operation

SWING

Swing* is a collection of lightweight components built on top of the AWT. Swing provides a wealth of components, such as:

- Borders
- Buttons
- ComboBoxes
- Icons
- Menus
- Scrollbars
- Scrolling support
- Tabbed panes
- Tables

Lightweight components are peerless and are rendered in their container's real estate. As a result, lightweights are less resource-intensive than their heavyweight counterparts and can also be transparent. All Swing components are lightweights.

SWING AND MODEL/VIEW/CONTROLLER

We've discussed MVC in this column before (see "Model/View/Controller," *Java Report,* Jan. 1997) where a simple MVC implementation was discussed. Our goal here is not to focus on MVC itself, but rather on how it is implemented in Swing.

---

*Not an acronym

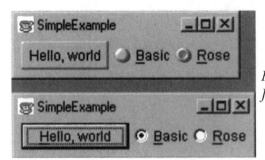

Figure 1.
JFC's pluggable look and feel.

PLUGGABLE LOOK-AND-FEEL

One of the most touted features of Swing components is their pluggable look-and-feel. All Swing components have the ability to take on different visual representations at runtime. For example, see Figure 1—an application that changes the look-and-feel of a button.

MVC

The ability to swap look-and-feels is the result of an underlying implementation of the MVC pattern. MVC divides software into three basic components:

- Model—maintains state information
- View—visual representation of the model (look)
- Controller—handles events (feel)

The look-and-feel of each component is encapsulated in view and controller classes. Many different types of views (looks) and controllers (feels) may be implemented for a single model. Each of the three objects in the MVC triad has specific areas of responsibility.

The model is charged with the envious task of simply tracking state information. For instance, the model associated with a Swing button maintains whether or not the button is currently pressed. Models also maintain lists of event listeners. When something in the model changes, a `ChangeEvent` is typically sent to all listeners interested in changes to the model.

Views are tasked with the more ambitious job of visually representing the model's state. A button's view, for example, is responsible for painting the button itself, both pressed and inset. Views are notified when changes occur to the model and must update themselves accordingly.

Finally, controllers listen for events, and react to them. From here out, I'll use the term listener instead of controller; event listeners in the AWT's dele-

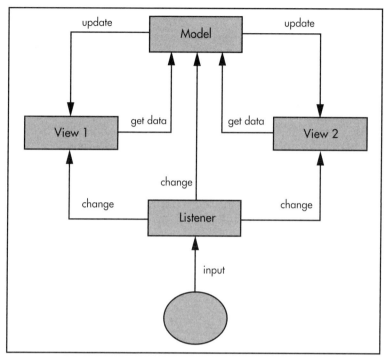

Figure 2. MVC communication.

gation event model are analagous to MVC's controllers. Buttons, for instance, fire change, item, and change events, and provide methods to register listeners for each type of event.

Figure 2 shows the flow of communication between a model, a listener, and one or more views. Input is detected by the listener, which then manipulates the model and/or its views. Changes to the model result in updates to the views.

Separating the responsibilities for views, models, and listeners results in objects that can be built from interchangeable parts. A button, for instance, may be fitted with a basic (Win95) type of view, a Macintosh view, or even a custom view. Swing provides the mechanisms for modifying the look-and-feel of a single component or all components recusively contained in a container.

JCOMPONENT

All Swing components ultimately extend Jcomponent. Jcomonent, in turn, extends java.awt.Container—as a result, Swing components are lightweight AWT containers. Jcomponent takes care of some housekeeping chores for all Swing components:

- Maintains listeners: Ancestor, PropertChange, and VetoableChange listeners
- Ability to set UI
- ToolTop
- Debug graphics

The handy features just listed are available with any extension of Jcomponent. By merely specifying a tooltip string, a Jcomponent can be fitted with a tooltip. Debug graphics slows graphical operations flashing intermittently while giving you the option to log information to a file.

Swing implements a common variation of the MVC architecture where view and listener pairs are combined in a look-and-feel module referred to simply as a ui. All Swing components delegate their look-and-feel to a ui, in much the same way that AWT components delegate their event handling to a layout manager.

The JComponent's ability to set its ui is the most interesting feature from our perspective, and is accomplished by invoking Jcomponent.setUI(ComponentUI).

ComponentUI

ComponentUI is a Swing interface whose methods are listed in Table 1. ComponentUI is responsible for painting a representation of a JComponent. An extension of ComponentUI overrides paint(Graphics, JComponent), and paints a representation of the component into the graphics it is passed. Component UIs are also responsible for computing the minimum, maximum, and preferred size of the Jcomponent of the microsecond.

The install()/deinstall() methods are used to inform a Component UI that it has been installed as some component's ui. ComponentUI extentions typically override installUI()/deinstallUI() to perform installation/deinstallation functionality, such as the registration and subsequent removal of event listeners to the JComponent at hand.

UI Factory

Swing components, meaning extensions of JComponent, obtain their ui through a UI factory when they are constructed. A UI factory typically creates ui objects that conform to a specific look-and-feel. Changing the UI fac-

Table 1. Component UI Interface.

Method	Description
void install UI(JComponent)	*this* ComponentUI installed as component's UI
void deinstallUI(JComponent)	*this* ComponentUI is no longer component's UI
paint(Graphics, JComponent)	paint into Graphics, representing component
Insets getInsets(JComponent)	return insets associated with component
Dimension getMaximumSize(JComponent)	return maximum size for component
Dimension getMinimumSize(JComponent)	return minimum size for component
Dimension getPreferredSize(JComponent)	return preferred size for component

tory results in changes to the look-and-feel of all objects subsequently created. As we've already seen, the ui for a single component can also be modified by invoking JComponent.setUI(ComponentUI).

A SIMPLE EXAMPLE

Listing 1 (see Listing 1 at end of chapter) is an example application that comes with the Swing release—Figure 1 shows the application in action. The key to the application is the code that handles radio button events by changing the ui of all the components in the application.

```
class RadioListener implements ActionListener {
    Pulic void actionPerformed(ActionEvent e) {
    String factoryName = null;

If (e.getActionCommand() == rose) {
            FactoryName = "com.sun.java.
            swing.rose.RoseFactory";
    }else{
            factoryName = "com.sun.java.
            swing.basic.BasicFactory"; }
```

```
try{
UIManager.setUIFactory(factoryName,
        (Container)frame);
        frame.pack();
}catch (ClassNotFoundException cnf){
System.err.println("could not load
Factory: "+ factoryName);
    }
  }
}
```

When a radio button is selected, the appropriate UI Factory is set for the frame. Setting the UI Factory causes the frame to fetch new ui objects from the UI Factory for all components residing in the frame. The RoseFactory churns out ui objects that have a Rose look-and-feel, while the BasicFactory outputs ui objects with a basic (Win95) look-and-feel.

It's a simple matter to implement a custom look-and-feel for a Swing component. In fact, it's such a simple matter that we're going to modify the application in Listing 1 so that it has a third ui to choose from: the Flat UI. We will implement a custom ui for buttons and then allow the button's ui to be set to the custom ui. You can see the modified application in Figure 3.

Implementing a Custom Look-And-Feel

Modifications to the original application are shown in Listing 2 (see Listing 2 at end of chapter). The first thing we do is create a FlatButton and a FlatUI, whose implementations we'll discuss shortly. An extra JradioButton is created in the SimpleExample constructor for the flat ui option. The radio button and the flat button are added to the SimpleExample panel.

Next up are the implementations of the FlatButton and FlatUI classes. FlatButton is straightforward—it is an extension of Jbutton that sets its tool tip text (just for fun) and constructs a FlatUI. Because JComponent.setUI() is a protected method, we relax the access to public for the setUI() method

Figure 3.
Adding a custom look and feel.

by overriding setUI() in FlatButton (methods can be overriden to be more pulic but not more private).

FlatUI implements ButtonUI, which is an extension of ComponentUI. FlatUI doesn't really have anything to do when it is installed or deinstalled as a component's ui, but it overrides the install/deinstall methods anyway so that we can see when the methods are invoked.

FlatUI takes care of painting a representation of the button by drawing a border around the edge of the button, and drawing the button's text centered in the button.

Notice that the event handling code for the flat radio button invokes JComponent.setUI() to set the ui for the button, instead of installing a factory, as is the case with the other two look-and-feels. Because we don't have a factory for our flat ui objects, we just set the button's ui directly.

ORCHESTRATING INPUT

Listing 3 (see Listing 3 at end of chapter) is a modified FlatUI that paints the button's border red when the mouse is pressed in the button and repaints the border black when the mouse is clicked. To accomplish this sleight of hand, FlatUI adds a mouse listener to the button when it is installed as the button's ui. When deinstalled, the listener is removed from the button.

In general, Jcomponents that are registered with a ui should be unchanged by the ui itself—the component after deinstallation should be indentical to the component just before installation. Therefore, we are sure to remove the event listener in the deinstall() method.

Notice that there is a clear distinction between event handling functionality and responsibilities that involve painting the ui. It is often acceptable to merge event handling into a ui class, and therefore merge the view and listener responsibilities, as we have done with the FlatUI class. On the other hand, we can easily encapsulate the listener responsibilities into a separate class as Listing 4 (see Listing 4 at end of chapter) shows.

SHOULD LISTENERS BE SEPARATED FROM UIS?

We've seen two ways to implement the UI for our flat button. One approach merges the listener functionality with the UI class, while the other encapsulates listener responsibilities in a separate class. The question is: Which approach is the best?

As with most things, it's difficult to state dogmatically that one approach is superior to another in any given situation. The best we can do is look at the trade-offs imposed by the two approaches.

Encapsulating event handling in a separate class results in event handling functionality that is available for others to use. Event handling code that is fused into a UI class is impossible to reuse without reusing the UI class.

On the other hand, it is often the case that UI classes and their event handling functionality are intimately tied to each other. For example, FlatUIListener maintains a reference to a FlatUI, and invokes FlatUI methods in response to mouse input. As a result, FlatUI and FlatUIListener are tightly coupled, and should probably be integrated into a single UI class.

As a general rule, if event handling functionality can be generalized so that it is not tightly coupled with a specific type of UI class, then it should be separated into its own class. Event handling that is tightly coupled to a specific type of UI class should be merged with the UI class.

Summary

The JFC classes are composed of the 1.1 (and later) AWT, the Swing components, the Java 2D API, and the Java Accessibility API.

Swing components are lightweight components that have pluggable look-and-feels. The pluggable look-and-feel is accomplished with the implementation of MVC architecture, which is part of the Swing infrastructure.

JComponents each have a ui that is created by a UI factory. The UI factory can be reset to produce ui components that conform to a specific look-and-feel, or the ui for individual components may be set.

Implementing a custom look-and-feel for a component involves implementing a ui class that paints the component in a particular manner. The feel is accomplished by event handling code, which can be implemented in the ui class itself or can be delegated to another object.

Implementing event handling code in the UI class itself reduces the chances for reuse of the event handling functionality. However, some UI classes are tightly coupled to their event handling code; in such a case it is often better to merge the event handling functionality into the UI class.

Listing 1.

```
public class SimpleExample extends JPanel{
    static JFrame frame;
    static String basic = new String("Basic");
    static String rose = new String("Rose");

    public SimpleExample() {
super(true);

// Create the buttons.
JButton button = new JButton("Hello, world");
        button.setKeyAccelerator('h'); // for looks only; button does nada

JRadioButton basicButton = new JRadioButton(basic);
basicButton.setKeyAccelerator('b');
basicButton.setActionCommand(basic);
basicButton.setSelected(true);

JRadioButton roseButton = new JRadioButton(rose);
roseButton.setKeyAccelerator('r');
roseButton.setActionCommand(rose);

// Group the radio buttons.
ButtonGroup group = new ButtonGroup();
group.add(basicButton);
group.add(roseButton);
/( Register a listener for the radio buttons.
RadioListener myListener = new RadioListener();
roseButton.addActionListener(myListener);
basicButton.addActionListener(myListener);

add(button);
add(basicButton);
add(roseButton); }

/** An ActionListener that listens to the radio buttons. */
class RadioListener implements ActionListener {
public void actionPerformed(ActionEvent e) {
    String factoryName = null;

    if(e.getActionCommand()== rose) {
      factoryName = "com.sun.java.swing.rose.RoseFactory";
    } else {
      factoryName = "com.sun.java. swing.basic.BasicFactory";
    }

    try {
            UIManager.setUIFactory(factoryName, (Container)frame);
            frame.pack();
        } catch( ClassNotFoundException cnf) {
            System.err.printIn("Could not load factory:" + factoryName); } } }

public static void main(String s[]){
```

(continued)

Listing 1 *(continued)*.

```
WindowListener l = new WindowAdapter(){
        public void windowClosing(WindowEvent e)
        {System.exit(0);}
};

frame  = new JFrame("SimpleExample");
frame.addWindowListener(l);
frame.add("Center", new SimpleExample() };
frame.pack();
```

Listing 2.

```
public class SimpleExample extends
JPanel{
   FlatButton button = new FlatButton("Hello world");
   FlatUI flatUI;
   ...
   static String flat = new String("Flat");
   ...

      public SimpleExample() {
   ...
   JRadioButton flatButton = new JRadioButton(flat);
           flatButton.setKeyAccelerator('f');
   flatButton.setActionCommand(flat);
   ...
   ButtonGroup group = new ButtonGroup();
   ...
   group.add(flatButton);
   ...
   RadioListener myListener = new RadioListener();
   ...
   flatButton.addActionListener(myListener);
   ...
   add(flatButton); }

   class FlatButton extends JButton {
     public FlatButton(String string) {
     setText(string);
     setToolTipText("button tooltip");
      flatUI = new flatUI(); }
     public void setUI(BasicButton UI cui) {
       super.setUI(cui); } }
   class FlatUI implements Button UI {
     public Insets getDefaultPad(AbstractButton ab) {
     return ab.getInsets(); }
     public void installUI(final JComponent jc){
        System.out.println("FlatUI.installUI()");
     }
     public void deinstallUI(JComponent jc) {
        System.out.println("flatUI.deinstallUI()"); }
     public Insets getInsets(JComponent jc) {
```

(continued)

Listing 2. *(continued)*

```
      return new Insets(5,5,5,5); }
   public void paint(Graphics g, JComponent jc) {
      FontMetrics    fm = g.getFontMetrics();
      Dimension      size = jc.getSize();
      Insets         insets = jc.getInsets();

      g.setColor(SystemColor.windowBorder);
      g.drawRect(0,0,size.width-1, size.height-1);

      g.setColor(SystemColor.controlText);
      g.drawstring(((JButton)jc).getText(),
         insets.left, insets.top + fm.getAscent()); }
   public Dimension getPreferredSize(JComponent jc) {
      Graphics g = jc.getGraphics();
      FontMetrics fm = g.getFontMetrics();
      Dimension rval = new Dimension();
      Insets insets = jc.getInsets();

      rval width = fm.stringWidth(((JButton)jc).getText()) +
            insets.left  + insets.right;
      rval.height = fm.getHeight() + insets.top  + insets.bottom;
      return rval; }
   public Dimension getMaximumSize(JComponent jc){
      return getPreferredSize(jc); }
   public Dimension getMinimumSize(JCompenent jc) {
      return getPreferredSize(jc); } }

class RadioListener implements ActionListener {
   public void actionPerformed(ActionEvent e) {
      String factoryName = null;

      if(e.getActionCommand() == flat) {
            button.setUI(flatUI);
         frame.pack();
         return; }
   ... }
   ... }
 ... }
```

Listing 3.

```
class FlatUI implements ButtonUI{
   final int RAISED=0, INSET=1, NONE=3;

   MouseAdapter listener;
   int border;

   public Insets getDefaultPad(AbstractButton ab) {
      return ab.getInsets(); }
   public void installUI(final JComponent jc ) {
      jc.addMouseListener(listener = new MouseAdapter() {
      boolean highlighted = false;

   public void mousePressed(MouseEvent event) {
```

(continued)

Listing 3. *(continued)*

```
        Graphics g = jc.getGraphics();
        if(g != null) {
        highlight(g, jc);
        highlighted = true;
        g.dispose(); } }
    public void mouseClicked(MouseEvent event) {
        Graphics g = jc.getGraphics();
        if(g != null) {
        unhighlight(g, jc);
        highlighted = false;
        g.dispose(); } } } ); }
public void deinstallUI(JComponent jc) {
    removeMouseListener(listener);
    System.out.println("FlatUI.deinstallUI()"); }
public Insets getInsets(JComponent jc) {
    return new Insets(5,5,5,5); }
public void paint(Graphics g, JComponent jc) {
    paintBorder(g, jc, SystemColor.windowBorder);
    paintText(g, jc); }
protected void paintBorder(Graphics g, JComponent jc, Color color) {
    Dimension sz = jc.getSize();
    g.setColor(color);
    g.drawRect(0,0,sz.width-1,sz.height-1); }
public void highlight(Graphics g, JComponent jc) {
    paintBorder(g, jc, Color.red); }
public void unhighlight(Graphics g, JComponent jc) {
    paintBorder(g, jc, SystemColor.windowBorder); }
protected void paintText(Graphics g, JComponent jc) {
    FontMetrics fm = g.getFontMetrics();
    String       s = ((JButton)jc).getText();
    Dimension   sz = jc.getSize();
    Dimension   strsz = new Dimension(fm.stringWidth(s),
            fm.getHeight() );
    g.setColor(SystemColor.textText);
    g.drawString(s, (sz.width/2)-(strsz.width/2),
        fm.getAscent()+(sz.height/2)-(strsz.height/2)(; }
public Dimension getPreferredSize(JComponent jc){
    Graphics g = jc.getGraphics();
    FontMetrics fm = g.getFontMetrics();
    Dimension rval = new Dimension();
    Insets insets = jc.getInsets();

    rval.width = fm.stringWidth(((JButton)jc).getText()) +
                insets.left + insets.right;
    rval.height = fm.getHeight() + insets.top + insets.bottom;
    g.dispose();
    return rval; }
public Dimension getMaximumSize(JComponent jc) {
    return getPreferredSize(jc); }
public Dimension getMinimumSize(JComponent jc) {
    return getPreferredSize(jc); } }
```

Listing 4.

```
class FlatButton extends JButton {
    public FlatButton(String string) {
        setText(string);
        setToolTipText("button tooltip");
        flatUI = new FlatUI(); }
    public void setUI(BasicButtonUI cui ) {
        super.setUI(cui); } }
class FlatUIListener extends MouseAdapter{
    FlatUI ui;

    public FlatUIListener(FlatUI ui) {
        this.ui = ui; }
    public void mousePressed(MouseEvent event) {
        JComponent jc = (JComponent)event.getSource();
        Graphics g = jc.getGraphics();
        if(g != null) {
            ui.highlight(g, jc);
            g.dispose(); } }
    public void mouseClicked(MouseEvent event) {
        JComponent jc = (JComponent)event.getSource();
        Graphics g = jc.getGraphics();
        if(g != null) {
            ui.unhighlight(g, jc);
            g.dispose(); } } }
class FlatUI implements ButtonUI {
    final int RAISED=0, INSET=1, NONE=3;

    FlatUIListener listener = new FlatUIListener(this);
    int border;

    public Insets getDefaultPad(AbstractButton ab) {
        return ab.getInsets(); }
    public void installUI(final JComponent jc) {
        jc.addMouseListener(listener);
        System.out.printIn("FlatUI.installUI()"); }
    public void deinstallUI(JComponent jc) {
        removeMouseListener(listener);
        System.out.printIn("FlatUI.deinstallUI()"); }
    public Insets getInsets(JComponent jc ) {
        return new Insets(5,5,5,5);  }
     public void paint(Graphics g, JComponent jc) {
        paintBorder(g, jc, SystemColor.windowBorder);
        paintText(g, jc); }
    protected void paintBorder(Graphics g, JComponent jc,Color color) {
        Dimension sz = jc.getSize();
        g.setColor(color);
        g.drawRect(0,0, sz.width-1, sz.height-1); }
    public void highlight(Graphics g, JComponent jc){
        paintBorder(g, jc, Color.red); }
    public void unhighlight(Graphics g, JComponent jc) {
        paintBorder(g, jc, SystemColor.windowBorder); }
```

(continued)

Listing 4. *(continued)*

```
protected void paintText(Graphics g, JComponent jc) {
    FontMetrics fm = g.getFontMetrics();
    String  s  = ((JButton)jc.)getText();
    Dimension sz = jc.getSize();
    Dimension strsz = new Dimension(fm.stringWidth(s),
            fm.get.Height());
    g.setColor(SystemColor.textText);
    g.drawString(sz.width/2) -(strsz.width/2),
            fm.getAscent() + (sz.height/2) -(strsz.height/2)); }
public Dimension getPreferredSize(JComponent jc ) {
    Graphics g = jc.getGraphics();
    FontMetrics fm = g.getFontMetrics();
    Dimension rval = new Dimension();
    Insets insets = jc.getInsets();

    rval.width = fm.stringWidth(((JButton)jc).getText())+
            insets.left + insets.right;
    rval.height = fm.getHeight() + insets.top + insets.bottom;
    g.dispose();
    return rval; }
public Dimension getMaximumSize(JComponent jc ) {
    return getPreferredSize(jc); }
public Dimension getMinimumSize(JComponent jc ) {
    return getPreferred Size(jc); } }
... }
```

PANEL STATES: A USER INTERFACE DESIGN PATTERN

ROGER SPALL

B ASED ON THE premise that individual design patterns are a powerful development tool, it stands to reason that combining several design patterns together is even more potent. A recent Java immersion program at the Object People (Object People is a provider of object-oriented training and development services in Smalltalk and Java. They are based in Ottawa, Ontario, Canada) proved this principle, and resulted in a design pattern that I am calling Panel States.

PROBLEM

The Panel State design pattern enables a group of user interface panels to be presented in a specific sequence. Each panel displays different information, captures user input, and determines the successive panel based on user choices.

For example, consider the Application shown in Figure 1, which provides a wide range of user functionality within the bounds of a single window frame. The window frame is divided into navigation/tool bar, main panel, and information line areas. Interactive content is presented in the main panel area, while the tool bar allows a user to navigate this content. The user interface is built around a collection of re-usable self-contained panels that are presented in this main panel area. As users complete their interaction with individual panels, further panels are displayed, thus the overall interaction may be seen as a network of interrelated panels.

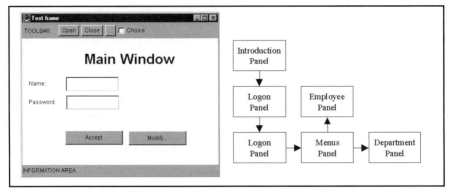

Figure 1. An example of a multi-panel application.

A common example of this type of problem is when a traditional mainframe client end-user interface is replaced with a Java client end-user interface. Many existing mainframe client applications are already panel based, and given users familiarity with an existing design, it may be advantageous to initially replace the legacy system with a similar "look and feel" Java application. In the longer term a more object-oriented design may better support the requirements of knowledge workers, especially as richer user-interface class libraries are added to Java.

SOLUTION

The Panel State design pattern combines both States Transition and Pluggable View controller patterns into a single extendible architecture. By way of review, the State Transition and Pluggable View controller patterns are first summarized.

STATE TRANSITION PATTERN

States represent "resting places" in an object's life cycle. All but the shortest-lived objects have at least one state and typically progress through many different states before reaching their final termination state. Each state progression is known as a *state transition*, and for important objects it can be useful to explicitly represent these transitions in a State Transition Diagram. For example, consider Figure 2, which represents a simplified digital watch with three states. Each node represents a separate state, while the arcs represent named events that cause the individual transitions.

In addition to specifying the individual transitions and the events that cause

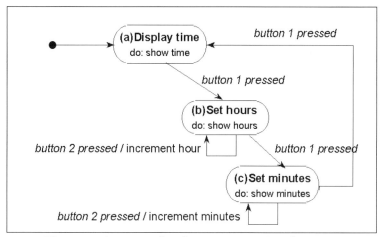

Figure 2. An example of a state transition diagram.

a transition, State Transition Diagrams may also include advanced syntax for nested and generalized states. Given their importance in object-oriented analysis and design, readers are directed to James Rumbaugh's OMT (*Object-Oriented Modeling and Design*, Prentice Hall International, 1991) book for a more complete description.

Applying conventional state transition terminology, each state may have associated activities, which are performed while the object is in that state. For example, while in state (a) a digital watch will repetitively update its internal time, and hopefully any associated user interface. Note that the same event may cause different state transitions depending on the current state, e.g., pressing button 1 will progress to state (c) if the watch is already in state (b). Also, the object's response to method calls will often vary depending on its current state. In fact, some methods may be unavailable while in certain states. Finally, specific actions may be associated with individual state transitions, e.g., progressing from state (a) to state (b) may cause a beep sound to occur.

Implementation of a State Transition Diagram for a specific object requires one or more member variables which together model the current state. State transitions may be implemented as member functions, that are called when an event occurs. Nested if/case statements are required to handle identical events, which cause different state transitions depending on the current state. In addition, other member functions may also require conditional logic to examine the current state in order to determine correct responses, which alter from state to state.

It is, therefore, common to utilize extensive conditional logic when implementing State Transition Diagrams. Unfortunately, besides being difficult to recognize the state transitions identified within an explicit state transition diagram, conditional logic such as ifs and case statements are typically "frowned on" in object-oriented circles. This is not to say that conditional logic is a "deadly sin," however, it is usually safe to hold it "guilty of poor design until proven innocent." Conditional logic may often be replaced with double/single dispatching and reliance on polymorphism to handle the individual cases. State transitions are an excellent opportunity to replace conditional logic in this way.

As discussed by John Vlissides (in Gamma, E. et al., *Design Patterns: Elements of Reusable Object Oriented Software*, Addison-Wesley, 1995) and shown in Figure 3, the key to a better implementation is explicitly identifying an object's individual states and implementing these states as separate objects encapsulated within another object. To clarify terminology, I will refer to this parent object as the *State Machine* and its component states as *State Objects*. A State Machine maintains a current state pointer that references a single State object. State Machine methods may then delegate their behavior by invoking methods on this current state pointer. As the current state pointer points to different State objects, polymorphism replaces the previous conditional logic.

Given this delegation model, each State object must share the same interface. This can be accomplished by a single State object class, with different instances representing the different states. However, this will again necessitate conditional logic in the State object's implementation, thus reducing the effectiveness of the pattern. It is better to implement each State object as a separate class that either inherits from a common State object abstract class, or implement a common Java Interface. The result is one Java State Interface or State abstract class per State Machine. Meanwhile, making use of Java inner classes, the individual state classes may themselves be hidden within the original object.

To complete this design, support must be provided to set the initial state, and to handle the individual state transitions. The former should be adequately managed

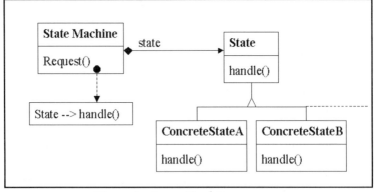

Figure 3. State Machine pattern.

by providing an appropriate State Machine constructor method, which takes the initial state as an argument. The latter is accomplished by providing a State Machine method, which takes a new state as an argument, e.g., changeState(State nextState). State objects requiring access to this method may easily do so if their corresponding classes are implemented as inner classes. Java Inner classes have access to all of their containing class' methods. Alternatively, a reference to the State Machine object could be included whenever a delegate method call is made to a State object.

This completes the introduction to the State Transition Pattern. Opportunities for improving the design include grouping the individual transitions into a single table maintained by the State Machine. In the form just described, each State object is alone responsible for progressing to the next state by calling the changeState method. This results in the state transitions being "spread" among the State objects and therefore more difficult to maintain as a single unit. These improvements are beyond the scope of this article; the reader is directed to John Vlissides *Design Patterns* and in *Pattern Languages* for further information.

PLUGGABLE VIEW CONTROLLERS

Based on the principle of separating the user interface from its underlying model, Pluggable View Controllers provide a similar abstraction to the Model View Controller design pattern familiar to most Smalltalk developers. The key to this pattern is separating the presentation, interaction, and application components of a system. As shown in Figure 4, a Java panel is used to group together the controls for a specific user interface. Each panel represents a combined View Controller in that it both controls the way in which information is presented to the user, and also the response of the user interface to any user interactions. All

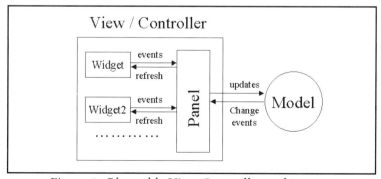

Figure 4. Pluggable View Controller architecture.

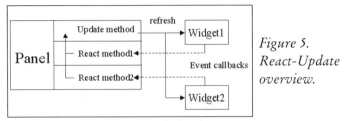

Figure 5.
React-Update
overview.

widget events are directed to the containing Panel, and the same Panel is responsible for refreshing widgets accordingly. The Panel is effectively responsible for managing all user interface control and refreshing. Applying the standard Java 1.1 event delegation model, all "interesting" widget events are directed to the Panel. The initial contents and layout for a panel are fixed when a new panel is created. At the same time, Java EventListeners are added to the panel widgets to call appropriate methods against the panel itself.

A Panel has a single reference to its model object to which it is effectively "plugged." Using this reference, a Panel may communicate changes to, and request information from the model. A model object has no reference to its panel, which minimizes design dependencies between objects and facilitates replacing a model's panel with little impact on the model itself. This design assumes that at most one panel exists per model. This assumption will become clearer, however, as a separate design pattern, Pluggable View Controllers can be further refined, for example, to include multiple panels per model.

Every user interface, or Panel, has at least two responsibilities:

1. To keep itself up to date with any changes in the underlying model.
2. To notify the model of any changes that occur in the user interface.

These requirements can be met using the React-Update pattern as a "pull mechanism" for keeping a panel synchronized with its corresponding model. When a panel is first built, it is provided with a model object on which to initialize. After storing a reference to the model, the panel adds its user interface components, sets their event listeners, and provides their initial contents using an aptly named *update* method. Finally, it returns an initialized instance of itself for any container Applet or frame to add to itself. As user interactions occur, all events are channeled to the panel. When necessary, the panel may update the model using its internal reference and the model's public interface. Whenever the panel performs such an update in reaction to a user interaction, it also has responsibility to call its own update method. This update method is responsible for synchronizing the panel with its model. A simple update method may assume that all aspects of the panel must be refreshed, regardless of whether they have actually changed or not. This assumption simplifies the react-update pattern, however, it may be inefficient, and a waste of time updating an entire panel, when only part of its content may be out of date. A more efficient update method can be written, which first compares existing panel values with current model values and only performs a user interface refresh for those aspects which have actually changed.

The term *Model* is used very liberally and does not necessarily mean a business object. Although a *Model* may represent a single business object, it may also represent a support, or intermediary object that "wrappers" one or more business objects to provide enhanced user interface specific behavior. This could include additional conversion behavior, and undo/redo extensions.

Note that Pluggable View Controllers are not the only technique for separating presentation and business logic layers. I will not attempt to compare different approaches in this article. Needless to say, the Panel States pattern can be integrated with other user interface design patterns provided they encapsulate the panel as a single entity, and allow the panel to be parameterized with a single business object.

PANEL STATES

Having described the basic patterns we can now combine the two to create the Panel States pattern. The object model and an interaction diagram are shown in Figures 6 and 7, while Appendix 1 contains sample code. The design can be broken into three pieces:

1. State Machine, which performs overall coordination function and is known as a NavigationMap.
2. An Applet or frame, which displays the current panel.
3. A collection of InterfacePanel/Panel Model pairs.

NAVIGATIONMAP

Given its role in controlling panel navigation, the State Machine class is called a NavigationMap and represents an implementation of the previously described State Transition pattern. A NavigationMap keeps track of its current state, which is a type of PanelModel. It also maintains a reference to a Java Applet or Frame in which it displays the InterfacePanel associated with its current PanelModel.

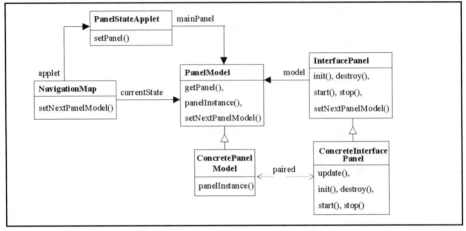

Figure 6. Panel States architecture.

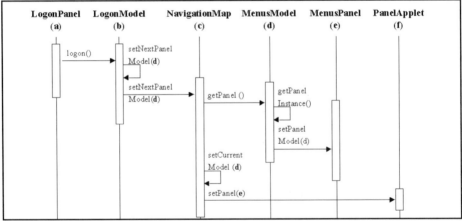

Figure 7. Interaction diagram for PanelChange.

The NavigationMap class is critical to the PanelModel pattern and coordinates most of the interactions between the various pieces.

PANEL STATE APPLET

As the simplest component, the Panel State Applet or frame extends a regular Java Applet or Frame and maintains a reference to the current panel instance that is being displayed. This reference to the current panel instance, is also required to forward appropriate init(), start(), stop(), and destroy() messages. This builds on the Java Applet design, and default init(), start(), stop(), and destroy() methods are provided by an abstract InterfacePanel class. These methods provide flexibility for further extension of the pattern, and use a familiar design, which is already part of the base Java AWT API.

INTERFACEPANEL/PANELMODEL PAIRS

Based on the previous Pluggable View Controller pattern, together, the InterfacePanel and PanelModel abstract classes provide the look and feel for each Panel. The PanelModel class represents an available NavigationMap state, and is associated with exactly one InterfacePanel representing its user interface. This is accomplished at the class level, with a PanelModel instance maintaining a reference to its corresponding InterfacePanel instance. A getPanel() method is provided for the PanelModel class, which calls an abstract panelInstance() method to return the InterfacePanel instance for a new PanelModel. This follows the Factory Method design pattern (see *Design Patterns*), requiring each PanelModel subclass to implement panelInstance() to return a new instance of its corresponding InterfacePanel. In addition, a PanelModel instance maintains a reference to its NavigationMap, and the abstract class provides a setNextPanelModel (PanelModel nextModelState) method, which may be called to progress to the next state, i.e., display the next InterfacePanel. In addition, a PanelModel may provide application-specific methods/fields, which keep track of an internal business model or object(s), and provide access to this object for its InterfacePanel.

Each InterfacePanel instance maintains a reference to its PanelModel instance and may use its corresponding public interface for updating and inquiring on the model. Default init(), start(), stop(), and destroy() methods are provided by the abstract InterfacePanel class, while individual InterfacePanel subclasses may provide their own initialization, cleanup, and efficient multi-threaded behavior as appropriate. The init() method is called once after a panel is created, but before it is displayed, and should contain panel logic that builds the actual panel by adding its components, and event callbacks. The destroy() method is also called once before a panel is destroyed and may contain necessary cleanup logic. Finally, the start() and stop() methods are called whenever an Applet gains or loses focus and may contain logic, which starts and stops various background panel tasks.

Developers using this pattern, must implement two concrete classes for each required panel: a subclass of PanelModel and a subclass of InterfacePanel. Furthermore, a panelInstance() factory method must be written in the PanelModel subclass, which returns an instance of the corresponding InterfacePanel subclass. Next, an init() method must be written in the InterfacePanel subclass, which adds the various user interface components to the new panel, sets its layout manager, and adds the necessary Java Event Listeners. In addition, the default start(), stop(), and destroy() may be overridden by the new InterfacePanel subclass. Finally, it is recommended that developers follow the react-update pattern previously described, requiring the writing of an InterfacePanel subclass update() method.

INTERACTIONS

When the Panel States pattern is first invoked, a Panel State Applet is created along with a single NavigationMap instance. The NavigationMap instance is provided an initial PanelModel instance representing the initial state, and the unidirectional reference between a NavigationMap and its Applet is established. Although special NavigationMap initialization logic is provided, whenever a NavigationMap's PanelModel is changed, essentially the same behavior occurs. The special initialization logic simply prevents the first InterfacePanel's start() method from being called twice: once when the first PanelModel is set, and again when the Applet starts.

A setNextPanelModel (PanelModel nextState) method is provided by the NavigationMap, to change the current PanelModel state. After modifying its currentState attribute to reference the next PanelModel, this method asks the nextState for its InterfacePanel using the getPanel() method, and expects an instance of an InterfacePanel in response. This InterfacePanel is then sent the init() message, and passed as an argument to the NavigationMap's setPanel(InterfacePanel) method call to its Applet. Finally, the new InterfacePanel instance is sent the start() message.

The Panel States Applet's implementation of the setPanel(InterfacePanel) method sends the stop() and destroy() messages to any existing panel, removes the existing panel from itself, replaces it with the new panel, and updates its internal reference. Finally, the Applet sends itself the validate() message forcing it to redisplay itself, including the replaced panel. In addition the Applet's start(), stop(), and destroy() method implementations call the same method against its mainPanel instance reference.

Once the NavigationMap has been initialized and the first InterfacePanel displayed in the Applet, control now passes to the initial InterfacePanel. Although InterfacePanel's are unaware of the NavigationMap, they may directly communicate with their PanelModel. The PanelModel does have explicit knowledge of the NavigationMap and may therefore request a transition to the next PanelModel state at any time. To accomplish this state transition, a PanelModel subclass may send the setNextPanelModel (PanelModel nextState) message to itself, invoking the method supplied by the InterfacePanel abstract class. The implementation for this method simply calls the same method against the InterfacePanel's NavigationMap reference. The resulting behavior is described above, thus completing the collaboration between PanelModel and NavigationMap classes.

DISCUSSION

The PanelModel pattern has already proven itself in several implementations. Once in place, it becomes relatively simple to add new InterfacePanel PanelModel pairs, and to quickly deploy a fully functional user interface. In hindsight, provision for an InterfacePanel init() method proved valuable, as many Java interface building tools automatically generate this method as a means for creating the visually constructed Applet or Panel at runtime.

Further refinements have been tested, including the ability to pass context information between state changes. In this case the setNextPanelModel (PanelModel nextState) is replaced with the setNextPanelModel (PanelModel nextState, Object contextInfo) method, and its logic is extended to include calling the setContext(Object context) method on the nextState. Meanwhile a default, empty implementation of the setContext() method is provided in the PanelModel abstract class. It has also proven easy to extend the pattern with nested PanelModels allowing panels within other panels, such as a panel containing a notebook with other panels as pages.

In reflection, further improvements may be made including grouping together the panel state transition logic. In its current form, individual state transitions are "hard-coded" into PanelModel methods. Managing these different transitions becomes difficult as more InterfacePanel PanelModel pairs are added. This could be improved by creating a state transition table in the NavigationMap class. This table would provide string indexes naming each state transition, and corresponding PanelModel class name.

Given that other objects (e.g., a toolbar) may also wish to change the current Panel in a Panel State Applet, additional logic is useful to provide "rights of denial" for state transitions to the next PanelModel. This is easily achieved by adding an additional default is ReadyToTransition() method in the **Pan-elModel** abstract class, which returns true. Subclasses may then override this with appropriate logic.

Finally, this Panel States pattern has been tested with other user interface implementation models such as that represented by the generated code for the IBM VisualAge for Java tool.

The complete source code listing is available from the Object People Web site, in addition to *Java Report Online* and as usual, your comments are invited and should be addressed to Roger@ObjectPeople.com.

SECURITY

Using the JavaSoft Security Package

Steve Burnett

L AST MONTH, Tim Matthews described how JavaSoft is developing a Java Cryptography Architecture (JCA) and extensions (Java Cryptography Extensions, or JCE). He described their contents and structure in the java.security package, and outlined their uses. This month I will present some actual code using the base functionality in the JCA, and next month will program using the JCE and use multiple Providers.

After reading this article, you will, I trust, be able to write a program in Java (an application or applet) that can sign or verify data using DSA with the security package. Beyond the specific DSA example presented here, though, I hope you will understand the JCA model enough to be able to quickly write code for any operation in the package.

Before beginning, however, it is important to note that the java.security package is not part of the JDK 1.0.2, only JDK 1.1 and above. Furthermore, there are significant differences between the security packages in JDK 1.1 and 1.2. This article (and next month's) describes features in 1.2. If you have not yet left 1.0.2 behind, now would be a good time to do so. After all, with 1.2, you are not only getting the security package, you are also getting improved cloning, serialization and many other features.

Now let's look at what a Java program needs to do to use the JCA. Most everything in cryptography begins with the random number generator. Such a tool is necessary to generate keys or other cryptographic components. So before getting to the DSA example, it is important to learn how to build an object that will produce the needed random values.

PSEUDO-RANDOM NUMBER GENERATION AND SecureRandom

More precisely, we will build a pseudo-random number generator (PRNG). Since a computer is a deterministic machine, when given a particular input, it will always produce the same output. The results of a PRNG will "look" random, that is, they will pass statistical tests of randomness, but since the results are reproducible, they cannot be called truly random. Hence the modifier "pseudo".

The PRNG will always produce the same results if given the same input. That input is known as the "seed," the cryptographic term for the user-input values (in Java generally a **byte** array) that get the PRNG started. If you build two objects using the same seed, the objects will produce the same pseudo-random values. If attackers know you used a particular PRNG to generate a key, rather than trying to reproduce the key, they can reproduce your PRNG. But they can only generate the same values if they can discover your seed. Therefore, you will want to use a seed the attacker cannot reproduce in a reasonable amount of time. There are several good seed-collecting techniques, but that is not the topic of this article, so for now assume that when we need a seed, we will have one. If you want to learn about good seeds, see *Suggestions For Random Number Generation In Software* by Tim Matthews in **RSA Laboratories' Security Bulletin** Number 1, January 22, 1996 at http://www.rsa.com/rsalabs/pubs/updates/bull-1.pdf. That article also lists other references.

In the JCA, the PRNG is known as SecureRandom. This is a subclass of java.util.Random. The random-generating techniques employed by SecureRandom have come under greater cryptographic scrutiny, so it is probably wiser to use it rather than the base class. To instantiate,

```
SecureRandom myRandom = SecureRandom.getInstance
("SHA1PRNG");
```

At this point you want to add the seed. Of course, in a real application, this would not be a good seed.

```
byte[] seed = { 4, 5, 6, 7 };
myRandom.setSeed (seed);
```

You can call this method as many times as you like, each call will add to the seed, not "replace" old material. If the object is never seeded, the first time it is called upon to generate some random bytes (such as with the nextBytes method) it will seed itself. That is, the object will call on a technique to generate 20 bytes of seed data. It is called autoseeding. Here is what JavaSoft says about the technique they employ.

> "We attempt to provide sufficient seed bytes to completely randomize the internal state of the generator… Note, however, that our seed generation algorithm has not been thoroughly studied or widely deployed. It relies on counting the number of times that the calling thread can yield while waiting for another thread to sleep for a specified interval."

There is also a method called getSeed (). This method executes the autoseeding algorithm, and returns seed bytes to you (it does not use those seed bytes on itself, though).

You might be thinking you might as well use their autoseed, right? Well, there is a downside, it takes a long time to execute. It will generally take a second or more (in my experience it usually takes three seconds and sometimes as much as five or six seconds) to generate the seed. That may be too slow for your application.

Incidentally, the SecureRandom in JDK 1.1 did not contain the getInstance method, only constructors. One constructor took no arguments and called the autoseed function. Another took a byte array, which was a seed. If you need to be compatible with JDK 1.1, you will probably want to instantiate by calling.

```
SecureRandom myRandom = new SecureRandom (seed);
```

A General Model

With the PRNG in hand, let's move on. Performing operations using the JCA, (and later the JCE) will generally follow a three-step process.

```
AlgorithmIndependentClass.getInstance ("algorithm");
AlgorithmIndependentClass.initialize (AlgorithmSpecificInfo);
AlgorithmIndependentClass.performOperation ( );
```

In other words, find the class that performs the operation desired and get an instance of it. Next, initialize the object to perform that operation using the specific algorithm information (which may be a key, a "Spec" or maybe even just an integer). Then call on the methods that perform that operation. The following example with digital signatures illustrates the process.

DIGITAL SIGNATURES

One of the most important features of the JCA is the digital signature. These cryptographic constructs are the "tamper-proof" seals and more of the digital world. When you attach your signature to the code, email, or data you send, the recipients can know whether the goods are arriving undamaged or not. A signature ensures more, though, it provides proof of the identity of the sender.

For example, Java has the concept of a "signed applet." After downloading an applet, the user can check the signature. If it verifies, the recipient can be confident it has not been corrupted. It has not, for example, been infected with a virus while in transit. Furthermore, the recipient can know that the applet is indeed from the appropriate source. If the applet is supposed to be from Acme Software, the Acme public key will verify that. If a signature does not verify, it may be because the applet is corrupt or the source is not who it is supposed to be. It does not matter, the recipient can simply know not to trust that applet.

But before we can create a digital signature, we must have a key pair: a public and a private key. The class that performs this function is **KeyPairGenerator**.

STEP 1: getINSTANCE

```
KeyPairGenerator dsaKeyPairGen =
  KeyPairGenerator.getInstance ("DSA");
```

The first thing to notice is the factory method used to instantiate. For security classes that have a protected constructor, you must use **getInstance ()** to obtain instances of them. With a constructor, you get an object of the specified class, but with the factory method, you get an object that satisfies the class requirements, and it can actually be an instance of any number of classes. The security package allows for multiple providers, and you may want to use a class produced by someone other than JavaSoft. The factory will be able to return to you an object from any number of providers.

The second thing to notice is the algorithm, DSA. When you get the JDK, you automatically get JavaSoft's version of DSA. If you do not install another provider's package onto your machine, that is the only choice of digital signatures you have. If you do want to use another algorithm, say RSA, you could call

---

Listing 1.

```java
// This Java program illustrates using the JCA to generate a DSA key pair and sign data.

import java.security.*;
import java.security.interfaces.*;

public class DSAExample {

 public static void main (String[] args)
 {
  try {
   // Build a PRNG
   byte[] seedBytes = { 0, 1, 2, 3 };
   SecureRandom myRandom = SecureRandom.getInstance ("SHA1PRNG");
   myRandom.setSeed (seedBytes);

   // Generate a key pair.
   // Step 1: getInstance.
   KeyPairGenerator dsaKeyPairGen =
   KeyPairGenerator.getInstance ("DSA");
   // Step 2: algorithm-specific initialization.
   dsaKeyPairGen.initialize (512, myRandom);
   // Step 3: perform the operation.
   KeyPair theKeyPair = dsaKeyPairGen.generateKeyPair ();

   // Compute a signature.
   byte[] dataToSign = { 8, 9, 10, 11 };
   // Step 1: getInstance.
   Signature signer = Signature.getInstance ("DSA");
   // Step 2: algorithm-specific initialization.
   PrivateKey thePrivateKey = theKeyPair.getPrivate ();
   signer.initSign (thePrivateKey, myRandom);
   // Step 3: perform the operation.
   signer.update (dataToSign);
   byte[] signature = signer.sign ();

   // Verifying the signature is left as an exercise for the reader.
  } catch (Exception anyException) {
   System.out.println ("Exception: " + anyException.getMessage()); } } }
```

```java
KeyPairGenerator rsaKeyPairGen =
KeyPairGenerator.getInstance ("RSA", "JsafeJCE");
```

Notice we added a second argument. It is the name of the provider. This will only work if you have the JsafeJCE provider and it is registered, either dynamically or in your java.security file (located in the lib\security directory of your JDK installation). Incidentally, the Provider package you get with the JDK goes by the name of "SUN".

Next month's article talks about alternate Providers, so for now, this sample will use the default security package from JavaSoft, which means using DSA.

STEP 2: ALGORITHM-SPECIFIC INITIALIZATION

Some algorithms require specific parameters, others do not. Without getting into excruciating detail about DSA, to generate a key pair, we need system parameters known as p, q, and g (prime, subprime, and base). JavaSoft offers a default p, q, and g for key sizes of 512, 768, and 1024 bits. It is not necessarily cryptographically unsecure to use system parameters other people use, unless too many people are sharing the same parameters (and just try to get a cryptographer to quantify "too many"). The object, dsaKeyPairGen, will use those default values unless instructed otherwise. For this example, we will use default system parameters (if you want to generate new parameters, use the AlgorithmParameterGeneratorClass).

        dsaKeyPairGen.initialize (512, myRandom);

The 512 is the length in bits of the key pair and the random object is there as a source of random values. Part of a DSA key pair is a value called "x", which is simply a random number.

Incidentally, 512 bits may not be sufficient security for a real application. Cryptographers generally recommend using at least a 768-bit key for DSA. Many real-world applications use 1024-bit keys. However, execution slows down as the key size increases. Since this example is not a real-world application, for convenience sake, we can use a 512-bit key pair.

STEP 3: PERFORM THE OPERATION

Now that the object knows what it needs to generate, we can call a generate method.

        KeyPair theKeyPair = dsaKeyPairGen.genKeyPair ();

And that's it. The private key consists of the system parameters p, q, and g, and the random value x. The public key consists of p, q, and g and the value $y = g^x \bmod p$.

One last note, if you generate your own system parameters (p, q, and g), your program may take quite a long time. The program would find two very large prime numbers, and that is rather time-consuming. Finding 1024-bit parameters can take two, three, or ten minutes. It might even take as long as 30 minutes.

Computing a Signature

Now that we have a key pair, we can compute a digital signature. What are we signing? In the real world you will sign files, email, code, whatever. For now, let's just sign some arbitrary data.

```
byte[] dataToSign = { 8, 9, 10, 11 };
```

If you do not know what happens when computing a DSA signature, here is a brief outline. The data to sign is digested using the SHA1 algorithm. The resulting 20-byte digest, plus a random value and the private key are the variables in a series of modular arithmetic operations. The result is a byte array that is the signature. To verify the signature, digest the data to verify using SHA1 and use the digest, the signature and the public key as the variables to another series of modular arithmetic operations. The result will determine if the signature on the data is valid. Actually, you will not have to digest the data explicitly. As you will see, the signing or verifying object will do that.

If you want to see a comprehensive description of DSA, there are several books on cryptography you could consult. Bruce Schneier's *Applied Cryptography* would be a good choice.

Step 1: getInstance

First we find the class that computes digital signatures. That's easy, it is Signature.

```
Signature signer = Signature.getInstance ("DSA");
```

Step 2: Algorithm-specific Initialization

With KeyPairGenerator, the algorithm-specific information was a key length and a random object. With Signature, the algorithm-specific information is the private key and a random object. When we generated the key pair, we received a KeyPair object containing a public and private key. We need only the private key here, but that is easy to get.

```
PrivateKey thePrivateKey = theKeyPair.getPrivate ();
signer.initSign (thePrivateKey, myRandom);
```

We pass in the random number generator at init time. Later on, the Signature object will use it to generate the random value necessary to compute a DSA signature.

STEP 3: PERFORM THE OPERATION

For digital signatures, the actual operation is a two step process. First, you call an update method with the data, then the sign method. Why two steps? Suppose you have an enormous file you want to sign, and you do not want to load the entire file into memory. You would want to break up the data into more manageable chunks. That is exactly what the update method allows you to do. It does not matter whether we pass in the data all at once, or in smaller increments (although the increments must be in the proper order), the signature will be the same.

```
signer.update (dataToSign);
byte[] signature = signer.sign ()
```

Incidentally, during update, the object is digesting the data only. During sign, the object computes the random value and performs the modular arithmetic.

Something else to note is that if you sign the exact same data again, you should get a different signature. That is how the DSA algorithm is supposed to behave. The signature depends on a random value, and for security reasons, each signature should use a different random value. Of course, if you compute a second signature with a new random object built with the same seed as before, you will get the same signature.

VERIFYING A SIGNATURE

The verification process is similar to the signing process. You use the public key and the result of the verify method is a true or false, indicating whether the signature verifies or not. The verification code is left as an exercise for the reader.

CONCLUSION

Adding java.security features to your program is relatively straightforward. All you need is a basic understanding of cryptographic concepts and the algorithms included in the JDK. This article has described a general model and applied that model to the digital signature. If you want to build other objects, you will be able to extend this model to other cryptographic constructs.

Sun has made substantial improvements to the security features in JDK

1.2. Writing applications that use cryptographic security will benefit greatly from them. Java will provide a solid and easy-to-use platform for the security developer.

The next step is encryption. Next month we will describe using alternate Providers and the JCE. We will also take a look at some of the other enhancements to JDK 1.2 and put them into the context of a security application.

Using the Java
Cryptographic Extensions

STEVE BURNETT

I N THE FIRST ARTICLE of this series, Tim Matthews described how JavaSoft
is developing a Java Cryptography Architecture (JCA) and extensions (Java
Cryptography Extensions, or JCE). He described their contents and structure in the java.security package, and outlined their uses. In the second installment, I presented some actual code using the base functionality in the JCA. This
third article describes programming using the JCE and multiple providers.

After reading this article, you will, I trust, be able to write a program in
Java (an application or applet) that can encrypt or decrypt data using DES
and create an RSA digital envelope with the extensions package. Beyond the
specific example presented here, though, I hope you will understand the JCE
model enough to be able to quickly write code for any operation in the package, and to be able to use multiple providers.

Before beginning, however, it is important to note that the security packages are not part of the JDK 1.0.2, only JDK 1.1 and above. Furthermore,
there are significant differences between the security packages in JDK 1.1 and
1.2. This article (and the previous) describes features in 1.2. If you have not
yet left 1.0.2 behind, now would be a good time to do so. After all, with 1.2,
you are not only getting the security packages, you are also getting improved
cloning, serialization and many other features.

There is an important change from JDK 1.1 to 1.2, the JCE is in a different package. The java.security package still contains the baseline functionality, but the extensions are in a new package, javax.crypto.

THE JCE PROVIDER

The JCE is only an API (application program interface). It describes what classes to build and what methods to call, but it does not actually perform the functionality. You write to the API and the tasks are performed by whatever provider's package is installed underneath. That was the same with the JCA, but when you downloaded the JDK, you automatically got a default provider, namely SUN.

Because the JCE contains cryptography, an export-controlled commodity, JavaSoft cannot release a JCE provider with the JDK. Hence, you must download the JCE and JavaSoft's provider separately. Once you have this package, you need to install it.

ADDING JAVASOFT'S JCE PROVIDER

A list of providers is in the java.security file (located in the lib\security directory of the JDK). The default SUN provider (for the JCA) is listed automatically.

    security.provider.1=sun.security.provider.Sun

If we downloaded the JCE, we need to add this new provider. Simply add the following line.

    security.provider.2=com.sun.crypto.provider.SunJCE

Now just make sure your CLASSPATH points to the JAR file possessing JavaSoft's JCE provider.

There is one other thing to note, the number (it is 1 for Sun, 2 for SunJCE in this example) is the preference order. Numbering begins at 1, so currently Sun is the preferred provider and SunJCE is next. If you call a getInstance without specifying a provider, it will search in that order. If you want to make SunJCE the number one choice, that's fine, just make sure all your providers have different preference numbers.

ENCRYPTING WITH DES

Encrypting data is one of the most important security features you can employ. To anyone without the appropriate keys, your data or the data you send to others looks like gibberish. This is one way to keep your private information away from prying eyes. The most common encryption algorithm in use today in the United States is DES, the Digital Encryption Standard, developed by IBM with the US government.

THE KEY OBJECT

DES, as with almost all ciphers, operates following the key model. The algorithm takes as input a "key" along with the plaintext to produce the ciphertext. The key is generally either a very large number or a series of random numbers. If you encrypt the same data with a different key, you will produce different results. DES is a symmetric cipher, which means that the key data used to encrypt is the only key data that can properly decrypt.

In order to encrypt using the JCE, we need to build a key object as well as an algorithm object.

THE GENERAL MODEL

In the previous article, I outlined a three-step process, which is the general model for operations in the security packages.

1. AlgorithmIndependentClass.getInstance ("algorithm");
2. AlgorithmIndependentClass.initialize(AlgorithmSpecificInfo);
3. AlgorithmIndependentClass.performOperation ( );

In other words, find the class that performs the operation desired and get an instance of it. Next, initialize the object to perform that operation using the specific algorithm information (which may be a key, a "Spec" or maybe even just an integer). Then call on the methods that perform that operation.

STEP 1: GETINSTANCE

There are several kinds of keys: public keys, private keys, symmetric keys (aka secret keys). DES is a symmetric encryption algorithm, so we will need a SecretKey. (Why did JavaSoft use the term "SecretKey" instead of "SymmetricKey"? Maybe it was to accentuate the point that such a key should remain hidden from prying eyes.)

To build a secret key, we need to use the SecretKeyFactory class.

```
SecretKeyFactory desKeyFactory =
    SecretKeyFactory.getInstance ("DES");
```

The first thing is to recall from the previous article that JCE objects are al-most always instantiated by the factory method. This allows for multiple providers. This current example uses the first provider available in the java.se-curity file (which in this example is "SunJCE"), since it does not specify a provider. The second thing to notice is the argument "DES". We are creating an object that will serve as a key for an encryption algorithm, the argument specifies which one. This allows the getInstance method to ask the provider whether it implements the desired algorithm.

STEP 2: ALGORITHM-SPECIFIC INITIALIZATION

Actually, we do not call a method with a name such as "init" or "initialize". We call generateSecret.

The class SecretKeyFactory is algorithm-independent. It does not know how to build keys for every type of encryption algorithm. We have created it specifying DES, but this class itself knows nothing about DES keys. That is because if it were to know about DES keys, it would have to know about every other type of key as well. So we need to set it with algorithm-specific information. Remember, the "DES" passed in at getInstance is only there to ask the provider if it implements this algorithm.

The most important algorithm-specific information is key size and the key data itself. A DES key is 8 bytes long (64 bits), no more, no less. With DES there is the concept of "parity bits" which means the actual number of key bits used in the encryption algorithm is 56. We still build a DES key with 64 random bits, it's just that the algorithm uses only 56 of them.

We need to pass in an algorithm-specific class, and with SecretKeyFac-tory it is a "Spec."

```
public final SecretKey generateSecret (KeySpec keySpec);
```

We need a KeySpec that possesses DES key data. Not surprisingly, it is called DESKeySpec. Actually, KeySpec (located in the package java.secu-rity.spec) is an interface, and DESKeySpec (located in the package javax.crypto.spec) is a class that implements it.

Looking at the DESKeySpec documentation, we see that it is instantiated by a constructor, not a factory, and that the constructor takes as an argument the key data. Why a constructor and not a factory? Well, this is a class that only holds data, so there is no sense in building it through alternate providers. As for the key data, with DES, the key should be random data. We need to generate 8 random bytes. In the previous article, I described the process for building a SecureRandom.

```
SecureRandom myRandom = SecureRandom.getInstance
  ("SHA1PRNG");
// A real world application would use a real seed.
myRandom.setSeed (new byte[4]);
byte[] keyData = new byte[8];
random.nextBytes (keyData);
```

Now we can build our DESKeySpec and use it in the SecretKeyFactory.

```
DESKeySpec desKeySpec = new DESKeySpec (keyData);
SecretKey desKey = desKeyFactory.generateSecret (desKeySpec);
```

Notice the result of the generateSecret method is a SecretKey. That is the key object we will want. Actually, SecretKey is an interface, the SecretKeyFactory returned us an instance of the provider's class that implements that interface. Because we have the key object, there is no Step 3.

THE ALGORITHM OBJECT

Now that we have a key object, we can build an algorithm object that employs the key object to perform DES encryption.

STEP 1: GETINSTANCE

We need an object that will encrypt. The JCE class that performs encryption is known as Cipher. Since this class is part of the JCE, in JDK 1.2 it is javax.crypto.Cipher.

```
Cipher desEncrypter = Cipher.getInstance
  ("DES/CBC/PKCS5Padding");
```

Notice the argument "DES/CBC/PKCS5Padding". We are creating an object that will perform encryption, the argument describes what specific type of encryption. The getInstance method is asking the provider if it can perform this operation. The "DES" part is clear, but what about the "/CBC/PKCS5Padding"? What does that mean?

DES is a block cipher. That means it can perform its operations only on blocks of data of a particular size. The size of a block for DES is 8 bytes. The implementation will break up the data into blocks of 8 bytes and operate on each individual chunk. This creates a particular problem, though, two blocks containing the same data will encrypt to the same ciphertext. That is, if your data to encrypt contains say, the letters "JavaSoft," in more than one place, depending on the offset, your encrypted data may contain the same 8-byte block in more than one place. This could aid an attacker in figuring out your message or even your key.

This problem is avoided by using a feedback mode. A feedback mode will prevent two blocks of the same plaintext from encrypting to the same ciphertext. The most popular feedback mode is Cipher Block Chaining, or CBC. It XOR's the current block of plaintext with the previous block of ciphertext before encrypting. If the current plaintext block is the first block, there is no previous ciphertext block, so CBC uses an initialization vector, commonly called the IV. After decrypting a block, XOR the result with the previous ciphertext block to recover the plaintext.

Another problem with block ciphers is that if there are fewer than "block size" bytes to encrypt, the algorithm cannot execute. With DES, we need 8 bytes of data before we can encrypt. If the total length of our input data is not a multiple of 8, say there are 3 leftover bytes, what happens? A padding scheme can append the last 5 bytes. When we decrypt, the padding scheme can strip the extra bytes. The most popular padding scheme for block ciphers is defined in PKCS #5. The PKCS is a series of cryptography standards adopted by much of the industry.

STEP 2: ALGORITHM-SPECIFIC INITIALIZATION

Here is the definition of Cipher's initialization method.

```
public final void init
 (int opmode, Key key, AlgorithmParameterSpec params);
```

The opmode is to specify encryption or decryption and the key is the key object we built (Key is an interface for all keys, SecretKey extends it). With the key factory, we passed in a KeySpec to initialize with algorithm-specific information. With Cipher, we use an AlgorithmParameterSpec. We need to build an AlgorithmParameterSpec that contains the DES/CBC/PKCS5Padding parameters. We would expect to find something called maybe DESParameterSpec, but there is no such class. That is because DES has no parameters. The padding algorithm also has no parameters, but CBC has parameters, the IV. So we use the IvParameterSpec.

```
byte[] initVector = new byte[8];
random.nextBytes (initVector);
IvParameterSpec ivParamSpec = new IvParameterSpec (initVector);
desEncrypter.init (Cipher.ENCRYPT_MODE, desKey, ivParamSpec);
```

STEP 3: PERFORM THE OPERATION

There are actually two methods to call to perform encryption, update and do-Final.

```
public final int update
  (byte[] input, int inputOffset, int inputLen,
   byte[] output, int outputOffset);
public final int doFinal (byte[] output, int outputOffset);
```

Why not just encrypt all at once? Suppose you had a 4-megabyte file you wanted to encrypt. You may not want to create a 4-megabyte input buffer and a 4-megabyte output buffer and perform the encryption. You might prefer to read some of the data from the input file, maybe 2048 bytes, process it and place the result into the output file. Then grab the next piece of data, and then the next and so on. With the update call, that is possible. When you have no more input, call doFinal and the object knows to append the padding.

```
byte[] dataToEncrypt = { 1, 2, 3, 4, 5, 6, 7, 8, 9, 10, 11};
int outputSize = desEncrypter.getOutputSize (dataToEncrypt.length);
byte[] encryptedData = new byte[outputSize];
int outputLen = desEncrypter.update
  (dataToEncrypt, 0, dataToEncrypt.length, encryptedData, 0);
outputLen += desEncrypter.doFinal (encryptedData, outputLen);
```

The data to encrypt was 11 bytes, but the output of encryption will be more. The extra bytes are for padding. With padded block ciphers, the output of encryption should be larger than the input. So how big should the output buffer be? Call the Cipher class's method getOutputSize.

DECRYPTING

Decrypting is very similar to encrypting. You build a key object the same way. Remember, though, that you must use the same key data to decrypt as was used to encrypt. In the example here, for our key used to encrypt, we generated random bytes. To get those bytes to use in building a key object for decrypting, either use the byte array that contained the data, or the DESKeySpec contains a method called getKey.

For the algorithm object, the code is pretty much the same, there are really only two differences. The first is that the IV must be the same as used in encryption, so as with the key, hard-code the data rather than generating random bytes. You can get the IV bytes either from the byte array holding the random bytes, or the Cipher class possesses a method called getIV. The second difference is that the init method takes the DECRYPT_MODE flag for the opmode argument.

Actual code that decrypts is left as an exercise for the reader.

OTHER SYMMETRIC ALGORITHMS

The previous example used DES, a block cipher. There are other block ciphers, such as RC2 or RC5. These use feedback modes and padding schemes as well. However, they require other parameters beyond the IV, and hence other AlgorithmParameterSpec's. RC5 also can operate on 8-byte or 16-byte blocks.

There are also stream ciphers, which behave slightly differently from block ciphers. A stream cipher does not use feedback modes or padding schemes. RC4 is an example of a stream cipher.

RC2, RC4, and RC5 have advantages over DES. They are significantly faster in software and they can take keys of varying length. The longer the key, the greater the security. DES is limited to 56 bits, but the RC series can use keys of up to 1024, 2048, and 2040 bits respectively. Since the RC series is not implemented by the default SUN provider, in order to use them you will have to find another provider. Also, DES is so widely implemented, if you use it, there is a greater chance your application will be able to interoperate with other applications.

If you want to use a symmetric cipher, you have a choice of algorithms, but when you choose an algorithm, you have to understand how it operates and what its parameters are.

THE DIGITAL ENVELOPE

Now that we can encrypt data with DES, suppose we want to send that data to a colleague. Since it is encrypted, attackers who intercept the message will not be able to understand the contents. But then again, without the key, neither will the recipient. We must send the key to our colleague as well. But if we send the key, the attackers can decrypt as well.

The solution is the digital envelope. We encrypt the DES key using the recipient's RSA public key. Only the recipient's private key can retrieve the DES key, and only the recipient has access to that key. Why not just send the entire message encrypted with the public key? RSA is not a fast algorithm. Encrypting one block of data with RSA would not be too time-consuming, but encrypting and then decrypting an entire message might be too great a performance hit.

Before we dive into the code, though, we have a problem, the default provider, SunJCE, does not offer an RSA implementation. If we want to use the RSA algorithm, we have to use another provider. Different companies produce the different providers. That means if you want to perform RSA, you must find a company that offers a provider that performs RSA and purchase their product.

For this example, assume we went to the Acme company and purchased their provider package, which supports RSA.

ADDING A PROVIDER

When instantiating a class, the getInstance method will look for a provider. If the provider's name is listed as one of the arguments to getInstance, that is the only place it will look. If not, it will look in the java.security file for a list of providers, then go down that list trying each provider in the preference order until it finds one that can perform the operation.

If you name the provider at getInstance and that provider is not listed in the java.security file, you will get an exception. Actually, there is a way around this requirement, you can add a provider dynamically. That will not change the java.security file, but while the program is running, any getInstance method will be able to find that provider if it needs to. Once the program stops running, the provider is lost.

First, let's add a provider to the java.security file. We actually did this already when adding the SunJCE package. To add another provider is almost identical. When we bought Acme's package, they should have told us what their master class name is. Say it is com.Acme.provider.Acme. To add Acme, edit java.security and search for

```
security.provider.2=com.sun.crypto.provider.SunJCE
```

Below that line, add

> security.provider.3=com.Acme.provider.Acme

Make sure your CLASSPATH points to the zip file or JAR possessing Acme's product.

If you do not want to edit the java.security file (maybe you are building an applet to be downloaded and you cannot edit the recipient's java.security file), you can add a provider dynamically. The java.security.Security class can do it, but only if a "trusted" program calls it, where trusted is a local application or an applet with appropriate permission. To get trusted status, your applet must be signed. Actually, there's a bit more to it than that, but code signing is not the focus of this article (see Javasoft's documentation at http://java.sun.com/security/usingJavakey.html and http://www.javasoft.com/products/jdk/1.1/docs/guide/security/index.html for more information on code signing), so let's just return to dynamically adding a provider.

The provider's master class (in this example, com.Acme.provider.Acme) is a subclass of java.security.Provider. Instantiate Acme's master class as a Provider object. The product's documentation should tell how, it will probably be a no-argument constructor. Then pass that object as an argument to the Security.addProvider method.

```
Provider newProvider = new com.Acme.provider.Acme ();
int preference = Security.addProvider (newProvider);
```

THE RSA PUBLIC KEY OBJECT

We now have our Acme provider installed, we can go ahead and use its functionality. We are using it to create an RSA digital envelope. That means we will encrypt data using the recipient's public key. Distribution of RSA public keys is generally done through the Certificate Authority infrastructure. Obtain the recipient's X.509 digital certificate and extract the encoding of their public key. The focus of this article is not digital certificates and certificate authorities (a good place to start would be questions 123 through 129 at http://www.rsa.com/rsalabs/newfaq), so let's simply assume we have the key in X.509 format.

STEP 1: GETINSTANCE

For a DES key, we used on SecretKeyFactory. For an RSA public key, we use KeyFactory.

```
KeyFactory rsaKeyFactory = KeyFactory.getInstance ("RSA",
                                                   "Acme");
```

We specify the provider, Acme. Remember, that means getInstance will look at only that provider. If we did not specify a provider, getInstance would look at all providers in the order of preference until it found one that could perform the operation. In addition, the "RSA" is there for getInstance to ask the provider whether it implements the algorithm.

STEP 2: ALGORITHM-SPECIFIC INITIALIZATION

As with the DES key, we do not call a method with a name such as "init" or "initialize." We call generatePublic.

```
public final PublicKey generatePublic (KeySpec keySpec);
```

We need a KeySpec for RSA public keys. It should come as no surprise that it is called RSAPublicKeySpec. Its constructor is the following.

```
public RSAPublicKeySpec
   (BigInteger modulus, BigInteger publicExponent);
```

We have a problem, the constructor calls for a modulus and public exponent, but we have the X.509 encoding of the key. It turns out there is another public key spec, X509EncodedKeySpec. This spec is actually valid for any public key in an X.509 certificate, Diffie-Hellman, DSA and elliptic curve as well as RSA. So assuming we have the public key in a byte array, the code will look like this.

```
byte[] encodedPublicKey;
X509EncodedKeySpec rsaKeySpec =
  new X509EncodedKeySpec (encodedPublicKey);
PublicKey rsaPubKey = rsaKeyFactory.generatePublic (rsaKeySpec);
```

THE ALGORITHM OBJECT

Now that we have a key object, we can build an algorithm object that employs the key object to perform RSA encryption.

STEP 1: GETINSTANCE

We saw that the JCE class that performs DES encryption is Cipher. It is the same class that will perform RSA encryption.

```
Cipher rsaEncrypter Cipher.getInstance ("RSA", "Acme");
```

STEP 2: ALGORITHM-SPECIFIC INITIALIZATION

It is the same init method that we used for DES, except this time we will use an AlgorithmParameterSpec for RSA. We would expect to find a class called RSAParameterSpec, but there is none. The RSA algorithm does not really have parameters. DES has an IV, DSA has p, q and g, but RSA has no parameters. So there are a couple options.

The first is to find out from Acme whether they have built an RSAParameterSpec class. The JCA and JCE are designed to be provider-independent, but since we have specified Acme, maybe they have released a ParameterSpec for RSA. It might even eventually be adopted by JavaSoft as the official RSAParameterSpec for the JCE. If Acme has such a class, we use it.

The second option is to pass null. If Acme does not have an RSAParameterSpec class and JavaSoft has not defined one, that means we do not need one.

```
rsaEncrypter.init (Cipher.ENCRYPT_MODE, rsaPubKey, null,
random);
```

Notice that this time when we called init, we passed in a random number generator. That is because in the JCE, RSA encryption is defined to follow PKCS #1, which specifies a padding scheme. This padding scheme relies on random numbers. There is the concept of "raw RSA" which does not require padding, but the JCE does not, as yet, indicate that it is an option. The JCE recognizes only PKCS #1 RSA, which means using the padding scheme specified in that standard, which means we must pass in a random number generator.

STEP 3: PERFORM THE OPERATION

Remember that what we are encrypting is the DES key data.

```
outputSize = rsaEncrypter.getOutputSize (keyData.length);
byte[] encryptedKey = new byte[outputSize];
int encryptedKeyLen = rsaEncrypter.update
    (keyData, 0, keyData.length, encryptedKey, 0);
encryptedKeyLen += rsaEncrypter.doFinal
    (encryptedKey, encryptedKeyLen);
```

Opening the Envelope

To open the envelope, we decrypt the encryptedKey using the RSA private key associated with the public key. Building a private key object is the same as building a public key object, except you will need to use a key spec that holds private keys. There is an **RSAPrivateKeySpec** and an **RSAPrivateKeyCrtSpec** which contain the components of a private key. For an encoded key (which is easier to store) there is a **PKCS8EncodedKeySpec**. Also, you must use the Key-Factory's method generatePrivate.

The algorithm object will look just like the one used to encrypt, except at init time, pass in the private key and set opmode to DECRYPT_MODE.

As with DES decryption, the code is left as an exercise for the reader.

Conclusions

Adding JCE features to your program is relatively straightforward. This article has described a general model and applied that model to the digital envelope. If you want to build other objects, you can extend this model to other cryptographic constructs.

Sun has made substantial improvements to the security features in JDK 1.2. Writing applications that use cryptographic security will benefit greatly from them. Java will provide a solid and easy-to-use platform for the security developer.

Listing 1.

```
/* This Java program illustrates using the JCE to create an RSA digital envelope. It calls
   on the fictional provider Acme. For this program to work, acquire a provder's package
   that performs RSA and replace "Acme" with the appropriate name. */

import java.security.*;
import java.security.spec.*;
import javax.crypto.*;
import javax.crypto.interfaces.*;
import javax.crypto.spec.*;
import COM.Acme.provider.*

public class RSAEnvelope {

  static byte[] encodedPublicKey = {
    (byte)0x30, (byte)0x81, (byte)0x8f, (byte)0x30,
    (byte)0x0d, (byte)0x06, (byte)0x09, (byte)0x2a,
    (byte)0x86, (byte)0x48, (byte)0x86, (byte)0xf7,
    (byte)0x0d, (byte)0x01, (byte)0x01, (byte)0x01,
    (byte)0x05, (byte)0x00, (byte)0x03, (byte)0x7e,
    (byte)0x00, (byte)0x30, (byte)0x7b, (byte)0x02,
    (byte)0x74, (byte)0x58, (byte)0x16, (byte)0xab,
    (byte)0xfc, (byte)0xf6, (byte)0x7c, (byte)0xfe,
    (byte)0xc5, (byte)0xa5, (byte)0xa2, (byte)0xe4,
    (byte)0x33, (byte)0x5b, (byte)0x69, (byte)0x04,
    (byte)0x74, (byte)0x84, (byte)0xc1, (byte)0x3b,
    (byte)0xe0, (byte)0xf4, (byte)0x7a, (byte)0xf1,
    (byte)0xcf, (byte)0x98, (byte)0xba, (byte)0x7e,
    (byte)0x0d, (byte)0xcc, (byte)0xf3, (byte)0x63,
    (byte)0x7b, (byte)0xf6, (byte)0x60, (byte)0xac,
    (byte)0xbf, (byte)0x47, (byte)0x97, (byte)0xa6,
    (byte)0x0a, (byte)0xa5, (byte)0x20, (byte)0x39,
    (byte)0x7d, (byte)0x0b, (byte)0xb2, (byte)0x42,
    (byte)0x36, (byte)0x5a, (byte)0x8a, (byte)0xe2,
    (byte)0xe6, (byte)0xd6, (byte)0x32, (byte)0x1c,
    (byte)0xf0, (byte)0x80, (byte)0x02, (byte)0xc8,
    (byte)0x93, (byte)0x14, (byte)0xe3, (byte)0xa4,
    (byte)0x22, (byte)0x51, (byte)0xe6, (byte)0x86,
    (byte)0x08, (byte)0xf5, (byte)0x41, (byte)0xce,
    (byte)0x26, (byte)0x4b, (byte)0x37, (byte)0x50,
    (byte)0x6c, (byte)0x84, (byte)0xf2, (byte)0xa6,
    (byte)0xef, (byte)0x83, (byte)0x2b, (byte)0x15,
    (byte)0xa2, (byte)0xfd, (byte)0x10, (byte)0xa4,
    (byte)0x1f, (byte)0x50, (byte)0x1f, (byte)0x0e,
    (byte)0xd4, (byte)0x54, (byte)0x13, (byte)0xd4,
    (byte)0x31, (byte)0xec, (byte)0x0b, (byte)0x83,
    (byte)0x22, (byte)0x23, (byte)0x18, (byte)0x15,
    (byte)0x7b, (byte)0xf4, (byte)0xf1, (byte)0x79,
    (byte)0xeb, (byte)0x99, (byte)0x6e, (byte)0xbb,
    (byte)0x62, (byte)0x2b, (byte)0x1a, (byte)0x69,
    (byte)0x5f, (byte)0x02, (byte)0x03, (byte)0x01,
    (byte)0x00, (byte)0x01 };

/* Although this example does not use the following private key, if you want to expand
   this example, here is the partner to the above public key. This is the PKCS #8 encoding
   of a private key, so its KeySpec is PKCS8EncodedKeySpec. */
```

Listing 1. *(continued)*

```
static byte[] encodedPrivateKey = {
  (byte)0x30, (byte)0x82, (byte)0x02, (byte)0x3b,
  (byte)0x02, (byte)0x01, (byte)0x00, (byte)0x30,
  (byte)0x0d, (byte)0x06, (byte)0x09, (byte)0x2a,
  (byte)0x86, (byte)0x48, (byte)0x86, (byte)0xf7,
  (byte)0x0d, (byte)0x01, (byte)0x01, (byte)0x01,
  (byte)0x05, (byte)0x00, (byte)0x04, (byte)0x82,
  (byte)0x02, (byte)0x25, (byte)0x30, (byte)0x82,
  (byte)0x02, (byte)0x21, (byte)0x02, (byte)0x01,
  (byte)0x00, (byte)0x02, (byte)0x74, (byte)0x58,
  (byte)0x16, (byte)0xab, (byte)0xfc, (byte)0xf6,
  (byte)0x7c, (byte)0xfe, (byte)0xc5, (byte)0xa5,
  (byte)0xa2, (byte)0xe4, (byte)0x33, (byte)0x5b,
  (byte)0x69, (byte)0x04, (byte)0x74, (byte)0x84,
  (byte)0xc1, (byte)0x3b, (byte)0xe0, (byte)0xf4,
  (byte)0x7a, (byte)0xf1, (byte)0xcf, (byte)0x98,
  (byte)0xba, (byte)0x7e, (byte)0x0d, (byte)0xcc,
  (byte)0xf3, (byte)0x63, (byte)0x7b, (byte)0xf6,
  (byte)0x60, (byte)0xac, (byte)0xbf, (byte)0x47,
  (byte)0x97, (byte)0xa6, (byte)0x0a, (byte)0xa5,
  (byte)0x20, (byte)0x39, (byte)0x7d, (byte)0x0b,
  (byte)0xb2, (byte)0x42, (byte)0x36, (byte)0x5a,
  (byte)0x8a, (byte)0xe2, (byte)0xe6, (byte)0xd6,
  (byte)0x32, (byte)0x1c, (byte)0xf0, (byte)0x80,
  (byte)0x02, (byte)0xc8, (byte)0x93, (byte)0x14,
  (byte)0xe3, (byte)0xa4, (byte)0x22, (byte)0x51,
  (byte)0xe6, (byte)0x86, (byte)0x08, (byte)0xf5,
  (byte)0x41, (byte)0xce, (byte)0x26, (byte)0x4b,
  (byte)0x37, (byte)0x50, (byte)0x6c, (byte)0x84,
  (byte)0xf2, (byte)0xa6, (byte)0xef, (byte)0x83,
  (byte)0x2b, (byte)0x15, (byte)0xa2, (byte)0xfd,
  (byte)0x10, (byte)0xa4, (byte)0x1f, (byte)0x50,
  (byte)0x1f, (byte)0x0e, (byte)0xd4, (byte)0x54,
  (byte)0x13, (byte)0xd4, (byte)0x31, (byte)0xec,
  (byte)0x0b, (byte)0x83, (byte)0x22, (byte)0x23,
  (byte)0x18, (byte)0x15, (byte)0x7b, (byte)0xf4,
  (byte)0xf1, (byte)0x79, (byte)0xeb, (byte)0x99,
  (byte)0x6e, (byte)0xbb, (byte)0x62, (byte)0x2b,
  (byte)0x1a, (byte)0x69, (byte)0x5f, (byte)0x02,
  (byte)0x03, (byte)0x01, (byte)0x00, (byte)0x01,
  (byte)0x02, (byte)0x74, (byte)0x10, (byte)0xb1,
  (byte)0xf3, (byte)0x54, (byte)0xd5, (byte)0x4e,
  (byte)0xa9, (byte)0x66, (byte)0xc2, (byte)0x56,
  (byte)0xd6, (byte)0x13, (byte)0x59, (byte)0xbe,
  (byte)0xd4, (byte)0xa6, (byte)0x54, (byte)0xc6,
  (byte)0xde, (byte)0xd7, (byte)0x6a, (byte)0xde,
  (byte)0xa6, (byte)0x57, (byte)0xe7, (byte)0x25,
  (byte)0x69, (byte)0x60, (byte)0xaa, (byte)0x38,
  (byte)0x72, (byte)0xe1, (byte)0x7a, (byte)0xb7,
  (byte)0xa5, (byte)0xe5, (byte)0xf6, (byte)0xe6,
  (byte)0xaa, (byte)0x04, (byte)0x98, (byte)0x79,
  (byte)0x3c, (byte)0x0c, (byte)0x14, (byte)0x1c,
  (byte)0x6b, (byte)0xea, (byte)0x2b, (byte)0x4c,
```

(continued)

Listing 1. *(continued)*

```
(byte)0xe9, (byte)0x66, (byte)0x40, (byte)0xb0,
(byte)0x6c, (byte)0xc5, (byte)0xb4, (byte)0x2d,
(byte)0x14, (byte)0x9a, (byte)0x4b, (byte)0xbf,
(byte)0x96, (byte)0xe8, (byte)0x67, (byte)0x68,
(byte)0x99, (byte)0xbf, (byte)0xa3, (byte)0x9e,
(byte)0x87, (byte)0xdb, (byte)0x2d, (byte)0xf8,
(byte)0x15, (byte)0x28, (byte)0x89, (byte)0xb7,
(byte)0xcf, (byte)0x81, (byte)0x6a, (byte)0x6f,
(byte)0x0d, (byte)0x66, (byte)0x98, (byte)0x0a,
(byte)0x64, (byte)0xd6, (byte)0x7f, (byte)0xfe,
(byte)0x49, (byte)0xad, (byte)0x06, (byte)0x69,
(byte)0x26, (byte)0xe0, (byte)0xe2, (byte)0xec,
(byte)0x9b, (byte)0x97, (byte)0x93, (byte)0x0d,
(byte)0xeb, (byte)0xc4, (byte)0x2d, (byte)0x6c,
(byte)0x93, (byte)0x1f, (byte)0x32, (byte)0x7d,
(byte)0xfe, (byte)0x59, (byte)0x6c, (byte)0x5f,
(byte)0xbb, (byte)0x59, (byte)0x02, (byte)0x3a,
(byte)0x61, (byte)0xa7, (byte)0xa2, (byte)0x10,
(byte)0xbd, (byte)0x4e, (byte)0xc6, (byte)0x2a,
(byte)0x9d, (byte)0x20, (byte)0x41, (byte)0xfa,
(byte)0xf5, (byte)0x60, (byte)0x11, (byte)0xe1,
(byte)0xb9, (byte)0xee, (byte)0x2d, (byte)0x30,
(byte)0xdc, (byte)0x4a, (byte)0xa3, (byte)0x48,
(byte)0xd5, (byte)0x1f, (byte)0xbf, (byte)0x6e,
(byte)0x7d, (byte)0x63, (byte)0x33, (byte)0x84,
(byte)0xd6, (byte)0xac, (byte)0x3c, (byte)0x81,
(byte)0xc8, (byte)0xb2, (byte)0x78, (byte)0xa5,
(byte)0xb4, (byte)0x16, (byte)0xfd, (byte)0x34,
(byte)0xc4, (byte)0xa1, (byte)0x1c, (byte)0x0b,
(byte)0x29, (byte)0x37, (byte)0x7c, (byte)0xf8,
(byte)0x10, (byte)0xbd, (byte)0x70, (byte)0x73,
(byte)0xaf, (byte)0x6d, (byte)0x02, (byte)0x3b,
(byte)0x00, (byte)0xe6, (byte)0xec, (byte)0x19,
(byte)0xcf, (byte)0x7c, (byte)0xc9, (byte)0x66,
(byte)0x29, (byte)0x53, (byte)0x8f, (byte)0xe7,
(byte)0x5a, (byte)0xf9, (byte)0x23, (byte)0x6d,
(byte)0x59, (byte)0x65, (byte)0xec, (byte)0x47,
(byte)0xcc, (byte)0x27, (byte)0x67, (byte)0xf8,
(byte)0xf4, (byte)0xf2, (byte)0xec, (byte)0x1e,
(byte)0x04, (byte)0x7c, (byte)0x3f, (byte)0xbb,
(byte)0x78, (byte)0x7c, (byte)0xb8, (byte)0x71,
(byte)0xcc, (byte)0x6d, (byte)0x84, (byte)0xfa,
(byte)0x77, (byte)0x95, (byte)0xb3, (byte)0xba,
(byte)0x00, (byte)0xef, (byte)0xbc, (byte)0xc0,
(byte)0x9a, (byte)0xf3, (byte)0xf1, (byte)0x05,
(byte)0xbf, (byte)0x42, (byte)0x58, (byte)0xd3,
(byte)0xc5, (byte)0xa0, (byte)0x7b, (byte)0x02,
(byte)0x3a, (byte)0x10, (byte)0xe6, (byte)0x1e,
(byte)0x60, (byte)0x9b, (byte)0x81, (byte)0x31, (byte)0xf9,
(byte)0x8e, (byte)0xf4, (byte)0x43, (byte)0xd9,
(byte)0xc7, (byte)0x20, (byte)0xe1, (byte)0x30,
(byte)0x16, (byte)0xfc, (byte)0xc2, (byte)0xdf,
(byte)0xa5, (byte)0x1d, (byte)0xe9, (byte)0xf8,
```

Listing 1. *(continued)*

```
(byte)0x99, (byte)0xa8, (byte)0xef, (byte)0xe6,
(byte)0x83, (byte)0xab, (byte)0x45, (byte)0x18,
(byte)0x6c, (byte)0x3b, (byte)0x6d, (byte)0xf0,
(byte)0xc6, (byte)0x90, (byte)0xc1, (byte)0x79,
(byte)0xa9, (byte)0x4b, (byte)0x21, (byte)0xd3,
(byte)0x4d, (byte)0x67, (byte)0x5d, (byte)0x6d,
(byte)0xe9, (byte)0xec, (byte)0x87, (byte)0x02,
(byte)0xa4, (byte)0x36, (byte)0xd9, (byte)0x61,
(byte)0x75, (byte)0x53, (byte)0x7d, (byte)0x02,
(byte)0x3a, (byte)0x4f, (byte)0xb1, (byte)0x21,
(byte)0x43, (byte)0x2a, (byte)0xc4, (byte)0x72,
(byte)0x5e, (byte)0x46, (byte)0xb9, (byte)0x3d,
(byte)0xd5, (byte)0x76, (byte)0x6f, (byte)0x54,
(byte)0x78, (byte)0x6a, (byte)0xa5, (byte)0x3d,
(byte)0x2d, (byte)0xe6, (byte)0x57, (byte)0x8a,
(byte)0x62, (byte)0x36, (byte)0x47, (byte)0x68,
(byte)0x20, (byte)0x92, (byte)0x24, (byte)0x88,
(byte)0x75, (byte)0x0f, (byte)0x4d, (byte)0xb3,
(byte)0xf0, (byte)0x21, (byte)0xc7, (byte)0xa7,
(byte)0x8c, (byte)0x87, (byte)0x7c, (byte)0x4b,
(byte)0xef, (byte)0xb0, (byte)0xcc, (byte)0x8a,
(byte)0x07, (byte)0xaf, (byte)0xb1, (byte)0xf9,
(byte)0x12, (byte)0xc5, (byte)0x39, (byte)0xd4,
(byte)0x73, (byte)0xba, (byte)0x6b, (byte)0x02,
(byte)0x3a, (byte)0x18, (byte)0xf2, (byte)0x6c,
(byte)0x8a, (byte)0x69, (byte)0xd5, (byte)0x96,
(byte)0xf7, (byte)0xc9, (byte)0x5c, (byte)0x57,
(byte)0x2b, (byte)0xb9, (byte)0x2a, (byte)0x3a,
(byte)0xab, (byte)0x4e, (byte)0x7a, (byte)0x0b,
(byte)0xae, (byte)0xc4, (byte)0xd9, (byte)0xc7,
(byte)0x71, (byte)0x7e, (byte)0xa0, (byte)0xc3,
(byte)0x5f, (byte)0xdb, (byte)0x46, (byte)0xe1,
(byte)0x88, (byte)0x7c, (byte)0xd2, (byte)0x36,
(byte)0xd5, (byte)0xee, (byte)0x8d, (byte)0xc4,
(byte)0xff, (byte)0xa0, (byte)0x5e, (byte)0xe5,
(byte)0xc7, (byte)0x3c, (byte)0x03, (byte)0xa6,
(byte)0x65, (byte)0x8c, (byte)0x76, (byte)0x1a,
(byte)0x67, (byte)0xb6, (byte)0x85, (byte)0x19,
(byte)0x40, (byte)0xf3, (byte)0x53 };

public static void main (String[] args)
{
 try
  /* Build a PRNG */
  byte[] seedBytes = { 0, 1, 2, 3 };
  SecureRandom random = SecureRandom.getInstance ("SHA1PRNG");
  random.setSeed (seedBytes);

  /* Build a DES key */
  SecretKeyFactory desKeyFactory =
   SecretKeyFactory.getInstance ("DES");
  byte[] keyData = new byte[8];
  random.nextBytes (keyData);
```

(continued)

Listing 1. *(continued)*

```
DESKeySpec desKeySpec = new DESKeySpec (keyData);
SecretKey desKey = desKeyFactory.generateSecret (desKeySpec);

/* Build an algorithm object that will perform DES */
Cipher desEncrypter =
  Cipher.getInstance ("DES/CBC/PKCS5Padding");
byte[] initVector = new byte[8];
random.nextBytes (initVector);
IvParameterSpec ivParamSpec =
  new IvParameterSpec (initVector);
desEncrypter.init (Cipher.ENCRYPT_MODE, desKey, ivParamSpec);

/* Encrypt arbitrary data */
byte[] dataToEncrypt = { 1, 2, 3, 4, 5, 6, 7, 8, 9, 10, 11};
int outputSize = desEncrypter.getOutputSize (dataToEncrypt.length);
byte[] encryptedData = new byte[outputSize];
int outputLen = zdesEncrypter.update
  (dataToEncrypt, 0, dataToEncrypt.length, encryptedData, 0);
outputLen += desEncrypter.doFinal (encryptedData, outputLen);

// Load up the Acme provider.
Provider newProvider = new Acme ();
int preference = Security.addProvider (newProvider);

// Build an RSA public key object.
KeyFactory rsaKeyFactory =
  KeyFactory.getInstance ("RSA", "Acme");
X509EncodedKeySpec rsaKeySpec =
  new X509EncodedKeySpec (encodedPublicKey);
PublicKey rsaPubKey = rsaKeyFactory. generatePublic (rsaKeySpec);

// Build an algorithm object that will     // perform RSA.
Cipher rsaEncrypter = Cipher.getInstance ("RSA", "Acme");
rsaEncrypter.init (Cipher.ENCRYPT_MODE, rsaPubKey, null, random);
outputSize = rsaEncrypter.getOutputSize (keyData.length);
byte[] encryptedKey = new byte[outputSize];
int encryptedKeyLen = rsaEncrypter.update
  keyData, 0, keyData.length, encryptedKey, 0);
encryptedKeyLen += rsaEncrypter.doFinal (encryptedKey, encryptedKeyLen);

/* Opening the envelope is left as an exercise for the reader */
} catch (Exception anyException) {
  System.out.println ("Exception: " + anyException.getMessage()); } } }
```

Java Application Server Security Using Capabilities

Greg Frascadore

T HE INTERNET HAS FOSTERED rapid growth in the use of application servers. Previously inaccessible outside private Intranets, application servers are increasingly appearing as the middle layer of three-tiered network applications. A GUI executing on a desktop establishes a session with an application server that implements product features on top of a third tier of legacy systems or databases. Supported by growing customer access to the Internet, the application server allows a business to rapidly deploy information products, and services. Java catalyzes the process by speeding the development of both the GUI and server software as well as making the GUI platform-independent.

Application server development is a complex undertaking. Supporting simultaneous GUI connections, application servers must protect the integrity of system data from malicious clients and the privacy of clients from each other. Traditionally this has been accomplished by guarding sensitive data with access control checks. Associated with each protected object, an access control list (ACL) names authorized principals and permitted operations. The server checks the ACL before taking potentially damaging actions. Although this is called an *access list approach,* its essential characteristic is not the use of a list, but the checking of permissions after granting a reference to the protected object. In this approach, the reference does not imply a right to use the protected object.

Described here is an alternative way of protecting objects based on a *capability approach*[1].

Capability designs are often less cluttered, more efficient, and more fail-safe than their access list counterparts. In computer science literature, a capability approach has often been applied within experimental operating systems, but the increasing number and complexity of application servers elevates the need for capabilities to the application level. Capabilities take some getting used to, but it turns out that the Java programming language provides a vehicle to implement them cleanly and efficiently. Capabilities have limitations. They are subject to the confinement problem described later in this article.

CAPABILITIES OVERVIEW

A capability combines access to an object's interface with permission to invoke the operations of that interface. Intuitively, a capability is like a car key; possession of the key is all you need to unlock the car and start the engine. A capability-based system concentrates on regulating the distribution of capabilities rather than on checking credentials. A theater ticket is another metaphor for a capability.

You can build a capability in Java using the *protection proxy*[3] design pattern. Figure 1 diagrams the technique. Ticket A and Ticket B are capabilities limiting access to the ProtectedObject. Each ticket grants a degree of access commensurate with the size of the interface it implements. Because capabilities protect interfaces, not individual operations, adding and layering interfaces are the techniques for creating security levels.

Java and the Java virtual machine (JVM) make an ideal environment for implementing a capability. C and C++ allow one to violate encapsulation by converting integers into pointers, casting pointer types, and exceeding array bounds. However, such improvisation is forbidden to Java programs. In Java, a client has no way to fabricate a ticket reference, exceed the ticket's interface, or wrongfully acquire direct access to the protected object. This is why Java is said to support language-based security[2].

ACCESS LISTS

Before examining capabilities further, let's look at an access list example (Listing 1) using the java.security.acl interfaces. Consider an odometer with protected operations increment and reset.

First we need a definition. A *principal* is an object that represents the accountable party to which privileges are granted. Principals frequently represent people or companies. The call to Session.getPrincipal at (2) fetches the principal on whose behalf the example code is executing. The variable name

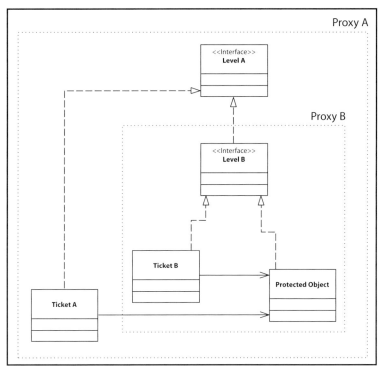

Figure 1. Implementing capabilities as protection proxies.

caller signifies we have fetched the principal attempting to increment or reset the odometer.

Given the principal, Listing 1's approach has some serious drawbacks. Permission to invoke increment or reset is checked by tests at (3) and (4). This technique promotes a defensive style of programming that is error-prone and unsafe. We must insert tests for the appropriate permission against the correct ACL at precise positions within the program. Mistakes result in granting access where it should be denied. This occurs because we are relying on a permission test to stop the client from using a reference already in its possession as a result of line (5). Obviously these tests also impact performance, and they certainly clutter the code with checkPermissions, ACLs, and exceptions.

Access lists have another shortcoming: they discourage delegation. When a client delegates work to a deputy, as the example does at (1), the deputy requires permission to use the protected object. In an access list approach, such permission is transferred separately. Either the client changes the ACL, or it

Listing 1.   Access list example.

```
public interface Odometer {
        Permission INCREMENT = new PermissionImpl("increment");
        Permission RESET = new PermissionImpl("reset");
        void increment();
        void reset(); }

public class Client {
        Odometer odometer;
        public void useOdometer (odometerFactory  odometerFactory) {
                try {
                        odometer = odometerFactory.newOdometer();
                        odometer.increment();
                        odometer.reset();
                } catch (SecurityException e) { } }
        public void delegateWork(Deputy deputy) {
(1)          deputy.work(odometer); } }

public class OdometerImpl implements Odometer {
        Acl acl;
        int counter = 0;
        public OdometerImpl(Acl acl) {
                this.acl = acl;
        }
        public void increment() {
(2)          Principal caller = Session.getPrincipal();
(3)          if (!acl.checkPermission(caller, INCREMENT))
                        throw new SecurityException();
                counter += 1;}
        public void reset() {
                Principal caller = Session.getPrincipal();
(4)          if (!acl.checkPermission(caller, RESET))
                        throw new SecurityException();
                counter = 0; } }

public class OdometerFactory {
        Principal owner;
        public OdometerFactory(Principal owner) {
                this.owner = owner; }
        public Odometer newOdometer() {
                Acl acl = new AclImpl(owner, ...);
                // fill Acl here
(5)          return new OdometerImpl(acl); } }
```

asks the ACL's owner to do so (thereby exposing the client's implementation), or we arrange for the deputy to possess the necessary permission in advance (like a UNIX *setuid* daemon). None of these choices is clean, but the last is the source of a particularly common type of security problem called a *Confused Deputy*[4]: a deputy with lingering permissions just waiting to be duped into acting on behalf of an hostile client.

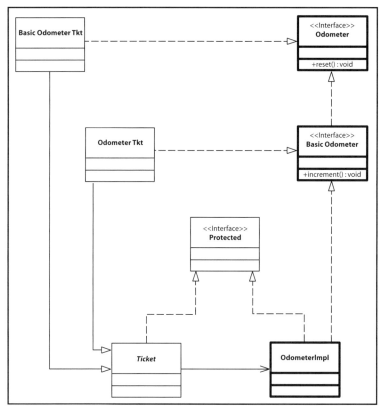

Figure 2.. Odometer capabilities and interfaces.

CAPABILITY APPROACH

A capability approach to the odometer example is sketched in Figure 2. A developer codes the class and interfaces with **bold** outlines. The types Protected and Ticket are from a class library.

Here we have partitioned the OdometerImpl's interface into layers (BasicOdometer and Odometer), and then used a post-processor (described) to create the tickets (capabilities). In practice, this is much easier than writing permission tests as the access list approach would have us do. Each ticket implements one of the layered interfaces. This allows its assignment to any variable of that interface type. A factory constructs the ticket as the rewritten odometer example in Listing 2 shows. The Client class is unchanged from Listing 1.

Note these differences from Listing 1:

Listing 2.   Odometer rewritten.

```
(6)   public interface BasicOdometer {
          void increment(); }

      public interface Odometer extends BasicOdometer {
          void reset(); }

      public class OdometerImpl implements Odometer, Protected {
          int counter = 0;
(7)       public void increment() {
              counter += 1; }
          public void reset() {
              counter = 0; } }

      public class OdometerFactory {
          public Odometer newOdometer() {
              Odometer odometer = new OdometerImpl();
(8)           return new OdometerTkt(odometer); } }
```

- (6) Callers obtain references to interfaces not permissions for individual methods
- (7) The increment and reset methods are not cluttered with permission tests
- (8) The returned ticket implies permission to use the ticket's interfaces

There are some details to discuss: how are the ticket classes generated? How does the OdometerFactory construct tickets? Doesn't newOdometer need to check an access list when deciding whether to grant the OdometerTkt?

TICKET CLASS GENERATION

The post-processor generates one ticket for every protected interface. Each ticket is a class with suffix *Tkt* (Listing 3).

The protected interfaces, like Odometer and BasicOdometer, are compiled first. The resulting class files are then post-processed in a manner reminiscent of rmic:

```
javac BasicOdometer.java Odometer.java
tgen BasicOdometer Odometer
```

You can obtain a copy of the **tgen** program from the Object Guild Web site. It operates using the following rules:

1. Assume Protected and Ticket are defined as shown in Listing 3. For each post-processed interface Foo, generate the beginning of a new ticket as follows:

Listing 3. Post-processor generated code.

```
// Protected and Ticket have fixed definitions

public interface Protected {/*empty*/}

public abstract class Ticket implements Protected {
    protected Protected obj;
    protected Ticket(Protected obj) {
                this.obj = obj; } }

// Post-processor generated code below

public class BasicOdometerTkt extends Ticket implements BasicOdometer {
    public static final String IFNAME = BasicOdometer.class.getName();
    public BasicOdometerTkt(Protected obj) {
        super(obj); }
    public void increment() {
        ((BasicOdometer)obj).increment(); } }

public class OdometerTkt extends Ticket implements Odometer {
    public static final String IFNAME = Odometer.class.getName();
    public OdometerTkt(Protected obj) {
        super(obj); }
    public void increment() {
        ((Odometer)obj).increment(); }
    public void reset() {
        ((Odometer)obj).reset(); } }
```

```
public class FooTkt extends Ticket implements Foo {
      public static final String IFNAME = Foo.class.getName();
      public FooTkt(Protected obj) {
            super(obj);
      }
```

2. For each **fooMethod** of interface **Foo** that returns void, generate an identically named method in **FooTkt** with the same arguments and exceptions, by replacing the body of **Foo.fooMethod** with a delegation through Ticket.obj as follows:

```
public void fooMethod(...) throws ... {
      ((Foo)obj).fooMethod(...);
}
```

3. For each **fooMethod** of interface **Foo** that returns a result, generate an identically named method in **FooTkt** with the same arguments, exceptions, and result type, by replacing the body of **Foo.fooMethod** with a delegation through Ticket.obj as follows:

```
public ResultType fooMethod(...) ... {
    return ((Foo)obj).fooMethod(...);
}
```

TICKET CONSTRUCTION

Factories construct tickets to encapsulate a reference to the protected object. To create the ticket, the factory must possess the reference beforehand. How does the factory obtain that reference in the first place? It must do so in a secure fashion otherwise a client, using some oversight like a public variable, could obtain the reference and act unchecked.

The factory obtains the reference in one of three ways:

- It constructs the protected object itself, safeguarding the reference in non-public variables
- It obtains the reference from non-public variables
- As the result of a non-public method

In our odometer example, the factory used the first of these when it constructed the OdometerImpl.

When protected objects are persistent, there seems to be a problem. Java's language-based security does not protect persistent state outside of the JVM. Here, the factory must use some additional mechanism, like file permissions or encryption, to protect that state. The factory can construct the protected object after retrieving, and possibly decrypting, the persistent state. It then builds a ticket around the resulting object reference.

GRANTING TICKETS

Capability systems concentrate on regulating the distribution of capabilities, so by this time someone is probably wondering how the factory decides whether to grant a ticket. In Listing 2 at (8), it always returns one. Certainly, there must be situations where more discretion is required.

There are three philosophies on this subject:

- purist: in a good design, no decision is necessary; just return a ticket
- bridge: ask another subsystem
- retro: check a voucher, possibly stored in an ACL

In a pure capability design, there is never a need for the factory to decide. Instead of working backwards from protected operations and deciding how to check whether the caller has permission, the pure approach works forward from where permission is granted. When an administrator configures an application server to grant a privilege, the server builds a capability and gives it to the grantee. In our example, when an administrator grants permission to reset an odometer, the server either builds an OdometerTkt and gives it to the client, or it gives the client a ticket to the OdometerFactory. The OdometerFactory would itself be a protected object and would not need to check if the client has permission; the ticket is all the evidence it needs. The purist approach is the cleanest, most efficient, and admittedly hardest to take. It requires a complete system design with capabilities in mind.

The purist approach is impossible when the application server is built on top of a non-capability infrastructure (like the Java API). Here a protected object can be an aggregation of components, each protected by other means. To handle this, you can code a bridge between capabilities and the other systems. Consider a database built using an instance of java.io.File.

```
public interface Database {
    // database operations
}

public class DatabaseFactory {
    public Database newDatabase(File db) {

        if (!db.canWrite())
            return null;
        ...
        return new DatabaseTkt(
            new DatabaseImpl(db));
    }
}
```

Here the call to File.canWrite is the bridge to the underlying Java permission system.

Listing 4.   Java API bridge.

```
public class System {
    ...
    public static Properties getProperties() {
        ...
        if (securityManager != null)
        securityManager.checkPropertiesAccess();
        ...
        return properties; }
```

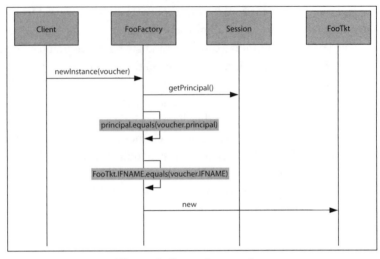

Figure 3. Retro interaction.

When using a bridge, sometimes the underlying permission system can re-voke access after a capability is granted. In the case of this database, the file could become unwritable and a SecurityException thrown upon using the capability—a situation at odds with the definition of a capability. To handle this, we could modify tgen to generate tickets that re-throw SecurityExcep-tions as RevokedTicketExceptions.

Interestingly, the Java API uses the bridge philosophy itself. Some system classes, like FileInputStream, Socket, and System have capability-like inter-faces. Internally the constructors defer to the SecurityManager using code similar to Listing 4.

Finally, the *retro* philosophy is useful when a seamless capability design is impractical. In retro, a ticket factory consults a voucher before returning a ticket. The voucher names a principal and a particular ticket type. The fac-tory compares the named principal against the caller's principal (from Ses-sion.getPrincipal), matches the ticket types, and returns a ticket if the tests succeed. See Figure 3. Essentially, the factory redeems vouchers for tickets after checking credentials.

While foregoing the cleanliness of a pure capability design, the retro ap-proach allows an application server to isolate permission testing code in the factory. Retro is particularly handy at dealing with cases where a client is sep-arated from its capabilities (on logout for example). A ticket is saved as a per-sistent voucher. An authenticated client can retrieve and redeem the voucher at a later time (at login). A useful trick is to use an ACL like a booklet con-taining a stack of vouchers. Each ACL entry implements one voucher:

> ## Netscape's Java Capabilities API
>
> Netscape uses the term *capabilities* when referring to its security API for signed applets, but that system does not involve capabilities as the term is used in this article or in the computer security literature.
>
> A Netscape capability[5] refers to a privilege to invoke an operation that would normally be denied to an applet running within the Java sandbox. A signed applet, running in Netscape Navigator, may request a privilege by calling PrivilegeManager.enablePrivilege. The parameter to this method designates a restricted operation, like File.write. If enablePrivilege returns normally, a privilege to use the operation is granted by Netscape's security manager.
>
> The Capabilities API is actually an access list approach. The Netscape security manager guards restricted operations with tests checking whether the invoking applet has enabled the proper privilege; enablePrivilege succeeds if the applet is signed by a principal authorized to possess the privilege. The use of the term *capabilities* in Netscape's name for this API should not be interpreted as meaning the system uses a capability model, one that unites access and permission in a single token conventionally called a capability. However, capabilities can be built on top of the Netscape API using the bridge philosophy as described in the main body of this article.

```
public class OdometerFactory {
    Acl acl;

    ...

    public Odometer newOdometer() {
        Principal caller = Session.getPrincipal();
        Permission perm =
            new PermissionImpl(OdometerTkt.IFNAME);
        if (!acl.checkPermission(caller, perm))
            throw new SecurityException();
        return new OdometerTkt(new OdometerImpl());
    }
}
```

CONFINEMENT PROBLEM

Capabilities have a serious limitation; it is called the *confinement problem.* In short, once a capability is granted, it is very hard to control where it propagates—if you lend out your car keys, they can easily wind up in the wrong hands. The previously mentioned support for delegation is the precursor to this symptom of over-delegation.

An application server can deal with confinement the way operating systems have done in the past: retain capabilities internally. The server can build a kind of keychain by linking capabilities to client sessions. The capabilities limit the client's activities: an operation proceeds if the client holds the proper capability. Internally, server classes delegate by passing capabilities around. However, the server never returns a capability to a client. In the best case, it doesn't even provide a mechanism (interface) to export capabilities outside itself.

CONCLUSION

Capabilities are efficient, uncluttered, and fail-safe. In our **Odometer** example, capabilities replace the permission tests that normally occur during every invocation of a protected operation. A post-processor can generate capabilities directly from the declarations of protected interfaces. As a result, the **increment** and **reset** methods take on an uncluttered appearance. By uniting access with permission, a capability approach is fail-safe, in contrast to an access list approach where mistakes result in granting access. Capabilities have an important limitation in the confinement problem. However, this is not an issue when they are used within an application server that provides no mechanism to pass them outside the server's boundary. Java and the JVM make an ideal environment for implementing a capability by nature of their support for language-based security.

ACKNOWLEDGMENTS

Thanks to Steve Senator, Chuck Suscheck, and Garrison Venn for their help with this article.

REFERENCES

1. Saltzer, J. H., and M.D. Schroeder, "The Protection of Information in Computer Systems," Proceedings of the IEEE, Vol. 63, No. 9, 1975, pp. 1278–1308.
2. Wallach, D., D. Balfanz, D. Dean, and E. W. Felton, "Extensible Security Architectures for Java," 16th Symposium on Operating System Principles, Oct. 1997, www.es.princeton.edu /sip/pub/sosp97/paper.html.

3. Gamma, E., R. Helm, R. Johnson and J. Vlissides, *Design Patterns*, Addison-Wesley, Reading MA. 1995.

4. Hardy, N., The Confused Deputy, www.cis. upeen.edu/~KeyKOS/ConfusedDeputy.html.

5. Java Capabilities API, Netscape, http://developer.netscape.com/docs/manuals/signedobj.

TESTING

Effective Test Strategies for Enterprise-Critical Applications

Kamesh Pemmaraju

J
AVA HAS QUICKLY evolved into more than a simple-minded language used to create cute animations on the Web. These days, a large number of serious Java developers are building enterprise-critical applications that are being deployed by large companies around the world. Some applications currently being developed on the Java platform range from traditional Spreadsheets and Word Processors to Accounting, Human Resources, and Financial Planning applications. Because these applications are complex and use rapidly evolving Java technology, companies need to employ a vigorous quality assurance program to produce a high-quality and reliable product. Quality assurance and test teams must get involved early in the product development life cycle, creating a sound test plan, and applying an effective test strategy to insure that these enterprise-critical applications provide accurate results and are defect-free. Accuracy is critical for users who apply these results to crucial decisions about their business, their finances, and their enterprise. I present a case-study of how an effective testing strategy, focused on sub-system level automation, was applied to successfully test a critical real-world Java-based financial application.

The Application

The application is being developed by a leading financial services company (hereafter referred to as *client*) and is targeted toward both individual investors and institutional investors, particularly those investors that are interested in managing their finances and retirement plans. Reliable Software Technologies (RST) provided the QA/Test services and the test team (hereafter referred to as the *QA/Test team*) to the client. Because RST carried out third-party independent testing of the client application, some details about the development of the product were missing. However, RST received enough information to perform an effective test cycle on the product.

The application to be tested is a personal financial planning package. In addition to investment planning, the package features financial planning for college, retirement, and estate. The software is designed for, and tested on, Windows 95, Windows 98, and Windows NT platforms and both Sun's JDK 1.1.6 and Microsoft's JVM. The application is a very complex, data-driven, and computationally intensive Java-based application capable of performing several thousand calculations while processing more than 1000 input variables. The number of calculations and their complexity almost rules out any manual validation and demands an automated solution to execute tests and an *Oracle* to verify the accuracy of the results. The Oracle is not to be confused with the popular database software of the same name; rather the Oracle is a *Reference Spreadsheet* that does the same calculations (for validation purposes) as the application under test. The Reference Spreadsheet is implemented in Microsoft Excel.

The client design team decided early on to separate the user-interface software and the business software (referred hereafter as the *backend*). This decision was in part due to the client management's goal to eventually deploy the application on the Web. For future Web implementation of the application, the design team decided to re-use the backend software (e.g., on the application server) and re-implement the GUI as a thin-client. A thin-client could be a simple Java applet or application that handles user input and display while the server software could perform all the complex calculations on a dedicated application server.

For testing purposes, the decision to separate the backend from the GUI proved to be crucial. The application performs hundreds of calculations behind the scenes and the user interface only partially shows what happens inside. Sometimes, a very complicated internal processing produces only a single final result. Clearly, in this situation, testing *only* through the GUI is not enough. Separating the GUI from the backend allowed comprehensive automated verification of the backend calculations at a much higher level of granularity.

During the design phase, the client application designers used Rational Rose to design the backend software and to develop use cases and Object Models for the application. Use cases are used as a means of describing the functionality of a system in object-oriented software development. Each use case represented a specific flow of events in the system. The description of a use case defined what should happen in the system when the use case is performed. These use cases were later used to define the Objects (Java classes) required in the system. At the end of the design phase, the backend consisted of nearly a hundred Java classes and several hundred use cases.

The client management made an important early decision: to develop a Reference Spreadsheet that can be used to validate the thousands of calculations performed by the backend. The Reference Spreadsheet was developed using several inter-linked Microsoft Excel worksheets that implemented the same functionality as the application under test. As described later, the creation of the Reference Spreadsheet proved to be extremely useful for automated validation of the calculations. The medium for automation here was Visual Basic for Applications (VBA).

Finally, the client development team created a data-dictionary that contained detailed information on the range and limits of all the input variables of the application. The data-dictionary proved to be an invaluable test entity that was later used for automatic generation of thousands of semantically correct and constrained test data. In addition, test data that fell outside the bounds of the defined ranges was generated. This test data was used to verify the error and range handling of the application. Because the data-dictionary was in Microsoft Excel, the test-data generation software was written in VBA.

Test Approach

Testing a relatively large Java application under an aggressive schedule requires that the QA/Test teams get involved early in the life cycle creating a sound test plan and then applying an effective test strategy. The following is a description of some factors that helped ensure a successful test life cycle for the application.

Early Life Cycle Testing

Test plan analysis and design during the initial stages of a software project aided in the success of the test implementation, efficiency, rigor, coverage, and overall quality of a product. The early life cycle testing approach employed was based on the development model of the project. The development model was evolutionary: the design team incrementally modeled the Use Cases, then carried out the OO design, and finally constructed and unit-tested the code. At the end of each iteration, the design team handed over the use cases, the OO models, and alpha code to the QA/Test team. Based on these documents, the QA/Test team identified a strategy that would improve the testability of the code (testability in this context is defined as the ability to minimize the effort required to apply the chosen test strategy to the system), evaluated tools that supported test automation, and prepared detailed test requirements.

Specifically, the QA/Test team's activities were: development of a use case test plan, development of class level test requirements, evaluation of Sun Microsystems's GUI test tool JavaStar for system-level GUI test, and some initial system level testing of the alpha versions.

A number of benefits were realized by the QA/Test team initiating quality assurance work early in the life cycle and concurrent with the development process:

- An early understanding of the design structure and functionality of the product and develop effective test strategies.
- Increased awareness of design issues to be considered along with items or issues, which were a high priority in facilitating early test planning.
- To execute a more rapid and effective response as the product moved to completion.

TEST STRATEGY

The test plan defined a multi-pronged approach consisting of the following five activities to test various aspects of the application:

- Sub-system level testing
- GUI Integration system testing
- System level testing
- Use case testing
- Range/Error handling testing

The test approach clearly defined exit criteria to determine when to stop testing activities and when to ship the product. Finally, all test activities focused on maximizing automation of tests whenever possible. What follows is a brief description of these five activities.

SUB-SYSTEM LEVEL TESTING OF THE BACKEND

Given the limited testing time and the large number of backend Java classes to test (nearly 100), an approach toward unit testing based purely on individual class-level testing was neither feasible nor cost-effective. Moreover, many individual classes served only as support classes or utility classes in the class framework (especially those at the lower end of the class hierarchy) and did not, therefore, produce application-level results that could be validated against the Reference Spreadsheet. Consequently, the QA/Test team chose a collection of class sub-systems to test at the "unit" level. The choice of sub-systems to test was made in the Reference Spreadsheet, which defined 25 distinct sub-systems.

The test approach for sub-system testing was essentially black box in nature requiring generation of test inputs, development of test drivers, and development of utilities for automated verification of the outputs against the Reference Spreadsheet. Unfortunately, black box testing has one notable drawback—it fails to exercise significant portions of the code. However, coverage measurement and analysis can determine the portions of the code unexercised by black box testing. The QA/Test team utilized Reliable Software Technology's Deepcover™ as its Java coverage tool to identify areas of inadequate coverage in the code. Additional test cases were created as needed to improve the coverage levels achieved.

A test framework was developed to support an automated verification of the backend subsystems. The framework consisted of the following components:

- Test Data Generation tool
- Test Drivers
- Comparator

The following is a brief description of these components:

Test data generation—The QA/Test team developed a test data generation tool that could automatically generate thousands of test cases containing constrained test data for each sub-system of the product. The tool was developed using VBA taking advantage of the powerful constraint satisfaction algorithms available in Microsoft Excel. To automatically generate test data, the tool used the information on the range and limits of the input variables in each sub-system. The tool obtained this information from the data-dictionary, which contained the range information for each input variable. The range information was available as minimum, maximum, typical minimum, and typical maximum values. The test data generation tool used this range information in the data dictionary to generate test data such as random values within the maximum range, random values within the typical range, inner bounds, and outer bounds. The data dictionary also defined error messages that should be displayed when the user inputs values outside the valid bounds. This error message information in the data-dictionary was later used for Range/Error testing.

Using the data generation tool, the QA/Test team generated 1500 test cases (a few test cases are defined next) for each of the 25 different sub-systems, totaling 37,500 test cases. Each test case consisted of a row of test data (see Table 1) used to populate the input variables of the sub-system under test. As shown in the table, the input variables are represented in columns and the test cases are represented in rows. The last column (**ErrorStatus**) shows whether the test case represents normal

Table 1. Example test case file.

Tests number	ID String	Contributions Double	Balance Double	StartYear Double	StopYear Double	ErrorStatus String
Testcase 1	RothIRA1	32.535055	5564695.596695	0.749640	0.061425	NORMAL
Testcase 2	RothIRA2	252.356084	6395447.850227	0.420031	0.978902	NORMAL
Testcase 3	RothIRA3	296.574927	2281296.253204	0.250895	0.633954	NORMAL
Testcase 4	RothIRA4	1000000.00	5363611.578941	0.235563	0.139361	ERROR

processing or exception processing. In this example, the last test case exercises the exception processing because the **RothIRA4** contribution ($1 million) exceeds the maximum allowable contribution. Notice the values for **StartYear** and **StopYear**: these are represented in random double values between 0 and 1 instead of regular year format. The test drivers (described next) use these random numbers and other context-sensitive dates (e.g., of birth, year of retirement, etc.) to generate the actual start and stop years. This was a simple and elegant way to deal with multi-constraint variables without complicating the process of data generation. The test data was stored in a flat file, one for each sub-system, in a fixed-width format so that it was easy to export it to a database or spreadsheet.

Test drivers—To exercise the backend code using the generated test data, the QA/test team developed component-level Java drivers for each sub-system. The test drivers read in the previously generated test data (see Table 1) from a file, used the set methods of the component to assign test data to the input variables, called the functions that calculate the results, and finally wrote the results to a file. Simultaneously, spreadsheet drivers were developed in VBA to perform this exact same process on the Reference Spreadsheet. The results of the Reference Spreadsheet were then compared with those of the backend. Unfortunately, sometimes the Reference Spreadsheet itself produced incorrect results. Nevertheless, discrepancies provided warnings and prompted further investigation.

After the sub-system level Java drivers were completed, a suite of Java integration drivers was developed, which incorporated methods in the module-level classes, as well as new functionality needed for integration testing. A similar process was followed for the spreadsheet drivers. Overall, 25 Java test drivers and 25 VB drivers were developed comprising 3,700 and 8,500 lines of test code, respectively. Together, the Java and VB test driver code accounted for 12,200 lines of code, which are almost 50% of the total lines of code of the backend. Studies have often shown that for well-tested applications, test code comprises 50% of all code written for a project.

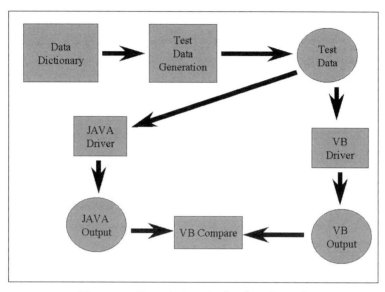

Figure 1. Examining the backend results.

Comparator—Because the calculations performed by the backend often produced hundreds of output variables, an automated comparison tool was developed in Visual Basic to examine and compare the backend results with those of the spreadsheet. The comparator tool discarded unneeded text strings before making comparisons of the output results. A backend-calculated value was deemed correct if it deviated by less than .0001% from the spreadsheet calculation. This represented a variation of, at most, one dollar in a million dollars and this was deemed acceptable if the variation is caused due to drifts in floating point accuracy in the Java system and Microsoft Excel. At the end of the entire test suite execution, the total number of actual comparisons of the backend results and the spreadsheet was close to *three-quarters of a million* (693,122). Nearly 98% of these comparisons passed. The overall scheme is illustrated in the Figure 1.

GUI INTEGRATION TESTING

GUI integration testing verified end-to-end functionality of the application. The input data was entered through the GUI and the results obtained were verified against the spreadsheet. GUI integration tests were automated using JavaStar in only one area of the application. Other areas were tested manually due to the limitations of JavaStar (these are described in "Lessons Learned" section) and lack of time.

Table 2. Test summary and statistics.

Total number of sub-system test cases	37,500
Total number of output comparisons	693,122
Number of passed comparisons	679,259 (Pass percentage = 98%)
Total lines of test code (Java and VB)	12,200 (50% of total backend code)
Total number of use cases verified	3200
Number of passed use cases	2880 (Pass percentage = 90%)
Total number of versions tested	30 (9 Alpha and 21 Beta)
Statement coverage obtained for the entire backend code	80.016% (43 modules out of 152 achieved 100% coverage)
Total number of defects found	162 (52% functional failures, 30% critical defects)

System Testing

System testing was performed to verify that the application as a whole performed correctly when used in real-life conditions. System-level testing was done manually due to limitations with JavaStar. Some of the difficulties faced with JavaStar are described next. Most problems found during system level testing were incorrect error messages, minor functionality failures, "look-and-feel" problems, and usability issues.

Use Case Testing

Use case testing verified specific paths through the application as specified by use case documentation provided by development team The use cases were executed at least once, with all outputs being analyzed for correctness and usability. More than 3,200 use case tests were executed manually against the application, and about 90% of these passed the tests. The remaining 10% of the use case tests were either not verifiable or did not behave correctly, and were therefore reported as bugs. The test results were tracked manually during the testing cycle and then cross-referenced in an Excel spreadsheet for further validation and verification.

Range and Error Handling Testing

The approach to range testing focused on testing maximum/minimum range values, invalid characters, and error handling.

- Minimum and maximum values were identified for each field in the application as specified by the data dictionary. Test cases ensured that values were within the specified range (including the boundary values) and all values outside the range produced appropriate error messages.
- Error messages were also validated based on incorrect input. By entering an invalid value, error messages were verified and analyzed for correctness.

Table 2 presents a summary of the test results and some interesting statistics on the test cycle.

LESSONS LEARNED

EARLY LIFE-CYCLE ISSUES AND DEVELOPER-TESTER INTERACTIONS

The QA/Test team had an opportunity early in the design process to review the Rational Rose design diagrams, the data dictionary, and the spreadsheet documentation. The data dictionary and the spreadsheet documentation were particularly useful in the development of the test data generation scheme and test requirements for class level testing. These documents were also very helpful for the development of the VB drivers. The data dictionary, however, was suitable for neither test data generation nor was it in a format amenable for data access from other applications. The QA/Test team modified the data dictionary so that it was possible to access the information in a uniform manner.

While this early involvement was clearly helpful in several ways, there are still some areas that could be improved. One is the lack of one-on-one interaction with the design/development team early in the life cycle. While use cases and object models were provided early, these were not sufficient. Without interaction with the design team—to understand the reasoning behind their design—it was sometimes difficult to effectively use the object models and use cases. One-on-one interaction between the QA/Test teams and the developers earlier in the life cycle would have provided several advantages:

- Complex development issues, such as understanding the object models, integration issues, etc., could have been quickly addressed.
- Certain financial algorithms, limits, maximums, and boundaries could have been better understood and thereby reduced the troubleshooting time of sub-system and Reference Spreadsheet drivers.

- Better understanding of the intended customers and their needs would also have helped to reduce troubleshooting time.

The early personal level of interaction would have also facilitated understanding of factors such as purpose of software, user requirements, typical environment, business logic, and performance requirements. This in turn could have helped the QA/Test team to create a much more effective and accurate test plan.

GUI-BACKEND SEPARATION

The separation of the GUI and the backend, enabled backend testing without requiring access to the GUI functionality. However, testing the GUI functionality and its communication with the backend was made difficult due to the tight coupling between the GUI and the backend. GUI integration testing checks to see whether the GUI communicates data to and from the backend correctly. If these two systems are tightly integrated, it is difficult to determine whether entered information is being processed, and passed on to the backend properly by the GUI. Providing hooks into the GUI and backend for accessing state information would also greatly enhance the value and efficiency of GUI testing.

ISSUES WITH THE REFERENCE SPREADSHEET

The Reference Spreadsheet was implemented by the client and contained the same functionality as the application under-test. The Reference Spreadsheet was just another implementation of a complex application and was therefore as faulty as the implementation of the software-under-test: it was not completely accurate and it did not always provide the correct answers. This is not surprising because if the Reference Spreadsheet has to provide the correct answers accurately and completely, it must be at least as complex (and hence likely to be as faulty) as the program under verification.

Nevertheless, the Reference Spreadsheet proved to be very useful for automated verification of results, as it was possible to write scripts to drive the Spreadsheet and obtain results from it. Moreover, the Reference Spreadsheet was the only specification for the backend calculations. Any discrepancies in the results from the backend and spreadsheet provided warnings. Sometimes the Oracle was incorrect, sometimes the backend was incorrect (real bug), and sometimes both were wrong. The analysis of these discrepancies often helped in identifying faults made in the backend and the spreadsheet and at times even caught errors of omission in the code and requirements that were totally overlooked.

Java Standards

There are several standard interfaces designed to be used by Java objects to aid in debugging and testing. Using these interfaces can increase efficiency of testing and debugging with minimal effort.

- **Java.awt.Component.setName()**

All GUI components that derive from **java.awt.Component** should use the **setName()** method to identify instances of the component. This allows GUI testing programs to identify the GUI component quickly, regardless of position on the page. This makes it possible to change the layout of a page without affecting GUI testing scripts.

- **Object.toString()**

The purpose of the **toString()** method, as stated in the Java specifications, is to provide a standard interface for displaying state information. Every class should provide a **toString()** method that dumps the values of current state variables, possibly also calling the **toString()** function of the superclass. This will speed both debugging and development of test drivers.

Issues with Test Automation Using JavaStar

Despite some initial drawbacks, JavaStar was deemed usable enough to support automated testing for use case, system, and integration testing. However, many problems surfaced throughout the test life cycle, which caused delays and hindered the testing effort. Because the GUI code-base did not explicitly name the GUI components using the **setName()** method, JavaStar automatically provided its own names. These names were usually incomprehensible because they had no correlation to the application names. For example, an "OK" button on the first GUI form was named **Nav3Button21()**. This posed a problem for long-term test script comprehension and maintenance. An effort was also made to use JavaStar for automated use case testing. Because use case scenarios involved testing of exceptions, it was attempted to synchronize the application's exceptions with JavaStar exceptions to facilitate the throwing of exceptions. However, JavaStar would catch the exceptions and terminate the test because it assumes that if an exception was thrown, the user did not want to continue. Because use case testing is not data driven and does not require as much repetition, JavaStar was abandoned because of these technical difficulties.

Extracting data from some screens of the application was also problematic. In one of the sections of the application, data was painted onto the screen and therefore could not be selected and copied into a results file for later comparison with Java driver generated results. The only solution was to write a traversal procedure and insert it unobtrusively into backend code to gather results. A call to the output function was inserted in the required class files for report generation.

Finally, JavaStar had problems handling warning pop-ups that the application was creating when exceptions were thrown. When encountering such a window, it would throw its own exception and terminate the current test as well as other tests. To handle these warnings, subroutines were written to check whether a warning window should come up in a certain case, at which time "OK" would be clicked on the warning window.

Summary

Using the approaches described in this article, the test team reached an average of 80% statement coverage for the *entire backend* code. Critical modules reached 100% statement coverage and less critical modules reached 95% statement coverage.

Several defects were uncovered and fixed during the test cycle. Java-specific tools for GUI testing (Sun Microsystem's JavaStar) and coverage measurements (RST's Deepcover) simplified the tasks of implementation and execution of tests. The high levels of test productivity achieved through automation and the demonstration of reliability of the product resulted in a highly satisfied client and a high-quality Java product.

PUTTING JAVABEANS TO THE TEST

David Houlding

J AVABEANS ARE REUSABLE software components that are assembled using a visual assembly tool to create Java applets or applications. The JavaBean standard provides a software component architecture for Java that promises to deliver rapid application development (RAD) by enhancing reuse and increasing the abstraction level of software development, enabling even non-programmers to develop Java applets and applications. JavaBeans derive power because one can configure and connect beans to achieve sophisticated functionality without knowing all of the internal details of beans themselves.

In principle, a bean may be used by just knowing "what" it does without necessarily knowing "how" it works. For example, a loan calculator bean can calculate the principal and interest due on a loan. Generally, this is sufficient information to use the bean without having to know the details of the algorithm the bean uses. However, this requires some measure of trust on the part of the person using the bean. To draw again on the loan calculator bean example—if the configured loan calculator bean says we need to make a payment of $550 per month for the term of the loan, we need to trust that this result is correct without meticulously working through the beans implementation to ensure it calculates correctly. Clearly, without this trust the bean loses much of its power as a software component for reuse and RAD, and worse still, fuels the "not invented here" syndrome. To earn this trust, the bean must behave in a robust, predictable manner and consistently deliver high quality services to other beans in a sometimes unpredictable environment. After all, it is generally impossible at the time of development to anticipate the beans reuse in every possible situation.

A common oversight made by a developer of a new bean is assuming that other beans using the services of the new bean will provide inputs to, and accept outputs from the new bean that are in the ranges the developer expects. Similarly, visual assembly tools allow developers to configure bean properties. Another common oversight of bean developers is assuming that the properties of a bean will be configured with values that are within expected ranges. In the past, JavaBeans were used primarily to implement GUI widgets. Oversights were not too dangerous, because if a component was not configured or was not behaving correctly, it was generally apparent from the visual nature of these GUI beans. However, more complex non-GUI "invisible" beans are now being developed for mission-critical enterprise systems and there is consequently an elevated need for beans to be more testable.

TESTING JAVABEANS

To develop reusable beans that behave in a robust predictable manner, it is important to provide facilities in the bean, which allow verification through testing that its inputs, outputs, behavior, and state are valid. However, it is desirable to provide these facilities in such a way that they don't compromise the beans' performance in a real implementation. The following discussion illustrates how some well established software testing strategies may be practiced during bean development in a way that is consistent with the JavaBean standard and development paradigm.

A JavaBean is effectively tested through two strategies: the first strategy includes preconditions, assertions, and postconditions, while the second strategy involves self-testing. The bean developer implements these testing strategies when the bean is created, and allows the bean to be tested either while it is under development or after it has been configured for use in a larger system. However, these strategies do require some software development discipline from the bean developer. Each of these strategies is discussed and illustrated in more detail.

PRECONDITIONS, ASSERTIONS, AND POSTCONDITIONS

Preconditions, assertions, and postconditions may be used to verify that the inputs, intermediate results, and outputs from JavaBean methods, respectively, are valid. For example, consider a utility bean implemented in a class named "Assert" that implements preconditions, assertions, and postconditions; and an example bean with a public method "calculateResult." These strategies may be used as shown in the following example:

```
public double calculateResult( double input )
{
Assert.precondition( input < 3.5,
   "input is too high: " + input );
:

:

Assert.assertion( intermediateResult.equals( "January" ) ||
   intermediateResult.equals( "February" ),
   "intermediateResult is invalid: " +
   intermediateResult );
:

:

Assert.postcondition( output > threshold,
   "output is too low: " + output );

return output;
}
```

Preconditions, assertions, and postconditions have similar method signatures where the first argument is an expression that evaluates to a boolean value and the second argument is some expression that evaluates to a string textual message. The behavior of these methods is to log the message if the boolean expression evaluates to *false*. The bean providing these services may also provide switches to conveniently turn preconditions, assertions, and postconditions *on* during testing or *off* during normal execution to improve performance. A simple example implementation of the Assert class as a JavaBean is shown in Listing 1.

Note that the Assert class is implemented as a JavaBean, allowing it to be used for interactive testing of beans using, for example, the BeanBox tool distributed with the Bean Development Kit (available from the Sun Web site).

Where preconditions, assertions, and postconditions evaluate to *false* an AssertFailedException is created but is used only to generate output rather than being thrown. This is desirable, because if these methods were to throw the exception, this would force any method preconditions, assertions, or postconditions to also throw the exception, making their use awkward and impractical. If a precondition, assertion, or postcondition fails, the Assert bean will produce output similar to this:

Listing 1.

```java
import java.io.*;

public class Assert implements Serializable
{
        private static boolean
        preconditionOn = false;
        private static boolean assertionOn = false;
        private static boolean
        postconditionOn = false;
        private static PrintStream
        outputStream = System.err;

        public static boolean precondition( boolean conditionTrue,String message ) {
            if( preconditionOn & ( ! conditionTrue ) ) {
                new AssertFailedException( "Precondition failed: " + message
                ).printStackTrace( outputStream ); }
            return conditionTrue; }

        public static boolean assertion( boolean conditionTrue, String message ) {
            if( assertionOn & ( ! conditionTrue ) ) {
                new AssertFailedException( "Assertion failed: " +
                message ).printStackTrace( outputStream ); }
            return conditionTrue; }

        public static boolean postcondition( boolean conditionTrue,

                        String message ) {
            if( postconditionOn & ( ! conditionTrue ) ) {
                new AssertFailedException( "Postcondition failed: " +
                message ).printStackTrace( outputStream ); }
            return conditionTrue; }

        public static void setOutputStream( PrintStream newStream ) {
            outputStream = newStream; }

        public  static PrintStream getOutputStream() {
            return outputStream; }

        public static void setPreconditionOn( boolean preconditionOn ) {
            Assert.preconditionOn = preconditionOn; }

        public static boolean isPreconditionOn() {
            return preconditionOn; }

        public static void setPostconditionOn( boolean postconditionOn ) {
            Assert.postconditionOn = postconditionOn; }

        public static boolean isPostconditionOn() {
            return postconditionOn; }

        public static void setAssertionOn( boolean assertionOn ) {
            Assert.assertionOn = assertionOn; }

        public static boolean isAssertionOn() {
            return assertionOn; } }
```

```
AssertFailedException: Precondition failed:
input is too high: 3.6
    at Assert.precondition(Assert.java:12)
    at MyBean.calculateResult(MyBean.java:5)
    at TestAssert.main(TestAssert.java:14)
```

By default the Assert output stream to which messages are logged is the standard error stream (System.err). This default may also be changed via the read/write "outputStream" property on the Assert bean. For example, this allows logging to a file or displaying a dialog instead of logging to the default standard error stream. The output generated by preconditions, assertions, and postconditions allows either the bean developer or the system developer using the bean to efficiently detect, locate, diagnose, and correct problems.

SELF-TESTING

Another established strategy for testing a component is to provide a public "self test" method on the component that tests the state and behavior of the component. An example of a signature for such a method is shown:

```
public synchronized void selfTest() throws TestFailedException
```

This method's behavior is to test the configured state and behavior of the bean on which it is implemented and simply return if successful, otherwise it should throw a TestFailedException. The behavior of the selfTest method should be to first verify that all member variables of the bean are valid, for example, by checking that they are non-null and have values that are within valid ranges. The behavior of the bean is then checked from the selfTest method by calling key methods on the bean and checking outputs and bean state after the method is called. If the self-test method fails, its behavior should be to throw a Test-FailedException with a meaningful message including key variable values where applicable. This exception will "bubble up the stack" to the level at which the self test method was first called and should be caught and handled at that point, for example, by displaying a dialog or logging the exception message. Note that the selfTest method should be synchronized to make sure it is thread-safe so that another thread doesn't modify the bean's state while it is being tested.

In the case of more complex self-tests, it may be necessary to initialize the state of the bean before testing its behavior (e.g., to test boundary conditions). Where the bean state is modified through testing, its original state should be cached before testing and later restored after testing to ensure that the testing does not corrupt the original bean configuration. A bean may also call the self-test method on, another bean it depends on, for example, in the case where one bean is an aggregation of other beans. However, if one bean calls the self-test method on another bean, the bean developer is cautioned to be careful not to allow a situation where two beans each call the self-test methods on each other. Because the self-test methods are synchronized, this will cause the self-test thread to lock. For example, this is analogous to a real world situation where testing a car implies testing its engine, but testing a car's engine does not imply testing the rest of the car.

CONCLUSION

JavaBeans hold great promise in delivering reusable components that may be used to reap RAD benefits in the development of Java applications. Furthermore, JavaBeans promise to enable non-programmers to participate in Java application development. However, before JavaBeans can grow to meet the challenges involved in developing more complex "invisible" non-GUI components for mission-critical enterprise applications, they need to be developed in such a way that they may be tested either at development time or during their use in larger systems. Testing is critical in allowing developers to verify that beans have been configured and are behaving correctly. My article has outlined how two established software testing strategies may be used by bean developers, within the context of the JavaBean standard and development paradigm. It is mandatory to work to improve the testability of beans so that they may grow into a software component architecture suitable for development of not only the GUI, but all aspects of future mission-critical enterprise software systems.

Test-Infected: Programmers Love Writing Tests

KENT BECK AND ERICH GAMMA

TESTING IS NOT closely integrated with development. This prevents you from measuring the progress of development—you can't tell when something starts working or when something stops working. Using JUnit you can cheaply and incrementally build a test suite that will help you measure your progress, spot unintended side effects, and focus your development efforts.

The Problem

Every programmer knows they should write tests for their code. Few do. The universal response to "Why not?" is "I'm in too much of a hurry." This quickly becomes a vicious cycle—the more pressure you feel, the fewer tests you write. The fewer tests you write, the less productive you are and the less stable your code becomes. The less productive and accurate you are, the more pressure you feel.

Programmers burn out from just such cycles. Breaking out requires an outside influence. We found the outside influence we needed in a simple testing framework that lets us do a little testing that makes a big difference.

The best way to convince you of the value of writing your own tests would be to sit down with you and do a bit of development. Along the way, we would encounter new bugs, catch them with tests, fix them, have them come back, fix them again, and so on. You would see the value of the immediate feedback you get from writing and saving and rerunning your own unit tests.

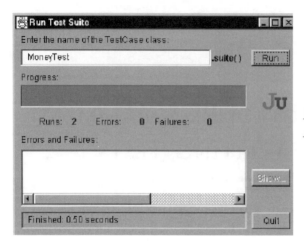

Figure 1.
A successful run.

Unfortunately, this is an article, not an office overlooking charming old-town Zürich, with the bustle of medieval commerce outside and the thump of techno from the record store downstairs, so we'll have to simulate the process of development. We'll write a simple program and its tests, and show you the results of running the tests. This way you can get a feel for the process we use and advocate without having to pay for our presence.

Example

As you read, pay attention to the interplay of the code and the tests. The style here is to write a few lines of code, then a test that should run, or even better, to write a test that won't run, then write the code that will make it run.

The program we write will solve the problem of representing arithmetic with multiple currencies. Arithmetic between single currencies is trivial, you can just add the two amounts. Simple numbers suffice. You can ignore the presence of currencies altogether.

Things get more interesting once multiple currencies are involved. You cannot just convert one currency into another for doing arithmetic because there is no single conversion rate—you may need to compare the value of a portfolio at yesterday's rate and today's rate.

Let's start simple and define a class **Money** to represent a value in a single currency. We represent the amount by a simple **int**. To get full accuracy you would probably use double or **java.math.BigDecimal** to store arbitrary-precision signed decimal numbers. We represent a currency as a string holding the ISO three-letter abbreviation (USD, CHF, etc.). In more complex implementations, currency might deserve its own object.

```
class Money {
   private int fAmount;
   private String fCurrency;

   public Money(int amount, String currency) {
      fAmount= amount;
      fCurrency= currency;
   }
   public int amount() {
      return fAmount;
   }
   public String currency() {
      return fCurrency;
   }
}
```

When you add two Moneys of the same currency, the resulting Money has as its amount the sum of the other two amounts.

```
public Money add(Money m) {
   return new Money(amount()+m.amount(), currency());
}
```

Now, instead of just coding on, we want to get immediate feedback and practice "code a little, test a little, code a little, test a little." To implement our tests we use the JUnit framework. To write tests you need to get JUnit (or write your own equivalent—it's not so much work). Download the latest copy from the Web.

JUnit defines how to structure your test cases and provides the tools to run them. You implement a test in a subclass of TestCase. To test our Money implementation we therefore define MoneyTest as a subclass of TestCase. In Java, classes are contained in packages and we have to decide where to put MoneyTest. Our current practice is to put MoneyTest in the same package as the classes under test. In this way a test case has access to the package private methods. We add a test method testSimpleAdd, that will exercise the simple version of Money.add() above. A JUnit test method is an ordinary method without any parameters.

```
public class MoneyTest extends TestCase {
   //...
   public void testSimpleAdd() {
      Money m12CHF= new Money(12, "CHF"); // (1)
```

```
    Money m14CHF= new Money(14, "CHF");
    Money expected= new Money(26, "CHF");
    Money result= m12CHF.add(m14CHF); // (2)
    assert(expected.equals(result)); // (3)
}
```

The testSimpleAdd() test case consists of:

1. Code that creates the objects we will interact with during the test. This testing context is commonly referred to as a test's *fixture*. All we need for the testSimpleAdd test are some Money objects.
2. Code that exercises the objects in the fixture.
3. Code that verifies the result.

Before we can verify the result we have to digress a little because we need a way to test that two Money objects are equal. The Java idiom to do so is to override the method equals defined in Object. Before we implement equals let's write a test for equals in MoneyTest.

```
public void testEquals() {
    Money m12CHF= new Money(12, "CHF");
    Money m14CHF= new Money(14, "CHF");

    assert(!m12CHF.equals(null));
    assert(m12CHF, m12CHF);
    assertEquals(m12CHF, new Money(12, "CHF")); // (1)
    assert(!m12CHF.equals(m14CHF));
}
```

The equals method in Object returns true when both objects are the same. However, Money is a *value object*. Two Monies are considered equal if they have the same currency and value. To test this property we have added a test (1) to verify that Monies are equal when they have the same value, but are not the same object.

Next let's write the equals method in Money:

```
public boolean equals(Object anObject) {
    if (! anObject instanceof Money)
        return false;
    Money aMoney= (Money)anObject;
    return aMoney.currency().equals(currency())
        && amount() == aMoney.amount();
}
```

Because equals can receive any kind of object as its argument, we first have to check its type before we cast it as a Money. As an aside, it is a recommended practice to also override the method hashCode whenever you override method equals. However, we want to get back to our test case.

With an equals method in hand we can verify the outcome of testSimpleAdd. In JUnit you do so by a calling assert, which is inherited from TestCase. Assert triggers a failure that is logged by JUnit when the argument isn't true. Because assertions for equality are very common, TestCase also defines an assertEquals convenience method. In addition to testing for equality with equals, it logs the printed value of the two objects in case they differ. This lets us immediately see why a test failed in a JUnit test result report. The value is logged as a string representation created by the toString converter method.

Now that we have implemented two test cases we notice some code duplication for setting-up the tests. It would be nice to reuse some of this test set-up code. In other words, we would like to have a common fixture for running the tests. With JUnit you can do so by storing the fixture's objects in instance variables of your TestCase class and initialize them by overridding the setUp method. The symmetric operation to setUp is tearDown, which you can override to clean up the test fixture at the end of a test. Each test runs in its own fixture and JUnit calls setUp and tearDown for each test so that there can be no side effects among test runs.

```
public class MoneyTest extends TestCase {
    private Money f12CHF;
    private Money f14CHF;

    protected void setUp() {
        f12CHF= new Money(12, "CHF");
        f14CHF= new Money(14, "CHF");
    }
}
```

We can rewrite the two test case methods, removing the common setup code:

```
public void testEquals() {
    assert(!f12CHF.equals(null));
    assertEquals(f12CHF, f12CHF);
    assertEquals(m12CHF, new Money(12, "CHF"));
    assert(!f12CHF.equals(f14CHF));
}
```

```
public void testSimpleAdd() {
   Money expected= new Money(26, "CHF");
   Money result= f12CHF.add(f14CHF);
   assert(expected.equals(result));
}
```

Two additional steps are needed to run the two test cases:

1. Define how to run an individual test case.
2. Define how to run a *test suite*.

JUnit supports two ways of running single tests:

- static
- dynamic

In the static way you override the runTest method inherited from TestCase and call the desired test case. A convenient way to do this is with an anonymous inner class. Note that each test must be given a name, so you can identify it if it fails.

```
TestCase test= new MoneyTest("simple add") {
   public void runTest() {
      testSimpleAdd();
   }
};
```

A template method (see Gamma, E., et al. *Design Patterns: Elements of Reusable Object-Oriented Software,* Addison-Wesley, Reading, MA, 1995) in the superclass will make sure runTest is executed when the time comes.

The dynamic way to create a test case to be run uses reflection to implement runTest. It assumes the name of the test is the name of the test case method to invoke. It dynamically finds and invokes the test method. To invoke the testSimpleAdd test we therefore construct a MoneyTest as shown below:

```
TestCase = new MoneyTest("testSimpleAdd");
```

The dynamic way is more compact to write but it is less static type safe. An error in the name of the test case goes unnoticed until you run it and get a NoSuchMethodException. Because both approaches have advantages, we decided to leave the choice of which to use up to you.

As the last step to getting both test cases to run together, we have to define a test suite. In JUnit this requires the definition of a static method called suite. The suite method is like a main method that is specialized to run tests. Inside suite you add the tests to be run to a TestSuite object and return it. A TestSuite can run a collection of tests. TestSuite and TestCase both implement an interface called Test, which defines the methods to run a test. This enables the creation of test suites by composing arbitrary TestCases and TestSuites. In short TestSuite is a Composite (see Gamma, E. et al.) The code below illustrates the creation of a test suite with the dynamic way to run a test.

```
public static Test suite() {
    TestSuite suite= new TestSuite();
    suite.addTest(new MoneyTest("testMoneyEquals"));
    suite.addTest(
        new MoneyTest("testSimpleAdd"));
    return suite;
}
```

Here is the corresponding code using the static way.

```
public static Test suite() {
    TestSuite suite= new TestSuite();
    suite.addTest(
        new MoneyTest("money equals") {
            protected void runTest() {
                testMoneyEquals(); }
        }
    );
    suite.addTest(
        new MathTest("simple add") {
            protected void runTest() {
                testSimpleAdd(); }
        }
    );
    return suite;
}
```

Now we are ready to run our tests. JUnit comes with a graphical interface to run tests. Type the name of your test class in the field at the top of the window. Press the Run button. While the test is run JUnit shows its progress with a progress bar below the input field. The bar is initially green but turns into red as soon as there is an unsuccessful test. Failed tests are shown in a list at the bottom. Figure 1 shows the **TestRunner** window after we run our trivial test suite.

After having verified that the simple currency case works, we move on to multiple currencies. As mentioned above, the problem of mixed currency arithmetic is that there isn't a single exchange rate. To avoid this problem we introduce a **MoneyBag**, which defers exchange rate conversions. For example, adding 12 Swiss Francs to 14 US Dollars is represented as a bag containing the two Monies 12 CHF and 14 USD. Adding another 10 Swiss francs gives a bag with 22 CHF and 14 USD. We can later evaluate a **MoneyBag** with different exchange rates.

A **MoneyBag** is represented as a list of Monies and provides different constructors to create a **MoneyBag**. Note, the constructors are package private because **MoneyBags** are created behind the scenes when doing currency arithmetic.

```
class MoneyBag {
    private Vector fMonies= new Vector();

    MoneyBag(Money m1, Money m2) {
        appendMoney(m1);
        appendMoney(m2);
    }

    MoneyBag(Money bag[]) {
        for (int i= 0; i < bag.length; i++)
            appendMoney(bag[i]);
    }
}
```

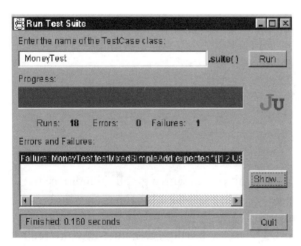

Figure 2. A failed test.

The method appendMoney is an internal helper method that adds a Money to the list of Moneys and takes care of consolidating Monies with the same currency.

MoneyBag also needs an equals method together with a corresponding test. We skip the implementation of equals and only show the testBagEquals method. In a first step we extend the fixture to include two MoneyBags.

```
protected void setUp() {
    f12CHF= new Money(12, "CHF");
    f14CHF= new Money(14, "CHF");
    f7USD= new Money( 7, "USD");
    f21USD= new Money(21, "USD");
    fMB1= new MoneyBag(f12CHF, f7USD);
    fMB2= new MoneyBag(f14CHF, f21USD);
}
```

With this fixture the testBagEquals test case becomes:

```
public void testBagEquals() {
    assert(!fMB1.equals(null));
    assertEquals(fMB1, fMB1);
    assert(!fMB1.equals(f12CHF));
    assert(!f12CHF.equals(fMB1));
    assert(!fMB1.equals(fMB2));
}
```

Following "code a little, test a little" we run our extended test with JUnit and verify that we are still doing fine.

With MoneyBag in hand, we can now fix the add method in Money.

```
public Money add(Money m) {
    if (m.currency().equals(currency()) )
        return new Money(amount()+m.amount(), currency());
    return new MoneyBag(this, m);
}
```

As defined above this method will not compile because it expects a Money and not a MoneyBag as its return value. With the introduction of MoneyBag there are now two representations for Moneys that we would like to hide from the client code. To do so we introduce an interface IMoney that both representations implement. Here is the IMoney interface:

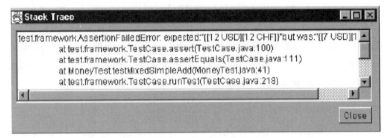

Figure 3. Failure details.

```
interface IMoney {
    public abstract IMoney add(IMoney aMoney);
    //...
}
```

To fully hide the different representations from the client we have to support arithmetic between all combinations of Moneys with MoneyBags. Before we code on, we therefore define a couple more test cases. The expected MoneyBag results use the convenience constructor shown above, initializing a MoneyBag from an array.

```
public void testMixedSimpleAdd() {
    // [12 CHF] + [7 USD] == {[12 CHF][7 USD]}
    Money bag[]= { f12CHF, f7USD };
    MoneyBag expected= new MoneyBag(bag);
    assertEquals(expected, f12CHF.add(f7USD));
}
```

The other tests follow the same pattern:

- testBagSimpleAdd—to add a MoneyBag to a simple Money
- testSimpleBagAdd—to add a simple Money to a MoneyBag
- testBagBagAdd—to add two MoneyBags

Next, we extend our test suite accordingly:

```
public static Test suite() {
    TestSuite suite= new TestSuite();
    suite.addTest(new MoneyTest("testMoneyEquals"));
    suite.addTest(new MoneyTest("testBagEquals"));
    suite.addTest(new MoneyTest("testSimpleAdd"));
```

```
    suite.addTest(new MoneyTest("testMixedSimpleAdd"));
    suite.addTest(new MoneyTest("testBagSimpleAdd"));
    suite.addTest(new MoneyTest("testSimpleBagAdd"));
    suite.addTest(new MoneyTest("testBagBagAdd"));
    return suite;
}
```

Having defined the test cases we can start to implement them. The implementation challenge here is dealing with all the different combinations of **Money** with **MoneyBag**. Double dispatch (see Beck, K., *Smalltalk Best Practice Patterns*, Prentice Hall, 1996) is an elegant way to solve this problem. The idea behind double dispatch is to use an additional call to discover the kind of argument we are dealing with. We call a method on the argument with the name of the original method followed by the class name of the receiver. The add method in **Money** and **MoneyBag** becomes:

```
class Money implements IMoney {
    public IMoney add(IMoney m) {
        return m.addMoney(this);
    }
    //...
}

class MoneyBag implements IMoney {
    public IMoney MoneyBag.add(IMoney m) {
        return m.addMoneyBag(this);
    }
    //...
}
```

In order to get this to compile we need to extend the interface of **IMoney** with the two helper methods:

```
interface IMoney {
//...
    IMoney addMoney(Money aMoney);
    IMoney addMoneyBag(MoneyBag aMoneyBag);
}
```

To complete the implementation of double dispatch, we have to implement these methods in **Money** and **MoneyBag**. This is the implementation in **Money**.

```
public IMoney addMoney(Money m) {
   if (m.currency().equals(currency()) )
      return new Money(amount()+m.amount(), currency());
   return new MoneyBag(this, m);
}

public IMoney addMoneyBag(MoneyBag s) {
   return s.addMoney(this);
}
```

Here is the implementation in MoneyBag, which assumes additional constructors to create a MoneyBag from a Money and a MoneyBag and from two MoneyBags.

```
public IMoney addMoney(Money m) {
   return new MoneyBag(m, this);
}

public IMoney addMoneyBag(MoneyBag s) {
   return new MoneyBag(s, this);
}
```

We run the tests, and they pass. However, while reflecting on the implementation we discover another interesting case. What happens when, as the result of an addition, a MoneyBag turns into a bag with only one Money? For example, adding -12 CHF to a Moneybag holding 7 USD and 12 CHF results in a bag with just 7 USD. Obviously, such a bag should be equal with a single Money of 7 USD. To verify the problem let's implement a test case and run it.

```
public void testSimplify() {
   // {[12 CHF][7 USD]} + [-12 CHF] == [7 USD]
   Money expected= new Money(7, "USD");
   assertEquals(expected, fMS1.add(new Money(-12, "CHF")));
}
```

When you are developing in this style you will often have a thought and turn immediately to writing a test, rather than going straight to the code.

It comes as no surprise that our test run ends with a red progress bar indicating the failure. So we fix the code in MoneyBag to get back to a green state.

```
public IMoney addMoney(Money m) {
   return (new MoneyBag(m, this)).simplify();
}
```

```
public IMoney addMoneyBag(MoneyBag s) {
   return (new MoneyBag(s, this)).simplify();
}

private IMoney simplify() {
   if (fMonies.size() == 1)
      return (IMoney)fMonies.firstElement()
   return this;
}
```

Now we run our tests again and voilà! We end up with green.

The code above solves only a small portion of the multi-currency arithmetic problem. We have to represent different exchange rates, print formatting, and the other arithmetic operations, and do it all with reasonable speed. However, we hope you can see how you could develop the rest of the objects one test at a time—a little test, a little code, a little test, a little code.

In particular, review how in the development above:

1. We wrote the first test, testSimpleAdd, immediately after we had written add(). In general, your development will go much smoother if you write tests a little at a time as you develop. It is at the moment that you are coding that you are imagining how that code will work. That's the perfect time to capture your thoughts in a test.

2. We refactored the existing tests, testSimpleAdd and testEqual, as soon as we introduced the common code. Test code is just like model code in working best if it is factored well. When you see you have the same test code in two places, try to find a way to refactor it so it only appears once.

3. We created a suite method, then extended it when we applied Double Dispatch. Keeping old tests running is just as important as making new ones run. The ideal is to always run all of your tests. Sometimes that will be too slow to do 10 times an hour. Make sure you run all of your tests at least daily.

4. We created a new test immediately when we thought of the requirement that a one element MoneyBag should just return its element. It can be difficult to learn to switch gears like this, but we have found it valuable. When you are struck by an idea of what your system should do, defer thinking about the implementation. Instead, first write the test. Then run it (you never know, it might already work). Then work on the implementation.

COOKBOOK

Okay, you are completely convinced that unit testing is a most fabulous idea. How can you write your own tests? Here is a short cookbook showing you the steps you can follow in writing and organizing your own tests using JUnit.

SIMPLE TEST CASE

How do you write testing code?

The simplest way is as an expression in a debugger. You can change debug expressions without recompiling, and you can wait to decide what to write until you have seen the running objects. You can also write test expressions as statements that print to the standard output stream. Both styles of tests are limited because they require human judgment to analyze their results. Also, they don't compose nicely—you can only execute one debug expression at a time and a program with too many print statements causes the dreaded "Scroll Blindness."

JUnit tests do not require human judgment to interpret, and it is easy to run many of them at the same time. When you need to test something, here is what you do:

1. Create an instance of TestCase:.
2. Override the method "runTest()".
3. When you want to check a value, call "assert()" and pass a boolean that is true if the test succeeds.

For example, to test that the sum of two Moneys with the same currency contains a value that is the sum of the values of the two Moneys, write:

```
public void testSimpleAdd() {
    Money m12CHF= new Money(12, "CHF");
    Money m14CHF= new Money(14, "CHF");
    Money expected= new Money(26, "CHF");
    Money result= m12CHF.add(m14CHF);
    assert(expected.equals(result));
}
```

If you want to write a test similar to one you have already written, write a Fixture instead. When you want to run more than one test, create a Suite.

FIXTURE

What if you have two or more tests that operate on the same or similar sets of objects?

Tests need to run against the background of a known set of objects. This set of objects is called a test fixture. When you are writing tests you will often find that you spend more time writing the code to set up the fixture than you do in actually testing values.

To some extent, you can make writing the fixture code easier by paying careful attention to the constructors you write. However, a much bigger savings comes from sharing fixture code. Often, you will be able to use the same fixture for several different tests. Each case will send slightly different messages or parameters to the fixture and will check for different results.

When you have a common fixture, here is what you do:

1. Create a subclass of TestCase.
2. Add an instance variable for each part of the fixture.
3. Override "setUp()" to initialize the variables.
4. Override "tearDown()" to release any permanent resources you allocated in setUp.

For example, to write several test cases that want to work with different combinations of 12 Swiss Francs, 14 Swiss Francs, and 28 US Dollars, first create a fixture:

```
public class MoneyTest extends TestCase {
    private Money f12CHF;
    private Money f14CHF;
    private Money f28USD;

    protected void setUp() {
        f12CHF= new Money(12, "CHF");
        f14CHF= new Money(14, "CHF");
        f28USD= new Money(28, "USD");
    }
}
```

Once you have the Fixture in place, you can write as many Test Cases as you'd like.

Test Case

How do you write and invoke an individual test case when you have a Fixture?

Writing a test case without a fixture is simple—override runTest() in an anonymous subclass of TestCase. You write test cases for a Fixture the same way, by making a subclass of TestCase for your set up code and then making anonymous subclasses for the individual test cases. However, after a few such tests you would notice that a large percentage of your lines of code are sacrificed to syntax.

JUnit provides a more concise way to write a test against a Fixture. Here is what you do:

1. Write the test case method in the fixture class. Be sure to make it public, or it can't be invoked through reflection.
2. Create an instance of the TestCase class and pass the name of the test case method to the constructor.

For example, to test the addition of a Money and a MoneyBag, write:

```
public void testMoneyMoneyBag() {
    // [12 CHF] + [14 CHF] + [28 USD] == {[26 CHF][28 USD]}
    Money bag[]= { f26CHF, f28USD };
    MoneyBag expected= new MoneyBag(bag);
    assertEquals(expected, f12CHF.add(f28USD.add(f14CHF)));
}
```

Create an instance of MoneyTest that will run this test case like this:

```
new MoneyTest("testMoneyMoneyBag")
```

When the test is run, the name of the test is used to look up the method to run. Once you have several tests, organize them into a Suite.

Suite

How do you run several tests at once?

As soon as you have two tests, you'll want to run them together. You could run the tests one at a time yourself, but you would quickly grow tired of that. Instead, JUnit provides an object, TestSuite, which runs any number of Test-Cases together.

For example, to run a single test case, you execute:

```
TestResult result= (new MoneyTest("testMoneyMoneyBag")).run();
To create a suite of two test cases and run them together, execute:
TestSuite suite= new TestSuite();
suite.addTest(new MoneyTest("testMoneyEquals"));
suite.addTest(new MoneyTest("testSimpleAdd"));
TestResult result= suite.run();
```

TestSuites don't only have to contain TestCases. They contain any object that implements the Test interface. For example, you can create a TestSuite in your code and I can create one in mine, and we can run them together by creating a TestSuite that contains both:

```
TestSuite suite= new TestSuite();
suite.addTest(Kent.suite());
suite.addTest(Erich.suite());
TestResult result= suite.run();
```

Testrunner

How do you run your tests and collect their results?

Once you have a test suite, you'll want to run it. JUnit provides tools to define the suite to be run and to display its results. You make your suite accessible to a TestRunner tool with a static method suite that returns a test suite.

For example, to make a MoneyTest suite available to a TestRunner, add the following code to MoneyTest:

```
public static Test suite() {
    TestSuite suite= new TestSuite();
    suite.addTest(new MoneyTest("testMoneyEquals"));
    suite.addTest(new MoneyTest("testSimpleAdd"));
    return suite;
}
```

JUnit provides both a graphical and a textual version of a TestRunner tool. Start it by typing java test.ui.TestRunner. The graphical user interface (GUI) presents a window with:

- a field to type in the name of a class with a suite method
- a Run button to start the test

- a progress indicator that turns from red to green in the case of a failed test
- a list of failed tests

In the case of an unsuccessful test, JUnit reports the failed tests in a list at the bottom. JUnit distinguishes between failures and errors. A failure is anticipated and checked for with assertions. Errors are unanticipated problems like an ArrayIndexOutOfBoundsException. Figure 2 shows an example with a failed test.

To find out more about a failure or an error select it in the list and press Show. This will show you a stack trace of the failure (see Figure 3).

There is also a batch interface to JUnit. To use it type java test.textui.TestRunner followed by the name of the class with a suite method at an operating system prompt. The batch interface shows the result as text output. An alternative way to invoke the batch interface is to define a main method in your TestCase class.

For example, to start the batch TestRunner for MoneyTest, write:

```
public static void main(String args[]) {
    test.textui.TestRunner.run(suite());
}
```

With this definition of main you can run your tests by simply typing java MoneyTest at an operating system prompt.

For using either the graphical or the textual version make sure that the test.jar file is on your CLASSPATH.

Testing Practices

Martin Fowler (private communication) makes this easy for you. He said, "Whenever you are tempted to type something into a print statement or a debugger expression, write it as a test instead." At first you will find that you have to create new fixtures all the time, and testing will seem to slow you down a little. Soon, however, you will begin reusing your library of fixtures and new tests will usually be as simple as adding a method to an existing TestCase subclass.

You can always write more tests. However, you will quickly find that only a fraction of the tests you can imagine are actually useful. What you want is to write tests that fail even though you think they should work, or tests that succeed even though you think they should fail. Another way to think of it is in cost/benefit terms. You want to write tests that will pay you back with information.

Here are a couple of the times that you will receive a reasonable return on your testing investment:

1. **During Development**—When you need to add new functionality to the system, write the tests first. Then, you will be done developing when the test runs.
2. **During Debugging**—When someone discovers a defect in your code, first write a test that will succeed if the code is working. Then debug until the test succeeds.

One word of caution about your tests. Once you get them running, make sure they stay running. There is a huge difference between having your suite running and having it broken. Ideally, you would run every test in your suite every time you change a method. Practically, your suite will soon grow too large to run all the time. Try to optimize your setup code so you can run all the tests. Or, at the very least, create special suites that contain all the tests that might possibly be affected by your current development. Then, run the suite every time you compile. And make sure you run every test at least once a day: overnight, during lunch, during one of those long meetings….

CONCLUSION

This article only scratches the surface of testing. However, it focuses on a style of testing that with a remarkably small investment will make you a faster, more productive, more predictable, and less stressed developer.

Once you've been test-infected, your attitude toward development is likely to change. Here are some of the changes we have noticed:

There is a huge difference between tests that are all running correctly and tests that aren't. Part of being test-infected is not being able to go home if your tests aren't 100%. If you run your suite ten or a hundred times an hour, though, you won't be able to create enough havoc to make you late for supper.

Sometimes you just won't feel like writing tests, especially at first. Don't. However, pay attention to how much more trouble you get into, how much more time you spend debugging, and how much more stress you feel when you don't have tests. We have been amazed at how much more fun programming is and how much more aggressive we are willing to be and how much less stress we feel when we are supported by tests. The difference is dramatic enough to keep us writing tests even when we don't feel like it.

You will be able to refactor much more aggressively once you have the tests. Though you won't understand at first just how much you can do. Try to catch yourself saying, "Oh, I see, I should have designed this thus and so. I can't change it now. I don't want to break anything." When you say this, save a copy of your current code and give yourself a couple of hours to clean up. (This part works best when you can get a buddy to look over your shoulder while you work.) Make your changes, all the while running your tests. You will be surprised at how much ground you can cover in a couple of hours if you aren't worrying every second about what you might be breaking.

For example, we switched from the Vector-based implementation of Mon-eyBag to one based on HashTable. We were able to make the switch very quickly and confidently because we had so many tests to rely on. If the tests all worked, we were sure we hadn't changed the answers the system produced at all.

You will want to get the rest of your team writing tests. The best way we have found to spread the test infection is through direct contact. The next time someone asks you for help debugging, get them to talk about the problem in terms of a fixture and expected results. Then say, "I'd like to write down what you just told me in a form we can use." Have them watch while you write one little test. Run it. Fix it. Write another. Pretty soon they will be writing their own.

So, give JUnit a try. If you make it better, please send us the changes so we can spread them around. A future article will double-click on the JUnit framework itself. We will show you how it is constructed, and talk a little about our philosophy of framework development.

We would like to thank Martin Fowler—as good a programmer as any analyst can ever hope to be—for his helpful comments in spite of being subjected to early versions of JUnit.

PERFORMANCE

Complex Java Applications: Breaking the Speed Limit

Allen Wirfs-Brock

A BASIC PROBLEM with most current Java implementations is that they were designed to support very small applet-style programs. The ability to effectively execute very large, computationally complex application programs is not currently an area of strength for Java. However, Java is now being used as a general-purpose language for implementing all types of programming problems including computationally intense applications. The translation and execution techniques used by current Java implementations do not necessarily scale to support the performance requirements of such programs. Static compilation with aggressive optimization is an implementation technique that is commonly used for languages such as C, C++, and FORTRAN but has not been widely used to implement Java. This article identifies some of the reasons for Java's performance problems and examines how static compilation and optimization techniques can be applied to Java to alleviate these problems.

Why Does Java Have Poor Performance?

Java's performance problems can be traced to two major sources: the inherent inefficiencies of object-oriented (OO) programming constructs and the use of a virtual machine (VM)-based implementation strategy. After explaining the details of these inefficiencies I show how static compilation technology is able to overcome them.

OO LANGUAGE INEFFICIENCIES

OO programming languages such as Java have been widely promoted as key tools for increasing programmer productivity. The productivity improvements of OO languages are generally achieved through code reuse. Using an OO language such as Java, a programmer needs to write less new code because OO languages support and encourage the reuse of existing code. Code reuse can be either local to a single program or global to many programs.

Local code reuse occurs within an individual program when a programmer uses Java's constructs to create groups of classes that are related through inheritance. Inheritance allows classes to share code. A subclass does not need to duplicate code that is implemented by its superclasses. When writing a subclass, a programmer only needs to write code that extends or modifies the code in the superclass.

Local code reuse also depends on Java's support for polymorphic method invocation. Using polymorphism, a programmer may implement generalized algorithms that can operate on a variety of data types defined using multiple classes. Using a procedural language, such as C, a programmer would have to write a specialized version of the algorithm for each different class of data. Using Java, only a single copy of the algorithm is needed because polymorphic method invocation allows the behavior of the code to dynamically vary depending on the specific class of the data.

Global reuse occurs when inheritance and polymorphism are used to create class libraries and OO frameworks whose functionality is applicable to many programs. Programmers improve their productivity by incorporating pre-existing class libraries or frameworks into an application instead of writing new code to implement the functionality

Unfortunately, the characteristics of OO languages that contribute to reuse have a negative impact on program performance and footprint. Part of this performance impact derives from the overhead of polymorphic method invocation. Polymorphic invocation requires an extra runtime computation each time a method call occurs in order to dynamically select the actual method that will be the target of the method call. The extra computation to determine the target method slows down each method call. In addition, the designs of modern pipelined processors such as the Intel Pentium are optimized for fixed call and branch targets. The performance of such processors decreases when a large percentage of method call targets must be dynamically computed. These problems are heightened by OO program design practices that encourage the creation of many small methods and a very high frequency of polymorphic method calls.

The negative performance impact of polymorphism goes beyond the actual overhead of polymorphic method invocation. Modern optimizing compilers for procedural languages use interprocedural analysis and inlining to improve compiled code performance. These techniques depend on the ability of the compiler to determine the actual procedure (method) that is the target for each call site within a program. A call site that uses polymorphic method invocation may have several methods that may be called from the site at different times during execution of a program. Because there is not a single target method for a call site, conventional interprocedural analysis and inlining cannot be used to optimize the program's performance.

Global reuse through class libraries and frameworks impact performance because of unused generalization. A class library or framework is usually designed to be used by a wide variety of programs. To accommodate a variety of uses, its functionality is broader and more general than what is needed by any single program that uses it. Any particular program will use only a subset of the available functionality. Yet, each program must carry the performance overhead of the fully generalized functionality. Part of this overhead is the extra memory footprint needed to accommodate unused methods and fields. Another form of overhead is in the performance of generalized algorithms that depend on the use of polymorphic method invocation. Often within a particular program such polymorphic invocations always resolve to a single method. In essence, they are not polymorphic within that program but they still impose the full performance penalty of a true polymorphic call site.

Assuming equivalent implementation technology, the overhead of polymorphism and unused generalization causes a Java program to have significantly poorer performance than an equivalent program written in a procedural language such as C. However, Java is not usually implemented using static optimization compiler technology such as is typically used for C or similar languages. Instead, most Java implementations make use of VM technology.

VM Inefficiencies

An executable Java program is typically distributed in the form of binary class files. A Java class file encodes the executable code of a Java class in the form of "bytecodes." Bytecodes are the instructions of a hypothetical computer that is specially designed for the execution of Java programs. Conventional computers cannot directly execute Java bytecodes. Instead, a software layer, called a VM, is required to actually execute Java programs.

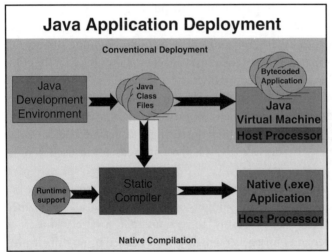

Figure 1.
Java application
deployment.

The simplest type of VM is a bytecode interpreter. An interpreter executes a program by successively fetching, decoding, and executing the semantic action specified by each bytecode. Interpreters are notoriously slow because the work of fetching and decoding each bytecode must be repeated every time that bytecode is executed. This computational work is pure overhead. It contributes nothing to the intrinsic function of the program. It is not unusual for interpreter-based execution to be an order of magnitude or slower than optimized C code.

One way to reduce the computational overhead of a VM is to separate the fetching/decoding of bytecodes from the execution of the semantic action of the bytecode. The overhead of decoding a particular bytecode then occurs only once each time the program is executed instead of once each time the bytecode is executed. A Just-In-Time (JIT) VM accomplishes this by translating bytecodes into native machine code as the application executes. All of the bytecodes in a method are translated into native machine code before the method is executed for the first time. The execution of the method then proceeds by executing the resultant machine code.

JIT-based VMs are usually significantly faster than interpretive VMs. However, they are still not as fast as optimized C code. There are two primary reasons for this: translator overhead and poor code quality. The process of translating the bytecodes of a method into machine code is itself a complex and computationally expensive operation. Because this translation takes place while the application programs are executing, the time it takes to perform the translation must be added to the total execution time of the program. Also, because translation takes place at execution time, the time taken to translate each method must be short enough that it does not introduce any user noticeable pauses or delays into the program. This means that the translator cannot incorporate the computationally-intensive code optimization algorithms that are used by C compilers. The machine code produced by a JIT VM is often several times slower than the code produced by an optimizing C compiler for an equivalent program.

JVMs also incur a significant memory footprint overhead that is not required by optimized C code. This overhead consists of the code and runtime data structured needed to implement the interpreter or JIT translator. A complex JIT-based VM may add several MBs to the runtime footprint of even the simplest Java programs.

HOW CAN STATIC COMPILATION IMPROVE JAVA'S PERFORMANCE?

Static compilation techniques can significantly improve the performance of Java programs by directly addressing the fundamental causes of poor Java performance. Using static compilation, the overhead of a VM is eliminated by converting the Java program into optimized native code for specific target processors. Most importantly, by using state-of-the-art optimization techniques, static compilation can eliminate the intrinsic OO language inefficiencies. For example, optimization techniques are capable of eliminating more than 90% of the polymorphic method invocations for most programs.

Several experimental or commercial statically-optimizing compilers have been created for Java. These compilers vary significantly in their architecture and the types of optimizations they are able to perform. The actual performance of a statically-compiled application may vary significantly depending on the specific compiler that is used. This article uses Instantiations Inc.'s JOVE compilation technology as an example to illustrate the performance improvements that are potentially obtainable using static compilation technology.

NATIVE COMPILATION

A statically-compiled Java application is not executed using a VM in the sense that the term is most commonly used. Java bytecodes are not interpreted or translated as the Java program executes. Instead, Java is treated more like a conventional language such as C++. Using a static compiler, a Java program is translated to optimized native machine code before the program is distributed to its users. Most static compilers for Java differ from compilers for languages such as C++ in that they do not process Java source code. Instead, they accept as input the same Java class files that would be used with a JVM. Because such static compilers operate on class files, they preserve Java's "write once, run anywhere" characteristic. An application is created in class file format using any conventional Java IDE. Those class files may then be distributed to run on any platform using a JVM. The very same class files can be processed by a static compiler to create an optimized native program for specific platforms.

The generation of a native code program eliminates the performance and footprint overhead of a VM. The work necessary to translate bytecodes into an executable form is only performed once before the program is delivered to its users. Because the translation from bytecodes to native code need not be accomplished in real-time, computationally-intensive optimization techniques can be used to improve the quality and performance of the generated code.

The quality of the code generated by an optimizing compiler is closely related to how much of the program is analyzed when making optimization decisions. Simple compilers only consider a single operation or statement when making code generation decisions. Slightly more aggressive compilers analyze sequences of statements called "basic blocks." Most modern commercial compilers analyze entire procedures or, in some cases, entire modules to make optimization decisions. However, conventional optimization techniques cannot eliminate Java's inherent OO inefficiencies.

The most aggressive static compilers, such as JOVE, are "whole-program" optimizing compilers. Such compilers build a model of an entire Java program including any core or third-party class libraries that are used by the program. This model is used to analyze the structure of the entire program before performing optimizations or code generation.

OO OPTIMIZATIONS

With a model of the entire program available, a static compilation can perform unique optimizations that eliminate most of the OO overhead of large Java programs. This is accomplished by performing a set of transformations on the program model that produce a more efficient version of the program. JOVE, for example, first performs Class Hierarchy Analysis (CHA) on the entire program. CHA determines which classes and methods are actually used by the program and also which methods are not polymorphic. For example, CHA may determine that an abstract class has only a single subclass, in which case the abstract class is essentially

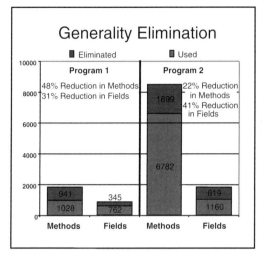

Figure 2.
Generality elimination.

equivalent to the subclass. It also ascertains which methods are not over-ridden by subclasses. Finally, it concludes which methods and fields are not used by the program and can be eliminated. Class Hierarchy Analysis is the first step in the elimination of unused generality from a Java program.

Figure 2 shows the effect of CHA on two Java programs that were compiled using JOVE. Program 1 is a small, but significant customer application with approximately 200 classes and 2,000 methods. Program 2 is a much larger, more complex program with more than 50,000 lines of code, approximately 600 classes, and almost 8,700 methods. Results presented are typical of applications that we have tested.

JOVE processes the body of each method using Polymorphic Type Elimination (PTE) and Data Flow Analysis (DFA) to determine a specific concrete class for each value in the program. PTE attempts to refine the declared type information for variables and methods to specific concrete classes while DFA is used to track the propagation of values (and their types) within a program. For example, the type of a variable might be declared as type Object but PTE and DFA may reveal that the only values that are ever assigned to the variable are instances of java.lang.String. In this case, the variable's polymorphic type, Object, is replaced with the concrete type java.lang.String.

The results of CHA, PTE, and DFA are then used for many purposes. For example, the precise type information is used to eliminate dynamic type checks introduced by casts and stores into Java arrays. This information is also used to eliminate runtime checks for null values. The most important use of this information is to perform Polymorphic Strength Reduction (PSR) on each polymorphic method call site. It may be the case that there are several different methods that could possibly be

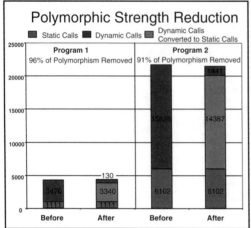

Figure 3.
Polymorphic strength
reduction.

invoked from any particular polymorphic call site. Polymorphic method calls require a dynamic method lookup based on the runtime class of the object that is the target of the method invocation to determine the specific method that will be executed for a particular invocation. PSR attempts to convert each polymorphic method call into a static method call. Static calls do not require dynamic method lookup because they directly reference individual methods. Figure 3 shows the results of PSR on the two sample programs. In each case, more than 90% of the polymorphic call sites requiring dynamic method lookup are converted into static calls.

While the elimination of the runtime overhead of dynamic method lookup is important, the most significant benefit of PSR is the ability to "inline" any method. When a method is inlined, calls to the method are replaced with the code that forms the body of the method. In essence, the method is "macro-expanded" at each of its call sites. Any method that is called from only one site (procedural decomposition) and small methods are good candidates for inlining. Small methods that access object state or delegate responsibility to other methods are particularly prevalent in well-structured OO programs. JOVE aggressively inlines methods. Figure 4 shows that more than 50% of the static method calls that exist after PSR are inlined.

The combined effects of the PSR and inlining are to significantly reduce both the total number of call sites and the polymorphic call sites within Java programs. Figure 5 shows the cumulative effect of these optimizations on call sites.

One concern about inlining is that it might significantly increase the runtime footprint of programs. This could be expected because inlining duplicates the code of a method at each of its call sites instead of having a single copy of the code that is shared by all call sites. In practice, this has not proven to be a prob-

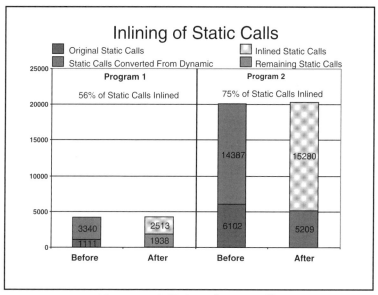

Figure 4. Inlining of static calls.

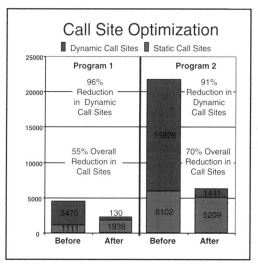

Figure 5.
Call site optimization.

lem. Figure 6 shows the cumulative effect of optimizations on the total number of intermediate instructions in each sample program. The total size of the program varies only slightly even in the presence of aggressive inlining.

The fact that inlining has a very small effect on the number of operations for most programs is less counter-intuitive if styles of method usage are considered. Well-designed programs use procedural decomposition to simplify and struc-

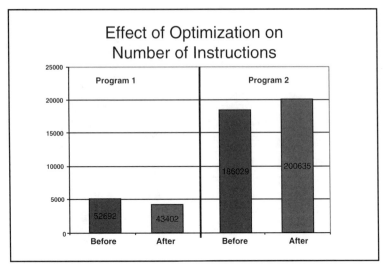

Figure 6.
Effect of optimization on the number of instructions.

ture the program's algorithms. This results in many procedures (methods) that are only called from a single site. The code to perform the invocation and the entry and exit code (prologue and epilogue) for such procedures are purely overhead. They contribute nothing to the actual computation. Inlining replaces such calls with the semantic body of the procedure. This completely eliminates the overhead of the call and the prologue and epilogue.

Well-structured OO programs contain many very small methods that only perform simple instance variable accesses or calls to other methods. For such methods, the sequence of instructions needed to call the method is often larger than the instructions that implement the bodies of the methods. By inlining, these calling sequences are replaced with the smaller body of the method.

The most important consequence of inlining is that it creates larger methods that are more amenable to conventional program optimization techniques. Optimizing compiler technologies were originally developed for procedural languages such as FORTRAN. Programs in such language are typically composed of large subroutines containing nested loops over complex computations. Conventional compiler optimization techniques attempt to improve the performance of such subroutines by identifying unnecessary or redundant computations and by moving computations outside of loops. This style of optimization usually has a significant positive performance impact on complex, FORTRAN-style subroutines. However, it may make little or no improvement for small, simple procedures. The presence of procedure calls within loops significantly complicates or even impedes the ability of a compiler to perform such optimizations. This is particularly true for polymorphic calls.

Through PSR and inlining, the many small, polymorphic methods of a well-structured Java program are transformed into a smaller number of large, FORTRAN-style subroutines. A static compiler can then apply more conventional optimization techniques to improve the performance of these subroutines.

CONCLUSION

The perception that OO languages are inherently inefficient has generally limited their usage to non-performance critical applications. Programmers continue to use conventional languages, such as C, for most performance-critical applications. This is similar to the situation that existed in the 1960s and early 1970s when many programs were still written in assembly language because higher level programming languages were considered to be too slow. The availability of optimizing compilers changed this perception to the extent that assembly language is now rarely used to create significantly-sized applications.

JOVE and similar technologies demonstrate that Java need not be inefficient. The availability of optimizing compiler technology enables the use of Java and its full OO capabilities for the most demanding of applications. Because of such technologies, we can easily foresee the day when non-OO languages are rarely used to create significantly-sized applications.

ARE DISTRIBUTED OBJECTS
FAST ENOUGH?

MATJAZ B. JURIC, ALES ZIVKOVIC, AND IVAN ROZMAN

J AVA IS BECOMING important for building real-world, mission-critical applications. Although Java is still not a perfect language, it is becoming more mature every day. We all know the advantages of Java, especially the "write once, run anywhere" approach, but we are also aware of the disadvantages (its performance being the most commonly offered reason for not using Java).

In spite of that, there are many large companies claiming they are developing their crucial business applications in Java. Modern applications are not monolithic programs, they are built of objects. Therefore, developers need a "glue" for bringing all the pieces together and coordinating them into a functional application. Object location independence is an advantage that gives developers the ability to structure the application into multiple tiers.

For building distributed applications in Java it is natural to choose the Remote Method Invocation (RMI), but there is another possibility—the Common Object Request Broker Architecture (CORBA). CORBA is a valuable alternative to RMI. We could describe CORBA as a superset of RMI, although both technologies are not compatible yet. Both CORBA and RMI allow remote method invocation independently of location, however, CORBA is more than just an object request broker. It offers programming language independence and a rich set of object services and common facilities all the way to the business objects.

There are multiple factors that can affect the decision. One of them is certainly the performance. To get an overview about the performance of RMI and CORBA we have done several measurements and experiments to simulate real world scenarios. We hope that this article will help you to get a clearer picture about both distributed object models.

TESTING METHOD

The goal was to measure the overhead that was introduced into method invocation by CORBA and RMI. Therefore, we have developed several testing patterns and methods with different basic data types of parameters and return values. As a basis for performed tests we used an Automatic Teller Machine (ATM) application that was developed for demonstration purposes for one of our banks.

The invocation time was measured for 6 methods with different return types. The main idea was to investigate the influence of data types on performance. The significant code with methods and corresponding classes is shown in Listing 1. As you can see, all the methods return just a value. We chose this approach to minimize the influence of time needed to execute the methods.

Listing 1. Methods used for performance measurement.

```
public class Atm {
    ...
    private long number;
    private boolean working=true;
    ...
    final public boolean Working() {
        return working; }

    final public long getAtmNo() {
        return number; } }
    ...
public class Card {
    ...
    private int number;
    ...
    final public int getNumber() {
        return number; } }
    ...
public class Account {
    ...
    private String type;
    private float balance=0f;
    private double limit;
    ...
    final public float getBalance() {
        return balance; }

    final public String getType() {
        return type; }

    final public double getLimit() {
        return limit; } }
    ...
```

The methods were invoked from an applet, which had a panel for displaying results and a button for start. Time was measured with the System.currentTimeMillis() method, which has returned time in milliseconds. To achieve more accurate results, methods were invoked several times. Listing 2 shows the skeleton of the testing applet.

To eliminate inaccuracy, we have repeated all the measurements 10 times and calculated the average values. To get an idea how the string size affected the performance, the method Account.getType() returned 2 different string sizes. First, the method returned a string with 1 character only. Then we repeated the test with a string of 10,000 characters.

All the test code was compiled and executed with Java Development Kit 1.1.4. For testing CORBA's performance we chose Visigenic's VisiBroker for Java Version 3.0.

For local measurements and all server-side tests we used a Pentium II, 233 MHz computer with 64 MB RAM and the Windows NT 4.0 Workstation as the operating system. At the client-side we used 200 MHz Pentium computers with 64 MB RAM and the same operating system. Because the trend today is to use applications over the Internet where the bandwidth is low, the computers were connected into a 10Mbps Ethernet network.

NATIVE JAVA PERFORMANCE

In the first step, we measured native Java performance for method invocation where we invoked all methods in a loop 1 million times to achieve the necessary accuracy. We found results (shown in Table 1) for data types integer, float,

Listing 2.   Client applet.

```
...
    boolean is_working=false;

    my_account.setBalance((float)50f);

    for(int j=0;j<10;j++) {

        long startTime=System.currentTimeMillis();

        for (n=0;n<NO_ITER;n++)
            is_working=my_Atm.Working();

        long stopTime=System.currentTimeMillis();

        tMessage.append("Elapsed time "+(stopTime-startTime)+"\n");        }
...
```

Table 1. Native Java performance.	
Data type	Time in ms
int	427,8
long	300,5
float	428,3
double	301,5
boolean	428,5
String (1)	428,6
Average	385,9

Table 2. RMI performance on a single computer.	
Data type	Time in ms
int	1,87
long	1,95
float	1,83
double	1,96
boolean	1,82
String (1)	1,85
Average	1,88
String (10.000)	108,00

boolean, and String (1 character) had identical values. Also, the results for types long and double were practically the same.

JAVA RMI PERFORMANCE

To measure the overhead that distributed processing introduces into method invocation, we reprogrammed tests using RMI. We defined interfaces, separated the functionality into a server process and changed the client applet to connect to the server objects. First we started both, the server and the client processes on the same Pentium II computer. As expected, the results showed very substantial performance degradation. In native Java an invocation lasts about 400 nanoseconds. When using RMI the time was not measured in nanoseconds but in milliseconds. Because of that, the client repeated all invocations 1 thousand times thus accurate times could be measured. We have repeated tests 10 times and reported the average values. The results of these tests are shown in Table 2.

The times for methods, which returned results of types integer, long, float, double, boolean, and String (1 character) were very close. A method invocation using RMI lasted around 1.9 milliseconds on the hardware configuration used for testing. When we increased the string size to 10,000 characters, the response time grew to 108 ms. The performance degradation factor was slightly over 58.

Second, the measurement was repeated (see Table 3 for the results) with server and client on separate computers. The server was the Pentium II computer and the client a Pentium 200. As already stated, the computers were connected using a 10Mbps Ethernet network.

When the methods were invoked over the network, the time on average was 12% slower than when they were invoked on the same computer. This

Table 3. Java RMI performance over the network.

Data type	Time in ms	Relative to local RMI
int	2,08	11,4%
long	2,13	9,0%
float	2,09	14,2%
double	2,14	9,3%
boolean	2,08	14,2%
String (1)	2,10	13,5%
Average	2,10	11,9%
String (10.000)	77,39	-28,3%

Table 4. Java RMI performance under 8-client load.

				Time in ms						
Data type	PC 1	PC 2	PC 3	PC 4	PC 5	PC 6	PC 7	PC 8	AVG	DEG %
int	9,16	8,88	8,68	8,00	8,54	7,94	8,81	8,59	**8,58**	312%
long	8,76	7,62	7,44	6,91	9,32	8,38	7,72	7,76	**7,99**	275%
float	7,16	8,06	6,64	8,10	7,45	7,90	7,80	7,59	**7,59**	263%
double	7,22	8,25	7,19	7,35	7,67	8,58	7,56	7,74	**7,70**	260%
boolean	8,36	7,85	8,91	8,58	8,47	8,14	8,45	8,11	**8,36**	302%
String (1)	8,38	7,93	8,15	7,60	8,22	8,28	8,56	8,42	**8,19**	290%
Average	**8,17**	**8,10**	**7,84**	**7,76**	**8,28**	**8,20**	**8,15**	**8,04**	**8,07**	284%
String (10.000)	226,38	208,43	310,95	198,60	200,22	228,98	298,56	317,42	**248,69**	221%

was true for all return values except for the string with 10,000 characters. When returning such a string the performance was approximately 28% better over the network. The blame probably went to the Java Virtual Machine (JVM), which appeared to be quite CPU-intensive. In our opinion it is possible to show that by using slower computers and method invocation over the network the measurement times will improve compared to local invocation.

To get more real performances of a client/server system we used 8 computers for the same tests. In the next test we tried to figure out the performance degradation under load imposed on the system. We configured 8 Pentium computers

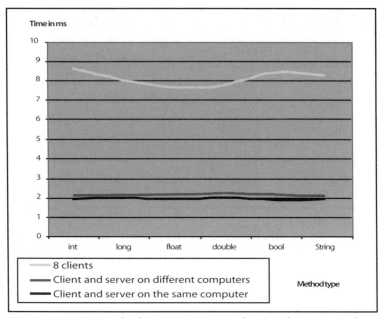

Figure 1. RMI method invocation time for simple return values.

to run the client applet. For the server-side we used the Pentium II computer. The client applets were running on all the client computers simultaneously. Each client invoked each test method one thousand times. All the tests were repeated 10 times to get an average value.

The clients invoked methods without any delays. This did not coincide with typical user interaction, therefore we assumed that this load represented more than 8 users. The results and relative performance degradation are presented in Table 4.

It was determined that the average response time increased 284% from slightly over 2 to about 8 milliseconds. A similar degradation occurred by string method with string size of 10,000 characters. The degradation there was slightly smaller, from 77 to 250 milliseconds (about 220%).

The results are graphically presented in Figure 1 and Figure 2. The first graph shows the response times for method invocations with different return types for a single computer scenario, a scenario with 2 and with 8 client computers. These are performances a developer might expect when using methods with short return values.

In Figure 2, you can find the invocation times for methods with large return values. For comparison, the graph also shows an average perfor-mance of methods with simple return values. Please note that the scales for both lines are different. In the graph you can see that the performance of

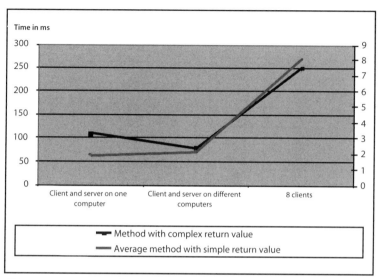

Figure 2. RMI method invocation time for large string method in comparison with average of simple methods.

Table 5. Typemapping.

Java type	IDL type
int	long
long	long long
float	float
double	double
boolean	boolean
java.lang.String	string

large string methods increased when we place the client and server on different computers. This is due to the CPU intensity of JVM.

CORBA PERFORMANCE

CORBA can be considered a more mature technology than RMI, because it has been around for years and there are numerous real-world projects using it. CORBA is a robust, scalable technology and its performances (especially in C++) are

---

Listing 3.   IDL definitions.

```
...                             ...
interface Atm {                 };
...                             ...
   boolean Working();           interface Account {
   long long getAtmNo();        ...
...                                float getBalance();
};                                 string getType();
...                                double getLimit();
interface Card {                };
...                             ...
   long getNumber();
```

Table 6.   CORBA performance with one client.

Data type	Client and server on the same computer (times in ms)	Client and server on different computers	Difference
int	2,20	2,31	5,0%
long	2,21	2,32	5,0%
float	2,20	2,27	3,2%
double	2,25	2,29	1,8%
boolean	2,02	2,23	10,4%
String (1)	2,24	2,30	2,7%
Average	2,19	2,29	4,6%
String (10.000)	19,59	28,12	43,5%

---

quite good. So it would be expected to get good results from the CORBA–Java connection as well. Until now, very little research had been done in this area. Therefore, we decided to compare Java RMI performance with Java–CORBA.

Numerous CORBA implementations exist today and most of them offer Java support. For this comparison we selected VisiBroker for Java Version 3.0 by Visigenic. It is one of the best CORBA implementations on the market and it has ORB bundled with Netscape Navigator 4.0. We adapted the tests described in the Java RMI chapter because our goal was to make the Java RMI and CORBA results comparable.

The first step in development of CORBA-compliant applications was the

Table 7. CORBA performance under 8-client load.

Data type	PC 1	PC 2	PC 3	PC 4	PC 5	PC 6	PC 7	PC 8	AVG	DEG %
				Time in ms						
int	8,36	8,18	6,72	7,09	7,87	7,32	7,59	8,60	7,72	234%
long	9,08	8,82	6,36	7,23	7,81	6,55	7,23	7,47	7,57	226%
float	6,51	7,45	7,32	7,75	6,92	7,89	7,51	7,50	7,36	224%
double	6,39	6,77	7,87	7,04	6,92	8,21	9,54	6,76	7,44	225%
boolean	7,79	7,75	7,91	8,05	8,24	9,76	8,04	7,16	8,09	263%
String (1)	7,41	8,10	7,77	7,89	7,41	8,03	7,69	8,12	7,80	239%
Average	7,59	7,84	7,32	7,51	7,53	7,96	7,94	7,60	7,66	235%
String (10.000)	105,64	91,85	88,45	101,00	98,92	178,25	123,60	113,99	112,71	301%

definition of interfaces in IDL (Interface Definition Language). Because the return types of methods had been already defined in Java, these types had to be mapped into IDL. The correct mapping is shown in Table 5.

The next step was the definition of interfaces and methods. In IDL, we defined the same interfaces and methods as in Java RMI. The important parts of IDL definitions are shown in Listing 3.

In both the client and the server code we made only CORBA-specific changes. The testing procedure was the same as when using Java RMI. Again, all the measurements were repeated 10 times and the applet at client-side has reported average values. In the first column of Table 6 you can see the times where server objects and client applet were on the same Pentium II computer. In the second column the times are given where server and client are communicating over network. In the third column the difference in percentage is calculated.

The average slow-down for using methods over network was smaller than 5%. Only the method that returned 10,000 characters was slower for 43.5%. Our next test was to measure the performance using 8 clients. The test was executed under the same conditions as when testing Java RMI. Again, on 8 client computers the applets were started simultaneously. The results are shown in Table 7.

On average it took 3.3 times longer to execute a method under load conditions, the execution times were around 7.7 instead of 2.3 milliseconds. Only the method that returned a large string executed 4 times longer. It took more than 112 milliseconds to complete (rather than 28). Figure 3 shows the re-

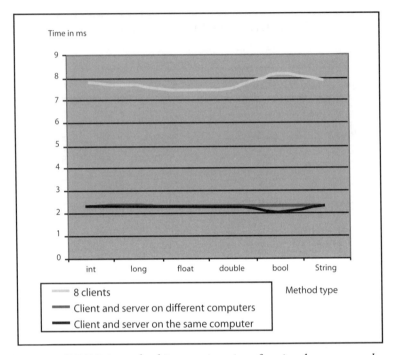

Figure 3. CORBA method invocation time for simple return values.

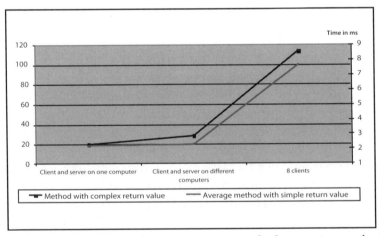

Figure 4. CORBA method invocation time for large string method compared to average of simple methods.

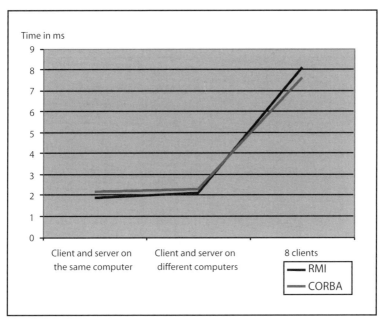

Figure 5. Average response time comparison between RMI and CORBA.

sponse times for methods returning different types for all the 3 scenarios used for testing. The Figure 4 shows the average response time of tested methods compared to the response time of large string method for all 3 scenarios. The scales for both lines are different.

CORBA vs. RMI

The results of tested performance were even more interesting when we compared RMI and CORBA. We could do this because the code used in both cases was the same. It differed only in the way the connection between the client and the server was established. Figure 5 shows an average response time of CORBA and RMI in 3 different testing scenarios.

The fact that RMI was slightly faster on one computer and on separate clients and servers was not surprising. CORBA is much more complex than RMI is. We should not forget that CORBA supports different programming languages and has more layers. On the other hand, the computers we used for testing were quite fast. The deficits of JVM, therefore, were not so obvious. When the results under the load of 8 clients were compared we found out that CORBA was faster. Still the difference was not significant. It is important to notice that the performance trade off by using CORBA was 235%. By using RMI, on the other hand, it was 284%.

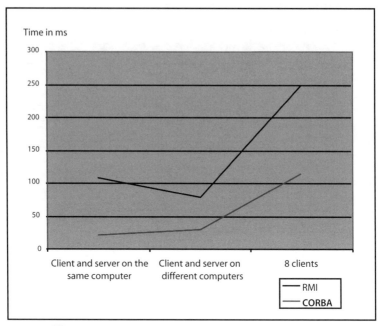

Figure 6. Large string response time comparison.

The assumption that CORBA is faster was confirmed when comparing responses by invoking a method, which returned a 10,000 character string. Figure 6 shows that CORBA was faster in all the situations. Under a load of 8 clients CORBA was more than twice as fast as RMI. The difference was even bigger on one computer, where CORBA was 5 times faster.

CONCLUSION

The performance tests gave us a picture about method invocation times using different data types of different sizes. We saw that both distributed object architectures introduced large overhead in method invocation. Therefore, developers should have this in mind when developing distributed applications, and should pay a great deal of attention to object design, as well as communications between them. When applications are poorly designed and the communication between objects is too heavy, the users will soon discover unacceptable performances. Improving them will be difficult and time-consuming.

We also saw that on fast computers Java RMI performance was acceptable, and in some cases, comparable to CORBA. This was true especially when small amounts of information were transferred between objects. By evaluation of numbers, we have to stress once again, that the tested CORBA implementation—VisiBroker—is not the only CORBA-compliant ORB. According to some unexamined sources, mainly on the Internet, VisiBroker is one of the best CORBA products available. We are already working on separate comparisons to get a better idea of how fast different CORBA products are.

And who is the winner? Unfortunately, it was not as easy to pick a winner as we hoped it would be. When the most important criteria was examined—and that was the performance degradation under heavy client load—CORBA was the winner. CORBA's performance degradation was lower than RMI's. On the other hand, it was once again proved that CORBA was a very complex product and this complexity was reflected in performance. This was why in simple cases (small client load, simple return values) on fast computers RMI was faster. This result is also congruent with the goals of both architectures.

In our opinion, RMI is very useful for simple applications, where it can offer acceptable performances. When applications become more complex, other reasons for choosing CORBA (besides performance) will have to be considered.

Based on the announcements of JavaSoft, in the near future RMI will accept the IIOP protocol and both architectures will become compatible. As soon as this happens we will not hesitate to make another performance comparison.

ACKNOWLEDGMENTS

We thank Mr. M. Hericko, B. Brumen, T. Domajnko, S. Beloglavec and Ms. A. Marinsek for their help and useful suggestions regarding performance measurements.

EFFICIENT TEXT
SEARCHING IN JAVA

LAURA WERNER

TEXT SEARCHING AND sorting is one of the most well researched areas in computer science. It is covered in an introductory algorithms course in nearly every engineering school, and there are entire books devoted to the subject. Why then, you might ask, is it necessary to publish yet another article about searching?

The answer is that most of the well-known, efficient search algorithms don't work very well in Unicode, which includes the char type in Java. Algorithms such as Knuth–Morris–Pratt and Boyer–Moore utilize tables that tell them what to do when a particular character is seen in the text being searched. That's fine for a traditional character set such as ASCII or ISO Latin-1 where there are only 128 or 256 possible characters.

Java, however, uses Unicode as its character set. In Unicode, there are 65,535 distinct characters that cover all modern languages of the world, including ideographic languages such as Chinese. In general, this is good; it makes the task of developing global applications a great deal easier. However, algorithms like Boyer–Moore that rely on an array indexed by character codes are very wasteful of memory and take a long time to initialize in this environment.

And it gets worse. Sorting and searching non-English text presents a number of challenges that many English speakers are not even aware of. The primary source of difficulty is accents, which have very different meanings in different languages, and sometimes even within the same language:

- Many accented letters, such as "é" in "café", are treated as minor variants on the letter that is accented, in this case "e".

- Sometimes the accented form of a letter is treated as a distinct letter for the purposes of comparison. For example, "Å" in Danish is treated as a separate letter that sorts just after "Z".
- In some cases, an accented letter is treated as if it were two letters. In traditional German, for example, "ä" is compared as if it were "ae".

Other difficulties arise when multiple characters compare as if they were one, such as in traditional Spanish where "ch" is treated as a single letter that sorts just after "c" and before "d", or when single characters such as the "Æ" ligature or the German "ß" are treated as if they were spelled out as "AE" or "ss".

All of the above might make the problem of sorting and searching international text seem hopeless. While not impossible, it is a difficult problem. Do not despair, however. Starting in JDK 1.1, the class java.text.Collator is here to help.

COLLATORS MADE SIMPLE

For JDK 1.1, Taligent, which has since been absorbed into IBM, contributed a number of international support classes to the Java Class Libraries. These classes are now maintained and enhanced by engineers at the IBM Center for Java Technology in Cupertino, CA. In combination with work done by Sun, they provide a powerful foundation for developing truly global applications.

Among the new classes introduced in JDK 1.1 were Collator and RuleBasedCollator, both in the java.text package. Collator provides an abstract interface for comparing text, while RuleBasedCollator is a concrete subclass that implements the comparison using a rule-driven algorithm.

Using these classes to compare two strings is quite straightforward:

```
Collator c = Collator.getInstance();
if (c.compare(string1, string2) == 0) {
    // Strings are the same
}
```

In a real program, of course, you would only call Collator.getInstance once and would then use the same collator object to perform as many comparisons as you wanted. Behind the scenes, getInstance determines the current default Locale, loads the appropriate collation rules, and constructs a Collator object that it returns. Currently, this object is always a RuleBasedCollator. However, in the future, different locales may require different classes with customized behavior,

Table 1. Example of the components of a collation element.

Character	Primary	Secondary	Tertiary
a	1	0	0
á	1	1	0
A	1	0	1
...			
B	2	0	1
...			
é	5	1	0

which is why you use a factory method to create instances of the more abstract Collator class.

UNDER THE HOOD

Internally, RuleBasedCollator.compare has an awful lot of bookkeeping to do. A byte-by-byte string comparison function like C's strcmp can walk though strings one character at a time and compare the bytes, but if Collator did something that simple it would rapidly get out of sync the first time it saw a contracting character like the Spanish "ch" or an expanding character like "Æ".

To keep track of this, RuleBasedCollator first translates strings into a series of *collation elements,* which correspond to single entities in the input string. In English, each character in the input maps to a collation element, but "Æ" produces two elements and the Spanish "ch" produces just one. This translation is done by the utility class CollationElementIterator, which uses a set of mapping tables built from the rules passed to the collator's constructor.

CollationElementIterator is a public class, and you can use it yourself to do searches, as we will see next. As an introduction, let's use it to iterate over the elements for a simple string:

```
RuleBasedCollator c = (RuleBasedCollator)Collator.getInstance();
CollationElementIterator iter = c.getCollationElementIterator("Foo");

int element;
while ((element = iter.next()) !=
    CollationElementIterator.NULLORDER) {
```

Listing 1.   The collation elements for the string Foo.

```
RuleBasedCollator c = (RuleBasedCollator)Collator.getInstance();
CollationElementIterator iter =
  c.getCollationElementIterator("Foo");

int element;
while ((element = iter.next()) != CollationElementIterator.NULLORDER) {
    System.out.println("Collation element is: " + element);
    System.out.println(" primary:
            " + Integer.toString(CollationElementIterator.primaryOrder(element), 16) );
    System.out.println(" secondary:
            " + Integer.toString(CollationElementIterator.secondaryOrder(element), 16) );
    System.out.println(" tertiary:
            " + Integer.toString(CollationElementIterator.tertiaryOrder(element), 16) ); }
```

```
        System.out.println("Collation element is: " +
                    Integer.toString(e,16) );
}
```

As you can see from this example, a collation element is a fairly simple creature; it's an int that describes where a character or group of characters falls in the sorting sequence. Higher-numbered elements are sorted after lower-numbered ones.

Of course, it's really a bit more complicated than that. Each collation element can be broken down into three components (also known as weights or orders): primary, secondary, and tertiary. The primary component of a collation element corresponds to which base letter the order represents, so "A" and "B" will have different primary weights. The secondary components typically correspond to accents, so "á" and "é" will have the same secondary weight, which is different from the secondary weight of "a". The tertiary components usually represent the case of a character, so "a" and "A" will have different tertiary weighting. (There is a fourth level, the normalized original string itself, which can be used for a final comparison, but you usually don't need to worry about this level.)

Table 1 uses simple, made-up numbers to illustrate the components of a collation element. In practice, the numbers are usually larger, because most collators have many more possible elements. To see what real collation orders look like, you can modify the last code example as follows. Listing 1 prints out the collation elements for the string Foo.

While this notion of three ordering levels seems complicated at first, it actually makes some tasks easier. If you want to do a case-insensitive comparison, you simply ignore the tertiary component of each collation element. If you also don't want to include accents, you can ignore the secondary component too.

Collator handles this by allowing you to set different strength levels using the setStrength method and constants such as Collator.PRIMARY.

```
Collator c = Collator.getInstance();
c.setStrength(Collator.PRIMARY);
if (c.compare(string1, string2) == 0) {
    ...                    // Strings matched
}
```

Text Searching in JDK 1.1

Now that you are familiar with the concepts behind collators and collation elements, we can put some of that knowledge to use. The same collation elements that RuleBasedCollator uses to perform string comparisons can be used to do string searching as well. The basic concept is quite simple: instead of searching through the characters in the string, we'll search through its collation elements.

Fast string-searching algorithms such as KMP and Boyer–Moore require the ability to back up or perform random access in the text being searched. Unfortunately, you can't do this with international text in JDK 1.1 because CollationElementIterator does not allow random access. It only has a **next** method and is lacking **setOffset** and **previous**. This means that Boyer–Moore searching cannot be implemented without a complicated buffering scheme that is very tricky to get right.

However, a traditional, brute-force string search is quite possible using the JDK 1.1 API. Essentially this comes down to comparing the search pattern against each individual character position in the text being searched. If the collation elements for the search pattern match the collation elements for that substring of text being searched, we've found a match. The outer loop looks like this:

```
/* What to search for */
String pattern = "for";
/* Text being searched */
String text = "Now is the time for all good men";

RuleBasedCollator c = (RuleBasedCollator)collator.getInstance();
CollationElementIterator patIter =
    c.getCollationElementIterator(pattern);

for (int i = 0; i < text.length(); i++) {
```

```
String substr = text.substring(i);
CollationElementIterator textIter =
    c.getCollationElementIterator(substr);
patIter.reset();
if (match(patIter, textIter)) {
    // They matched!  Do something.
}
}
```

Of course, I left out the hard part, the function match that decides whether two sequences of collation elements are equivalent. A simple, naïve implementation would loop through both iterators and ensure that the elements they return are the same:

```
boolean match(CollationElementIterator text,
        CollationElementIterator pattern)
{
    while (true) {
    int patternElement = pattern.next();
    int targetElement = text.next();
    if (patternElement = = CollationElementIterator.NULLORDER) {
    break;   // End of the pattern
    } else if (patternElement != = targetElement) {
        return false;      // Mismatch
        }
    }
    return true;   // No mismatches
}
```

This will work, but only if you want to treat any difference, be it primary, secondary, or tertiary, as significant. In most applications, that is not enough; users will want an "Ignore Case" option, and possibly an "Ignore Case and Accents" option as well. Fortunately, this is fairly easy to do. Collator provides the constants PRIMARY, SECONDARY, and TERTIARY that you can use to represent the level of comparison you want, and CollationElementIterator provides methods to break down a collation order into its three components.

All we need to do is create a variable, e.g., weight, that stores the desired level of comparison. If weight is PRIMARY, we check only the primary component of each collation element. If weight is SECONDARY, we check both the primary and secondary components, and if it is TERTIARY we check all three. For-

Listing 2. Masking unwanted portions of the collation element.

```
// Return a mask for the part of the order we're interested in
static final int getMask(int weight) {
        switch (weight) {
                case Collator.PRIMARY:
                        return 0xFFFF0000;
                case Collator.SECONDARY:
                        return 0xFFFFFF00;
                default:
                        return 0xFFFFFFFF; } }
boolean match(CollationElementIterator text,
                CollationElementIterator pattern)
{
        int mask = getMask(weight);
        int done = CollationElementIterator.NULLORDER & mask;

        while (true) {
                int patternElement = pattern.next() & mask;
                int targetElement  = text.next()   & mask;

                if (patternElement == done) {
                        break;      // End of pattern
                } else if (patternElement != targetElement) {
                        return false; // Mismatch } }
        return true;           // No mismatches }
```

tunately, the values of these constants are in ascending numerical order, so we can use simple comparisons such as "if (weight > Collator.PRIMARY) ...".

To add this extra functionality we have to modify our match function a bit, but it is still fairly simple. Because the documentation for CollationElementIterator promises that "the first 16 bits of a collation order is its primary order; the next 8 bits is the secondary order and the last 8 bits is the tertiary order," we can simply mask away the portions of the collation element that we're not interested in (see Listing 2).

IGNORE THAT CHARACTER!

As you've probably guessed, something was left out again. There's one last complication: ignorable characters. In Unicode, an accented character can be represented in two different ways. The single Unicode character \u00e1 represents "á", but the pair of Unicode values \u0061\u0301 also represents "á". The \u0061 is just a lowercase "a", but the \u0301 is special. It's a "combining acute accent" that combines with the value before it to create the single "user-level" character "á".

These combining characters need special processing during a comparison. Because \u0301 is only an accent, its collation element has a secondary com-

Listing 3. Settings to re-use and compare the current pattern element, thus skipping the current text element.

```
boolean match(CollationElementIterator text,
        CollationElementIterator pattern)
{
        int mask = getMask(weight);
        int done = CollationElementIterator.NULLORDER & mask;

        boolean getPattern = true, getTarget = true;
        int patternElement = 0, targetElement = 0;

        while (true) {
                if (getPattern) patternElement = pattern.next() & mask;
                if (getTarget) targetElement  = text.next()   & mask;
                getTarget = getPattern = true; // By default get both

                if (patternElement == done) {
                    break;        // End of pattern
                } else if (targetElement == 0) {
                    getPattern = false;    // skip targetElement
                } else if (patternElement == 0) {
                    getTarget = false;              // skip patternElement
                } else if (targetElement != patternElement) {
                    return false;     // Mismatch } }
        return true;           // No mismatches }
```

ponent but no primary or tertiary component. In a comparison that does not involve accents, we must ignore this element entirely. If we did not, we might end up comparing an accent in one string to a base letter in another string, which would give invalid results. For example, when doing an accent-insensitive comparison of "a\u0301b" and "ab", we want to skip the "\u0301" and go on to the next character; otherwise we'd compare "\u0301" and "b".

This logic is relatively straightforward, but it does make the code a bit more complicated (see Listing 3). The boolean variables getTarget and getPattern are used to decide whether to fetch the next collation element in the text and the pattern each time through the loop. Normally, both variables are true, but one or the other can be set to false if we want to skip an element. For example, setting getPattern to false and getTarget to true causes the current pattern element to be re-used and compared with the next text element, thus skipping the current text element.

This is about the best you can do with the JDK 1.1 API. You can add bells and whistles, such as searching backward though text by reversing the order of the outer loop that calls match, but you can't really implement a more efficient search without a lot of work.

It's Better in Java 2

In Java 2, we are making quite a few improvements to the international classes in java.text and java.util. Among them are enhancements to CollationElementIterator that make it possible to write faster and more powerful search routines. These changes are present in JDK 1.2 beta3 and now in Java 2. You can download the latest version from the Java Developer Connection Web site.

There are two major problems with the searching mechanism just outlined. First, it uses an inefficient algorithm that can, at worst, compare every character of the pattern against every character of the target, requiring a number of comparisons that is proportional to the size of the text being searched multiplied by the size of the pattern. (In practice, it's usually not quite that bad, however.) In computer science terms, if the size of the text is T and the size of the pattern is P, the search time is proportional to $T \cdot P$, or is $O(TP)$. Modern searching algorithms can do much better.

The second, and more obvious problem is that there is an awful lot of object creation going on in the last few examples. Every time through the outer loop we call substring, which creates a new String object, and then we create a new CollationElementIterator. This happens at every single position in the target string, which is woefully inefficient given the cost of object creation in Java (and in most other languages, for that matter).

This second problem is solved by two new CollationElementIterator methods that we have added in Java 2:

```
public void setOffset(int newOffset)
public int  getOffset()
```

These methods allow you to change the text position to which an iterator points and to retrieve its current position. With this flexibility, we can avoid all of the calls to substring and all of the extra iterator objects that we were creating before. The outer searching loop now looks like this:

```
String pat = "for";
/* What to search for */
String text = "Now is the time for all good men";
// Text to search in
RuleBasedCollator c = (RuleBasedCollator)Collator.getInstance();
CollationElementIterator patIter = c.getCollationElementIterator(pat);
CollationElementIterator targIter = c.getCollationElementIterator(text);
```

```
for (int i = 0; i < text.length(); i++) {
    targIter.setOffset(i);
    patIter.reset();            // Or setOffset(0)
    if (match(patIter, targIter)) {
        // They matched!  Do something.
    }
}
```

This will be much faster because we're no longer creating new objects each time through the loop. The algorithm is still O(TP), but the overhead per iteration is considerably lower, so the running time will be a lot better.

OPTIMIZED SEARCHING

We have solved the easier of our two efficiency problems; now it's time for the hard one. As explained, the brute-force algorithm we're using is O(TP). String searching is a well-researched area, and there are algorithms that can do considerably better. Perhaps the best is the Boyer–Moore method, which is never worse than O(T+P) and in practice is often proportional to T/P. That's right: the size of the text divided by the size of the pattern. Rather than forcing us to examine characters in the text multiple times, this algorithm actually lets us skip characters.

Boyer–Moore can be a little bit tricky to explain, but once you "get" it, it seems almost too obvious. The trick is that instead of comparing the strings starting at the beginning of the pattern, you compare them starting at the end. If the characters don't match, we still gleaned a bit of useful information: we now know what character occurs at that position in the text being searched. Often, we can take advantage of that information to skip several characters in the target text rather than simply sliding the pattern along by one position and trying again.

An example will make this more clear. Imagine that you're searching for the word "string" inside the phrase "silly spring string." To start off, you line up the beginning of the pattern with the beginning of the target, but you start comparing at the end, like so:

silly spring string
string

We compare the **g** in the pattern with a space character in the target, and there's no match. So far, there's nothing special. However, we know something else as

Table 2. Boyer–Moore Shift Distances.

Input Character	Distance
s	5
t	4
r	3
i	2
n	1
g	0
others:	6

well: the character at index 5 in the target is a space, and there are no space characters anywhere in the pattern we're searching for. Combining these two facts, we can slide the pattern over by six characters and try again:

silly **spring** string
    string

This time, there is a match between the pattern and the text. Because we're going backwards, we now compare the **n**, **i**, and **r** and find that they match too. However, the **p** and the **t** do not. We know that there is not a **p** anywhere in the pattern, so we can slide it over again:

silly spring **s**tring
    string**g**

This time, we see an **s** in the text. It's not a match, but we do know that there is an **s** at the beginning of the pattern. Therefore, we slide the pattern over five spaces. Now we have the following, which gives us a match.

silly spring **string**
    string

To implement this efficiently, you need to have a table that, for each possible character in the text, tells you how far from the end of the pattern that character first occurs. This is the distance by which the pattern can be shifted when that particular character is seen in the input. For the previous example, it would look like Table 2.

This table can be computed once, before the search is started, by making a single pass through the pattern. After that, it can be used each time we search for that pattern, leading to a huge performance win.

Listing 4. Calculating Boyer–Moore shift distances with Java 2.

```
/* Member variables for storing precomputed pattern data */
private int   patLen;
private int[] patElem;
private int[] shifts;

/* Map a collation element to an array index */
int hash(int order) {
        return CollationElementIterator.primaryOrder(order) % 256;
}

/* Initialize the Boyer-Moore shift tables */
void initialize(RuleBasedCollator c, String pat)
{
        /* First find out how many elements we're dealing with */
        patLen = 0;
        CollationElementIterator iter = c.getCollationElementIterator(pat);
        while (iter.next() != CollationElementIterator.NULLORDER)
                patLen++;

        /* Allocate space to store the pattern elements and the shift tables */
        patElem = new int[patLen];
        shifts = new int[256];

        /* Elements not found in the pattern get the maximum shift distance */
        for (int i = 0; i < 256; i++) {
                shifts[i] = patLen;
        }

        /* Now compute the shift distances for the elements in the pattern. While we're at it,
           save the elements themselves for quick access. The "-1" is in the calculation be-
           cause Java indices are 0-based. */
        iter.reset();
        for (int i = 0; i < patLen; i++) {
                patElem[i] = iter.next();
                int index = hash(patElem[i]);
                shifts[index] = Math.min(shifts[index], patLen - i - 1); } }
```

BOYER-MOORE VS. UNICODE

But wait! At the very beginning of this article, I said that this kind of algorithm doesn't work well with Unicode because it has 65,535 possible character values, which would make the table too large. Actually, it's worse, because we're concerned with collation elements, which are 32-bit integers, not with the Unicode values themselves. That's true, but (of course) there's another trick...

First, consider what happens when a letter occurs twice in the search pattern. There are two possible shift distances for that letter, one for each occurrence. To make the Boyer–Moore algorithm work, we always want to enter the smaller of the two shift distances in the table. If we used the larger one, we

Listing 5. Boyer–Moore searching with Java 2.

```
public int find(String text, String pattern)
{
        RuleBasedCollator coll = (RuleBasedCollator)Collator.getInstance();
        CollationElementIterator targIter =
            coll.getCollationElementIterator(text);

        /* build the shift table and the constants we need */
        initialize(coll, pattern);
        int mask = getMask(weight);
        int done = CollationElementIterator.NULLORDER & mask;

        /* Start at the text position corresponding to the end of the pattern */
        int textIndex = pattern.length();

        while (textIndex <= text.length()) {
                boolean getPattern = true, getTarget = true;
                int targetElement=0, patternElement=0;

                iter.setOffset(textIndex);
                int patIndex = pattern.length();

                /* Iterate backward until we hit the beginning of the pattern */
                while (patIndex > 0)
                {
                        if (getTarget)  targetElement  = targIter.previous() & mask;
                        if (getPattern) patternElement = patElem[—patIndex] & mask;
                        getTarget = getPattern = true;

                        if (targetElement == 0) {
                            getPattern = false;              /* skip targetElement */
                        } else if (patternElement == 0) {
                            getTarget = false;               /* skip patternElement */
                        } else if (targetElement != patternElement) {
                            /* There is a mismatch at this position. Decide how far over to shift the
                            pattern, then try again. */
                            textIndex = iter.getOffset() +
                                            shifts[hash(targetElement)];
                            break; } }
                if (patIndex == 0) {
                    /* We made it back to the beginning of the pattern, which means we
                    matched it all. Return the location. */
                    return targIter.getOffset(); }
                /* Otherwise, we're here because of a mismatch, so keep going.... */ }
        return -1;        /* No match.*/ }
```

might shift the pattern too far and miss a match. In a sense, the shift table is not required to be perfectly accurate, and conservative estimates of shift distances are OK. As long as we don't shift the pattern too far, we're fine.

This realization leads to a simple technique for applying the algorithm to Java collation elements: simply map all possible elements down to a much smaller set of shift table indices (say, 256). If two or more elements in your pattern happen to collide and end up with the same index, it's not a problem as long as you enter the smaller of the shift distances in the table.

A simple way to map the collation elements to 256 values is to use the low byte of the element's primary component. There are other approaches that will lead to a better distribution of values throughout the shift table and will thus give slightly better performance, but in practice this approach is usually good enough.

To implement Boyer–Moore searching with Java 2, we first need to construct a shift table that tells us how far to shift the pattern when a particular collation element is seen in the text (see Listing 4). The hash function is used to map from a 32-bit collation order down to an index in the 256-element array.

Once we have the tables, the search routine is straightforward. It uses another new method: CollationElementIterator.previous. Also note that there is no longer an outer loop that calls a separate match method, because that only worked well when we were marching through the text one character at a time. Now that we can skip ahead an arbitrary distance through the text, it is easier to combine all of the logic into one method (see Listing 5).

There you have it: a way to do fast, linear-time, international-friendly string searching in Java.

The Real Stuff

I hope I have given you a good idea of how you can use collators to add language-sensitive sorting and searching to your own Java applications. It is not that hard and the benefits can be enormous, because global markets are becoming increasingly more important to the computer industry. For example, according to IBM's first quarter 1998 financial statement, more than half of IBM's revenue came from outside North America. Using the international features of the JDK can help you begin to tap into this huge market.

The code examples listed in this article were intended primarily for their educational value, but they do work. However, for clarity I have ignored a few remaining issues to make the code easier to understand. Expanding ("ä" to "ae") characters in the pattern are the chief difficulty. If the shorter, non-expanded version of the character occurs in the text being searched, you can end up shifting too far and missing a possible match. However, it is not too hard to compensate for this by using the getMaxExpansion method (also new in Java 2) of CollationElementIterator to decrease the shift distances when expanded characters are seen in the pattern.

The other major feature I have left out is the ability to tell how much of the text matched the pattern. All of the code examples search for location in the text where a match starts, but they do not return the length of the text that matched. You would need to know this if you were writing a search and replace function in an editor, for example. In Java 2, it is easy to tell where the match ends: just call the iterator's getOffset method. With the JDK 1.1 API, it is harder; you basically have to resort to the brute-force technique of comparing longer and longer substrings of the text to the pattern and stopping when the collator says that they are equal.

If you want to see real, production-quality code that uses the same algorithms and solves these last few problems, visit the IBM alphaWorks Web site and download our fully-functional StringSearch class based on the JDK collation API. It supports case- and accent-insensitive searches, backward searches, and "whole word" searching among other features. alphaWorks also contains several other Java internationalization utilities that you might find useful, as well as a large number of JavaBeans, utility classes, and even a free XML parser written in Java.

ACKNOWLEDGMENTS

The patented technique for applying the Boyer–Moore search algorithm to collation elements was developed by Dr. Mark Davis of IBM. Kathleen Wilson, the manager of the text and international groups at IBM's Center for Java Technology in Silicon Valley, was very indulgent of the time I spent working on this article and the accompanying code. I would also like to thank Mark, Kathleen, Michael Pogue, John Raley, and Helena Shih for reviewing drafts of this article.

RECOMMENDED RESOURCES

Sedgewick, R., *Algorithms in C, 3rd ed.*, Addison-Wesley, 1997—Has a good overview of the Boyer–Moore search algorithm as applied to small character sets. He also covers a number of other search algorithms.

Chan, P., R. Lee, and D. Kramer, *The Java Class Libraries, 2nd ed., Vol. 1*, Addison-Wesley, 1998—Has a nice description of CollationElementIterator.

Making your Java/C++/C Applications Global, at www.ibm.com/java/education/international-unicode/unicode1.html—Is a good overview of some of the issues involved in writing global applications.

The Unicode Consortium's *The Unicode Standard, Version 2.0*, Addison-Wesley, 1996—Has lots of useful information on processing international text. In particular, section 5.15 covers sorting and searching.

The Unicode Consortium Web site at www.unicode.org has lots of useful information. If you want an even more detailed explanation of Unicode collation, see www.unicode.org/unicode/reports/tr10.

Enterprise Applets and Archive Functionality

John Cerwin

T HE PROMISE OF Java as a truly distributed software platform is now a step closer to reality. The recent integration of Java archive functionality significantly improves the ability of developers to manage and transfer disbursed data over large networks. Specifically, Java now provides two disparate areas of archiving functionality that address the same issue: an improvement in download time—but through different means. Java Archive files, or JAR files, allow an entire applet's dependency list to be transferred in the form of a single compressed file, while Java's archiving classes provide functionality for the programmatic manipulation of files in various compression formats. Given the benefits of archives in a distributed model, I will detail some of these newly integrated features, as well as demonstrate how archive functionality can improve enterprise applet performance.

JAR FILES

Introduced with the JDK 1.1, Java Archive files provide a vastly improved delivery mechanism for applets. An entire applet's dependency list (all .class files, images, sounds, text, etc.) can now be aggregated into a single compressed file, which can then be transferred over a single HTTP connection. Once downloaded, JDK 1.1-compliant browsers can then seemly decompress and run the applet. The result of this process is a marked decrease in the time it takes to launch an applet, due in part to a reduction of both the bytes transferred and number of dependency-based HTTP transactions.

Java Archive files are based on the popular ZIP archive format as defined by PKWare. Although they can be used in general, non-Java related archiving, it should be noted that they were developed with the express purpose of packaging an applet and its requisite components. One factor that validates this claim is the capability of JARs to be digitally signed. A digital signature provides a convenient method for authenticating the origin of the code contained within the archive.

The process of creating and distributing an applet in a JAR file is actually quite simple. Included in the JDK 1.1 is a tool called JAR.EXE. This utility allows an applet's dependent files to be aggregated into a single .jar file (see Listing 1 for the syntax and common switches). Once the JAR file is created, it can then be specified and used in HTML via the "archive" tag:

```
<APPLET CODE=foo.class ARCHIVE=foo.jar></
APPLET>
```

For more information on working with archives, see the JAR guide in the JDK documentation under ...\docs\guide\jar\jarguide.html.

WHAT'S IN PACKAGE ZIP?

Providing advantages similar to JAR file applet distribution, package ZIP represents Java's version of a network-oriented compression library. Included within its contents are classes that afford compression, decompression, filtering, and streaming capabilities for archives in the JAR, ZIP, and GZIP formats.

Package java.util.zip provides a compact, extremely simple means for the programmatic manipulation of archives in both a local and distributed format.

At the heart of package ZIP are the Deflater and Inflater classes. These two classes represent native functionality for compression and decompression of archives. Although Inflater and Deflater are not used directly, they do serve as the basis for InflaterInputStream and DeflaterOutputStream. These streaming classes combine Deflater and Inflater's native archiving capabilities with Java's traditional FilterInputStream and FilterOutputStream. An archive can thus be inflated by invoking method read() on an InflaterInputStream instance, and deflated by invoking method write() on an instance of DeflaterOutputStream. If you look in the JDK source code you will notice that each compression format has a corresponding set of classes that are extended from InflaterInputStream and DeflaterOutputStream. Archives in a ZIP format, for example, would use ZipInputStream and ZipOutput-

Stream, while GZIP archives would use the GZIPInputStream and GZIPOutputStream.

Arguably, the two most common classes in package ZIP are ZipFile and ZipEntry. A ZipFile object represents a physical file in an archive format, and provides a series of methods for performing high-level operations on that file. Listed below are some of the more common methods contained in class ZipFile:

- getName()—Returns the name of the archive file.
- entries()—Returns an Enumeration object that represents the entities in the archive file.
- getInputStream()—Returns an InputStream object that represents the method's ZipEntry parameter.

ZipFile objects are usually comprised of several ZipEntry objects, each of which represent an actual entity that is part of the archive itself. In the case of an applet, a particular ZipEntry might represent a physical .class, .au, or .gif file. Most of the methods provided for class ZipEntry are accessor related, allowing a developer to get or set specific entry-related information. Here is a list of ZipEntry's more prevalent methods:

- getName()—Returns the name of the entry.
- getSize()—Returns the uncompressed size of the entry's data.
- getCompressedSize()—Returns the compressed size of the entry's data.
- setTime()—Sets the modification time for the entry.
- setComment()—Sets an optional comment string for the entry.

Listing 2 provides an example of how class ZipFile and class ZipEntry are used in conjunction with each other to elicit information about an archive.

ENTERPRISE APPLETS AND PACKAGE ZIP

So, how can package ZIP improve on enterprise applet performance? Here is a classic example I recently came across.

While attempting to use JAR file distribution in the design of an enterprise-scale applet, I realized that several dependencies would essentially be optional. Specifically, each instance of the applet (or each *user*) could employ different combinations of image, audio, and text files. Given that the dependencies were elective, numerous, and quite large (typically 400k+), I faced a classic computing problem—do I *punish* the user up front by requiring *all* possible de-

Listing 1.

```
Switch      Use
c           Create a new archive.
x           Extract files from an archive.
t           View the archive table of contents.
f           Specify the archive's file name.
o           Do not use compression.
```

The example in Listing 2 creates a new JAR file in the current directory called foo.jar. All .class, .gif, and .au files that reside in that directory are incorporated in the foo.jar. Jar −cf foo.jar *.class *.gif *.au

Listing 2.

```
public class JarView {

    public static void main(String args[]) {
        if (args.length == 0) {
        System.out.println("No filespecified!");
        System.exit(0); }

        try {
        // Create a ZipFile object...
        ZipFile zFile = new ZipFile(args[0]);
        Enumeration enumEntries = zFile.entries();
        System.out.println ("Opening " + zFile.getName() + "...");

        // Enumerate and display the ZipFile entries...
        while(enumEntries.hasMoreElements()) {
        ZipEntry zEntry = (ZipEntry) enumEntries.nextElement();
        System.out.println("");
        System.out.println("Entry Name:\t" + zEntry.getName());
        System.out.println("Compressed:\t" + zEntry.getCompressedSize() + "kb");
        System.out.println("Uncompressed:\t" + zEntry.getSize() + "kb"); } }
        catch(IOException e) {
        System.out.println("Error opening " + args[0]); } } }
```

pendencies to be downloaded, or do I force the user to wait for dependencies during execution (to be loaded as needed)? The problem was further compounded by the advantages of JAR files. The compression ratio on many of the dependencies (especially the text files) was greater than 70%, which significantly reduced the transfer time, and, correspondingly, made me much less willing to exclude anything from a compressed form of distribution.

The dilemma ultimately came down to a question of on-demand zip loading. No matter how good the compression ratio, it just seemed wasteful to download everything in the beginning—as some items would never be used. However, if I could load a dependency in a compressed format as *needed*, I could still capitalize on the advantage of JAR file distribution, while avoiding the issue of dis-

Figure 1. Terminator.jpg extracted and displayed using JZipLoader.

tributing everything up front. What I needed was a class that could dynamically load and create different types of objects from a JAR (or ZIP) file on a server, and fortunately the JDK already contained many of the tools I required.

CLASS JZipLoader

The functionality behind JZipLoader is quite simple: use a stream to download a compressed resource, decompress that resource's bytes, and then create the resource. The class also doubles as a caching mechanism to further extend its functionality. Here is a quick summary of the JZipLoader methods that we will look at in detail:

- Public method getZipInputStream() is responsible for converting a resource URL (i.e., http://mysite/myapplet/images/image.jar) into an input stream with a filter for reading zip files.
- Public method getBytes() maintains the task of finding a specified entry (a *resource*) in a zip stream and then, if found, calling the necessary methods to convert it into a resident byte array.

Listing 3.

```
public ZipInputStream getZipInputStream(URL urlZipFile) {

    ZipInputStream zipStream = null;
    try {
        // Convert the archive into a ZipInputStream
        URLConnection urlConnection = urlZipFile.openConnection();
        urlConnection.setAllowUserInteraction(false);
        zipStream = new ZipInputStream(urlConnection.getInputStream()); }
    catch(IOException e) {
        System.out.println("IOException in JZipLoader.getZipInputStream, " + e.toString());
        }
    finally {
        return zipStream; } }
```

Listing 4.

```
public ZipInputStream getZipInputStream(String sJarFileName) {

    InputStream stream = getClass().getResourceAsStream(sJarFileName);
    return new ZipInputStream(stream); }
// Note that ClassLoader.getResourceAsStream() was not working properly in Netscape
// Navigator v4.03 (w/JDK 1.1 beta) as of the writing of this article.
```

- Public method readZipEntry() contains the actual functionality for de-compressing a ZipEntry into a byte array. This method is normally called by getBytes().

Public method getZipInputStream() accepts one parameter, a reference to a URL. If the URL is valid, a connection is opened to it, and the corresponding input stream is converted into an instance of ZipInputStream. The method then returns the newly created zip stream (see Listing 3). It should be noted that there are a variety of ways to convert a server file into a generic input stream. I elected to use a URLConnection object because it's common, but another technique involves the use of Class.getResourceAsStream(). This method accepts a single parameter, a string that represents a file on the server. It is somewhat easier to use because it hides a lot of the file-streaming grunt work, but is limited because the resource search rules are determined by the calling class' ClassLoader object. For a more detailed explanation see the JDK API help file. Listing 4 demonstrates a converted version of getZipInputStream() that uses getResourceAsStream().

Method getBytes() (see Listing 5) requires two parameters, a string representing a resource name, and an instance of a ZipInputStream object. The method starts by iterating the zip file to look for the specified resource. This is a simple process that employs the use of getNextEntry(), which is a public method of Zip-

---

Listing 5.

```
public byte[] getBytes(String sResourceName, ZipInputStream zipStream) {

   /* Return the uncompressed bytes of the specified resource... */
   ZipEntry zipEntry  = null;
   byte bBuffer[]  = null;

   try {
      while( (zipEntry = zipStream.getNextEntry()) != null) {
      /* Found resource yet? */
      if (zipEntry.getName().equalsIgnoreCase(sResourceName)) {
         /* The resource has been found, read it into a buffer */
         bBuffer = readZipEntry(zipStream, zipEntry);
         break; } }

         /* Did we find the resource? */
         if (zipEntry == null) {
            throw new ZipException("cannot find resource '" + sResourceName + "'"); } }
   catch(Exception e)   {
   System.out.println("Exception in JZipLoader.getBytes, " + e.toString()); }
   finally {
      return bBuffer; } }
```

InputStream. This method will return an instance of class ZipEntry if the resource is successfully located. Conversely, if none of the entries represent the resource name passed to getBytes(), a ZipException is thrown and null value is returned.

Once a valid ZipEntry exists for the specified resource, method readZipEntry() is called (see Listing 6), and the transfer and decompression process begins. The first step involves the allocation of a buffer as a placeholder for the resource. The size of the placeholder is normally determined by the reported size of the ZipEntry, although the operation can become somewhat more complex. Method getSize(), a member of ZipEntry, offers no guarantees that it will even know the entry size. Thus, if ZipEntry.getSize() returns –1, the buffer that serves as a place-holder for the decompressed resource must be resized dynamically. I was surprised to find during experimentation that although files in the traditional ZIP format do return a valid entry size via getSize(), JAR files often do not!

The actual process of transferring and decompressing the file into its local placeholder is encapsulated in ZipInputStream's overridden method read(). This form of read() is similar to others in that it accepts as an argument the buffer (or placeholder) we want to fill, and, correspondingly, returns the number of bytes read into that buffer. If the entry size was *unknown* up front, then the buffer is resized until method read() returns –1. If successful, the method terminates by returning a raw decompressed resource in the form of a byte array.

If you look at Listing 6 in detail you will notice that the buffer realloca-tions are performed by using a method called resizeBuffer(). This utility func-

Listing 6.

```
public byte[] readZipEntry(ZipInputStream zipStream, ZipEntry zipEntry) {

int iTotalRead = 0, iBytesRead = 0;

        /* Get the size of the entry, may be unknown! */
        int iEntrySize = (int) zipEntry.getSize();

        /* Establish a buffer for the entry to decompress into */
        int iBuffersize = (iEntrySize < 0) ? 10240 : iEntrySize;
        byte[] bBuffer = new byte[iBuffersize];

    try {

        /* Read the zip stream until its complete... */
        while((iBytesRead = zipStream.read(bBuffer, iTotalRead, bBuffer.length -
          iTotalRead)) >= 0) {

        /* Increment the read count */
        iTotalRead+=iBytesRead;

        /* Is this current read complete? */
        if (iTotalRead == bBuffer.length) {

            /* Are we working with a valid entry size? */
            if (iEntrySize < 0) {
            /* Entry size is unknown, double the buffer size and keep reading until
                zipStream.read is < 0! */
            bBuffer = resizeBuffer(bBuffer, 2 * iTotalRead); }
            else {
            /* Valid entry size, done reading */
            break; } } }

    /* Are we working with a valid entry size? */
    if (iEntrySize < 0) {
        /* The entry was read and the exact size is now known — strip any unused
            bytes */
        bBuffer = resizeBuffer(bBuffer, iTotalRead); } }
    catch(IOException e) {
        System.out.println("IOException in JZipLoader.readZipEntry, " + e.toString());}
        finally {
            return bBuffer; } }
```

Listing 7.

```
private byte[] resizeBuffer(byte[] bBuffer, int iNewBufferSize) {

    byte[] bTempBuffer = new    byte[iNewBufferSize];
    System.arraycopy(bBuffer, 0, bTempBuffer, 0,
      bBuffer.length);
    return bTempBuffer; }
```

Listing 8.

```java
public Image getImage(String sImageFileName, URL urlZipFile) {

/* Check the cache for the image... */
    Image image = (Image) m_hashtableCache.get(sImageFileName);
    if (image != null) {
        return image; }

    /* Convert the archive into a ZipInputStream */
    ZipInputStream zipStream = getZipInputStream(urlZipFile);

    /* Create the image... */
    if (zipStream != null) {
        byte bBuffer[] = getBytes(sImageFileName, zipStream);
        if (bBuffer != null) {
            image = Toolkit.getDefaultToolkit().createImage(bBuffer);
            m_hashtableCache.put(sImageFileName, image); } }

    return image; }
public String getText(String sTextFileName, URL urlZipFile)
{

    /* Check the cache for the text... */
    String text = (String) m_hashtableCache.get(sTextFileName);
    if (text != null) {
    return text; }

    /* Convert the archive into a ZipInputStream */
    ZipInputStream zipStream = getZipInputStream(urlZipFile);

    /* Create the String... */
    if (zipStream != null) {
        byte bBuffer[] = getBytes(sTextFileName, zipStream);
        if (bBuffer != null) {
            text = new String(bBuffer);
            m_hashtableCache.put(sTextFileName, text); } }

    return text; }
```

---

tion (found in Listing 7) allows a byte array to be dynamically resized, while concurrently maintaining the original array contents. Because such an operation could potentially be expensive, it's worth noting that resizeBuffer() is really just a call to the JDK's System.arrayCopy(). This static method provides a very fast, efficient way to copy the contents of an entire array into another. Although it might be tempting for a developer to implement the same functionality in the form of a *for loop*, System.arrayCopy() is machine-code based, and thus, much faster than slower byte-code (*Kick Ass Java Programming*, Espeset, T., Coriolis Group, 1996). Generally speaking, the Java API will always be faster than routines written from scratch.

USING JZipLoader

Because JZipLoader ultimately turns a compressed ZipEntry into an array of decompressed bytes, the process of recreating a resource is very straightforward. Most of the resource-related classes under Java include methods that provide for creation directly from a byte array. JZipLoader thus furnishes a series of type-specific, resource helper methods that are used to convert raw bytes into an object. Take a look at JZipLoader's getImage() and getText() methods (Listing 8), which use Toolkit.createImage(byte[]) and String(byte[]) respectively. You will notice as well that each of the type-specific, resource helper methods check JZipLoader's "cache" before streaming a compressed server resource. This cache is simply a Hashtable that saves a local copy of every requested resource. To use JZipLoader, simply create an instance and invoke one of the resource helper methods on it (Listing 8). A sample applet is shown in Figure 1, with the associated source code in Listing 9. The entire source code listing for JZipLoader and JZipLoaderApplet can be found at *Java Report Online*.

THE FUTURE

So, if downloading and decompressing an image or text file is so simple, can we perform the same technique with a Java .class file? This is probably the question that next comes to mind for most developers, and the answer is, fortunately, yes. In fact, if you look at the early release specs (available at Sun's Web site) for the JDK 1.2 you will find a new package called java.util.jar. (The JDK 1.2 was in beta 2 as of the writing of this article. Some functionality may change in the actual release version.) Package JAR is loosely based on package ZIP in that it closely mirrors ZIP's classes and functionality—but is specifically designed for the unique characteristics of a .jar file. Package JAR can be used in conjunction with the new JarURLConnection and URL-ClassLoader classes to dynamically load a .class file from an archive. Although JZipLoader's functionality could be extended to handle .class files, JavaSoft has already anticipated the need for dynamic class loading from a .jar file, and should be releasing it with the JDK 1.2. Also included in this release (as of the writing of this article) are methods for accessing .jar file resources. JarURLConnection.getJarFile() returns a JarFile object for a given physical .jar file, and JarURLConnection.getEntry() returns an archived resource in the form of a JarEntry object.

CONCLUSION

Although it is considered one of the more obscure sets of functionality in the JDK, package ZIP can dramatically improve the performance of Java over a network. This is especially true when used in conjunction with JAR-based applet distribution. It is obvious as well that archive functionality will continue to be a big part of Java's future. As the size, scope, and scale of enterprise applets continues to widen, archives will become much more commonplace, and their advantages much more apparent. The tools for fulfilling the promise of Java as a truly distributed software platform are coming of age, so don't hesitate to use them!

REALITY CHECK

Primitive Types Considered Harmful

Sherman R. Alpert

HE JAVA DEVELOPERS' slogan is "100% Java," meaning "Don't taint your Java software by incorporating non-Java components." Yet, Java itself is neither 100% pure object nor 100% pure object-oriented; it is "tainted" with components of the procedural programming paradigm. The Java designers have borrowed many ideas from diverse sources—other object-oriented languages, especially C++ and Smalltalk, design patterns (see Gamma, E. *et al. Design Patterns: Elements of Reusable Object-Oriented Software*, Addison-Wesley, 1995), and basic object-oriented design principles—picking and choosing good ideas from each. And they've done a truly fine job. However, at one particular juncture, I believe the language architects made the wrong choice, and that was the decision to incorporate non-object primitive types into the otherwise uniform object-oriented language model.

There are two types of types in Java. By primitive types, I mean elementary variable types such as int, boolean, float, long, short, and so on. These are sometimes referred to as "built-in" types. The other type of type is objects: a variable can be declared to be of type Object or String or any other class. Referring to the two types of types as *metatypes*, we have primitive and object metatypes (the truth is, the two metatypes are primitive and reference, which includes not only objects, but interfaces and arrays—more on why they are "reference" types later). By incorporating both metatypes, Java is not populated purely with objects.

The result, as would be expected, is that Java is also not 100% object-oriented. Programmers operate on objects by sending them messages and accessing their subsumed fields using dot notation. We operate on primitive variables with operators built into the Java language, such as +, *, and ++. [There are exceptions: in some (very few) cases, we can also act on objects using language-level operators, such as + (concatenation) for **String** instances; this actually only adds to the potential confusion because the language is thus all the more inconsistent.]

So, what's the problem? By building a world in which objects co-exist with primitive types and procedural programming constructs co-exist with object-oriented mechanisms, Java offers a single world with a dichotomy of semantics. It mixes procedural semantics into an otherwise uniform object-oriented model. Primitives are not first-class objects, yet they exist in a language that involves, primarily, first-class objects. Researchers have conjectured that mixing programming paradigms in a single language can be problematic, and a uniform model should be more comprehensible and usable. (See Rosson, M.B. and S.R. Alpert, "The Cognitive Consequences of Object-Oriented Design," *Human-Computer Interaction* (5)4, Lawrence Erlbaum Associates, Inc., 345-379, 1990.) I will offer concrete examples of why mixing paradigms is problematic in Java. My primary goal is to illustrate how incorporating primitive types into Java causes problems for programmers, and hopefully motivate the Java designers to rectify the problem. Secondarily, I will offer a solution to this problem as grist for the Java designers' mill.

Why Primitive Types?

It was certainly not illogical for the Java designers to include primitive types. There are several possible reasons they may have done so. The first potential reason is consistency—many of Java's ideas originate in C++ and in C++ objects and primitive types also co-exist. When object-oriented constructs were grafted onto the C language, C's data types remained as is. The motivation behind this is that Bjarne Stroustrup, C++'s designer, wanted to be as consistent as possible with the base C language, hoping to capitalize on programmers' pre-C++ knowledge. "*Unfortunately*, user-defined and built-in types cannot be made to behave in a completely uniform manner. The reason is that the irregularity of the built-in types cannot be removed without causing serious incompatibilities with C" (emphasis mine)—see Stroustrup, B., *The Design and Evolution of C++*, Addison-Wesley, 1994, p. 380.

For Java, this is a debatable issue. There is no base language with which Java ought to be consistent. On the other hand, Java programmers do have experience programming in non-object-oriented languages and are thus accustomed to using primitive data types.

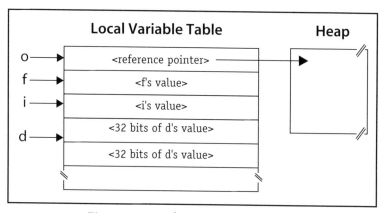

Figure 1. Local variable table entries.

Another point arguing against defining elementary types as objects (that is, as instances of some class) is, do we really want multiple instances of elementary types with the same value? For example, do we really want multiple integers whose value is 1? If primitive types such as integers are objects, then we might be able to have two *different* integer objects whose value is identical.

But really, the most important reasons for handling primitive types differently than objects are performance and verification. Primitive types such as integers, booleans, and floats are part of the "hard currency," the constantly used bread-and-butter of an imperative language like Java. Simply then, we want operations involving variables of these types—operations that are at the heart of our computing model—to run fast.

The Java virtual machine (JVM) maintains an execution stack for each thread. This *Java stack* is populated with *stack frames*: each time a method is invoked, a new stack frame is pushed onto the thread's stack. The stack frame represents the state of the method, including a local variable table (with entries for this— the object in which the method is running, the method's parameters, and variables declared within the method), a dynamic operand stack, and various data involved in invoking and returning from the method (such as a pointer to the invoker's stack frame). Variables declared in a Java program are represented inside the JVM by entries in the local variable table and operand stack. As mandated by the JVM specification, entries for primitive variables in the variable table and operand stack contain the actual values of those variables.*

Objects are represented on the stack quite differently. An entry for an object

---

* For economy of expression, I'll refer to both variable table and operand stack entries as "stack" entries from here on.

contains not the object itself, but a pointer into memory (into the heap) where the object resides. Figure 1 shows the local variable table entries for the following declorations (assuming a 32-bit stack word):

```
object o = new object();
floatf;
int i;
doubled;
```

Hence, accessing an object referenced in an operand stack entry requires at least an access of that stack entry to retrieve the memory pointer and another access of the object in the heap itself. (Actually, the JVM specification does not mandate any particular heap access mechanism; hence, accessing an object may require even more memory lookups, depending on the JVM's implementation. See Venners, B., *Inside the Java Virtual Machine*, McGraw-Hill, 1998 and Lindholm, T. and F. Yellin, *The Java Virtual Machine Specification*, Addison-Wesley, 1996 and also the Sun JVM specification Web page.) The upshot of all this is that accessing the values of primitive variables is faster that accessing data in objects because primitives require fewer memory fetches.

Note that while the JVM specification dictates the numerical magnitudes for all primitive types (e.g., an int must contain 32 bits of data, a short must have 16), it does not specify the actual size of a stack word beyond the criterion that it must be at least 32 bits. Often, the size of a word on the VM's stack is the native pointer size of the platform on which the JVM is implemented. (See Venners; Lindholm, and Yellin.) For example, in a typical Windows 95 JVM, single precision primitives reside in one 32-bit entry, and doubles and longs, which must be 64 bits wide, occupy two contiguous slots (see Figure 1). On platforms with a 64-bit native word size, a JVM could place all primitive variables (including doubles and longs) in a single stack word, which would leave some bits unused for all primitive variables [because, as per the JVM specification, doubles and longs must occupy two stack words regardless of the word size (see Lindholm and Yellin)]. For the rest of our discussion, I'll assume a 32-bit word size.

The other efficiency issue is speed of execution of operations. Sending a message to an object requires the JVM to perform multiple memory accesses to retrieve the object from the heap, several more to retrieve the method (based on pointers from the object to its class and possibly one or more superclass-chain pointers), and then executing the method using a generic method-invocation mechanism. On the other hand, the value of a primitive variable is right in the stack, plus the JVM has specific opcodes for specific primitive operations, such as adding two ints. These primitive-specific opcodes are executed directly by the VM; they do not require accessing and executing a method defined in a class.

Type-specific opcodes also facilitate one aspect of security, specifically, a portion of code verification. Bytecode verification includes making sure opcodes are type safe and consistent. So, for example, if opcodes in an applet tell the JVM to "load int from local variable 1 onto the operand stack" immediately followed by "store double into local variable 1," the bytecode verifier would fail. Because doubles occupy two words, storing a double implies storing the top *two* operand stack words into the *two* variable table entries starting at entry 1. This would result in overwriting whatever variable is currently in slot 2 of the variable table. This could be used to store pointers into unsecured portions of memory. So, the types encoded into Java opcodes play an important role in bytecode verification.

Clearly then, we do not wish to completely conceptually eliminate primitive types from the JVM. But we may want to eliminate them from Java source programs. Let's see why.

CONCRETE EXAMPLES OF THE PROBLEM

Performance and security notwithstanding, including primitive types in Java is problematic. Let's look at some concrete examples of why this is so. We'll consider these in, more or less, increasing severity of magnitude.

DICHOTOMY OF BASIC SEMANTICS

In Java, not only do we have different entities—objects and primitives—populating the same world, but features of the language itself have different meaning depending on the type of entity they are being applied to. At first blush, it may appear that this gulf of semantics—two possible meanings for a single language feature—could cause confusion and programming errors. Perhaps surprisingly, I'm going to begin by arguing that some of these basic differences are, in fact, not problematic per se, and thus are not part of the "harmful" aspects of mixing primitive and object metatypes. However, I will discuss problems *associated with* these semantic disparities.

The most basic difference is how we operate on the two different Java data entities. As I noted earlier, we operate on objects principally with dot notation mechanisms, resulting in sending messages to the objects or accessing their public member fields. Contrarily, we work on primitive variables with operators that are part of the Java language itself (+, *, etc.). The latter is probably a good thing: it capitalizes on programmers' previous experience with other languages and it is probably more natural. In a pure object-oriented language like Smalltalk, even mainstream operators such as +, are really messages sent to objects—anInteger + someOtherInteger means send the + message to anInteger with someOtherInteger as the argument. Many novice Smalltalk programmers have problems accepting and appreciating this concept. Nonetheless, *the real problem* derives from the inability to send messages to primitive typed variables. We'll see later that this prevents our use of polymorphism and basic object-oriented design strategies.

I'm going to provide a couple of other examples of the dichotomy of semantics caused by having two basic types of program entities. These boil down to the same issues. First, value versus reference semantics: as we've already seen, variables that are declared to be a primitive type actually contain their values whereas variables declared to be instances of some class contain a reference (pointer) to the actual object. Second, all primitives are immutable whereas most objects are not. You can always change what a variable references by reassigning the variable. But, you can also change mutable objects in place by sending messages or accessing public fields. That is, you can modify an object referenced by a variable without changing the variable (which object it points to) at all. You cannot modify immutable entities, including *all* primitives.

== != ==

The built-in language-level operator = = means two different things depending on whether its operands are objects or primitive types. In one case, = = tests for *identity*, in the other, for simple *equality*. If code compares two variables whose declared type is a class, that means "Do the two variables *point to* the *same object*?" Comparing two primitive variables means "Are the two variables logically equal, that is, do they *contain* the same *value*?" To be concrete, in the following code snippet we're testing whether a and b reference the identical object:

```
Object a, b;
...
if (a == b) ...
```

And here we're testing whether x and y have the identical value:

```
int x, y;
...
if (x == y) ...
```

The truth is, there really is no difference in how = = works—under the covers, it operates the same for both primitives and objects. The expression a = = b really means "Do the variables a and b (that is, the stack entries representing variables a and b) contain precisely the same bits?" It just so happens that in the case of primitive variables those bits represent the variables' values (do the variables contain the same value?), whereas for objects those bits represent pointers into the heap (do the two variables contain the same object reference, i.e., do they point to the identical object?).

The rest of the truth is that this really isn't a problem. The semantics of the = = operator are actually, "Do two variables refer to the same *thing*?" In a very real sense, asking whether 3 = = 3 *is* asking whether the thing on both sides of the = = is the same "object." After all, the Java world really possesses a *single* 3 "object." So logically, = = means the same thing for primitives as for objects.

We do, in fact, want the ability to check whether two variables reference the identical object—this is useful in a number of situations (for example, for comparing two instances, which have identical fields but are different: say, two Employees with the same name or when using similar objects as Dictionary keys). So, the semantics of = = for objects are just fine as is. *The real problem*, or at least confusion, with regard to the primitive vs. object dichotomy arises in the primitive wrapper classes. Java includes a wrapper class for each primitive type: the Integer class corresponds to ints; Boolean is used to wrap booleans, Float instances are used for floats, etc. The problem proceeds from the fact that multiple instances of these basic wrapper classes may have the identical value but not be = =. For example, the following expressions are false!

```
new Boolean(true) = = new Boolean(true) //false
new Integer(2) = = new Integer(2)     //false
```

On the other hand, when the = = operator compares two primitive types, the result is based on the logical equality of the operands:

```
int int1 = 2, int2 = 2;
boolean b1 = true, b2 = true;
int1 == int2    //true
b1 == b2        //true
```

The two Integer objects above are not the same object, but they should be. There ought to be only *one* instance of Integer with a value of 2, just like there is "one instance" of int with a value of 2. The same should hold for other primitive wrapper classes. In the first example, we're not interested in whether the two Integers are the same *object* but rather whether they're logically equivalent. To determine this, we can't use an "equals" test; we have to use an equals() test. That is, we can't use the = = operator; we have to remember, instead, to send a message to one instance asking that it compare itself to the other:

```
new Integer(2).equals(new Integer(2))    //true
new Boolean(true).equals(new Boolean(true)) //true
```

Passing Arguments by Reference vs. by Value

When actual arguments are passed to a Java method, they are passed either by value or by reference—primitives are passed by value, objects by reference. This is the story often told to new Java programmers—in fact, you'll find many Java books that say just this. But it's a lie. The truth is that all variables are passed by value—an invoked method cannot change the contents of the actual parameters. It just happens that some variables possess reference semantics. Primitive variables contain a value, object variables contain an object reference, *both* are passed by value. The method may reassign its local copy of this variable but this will not change the actual parameter in the caller's scope:

```
void doesNotChange (int anInt) {
   // Primitive type version of doesNotChange()
   anInt = 5;
}

/* calling doesNotChange(): */
int i = 1;
doesNotChange(i);
// At this point i has not changed. Its value is still 1. */

void doesNotChange (String aString) {
   // Object version of doesNotChange()
   aString = "xyz";
}

/* calling doesNotChange():
String s = "abc";
doesNotChange(s);
/* At this point s has not changed. It is still "abc". */
```

However, passing an object reference gives the invoked method a pointer to the actual object. Even though the method cannot *reassign* this variable to a *different object* in the caller's scope, it can send messages to the object or directly modify public fields inside that object. So, here's the difference: while primitives passed as parameters to a method cannot be changed in any way, objects passed in the same fashion can be "permanently" modified *in situ*. Here's an example (assume a class named Zot with a public field named field1):

```
void doesChange (Zot aZotObject) {
   aZotObject.changeYourself();
```

```
aZotObject.field1 = 2; }

/* calling doesChange:
Zot z = new Zot();
z.field1 = 1;
doesChange(z);
/* At this point z has changed. In addition to side
effects in changeYourself(), the value of z's "field1" field is now 2. */
```

So, there is no fundamental difference between primitives and objects with respect to being passed as arguments; the real difference is, once again, we can send messages to objects or access their internal fields *and* these actions may result in changing those objects. Hence, *the real problem* is simply that programmers must be cognizant of the potentially different results depending on whether method arguments are primitives or objects. Anything that a programmer has to remember is a potential source for errors.

The semantics of the = operator are quite similar to what we've just discussed. Two variables may reference the same object, in which case changing one implies changing the other (by definition). But, reassigning one does not affect the other—just as with primitives.

Round Pegs in Square Holes

Let's move on to the weightier problems caused by mixing primitives and objects. The first is that we cannot use primitives where objects are expected.

Because Java is strongly typed, an object's member fields are declared to be of specific types; when the type of a field is defined as Object or some subclass thereof, a primitive type may not be assigned to or used in that field. This is particularly problematic in the case of container classes (by that I do not mean the AWT Container components, but rather classes whose instances can contain collections or lists of other objects). Let's get concrete. Vector is a commonly used container class. A Vector provides the functionality of an ordered collection of elements, with the ability to add, insert, remove, and find elements at any position in the list. Hence, it has many desirable features and capabilities beyond a simple array. As a result, we may want to use a Vector's functionality for flexibly storing and accessing objects or primitives. The problem, of course, is that the Vector class is defined to contain elements of type Object. We cannot have a Vector with elements of type int, nor any other primitive type. *The real problem* is primitives and objects are fundamentally incompatible. Primitive types cannot be used where objects are expected—yet they coexist in the same environment.

As a result, if we desire a Vector's capabilities, we are forced to do extra object creation and casting. The objects involved are instances of the primitive wrapper classes defined by Java's developers precisely because of this incompatibility problem. To store an int in a Vector, we must first create a new instance of Integer to "wrapper" the int. We start by declaring the Vector and int variables:

```
Vector myNumbers = new Vector(100);
int i;
```

What we would like to do after assigning a value to i is simply:

```
myNumbers.addElement(i);
```

But this causes a compile error—there is no method addElement() with an argument of type int. And with good reason: a Vector may only contain Objects, not primitives. Vector's only addElement() method expects an Object parameter. So, instead of the above, we create and store an Integer based on i's value:

```
myNumbers.addElement(new Integer(i));
```

In later code, when we want to access the integers contained in the Vector, we must undo the type conversion we have just performed (note that we first cast the element to class Integer because as far as the Vector is concerned, it contains elements whose type is Object):

```
/* Retrieve the Integer object and then convert it to int: */
Integer temp = (Integer)myNumbers.elementAt(index);

i = temp.intValue();
```

What we would rather have done is something like:

```
i = (int)myNumbers.elementAt(index);
```

Of course, this causes a compile error as well because of the type mismatch: we cannot cast (with the explicit cast) or convert (without the cast) from type Object to int.

This may be a relatively minor problem, but nonetheless we've incurred two types of unnecessary overhead. First, cognitive overhead for the programmer who must remember that primitives cannot be used where objects are expected and to add wrapping and unwrapping code as necessary. Second, we have the runtime overhead of casting primitive types to and from wrapper objects.

GOOD OBJECT-ORIENTED DESIGN ABROGATED

The existence of primitive types also necessitates special case code, the effect of which is the undoing of polymorphism. Contrary to principles of good object-oriented design, we often must test for and write extra code specially for primitive operands. We cannot simply write code that sends a single polymorphic message that is understood (though perhaps implemented differently) by many different types of objects. Let's look at an example.

The String class has an overloaded static method named valueOf() that produces a String representation of its argument. For object arguments, the object's toString() method is invoked:

```
public static String valueOf(Object obj) {
    return (obj == null) ? "null" : obj.toString();
}
```

Hence the decision as to "How should a particular object appear when printed" is up to the object being printed (it's in the toString() method defined in or inherited by each object's class). So, this design adheres to good object-oriented design because it places responsibilities where they ought to be: the client merely asks the object for its printable representation and the object has the responsibility of providing its own printable form. This design also facilitates changing the way objects of a particular class print—we merely override the default version of toString() inherited from the class's superclass chain. This is nice because an object's toString() method can be, and is, called from numerous code locations. Thus, to change the way objects of a particular class print, we can change code in a single location, that class's toString().

The method shown above *should be* the entire implementation of valueOf(). We should only require a *single* valueOf() method in the String class. valueOf() simply sends the toString() message to its argument, placing the responsibility for how an object should print with the object itself. However, because we have primitives to worry about—and we can't send messages (such as toString()) to them—String is forced to overload valueOf() to handle primitive type arguments. Hence, String implements methods like the following, which adopts a decidedly procedural approach: the client code decides how some type should be printed, rather that the type itself.

```
public static String valueOf(boolean b) {
    return b ? "true" : "false"
}
```

Of course, String also implements a valueOf() for an int argument, another for a float argument, and so on.

If I'm an object, the behavior for deciding what I should look like when printed is *in* me (the object) as it should be in an object-oriented language. For primitives, the model is procedural: the decision is made by code separate from the data, acting on those data. Because they do not decide for themselves (with their own method), we cannot change this behavior in a single location. If we always want booleans to print as "T" or "F" rather than "true" or "false," we have to find every place that code is implemented and modify them all.

But, more importantly, *the real problem* here is that we cannot write programs using sound object-oriented design practices such as exploiting polymorphism because we cannot send messages to primitive variables.

THE MIRROR IS CRACK'D

Long after the decision to include two metatypes in the Java language, Java's developers realized the need for reflective capabilities. Reflection is the ability of a program to find out things about itself and its components at runtime. Java now includes classes such as Class, Field, and Method, which allow a program to determine the class of an object, the names and types of fields within an object, the names of messages understood by an object, to dynamically retrieve and invoke a specific method in an object, and so forth.

Let's consider an example. Every object is an instance of a class and we can ask an object for its Class object. The problem is that a primitive type is not an instance of any class. So what does it mean, for example, to ask a primitive variable for its class?

```
Equation eq = new Equation("x = y + 4");
Class c = eq.getClass();
```

As we'd expect, this getClass() call returns a Class object representing the Equation class. But, how about primitives?

```
int i = 1;
i.getClass()  // compile error:
/* "The method getClass invoked for type int with arguments
   () is not defined." */
```

But we *can* retrieve a Class object—sort of—for an int field, as follows. If we define a class with a field named i of type int, we can ask the Class for the Field named i. What do we get? The answer is, we get some sort of hybrid class/primitive type thing:

```
class Test {
    public int i;
}
Test test = new Test();
/* retrieve the Test Class object:
Class c = test.getClass();
/* retrieve the Field named i:
Field fieldI = c.getField("i"); */

/* Now ask for field i's class:
Class classForI = fieldI.getType(); */
```

We now have a Class object for int! We can ask it its name, and we find that we have a Class named "int".

```
classForI.getName()   /* returns "int" */
```

Realizing part of the problem, the developers of Class included a message to ask if the Class is a primitive:

```
classForI.isPrimitive()   /* returns true */
```

But, how can a Class be a primitive? Let's confuse things a bit more. We can access the Class object representing a defined class by coding, say:

```
Equation.class   /* returns the Equation Class object */
```

But, we can also say:

```
int.class
```

and obtain a Class object whose name is "int". Note we have not sent the getClass() method to an object; we have used the reserved word for a built-in primitive type (int) and, using dot notation, accessed its class "field." And this returns a Class object!

You can also ask for a Class instance by name:

```
Class.forName("java.lang.String")
/* Returns the Class object:
    (java.lang.Class) class java.lang.String */
```

But as you might expect, doing the same sort of thing fails for primitive type names:

```
Class.forName("int")
/* throws ClassNotFoundException */
```

We can retrieve a Class instance whose name is "int" using yet another approach. Here we do so by asking the corresponding wrapper class for its type (and we can do the same with all the primitive wrapper classes):

```
Integer.TYPE;
/* Returns the Class object:
   (java.lang.Class) int */
```

There are times, when using the reflection API, that "magic" happens with regard to primitive types and wrapper classes. Sometimes we expect a primitive, but get instead an instance of one of the wrapper classes. Conversely, at times we must remember to wrap primitives before passing them as arguments to reflection methods. Let's look at some examples. Assume first the following class definition:

```
public class Tester {
   public boolean test (int i) {return i > 3;
   }
}
```

We can retrieve a Method object (in this case the one representing test()) as follows:

```
Tester t = new Tester();             //line 1
Class[] argTypes = new class[1];     //line 2
argTypes[0] = Integer.TYPE;          //line 3
Method m = t.getClass().getMethod("test", argTypes);   //line 4
```

To retrieve the Method, we send getMethod() to the Class (line 4). The second parameter to getMethod() is an array containing the types of the formal parameters of the method we're trying to retrieve. Even though the argument to test() is of type int, getMethod() requires an array of Classes for the argument types. We declare and create the array in line 2, and then have to ask the appropriate wrapper class for its TYPE (as above, this retrieves a Class) (line 3).

Now that we have a Method object, we can invoke it. Using Java's reflection API, we invoke a method using invoke(). test() has one formal argument whose type is int, but, invoke() expects an array of Objects containing the actual parameters. Again we can't use the expected primitive per se; we must instead use an instance of the appropriate wrapper class:

```
Object[] actualArguments = new Object[1];
actualArguments[0] = new Integer(3);
m.invoke(t, actualArguments);
/* above line equivalent to "t.test(3)" */
```

Finally, test() returns a primitive, a boolean. But, invoke() returns an Object! invoke() automatically wraps primitive return types rather than returning a primitive per se. Hence, the result of m.invoke(...) is an instance of the Boolean wrapper class.

I could provide many more examples, but I think you can see *the real problem*: The inclusion of primitive types forces Java's reflection mechanisms to incorporate what amount to kludges to handle these non-object types.

FIXING THE PROBLEM: A PROPOSAL

As I noted, my main goal in writing this article was to assert and support the notion that Java's inclusion of primitive types causes problems for programmers and designers. Hopefully, I have provided the Java language designers with the motivation to correct the problem and hopefully they will devise a clever solution. Having said all this, however, I feel obligated to offer at least one potential solution.

Before discussing a fix, let's review the core problems:

1. We should be able to use primitive variables wherever objects can be used; we should be able, for example, to have a Vector or a Stack of ints. And we should be able to do so without giving it a second thought, without having to convert to primitive-wrapper objects into and out of the Vector or Stack.

2. We should be able to write code that sends a single polymorphic message regardless of the type of the message receiver. Otherwise, polymorphism— and thus a big piece of good object-oriented design—is defeated and we need to code special cases for primitives.

2a. Hence, we should be able to send messages to primitive typed variables.

3. Java's reflection code has incorporated an assortment of kludges to be able to handle primitives. Reflection should be uniform and consistent regardless of metatype.

My basic proposal to remediate these problems is derived from the approach used in many modern Smalltalk environments. First, the primitive declaration types int, boolean, float, etc. should be deprecated. All such variables should henceforth be declared the type of the currently associated primitive wrapper class. Thus, integer variables should be declared of type Integer rather than int, booleans should be type Boolean rather than boolean, variables containing a single-precision floating point should be Float instead of float, and so forth.

This immediately solves problems 1 through 3! However, a few problems immediately jump right out at us. First, what about literals? Currently, this is legal Java code:

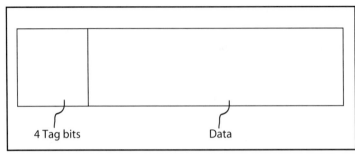

Figure 2.
Proposed JVM
variable
representation.

```
int i = 5;
i = 1;
```

Based on my proposal, the following would have to be legal instead:

```
Integer i = 5;
i = 1;
```

But this is no big deal at all. Java already creates objects based on literals. In the following statement, the literal "abc" results in a String object (a *new* String instance is created if this is the first "abc" literal encountered in the compilation; otherwise s is pointed to an existing String that contains the characters "abc"— but a String *object* nonetheless):

```
String s = "abc";
```

Java also provides language-level support for array creation based on literals, though arrays are reference variables, with a reference pointer in the stack and the actual data in the heap.

What about performance and verification? If all primitive variables are now treated like objects, what about the performance advantages of having primitive values reside directly in the stack and having specific JVM opcodes for them, as well as the bytecode verifier's usage of these type-specific bytecodes? The answer is, treat primitive *as if* they were objects when required, and treat them *as if* they're primitives when possible. All variables of the "primitive" type (note quotes; this means all variables declared as one of the primitive wrapper classes, Integer, Boolean, Float, etc.) should continue to contain the value of variable, not a reference—that is, exactly as done now, variables declared a "primitive" type will have their values reside directly in the stack. With regard to opcodes, the compiler knows when an operation involves "primitive" variables. It can thus generate opcodes accordingly, that is, the identical code it generates now for primitives. So, hard-currency operations like + will generate the same efficient bytecodes as they do now. Nonetheless, if we send a message to a "primitive" variable, the corresponding method in the declared class (Integer, Boolean, Float, etc.) would be invoked.

Again, this is not a far leap for Java. Arrays are already handled as the primitives are with respect to opcodes. The Java compiler generates array-specific bytecodes that the JVM can execute more efficiently than generic method invocation. Yet, we can send messages to arrays—arrays inherit and understand all messages defined in class Object. They also have a public member field named length accessible using dot notation—e.g., myArray.length. Arrays can be used anywhere an object can—for example, as elements in a Vector.

What about multiple different instances of the same primitive entity? As mentioned, we don't want two different integer objects with the value 2. These entities are internal, hard-wired—we don't want multiple "copies" of them. This is solved by handling "primitive" objects as in Smalltalk. Smalltalk behaves as if it implements the Flyweight design pattern for "primitive" classes. In the Flyweight pattern (see Gamma, E. *et al.*), clients of a class ask the class to create new instances with a particular value but hidden within its implementation the class determines if an instance with that same value already exists; if so, that pre-existing instance is returned rather than creating a new one. This is discussed in greater detail in *The Design Patterns Smalltalk Companion* (Alpert, S. R., K. Brown, and B. Woolf, Addison-Wesley, 1998), but briefly, Smalltalk has only one integer 3 (for example); in Smalltalk, the following is the case (Smalltalk is weakly typed, and hence there are no declared types):

```
i1 = 3.
i2 = 3.
i1 == i2    "true"
```

But, as discussed, in the current implementation of Java, two Integer objects with the same internal int value are not = =. All the primitive wrapper classes behave similarly. Under my proposal, the following would be the case instead:

```
Integer i1 = 3;
Integer i2 = 3;
i1 == i2    // true
```

Once again, this is not a big leap for Java. Java currently behaves similarly with respect to String literals. If the same String literal is encountered twice in a single compilation unit (typically, a single class), the compiler generates code to have them both reference the identical String instance, rather than creating a new instance for each. That is, the generated code results in the same behavior as the Flyweight pattern. So, for example:

```
String s1 = "abc";
String s2 = "abc";
s1 == s2   // true
```

Instances of the "primitive" classes should also be immutable. We don't want to be able to tell 3 to become 4 (of course, we can assign 4 to an Integer variable whose value is currently 3—we just cannot mutate the 3 object per se). We also want to be able to put an Integer in, say, a Hashtable, knowing its value (and thus its hash value) won't change.

So far, what I've proposed is easily implemented. There's one significant outstanding problem, however. Anything we can put in containers such as Vectors will eventually be removed from those containers. And when they are, we need to know each such object's exact class so we can send messages to them and invoke the appropriate method. The proposed "primitives" are instances of classes. But, based on this proposal, "primitive" variables are not represented inside the JVM (in the stack) as other objects. Non-"primitive" object variables are represented on the stack as references that point to the actual objects, which maintain class information about their class. But we want "primitive" variables to be represented as primitive types are currently with only their values in the stack. This works fine for "stand-alone" instances—if you declare a variable type Integer, the compiler knows to invoke methods in the Integer class for message-sends and to generate int opcodes for language-level operations (like +). But, when we place an Integer in a heterogeneous Vector containing objects of various classes and then remove those objects, how do we know when we have an Integer? Consider this code:

```
Vector stuff = new Vector(100);
Integer i = 1;
String s = "abc";
stuff.addElement(i);
stuff.addElement(s);
...
for (Enumeration e = stuff.elements();
    e.hasMoreElements(); )
    System.out.println(e.nextElement().toString());
```

We need to know which toString() to invoke for each element in the Vector. When we retrieve the stored Integer, how does the JVM know it's an instance of the Integer class?

One proposal is to emulate what some modern Smalltalk VMs do. As I mentioned earlier, many Smalltalk environments implement just what I've proposed so far. In Smalltalk, *everything* is an object and all "primitives" are instances of a class such as Integer and Boolean. But Smalltalk's "primitive" variables maintain their value, rather than an object reference, in the stack (these are known as *immediate* objects; see Lui, C. *Smalltalk, Objects, and Design*, Prentice Hall Press, 1996). To handle the class-identification problem, all variables on the stack contain tag bits (this is, in turn, based on earlier research on improving Smalltalk's efficiency; see Ungar, D.M., *The Design and Evaluation of a High Performance Smalltalk System*, ACM, NY, 1987. Different configurations of tag bits represent different "primitive" classes with one distinguished configuration meaning "this is an object reference."

For Java, we need eight different tag values for the eight primitive types, plus one for the "this is really a reference pointer" value. The latter could be tag value 0. So we need values 0 through 8: four bits. If we wish to retain the JVM's word size, this may mean a loss of precision for some "primitive" variables. Some but not all. Boolean (boolean), Character (char), Byte (byte), and Short (short) variables contain 16 bits or less of actual data but occupy a full word on the JVM's stack. Hence, even in a JVM with a 32-bit word size, using four bits for class information would not affect the values of such variables. For Integer (int), Long (long), Float (float), and Double (double), we would lose four bits of information on a 32-bit platform (of course, double word variables—Doubles and Longs—require tag bits in only one word). A potential alternative is to increase the width of the stack Figure 2 shows the proposed JVM variable representation.) Again, the JVM specification does not mandate a specific word size for the stack: "Implementation designers must...choose a word size that is at least 32 bits, but otherwise they can pick whatever word size will yield the most efficient implementation" (see Venners). Further, JVMs that already have a larger word size may wind up forfeiting no data bits: in the 64-bit implementation mentioned earlier, there would already be more than four unused and available bits for all "primitive" variables on the stack.

One small problem remains. In the general case, objects can be tested to determine whether they are equal to null. However, because "primitives" have no reference pointer, they cannot be compared to null using the JVM's current mechanisms. Hence, an additional change to the JVM would be required or we might have to disallow such comparisons. In fact, a potential alternative to non-heap-resident "primitive" objects with tag bits is a proposal by James Gosling. He has suggested the implementation of an immutable class modifier (as in immutable class Complex {...}; see "Efficient Classes" in Gosling, J., *The Evolution of Numerical Computing in Java*, available at Gosling's Sun Web site). Instances of classes so flagged are not allocated on the heap and cannot be compared to or assigned null (see Gosling, for other characteristics of immutable classes). Hence, "primitive" classes might be defined as immutable as per Gosling's proposal.

I've offered one solution that attempts to enable good object-oriented design while retaining the advantages of efficiency and verification. But, of course, every design decision involves trade-offs. We gain by eliminating the disadvantages of primitive types enumerated in this article; we lose four bits of information for some "primitives." Nonetheless, the more important point is that primitive types, as is, bear multiple disadvantages for object-oriented—and specifically Java—programmers.

Getting the Numbers Right, a Cautionary Tale

KEN DICKEY

T HERE IS A widespread myth that computers, being fast adding machines, do math well. We all know that this is not true but sometimes we believe anyway. Sometimes we forget that the numeric answers we get have high precision but perhaps no accuracy. I know that I should do the error analysis on each and every floating point operation but sometimes I don't.

I have always believed in "consumer arithmetic." (i.e., I don't care how fast I get the wrong answer. I care how fast I get the right answer.) And I really believe that programming language libraries should support math at least as good as high school algebra. When I get a numeric problem, I want the computer to tell me it can get the answer, it can get close, or it can't solve the problem to the accuracy I want given the data I have. What I don't want is a string of digits, which may or may not have any meaning, with no indication if they have meaning or not.

I will explore one small corner of the universe and how math happens in the Java language. I use a specific example from a talk I heard on Interval Arithmetic—more on that later. I'll warn you now that I consider myself a user of numbers rather than a mathematician, but we'll definitely do some math along the way.

EXAMPLE

Here is a simple polynomial function.

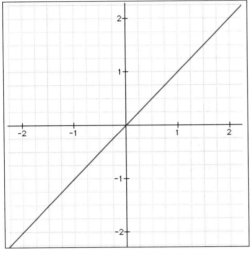

Figure 1.
$y= x\ (x-1-10^{\wedge}-9)/(x-1)$.

F(x,y)= 333.75 y^6
  + x^2 (11 x^2 y^2 - y^6 - 121 y^4 - 2)
  + 5.5 y^8 + x / (2 y)

I want the answer to its value at

F(77617, 33096)

G. W. Walster, who gave the talk I listened to on Interval Mathematics, reported that one implementation of IBM FORTRAN gave the following results.

	precision
f = 1.17260...	single
f = 1.1726039400531...	double
f = 1.172603940053178...	extended

Looks like a pretty good result, doesn't it? Calculate in higher precision and get more digits.

Let's take a look at calculating **F** in some other languages (See Listing 1). Java 1.1 double precision on both a Power PC and Pentium gives:

f = -1.1805916207174113e21

Gambit Scheme (generic arithmetic) gives:

f = -54767/66192

Squeak Smalltalk (generic arithmetic) gives:

f = -54767/66192

Macintosh Common Lisp (generic arithmetic) gives:

```
f = -54767/66192
```

As you may have guessed by now, not all of these answers are correct. The exact answer is:

```
-54767/66192
```

or, if you like decimals (first 100 digits)

```
-0.82739605994682136814116509547981629199
903311578438481991781484167270969301426154218032390621223
10854
```

Rounded to double precision, let's call it good at

```
-0.827396059946821.
```

Let's take a closer look at what is happening by breaking up the calculation into pieces.

```
A= 333.75 y^6
B= x^2 (11 x^2 y^2 - y^6 - 121 y^4 - 2)
C= 5.5 y^8
D= x / (2 y)
F = A+B+C+D
```

Java double arithmetic gives the following results.

```
x= 77617
y= 33096
A=    4.386057508463931e29
B= -  7.917111779274712e36
C=    7.91711134066896e36
D=    1.1726039400531787
double  F() - 1.1805916207174113e21
```

Now it is obvious what happened. Adding B and C produced what is called *catastrophic cancellation*, where most of the precise digits cancel each other out and we get a case of double precision (plenty of digits) but zero accuracy (no digits are correct). Because B and C are the largest numbers, they have the largest effect on the calculation.

The reason that Scheme, Smalltalk, and Mac Common Lisp give the correct answers is that they use Bignum and Rational Arithmetic. They calculate with full accuracy using big integers rather than automatically converting to IEEE floating point, where accuracy is easily lost. Many people consider IEEE floats as "the wrong answer fast."

Now some of you may have noticed that Java 1.1 added a new package called java.Math, which contains BigInteger and BigDecimal classes. We'll take a look at BigDecimal below, but before I get into that I'd like to take a side trip into Interval Arithmetic.

INTERVAL ARITHMETIC

The basic idea of interval arithmetic is that instead of rounding to the nearest IEEE floating point representation, you keep the largest and smallest bounds that a number can be using the IEEE rounding modes set to round-up or round-down as appropriate. So, one really does all the math at least twice, one rounding up, the other rounding down, while all the time keeping the largest and smallest possible values. Thus, interval math bounds the errors involved and the true answer must lie somewhere within the interval. As computing power doubles every 18 months, isn't it time to take some of this power and make sure we get the answers right?

The nice thing about intervals is that in cases where one really measures

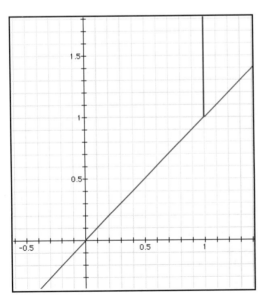

Figure 2.
Same as Figure 1 but with more samples, catching part of the discontinuity.

things, we can state what is really measured. We can easily specify the measurement error, e.g., 24 1/4 inches +/- 1/8 inch gives an interval of [24.125 24.375].

Another, often overlooked, problem is input error. Many decimal numbers cannot be represented as a finite binary number. (For example, 0.1 cannot.) If you use an input routine that bounds the error you will notice this:

```
    new Interval( "0.1" ) ;
 => [0.09999999999999999, 0.1]
    (new Interval(1)).div(new Interval(10)) ;
 => [0.09999999999999999, 0.1]
```

To keep things simple, I have just implemented intervals using Java double's (see Listing 2), but more complete methods are available at Interval Computing's Web site. Let's look at the result in interval math (Listing 3). The results follow. I have printed out both endpoint, [low, high], and <center +/- radius format>.

```
Interval F()=
[-1.1805916207174113e22,7.083549724304469e21]
=
<-2.361183241434822e21 +/-
  9.44473296573929e21>
```

Here the result shows that we don't have any precision left. The center point of the answer is a smaller magnitude than the radius.

The beauty of interval math is that you don't have to do the error analysis, instead you do the error calculation. If the number is good, use it. If not, we know we need to try something different—which we will do in a moment.

Before going on, here are the intermediate calculations using intervals.

```
A= [4.3860575084639306e29,
     4.3860575084639334e29]
   =4.386057508463932e29 +/- 1.40737488355 328e14>

B= [-7.917111779274718e36,
     -7.917111779274708e36]
   = <-7.917111779274713e36 +/-   4.722366482869645e21>
```

C=   [7.917111340668956e36,
      7.917111340668964e36]
    = <7.91711134066896e36+/-   4.1320706725109396e21>

D= [1.1726039400531785,
    1.1726039400531787]
  = <1.1726039400531785+/-   - 1.1102230246251565e-16>

Interval F()=
    [-1.1805916207174113e22,
     7.083549724304469e21]
  = <-2.361183241434822e21 +/-   9.44473296573929e21>

Now looking at B and C we find that we initially have plenty of accuracy (8e36 +/- 4e21 implies about 15 accurate digits before the addition). But because of the cancellation, we lose that accuracy. Note, however, that we keep the error. The magnitude of the error of the result is of the same order as for our largest numbers, B and C.

For numeric models it is frequently possible to do the error analysis, but what about when a user types an arbitrary expression in a spreadsheet? Intervals can give a good indication whether or not some other approach should be taken and they can be checked by the program doing the calculations.

Now, as with any other solution, there are interesting gotchas with intervals. Say one divides an interval by another interval that happens to span zero. One can end up with two intervals, each bounded by a number on one side and an infinity on the other. Intervals can also overstate the error.

But intervals can also give good results where floating point calculations fail. In finding function minima and maxima, intervals are often more efficient—they can converge faster and can find global rather than local minima and maxima. Interval valued functions—functions with interval arguments and interval answers—can determine that f([xMin, xMax]) does or does not cross 0, whereas millions of floating point evaluations off(x) at various points may fail to determine this. (See Figures 1-3.)

It is very interesting to use intervals to find out just how accurate answers to your favorite calculations are.

Okay, Intervals are interesting, but how about Java's new BigDecimal class?

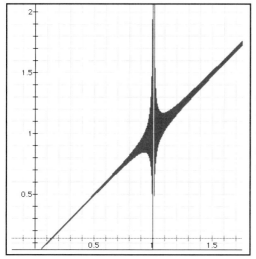

Figure 3.
Same as Figure 1
but using internal
math to show the
error bounds.

BIG DECIMALS

BigDecimals have some quirks and the user interface is horrible, but you do get much better accuracy.

The way that the precision is specified is not very clear. One of the basic maxims of user interface design is that if you use one control for two purposes, users will get confused. BigDecimals use "scale" for two purposes: [1] to scale a number by "moving the decimal point" and [2] to control the number of decimal digits after the decimal point.

Here is an example.

```
BigInteger i =
   new BigInteger("1234567890") ;
BigDecimal d =
   new BigDecimal( i, 5 ) ;
```

In this case, d takes the integer value, 12345, and scales by 5 powers of ten—i.e., it moves the decimal point over 5 places to give the value of

```
d == 12345.67890
```

The basic idea is that one keeps a BigInteger and a "scale", which tells where the decimal point is. When arithmetic is done on BigDecimals, the scale is used to know how many digits to keep after the decimal.

But what happens when you want to change this precision?

There is a method, setScale(), which allows you not to change the scale, but to get a new BigDecimal with the specified number of digits after the decimal. The argument to setScale() is also called "scale" but it does *not* scale the original value. Instead, it changes the number of digits kept (i.e., the scale argument to the BigDecimal constructor changes the position of the decimal point), but the scale argument to setScale() does not. So, setScale() should have really been called something like newWithDigits(). Note that when reducing the number of digits kept, one must specify how to round the value if precision is lost. Also note that BigDecimal numbers are immutable, so, setScale() does not change the original number or its scale, but yields a new BigDecimal number with the specified precision.

```
d = new BigDecimal(
       new BigInteger("1234567890"), 5)
    /* => 12345.67890 */


d.setScale( 2, BigDecimal.ROUND_HALF_EVEN )
/* => 12345.68 */


d.setScale( 6 )
/* =>12345.678900 */


d.setScale( 2,
    BigDecimal.ROUND_HALF_EVEN ).setScale( 6 ) */
/* => 12345.680000
```

Now, given that we know how to set the precision—the constructor is not too helpful here—lets look at a BigDecimal result. Remember that the first digits of the exact result are

```
-0.82739605994682136814116509547981629199
9903311578438481991781484167270969301426154218032390621223
1085327532028039642252840222383336959149141890258641 5...
```

ROUND_HALF_EVEN

```
BigDecimal F()=
-0.82739605994682136814116509547981629199
9033115784384819917814841672709693014261542180323906212231 08
532753202803964225284000000000000000000000000000000000000000
00000000000000000000000000000000000000000000000000000000000
```

```
00000000000000000000000000000000000000000000000000000000000
00000000000000000000000000000000000000000000000000000000000
00000000000000000000000000000000000000000000000000000000000
00000000000000000000000000000000000000000000000000000000000
00000000000000000000000000000000000000000000000000000000000
00000000000000000000000000000000000000000000000000000000000
00000000000000000000000000000000000000000000000000000000000
00000000000000000000000000000000000000000000000000000000000
00000000000000000000000000000000000000000000000000000000000
00000000000000000000000000000000000000000000000000000000000
00000000000000000000000000000000000000000000000000000000000
00000000000000000000000000000000000000000000000000000000000
00000000000000000000000000000000000000000000000000000000000
00000000000000000000000000000000000000000000000000000000000
000000000000000000000000
```

So, aside from the fact that String() does not yet trim trailing zeros from BigDecimals, the numeric result looks darn good.

I won't take the space here, and your eyes may be a bit strained numerically at this point, but the code in Test Class (Listing 4) lets you play with precision and amazing number of rounding modes in the BigDecimal class.

Given that the BigDecimal class was created for "reliable monetary calculations" they do a very reasonable job. For doing numeric calculations with numbers, which are very large, or in particular, very small, using BigDecimals may not be a convenient way to get the precision you require.

RECOMMENDATIONS

Math in Java breaks another user interface maxim: "similar things/operations should look similar." I found the syntax of working with numbers in Java to be awkward, to say the least. After some initial confusion, I created a class called Dribble (Listing 5), which boxes Java doubles. I then used Dribble expressions to check that I got the same answers as doubles—initially I did not! It took me much more time than I expected to get the expressions right. Once I fixed the equation by cutting and pasting—Java requiring code duplicated for each type signature—I had "the same" equations for Intervals and, with slight modifications, BigDecimals. If I did this much, I would certainly write a translator that parsed the standard operators and wrote the final code. Looking back, it would have probably been faster to do this and debug the translation than it took initially to debug the equational correspondence without it.

Another source of confusion for me was the fact that expressions like "(1/2)" do not yield a rational (fraction) or floating point result, but do yield truncated integer division. So, remember that (1/2) == 0 in Java! As a user, I find this kind of math to be very strange.

I think it obvious at this point that anyone doing heavy duty numerical calculations might look to Maple or Mathematica. When doing calculations in Java, one should think seriously about getting a commercial package by someone who has already done the legwork in this area—and testing it against various usage scenarios, e.g., using interval arithmetic.

CONCLUSION

Java has grown rapidly to fill a large space of design requirements. As implementations get faster and APIs evolve, I look forward to improvements in the usability of Java's math packages. In the meantime, as the saying goes "it is a wise man who learns from his mistakes, but a wiser one who lets the rattle snake bite the other fellow." I hope in sharing some of my experience in the Java math space that more of you will get the right answers.

RECOMMENDED READING

Elementary Numerical Computing with Mathematica, R. Skeel and J. Keiper, McGraw-Hill, 1993, ISBN 0-07-057820-6.

Improving Floating-Point Programming, Peter Wallis, editor, J. Wiley, 1990, ISBN 0-471-92437-7.

Numerical Toolbox for Verified Computing, Hammer, R., et al., Springer Verlag, 1993, ISBN 0-387-57118-3.

Precise Numerical Analysis, Oliver Aberth, W. C. Brown,1988, ISBN 0-697-06760-2.

INDEX